# WORKING WITH STUDENTS WITH EMOTIONAL AND BEHAVIOR DISORDERS

## CHARACTERISTICS AND TEACHING STRATEGIES

Terry L. Shepherd

*Indiana University–South Bend*

**Merrill**

Upper Saddle River, New Jersey
Columbus, Ohio

**Library of Congress Cataloging in Publication Data**

Shepherd, Terry L.
    Working with students with emotional and behavior disorders / Terry L. Shepherd.
       p. cm.
    ISBN-13: 978-0-13-229859-9
    ISBN-10: 0-13-229859-7
    1. Mentally ill children—Education.    2. Problem children—Behavior modification.    3. Behavior disorders in children.
    I. Title.
    LC4165.S49 2010
    371.94—dc22

                                                                                                        2008046838

**Vice President and Editor in Chief:** Jeffery W. Johnston
**Executive Editor:** Ann Castel Davis
**Editorial Assistant:** Penny Burleson
**Senior Managing Editor:** Pamela D. Bennett
**Senior Project Manager:** Sheryl Glicker Langner
**Project Coordination:** Nitin Agarwal, Aptara
**Photo Coordinator:** Lori Whitley
**Art Director:** Candace Rowley
**Cover Image:** Super Stock
**Cover Design:** Diane Lorenzo
**Senior Operations Supervisor:** Matthew Ottenweller
**Operations Specialist:** Laura Messerly
**Vice President, Director of Sales & Marketing:** Quinn Perkson
**Marketing Manager:** Erica DeLuca
**Marketing Coordinator:** Brian Mounts

This book was set in Garamond by Aptara. It was printed and bound by Bind-Rite Graphics. The cover was printed by Bind-Rite Graphics.

**Chapter Opening Photo Credits:** Index Open, p. 1; Comstock Royalty Free Division, p. 22; Getty Images–Stockbyte, Royalty Free, p. 39; George Dodson/PH College, p. 63; Bob Daemmrick/Bob Daemmrich Photography, Inc., pp. 89, 214; T. Lindfors/Lindfors Photography, p. 109; Anthony Magnacca/Merrill, pp. 136, 238; Anne Vega/Merrill, p. 158; Laura Bolesta/Merrill, p. 184; Lori Whitley/Merrill, p. 201.

**Pearson**® is a registered trademark of Pearson plc
**Merrill**® is a registered trademark of Pearson Education, Inc.

Pearson Education Ltd., London
Pearson Education Singapore, Pte. Ltd.
Pearson Education Canada, Inc.
Pearson Education—Japan
Pearson Education Australia PTY, Limited

Pearson Education North Asia, Ltd., Hong Kong
Pearson Educación de Mexico, S.A. de C.V.
Pearson Education Malaysia, Pte. Ltd.
Pearson Education Upper Saddle River, New Jersey

**Merrill**
is an imprint of

www.pearsonhighered.com

10 9 8 7 6 5 4 3 2 1
ISBN 13: 978-0-13-229859-9
ISBN 10:    0-13-229859-7

I would like to dedicate this book to my father, AB Shepherd, who through his example taught me the midwestern work ethics that resulted in the completion of this book.

# PREFACE

On my very first day as a teacher of students with emotional and behavior disorders, I had a student attempt suicide. Although I had 5 years of experience teaching history at a residential treatment facility for troubled teenagers, I had an emergency special education teaching certificate. The only training I had was an introduction to special education course I had taken as an undergraduate. I knew little of the theories of Piaget, Erickson, Bronfenbrenner, or others, and I did not completely grasp the devastating effects of post-traumatic stress disorder, depression, and child abuse. All of these issues affected my student with suicidal ideation.

When my student staggered into the classroom, I contacted my principal, and the student was rushed to the hospital where her antidepressant medication was removed from her stomach. I saw her only once after that. It was at a case conference where the decision was made to place her at a residential treatment center for troubled teenagers. And so began my journey into emotional and behavior disorders those many years ago.

Students with emotional and behavior disorders do not receive the services they need in our education system. As a result, many of them are unsuccessful in school or drop out of school, and they have higher unemployment rates than other individuals with disabilities. Just as distressing, the attrition rate for teachers of students with emotional and behavior disorders is higher than that of general education teachers and other special education teachers. I used to joke that I left the classroom because I was becoming emotionally disturbed myself, but for a number of teachers, there is some truth in that statement.

The purpose of this book is to help you to become an effective general or special education teacher, paraprofessional, or administrator of students with emotional and behavior disorders. I hope that, as one of these effective professionals, you will help students with emotional and behavior disorders become successful in school and beyond, which is the ultimate purpose of schools.

This book is intended to be a practical guide that will combine theory, best practices, strategies, and interventions. It is written for beginning teachers, seasoned teachers, alternatively certified teachers, counselors, parents, and administrators. The book is about children who have been identified as having emotional and behavior disorders, those who have not been identified, those who are depressed and suicidal, and those who display aggressive behavior in the classroom.

Is this book the final word on emotional and behavior disorders? I would like to think so, but no, it is not. It is impossible for any book to contain all the information that teachers and educators need. The research is ongoing and subject to change as new solutions are found to old problems. However, I hope that this book will provide you with the information you need to meet the needs of students with emotional and behavior disorders and to change their lives.

And the journey continues. . . .

## TEXT ORGANIZATION

In writing this book, I attempted to cover the complex issues that are specific to teaching students with emotional and behavior disorders without providing a Pollyanna image of the typical student or of the responsibilities of the professionals who work with these students.

The book is organized differently from other textbooks and contains content that is generally not included in other books. It is divided into three sections. The first section, "Foundations of Emotional and Behavior Disorders," provides an overview of the definition, characteristics, and theoretical explanations of emotional and behavior disorders. The inclusion of developmental theories is crucial. Theories help us understand the causes of emotional and behavior disorders and provide the basis for practical applications.

The second section is "Teaching Students with Emotional and Behavior Disorders." Many schools address the behavioral and academic needs of students with emotional and behavior disorders, but the needs of these children go beyond the basic academic and behavioral interventions. Interventions should holistically encompass the behavioral, social, academic, and emotional needs of the students.

The last section of the book is "The Successful Teacher." This section provides information regarding collaboration and special education law. More importantly, it provides suggestions for the emotional, social, and physical well-being of teachers, an area usually neglected in textbooks about teaching students with emotional and behavior disorders.

## ACKNOWLEDGMENTS

As in the creation of any textbook, a number of individuals have given a lot of personal and professional time to the completion of this book, and I would like to express my utmost appreciation to them. I would like to thank Allyson Sharp for her tireless assistance in developing the proposal that would eventually become this book and Penny Burleson for her support and advice. I especially want to thank Ann Davis for her patience, constructive criticism, and emotional support. I want to acknowledge all the reviewers who provided suggestions to improve this book: Amelia Blyden, The College of New Jersey; Dawn Behan, Upper Iowa University; Britt Ferguson, Minnesota State University; Joan Henley, Arkansas State University; Beverly Johns, MacMurray College; Karen Kirk, Brunswick Community College; Deborah Russell, University of Nevada, Las Vegas; Ralph Scott, University of Northern Iowa; Sarah Summy, Western Michigan University; William Sweeney, The University of South Dakota; Raymond Waller, Piedmont College; Elizabeth West, Boise State University; and Thomas Williams, Virginia Tech. In the public school realm, I want to thank Tom Dulle for his mentorship and friendship while I was the sole high school teacher for students with emotional and behavior disorders in a 10-school cooperative, and Janet Robison for being the best paraprofessional I ever had and for helping me understand her role in the classroom.

I also would like to thank my family, who allowed me to spend an inordinate amount of time at home staring at the computer. I want to thank my wife, Melanie, who read through every draft without complaint and offered a number of valuable suggestions. I also want to acknowledge my children, Shaun, Bessie, Tony, Christy, Jared, and Samuel. I promise not to engage in another major project for at least 3 months.

# BRIEF CONTENTS

# CONTENTS

Note: Every effort has been made to provide accurate and current Internet information in this book. However, the Internet and information posted on it are constantly changing, so it is inevitable that some of the Internet addresses listed in this textbook will change.

# CHAPTER 1

# Defining Emotional and Behavior Disorders

**After reading this chapter, you should be able to**

- Explain why all teachers should have some understanding of the nature and characteristics of emotional and behavior disorders.

- Discuss how events in history have influenced the way that teachers and administrators view and educate children with emotional and behavior disorders today.

- Explain why it is so difficult to define emotional and behavior disorders.

- State the federal definition of *emotional disturbance*.

- Examine how societal and cultural expectations influence the way that children with emotional and behavior disorders are perceived.

## THE IMPORTANCE OF UNDERSTANDING EMOTIONAL AND BEHAVIOR DISORDERS

One of the most difficult challenges facing teachers today is teaching students with emotional and behavior disorders. No matter what subject or grade level they teach, at some point teachers will have a child with some degree of emotional and behavior disorder. Often these students are not identified as having disorders or do not qualify for special education services, but today's teachers will still have to contend with the students' behavior. As a result, teachers will spend an inordinate amount of time trying to manage the behavioral, social, academic, and emotional needs of these students.

Students with emotional and behavior disorders display a wide range of behaviors. It is easy to identify students who display inappropriate behaviors such as defiance, aggression, and anger, but not so easy to identify students who are depressed or who do not display challenging behaviors overtly. The difficulty lies in understanding the characteristics and nature of students with emotional and behavior disorders and coping with attitudes and perceptions toward individuals with disabilities.

Teachers often feel that they do not have the skills and strategies to teach these children in their classrooms. More and more universities and colleges provide noncategorical training for individuals pursuing careers in special education. *Noncategorical* refers to the inclusion of all disabilities, rather than a focus on specific disabilities. While noncategorical training is beneficial in that it gives special education teachers a broad understanding of special education, it does not make them experts in any particular disability category. Expecting special education teachers to have expertise in a specific disability would be like asking a general practitioner to perform open-heart surgery.

Teachers who receive teaching certificates through alternative certification programs may receive even less specific training than teachers who receive noncategorical training. Many individuals completing alternative certification programs for critical areas already have degrees in math or science that allow them to teach in their chosen subject areas, but very few individuals completing alternative programs have backgrounds in special education (Shepherd & Brown, 2003; Tissington & Grow, 2007). Alternative certification programs may have potential to meet the need for other types of teachers, but they may not be as useful for producing teachers of students with emotional and behavior disorders (Henderson, Klein, Gonzalez, & Bradley, 2005). Comprehensive pedagogy and mentoring programs are critical components of high-quality teacher programs, but many alternatively certified teachers do not acquire the pedagogical and content skills necessary to meet the needs of children with disabilities (Darling-Hammond, 2002; Greeman, 2005).

General education teachers receive even less training in special education, unless they receive their certifications from a dual-license program such as elementary and special education. Normally, most teacher certification programs provide one course in special education, usually an introductory course, and only one or two class lectures within that course are devoted to the teaching of students with emotional and behavior disorders. School districts provide teachers with further training through in-services, but often it is the special education teachers who receive special education training, not the general education teachers.

With an estimated 2% or more of the student population having some type of emotional and behavior disorder, it is unfortunate that many teachers lack the training to work with and the understanding of students with emotional and behavior disorders. Students who have the physical characteristics of Down syndrome or cerebral palsy are recognized as having disabilities, whereas students with emotional and behavior disorders are not readily perceived as having disabilities. Teachers believe that students who display acting-out behaviors are capable of controlling their behaviors if they choose (Liljequist & Renk, 2007). These students are viewed with apprehension because they create havoc within the classroom.

Teachers must understand that students who have emotional and behavior disorders have disabilities and special needs. By understanding the nature of emotional and behavior disorders and by acquiring the tools to teach students with these disabilities, teachers will be better prepared to educate students who have emotional and behavior disorders.

## HISTORY OF EMOTIONAL AND BEHAVIOR DISORDERS

Congress passed the Education for All Handicapped Children Act (PL 94–142) in 1975, a law that eventually evolved into the Individuals with Disabilities Education Improvement Act of 2004 (IDEA; PL 108–446). This far-reaching legislation guaranteed that all children with disabilities would have a free and appropriate education in the public schools. Still, special education did not emerge overnight. The evolution of special education has been progressing since the beginning of civilization, but services and provisions for individuals with disabilities, especially those with emotional and behavior disorders, have not always existed.

### Ancient Practices and the Genesis of Special Education

Rather than trying to help children with disabilities, many ancient cultures practiced infanticide. A child who was deemed incapable of serving in the Spartan army was left to the elements and perished. In Rome, the father of a child with a disability would throw the child into the Tiber River so that the child would not become a burden to society (Winzer, 1993).

In ancient Greece and Rome, mental and behavior disorders were attributed to natural causes. Another explanation for these disorders was demon possession. Individuals with disabilities often faced lengthy and sometimes painful exorcisms. As society was gripped with a growing fear of the influence of the Devil and his minions during the late 1400s, many people with disabilities were accused of being witches. Even John Calvin, one of the great Protestant divines, preached that individuals with mental retardation were possessed by Satan. Martin Luther, the leader of the Reformation, declared that these individuals were without souls (Kanner, 1973).

The treatment of children with emotional and behavior disorders was often inhumane. In 1713, a 7-year-old girl was declared insane by a local physician because her behavior offended her stepmother. The girl would not participate in prayer, became agitated in the presence of black-robed preachers, and avoided contact with people by hiding in the closet. Her parents placed her in the custody of a minister who saw her behavior as evidence that she was being controlled by a baneful and infernal power. The minister laid her on a bench and beat her, locked her in a dark pantry, subjected her to a period of starvation, and clothed her in burlap. When she died a few months later, everyone was relieved, and the minister was amply rewarded for his efforts by the parents (Keller, 1921). There were other instances in which children with emotional and behavior disorders were subjected to exorcisms or sent to convents.

Despite these harsh treatments most individuals with disabilities were treated harshly, some people made efforts  was made to improve their lives. In 1578, Pedro Ponce de León, a Benedictine monk from San Salvador, Spain, began teaching sign language to children who were deaf. This marks de León as the first special education teacher. Jean Pablo Bonet continued this work by adding developing a hand-signed alphabet, additional signs, and techniques for teaching writing, speech, and lip-reading to deaf individuals. In 1620, he published *Simplification of the Letters of the Alphabet and a Method of Teaching Deaf Mutes to Speak*, the first special education text on teaching individuals with hearing impairments (Winzer, 1993).

The beginning of special education services is attributed to Jean Marc Gaspard Itard, a young doctor who tried to educate the *wild boy of Aveyron*. In 1799, three sportsmen were exploring woods in Aveyron, in southern France, when they found an 11- or 12-year-old boy who was filthy, naked, and covered with scars. They were able to capture the boy and bring him to the care of a widow in a nearby village. The boy escaped and spent the winter roaming the woods. Eventually he was recaptured and taken to Paris, where he was studied as a primitive (Itard, 1801/1962). Prominent physicians and psychiatrists declared that the boy was mentally deficient and "an incurable idiot." Itard believed that the boy's mental deficiency was due to a lack of human interaction. He developed the first individualized educational program. The boy made some marginal improvement over the course of 5 years, but Itard was disappointed that his progress was not more significant (Indiana University, 2003).

## Early Reformation

During the first part of the 19th century, progress in the treatment of individuals with mental illness was limited. Yet a few advocates were able to advance reforms in this area.

Dorothea Dix was an effective advocate of the rights of incarcerated people who fought for humanitarian reforms in mental institutions. She visited jails and almshouses (or workhouses), took extensive notes, and presented her findings to the general public and legislatures in over 20 states. Her radical work with individuals who had mental illnesses showed that bettering their environment improved their mental conditions. Dix was responsible for establishing 32 mental hospitals, 15 schools for people with mental deficiencies, a school for the blind, and numerous training facilities for nurses.

Compulsory attendance laws were passed in many states in the 1800s. These laws were enacted to curtail child labor, but they also served to socialize thousands of children immigrating to the United States. Students of different ages, abilities, and backgrounds were educated in one-room schools. These inclusionary schools were the sites where special education in the public schools originated. As graded schools replaced the one-room schools and academic requirements were established, many students with disabilities were placed in segregated special classes or placed in institutions.

By the end of the 19th century, textbooks began focusing on the causes of emotional and behavior disorders in children, especially in Europe. *Physiology and Pathology of the Mind* (Maudsley, 1880) had a 34-page chapter on "Insanity of Early Life" that tried to correlate symptoms of illness with the developmental status of the individual at the time of onset (Kanner, 1962). Many people protested this theory of infantile psychosis because they believed that children could not have mental illnesses. Meanwhile, other individuals attempted to organize monographs detailing the mental disorders of children and young adolescents. While many of these writings focused on degeneracy, masturbation, and religious preoccupation as causes of psychiatric disorders (Kanner, 1962), children with emotional and behavior disorders were beginning to be recognized as individuals deserving treatment.

## Services and Research

The first White House Conference on Children was held in 1910. This conference increased interest in educating children with disabilities in public school settings (Yell, Rogers, & Lodge Rodgers, 1998). As a result, the number of permanent segregated classes increased in public schools between 1910 and 1930 (Winzer, 1993). Educators believed that the smaller

# Case Study 1.1

## A Mind That Found Itself: Clifford Beers

Clifford Beers was a graduate from Yale University and a young businessman who suffered a mental breakdown brought about by the illness and death of his brother. In 1900, he was hospitalized in a private Connecticut mental institution after trying to commit suicide. For the next several years, Beers was hospitalized in various institutions, and was at the mercy of untrained, incompetent attendants. He was subjected to debasing treatment and witnessed the abuse of other patients.

"Of all the patients known to me," Beers wrote, "the one who was assaulted with the greatest frequency was an incoherent and irresponsible man of sixty years. This patient was restless and forever talking or shouting, as any man might if oppressed by such delusions as his. His monotonous recital of his imaginary troubles made him unpopular with those whose business it was to care for him. They showed him no mercy. Each day, he was belabored with lists, broom handles, and frequently with the heavy bunch of keys which attendants usually carry on a long chain."

Beers also wrote that another patient's "arch offense—a symptom of his disease—was that he gabbled incessantly. He could no more stop talking than he could right his reason on command. Yet his failure to become silent at a word was the signal for punishment. On one occasion an attendant ordered him to stop talking and take a seat at the further end of the corridor, about forty feet distant. He was doing his best to obey, even running to keep ahead of the attendant at his heels. As they passed the spot where I was sitting, the attendant felled him with a blow behind the ear; and, in falling, the patient's head barely missed the wall."

Beers often wrote of his own experiences. "It was after one of these wrangles that I was placed in a cold cell in the Bull Pen at eleven o'clock one morning. Still without shoes and with no more covering than underclothes, I was forced to stand, sit, or lie upon a bare floor as hard and cold as the pavement outside."

After being released, Beers began writing a book of his ordeals in the mental institutions. *A Mind That Found Itself* had a major influence on mental health reforms. That same year, Beers rounded the Connecticut Society for Mental Hygiene, which grew into the National Committee for Mental Hygiene. The goals of the society were to improve attitudes toward mental illness and the mentally ill, to improve services for the mentally ill, and to prevent mental illness and promote mental health. This committee produced a set of model commitment laws that were adopted by several states and conducted studies on mental health. Later, the National Committee for Mental Hygiene merged with two other organizations to form the National Association of Mental Health. Renamed the National Mental Health Association in 1979, the organization continues to strive to fulfill Clifford Beers' goals of understanding and tolerance of mental illness, improving services for the mentally ill, preventing mental illness, and promoting mental health.

Beers, 1981; National Mental Health Association, 2005

class sizes would allow more individualized instruction and would be beneficial to students with disabilities. In 1914, Michigan established the first teacher-training program in special education, and in 1919, Ohio passed a law providing for the statewide care of children with disabilities (Kauffman, 2005). Unfortunately, despite this progress, many children with disabilities were never identified and so did not receive treatment, while others had been excluded from school or had dropped out.

During this period, two professional organizations were founded. In 1922, the Council for Exceptional Children (CEC) was created by a group of administrators and supervisors attending the summer session at Columbia University. Composed primarily of parents and educators, CEC lobbied for the rights of individuals with disabilities. CEC was a prominent force in the passage of the first federal special education legislation. Today, CEC holds annual state and national conferences to disseminate current trends and information regarding the education of children with disabilities and continues to play a role in lobbying for the rights of children with disabilities.

The second organization was the American Orthopsychiatric Association, formed in 1924 by a small group of psychiatrists to unite professionals engaged in the study and treatment of human behavior. This organization supports research relating to family and group therapy, mental health, and services and treatment for children.

Multiple attempts to study the diagnosis, etiology, therapy, and prognosis of children with emotional and behavior disorders were made in the 1930s. Most of these studies focused specifically on childhood schizophrenia (Coleman & Webber, 2002; Kanner, 1962) and not on children with emotional and behavior disorders in general. Still, there was some notable progress toward helping children with emotional and behavior disorders during this time. Classrooms for such children were established at Bellevue Hospital in 1935. During the 1940s, schools for children with emotional and behavior disorders were opened in Chicago and New York. Pioneer House, a residential treatment facility in Detroit for delinquent and aggressive boys, was also opened during this period. Treatment at Pioneer House included group therapy and a structured, psychologically sound environment (Redl & Wineman, 1951).

Several attempts were made to define emotional and behavior disorders in children. In 1943, Leo Kanner of Johns Hopkins University Medical School outlined the syndrome of early infantile autism, which would later be called autistic spectrum disorder. Margaret Mahler described a disorder that she named symbiotic infantile psychosis, and Lauretta Bender identified the different levels of childhood schizophrenia (Kanner, 1962). Yet these attempts did not lead to a specific definition that could be used to identify children with emotional and behavior disorders, and despite the progress that had been made in educating children with disabilities, states still excluded them from public classrooms. In the *Department of Public Welfare v. Haas* (1958), the Illinois Supreme Court held that children with disabilities who could not benefit from a good education were not required to go to school (Yell et al., 1998), but events outside the realm of special education were about to change the face of public schools.

The ruling in *Brown v. the Board of Education of Topeka* (1954) had a major impact on the rights of children with disabilities. In *Plessy v. Ferguson* (1896), the Supreme Court had ruled that the states must "provide equal but separate accommodations for the white and colored races." The plaintiffs in the *Brown* case maintained that segregating schools was inherently unequal and that the practice denied educational opportunities to minorities and violated the Fourteenth Amendment (Rothstein, 2000; Yell, 2006; Yell et al., 1998). When the case was decided in their favor, the ruling eventually applied to children with disabilities and made the state-sanctioned segregation in the public schools or exclusion of these individuals from schools unconstitutional.

## Rights for Individuals with Emotional and Behavior Disorders

At the beginning of the 1960s, all the existing information on programs relating to children with emotional and behavior disorders was gathered into a body of research that resulted in a number of books. *The Early Identification of Emotionally Handicapped Children in the School* (Bower, 1960/1981) proposed the definition of emotional disturbance that was incorporated into the Education for All Handicapped Children Act in 1975 and maintained in the Individuals with Disabilities Education Improvement Act of 2004 (IDEA). *Educating Emotionally Disturbed Children* (Haring & Phillips, 1962) provided explicit instructions for establishing public school classrooms for children with emotional disturbances using behavioral principles and a structured environment. The first attempt to integrate the divergent views of psychodynamic, psychoanalytic, and behavioral theory was represented in *Conflict in the Classroom* (Long, Morse, & Newman, 1965).

The Council for Exceptional Children's 40th annual convention in 1962 featured an organizational meeting to discuss forming a new division that would focus on educational services for children with emotional and behavior disorders. By 1964, the Council for Children with Behavioral Disorders (CCBD) had 200 members (Wood, 1999). CCBD now has more than 9,000 members and is dedicated to the education and the social and emotional welfare of children with emotional and behavior disorders (CCBD, 2005).

The civil rights movement of the 1960s undoubtedly influenced parents, advocates, and professionals to seek rights for individuals with disabilities. One noteworthy event was a class action lawsuit brought by the Pennsylvania Association for Retarded Children (PARC) against the Commonwealth of Pennsylvania (*Pennsylvania Association for Retarded Citizens v. Pennsylvania*, 1972). The association challenged the Pennsylvania state law that denied public school education to students with mental retardation. The suit established that children with disabilities could benefit from public school attendance. By denying them a free and appropriate public school education, the state was violating their constitutional rights. The court ruled that all children with mental retardation between the ages of 6 and 21 years must be provided a free public education and must be educated in programs similar to those provided for children without disabilities. Soon after the PARC decision, another class action suit was filed against the District of Columbia's board of education on behalf of students with disabilities who were excluded from public education without due process (*Mills v. Board of Education*, 1972). The court ruled that school districts must develop due process procedures for parents and must create comprehensive plans for identification, assessment, and placement of students with disabilities.

## Legislative History (Mid-1970s to Present)

**SECTION 504.** Section 504 of the Rehabilitation Act (1973) was the first major federal legislation to protect individuals with disabilities against discrimination. It states that any program receiving federal financial assistance may not discriminate against students with disabilities on account of their disabilities. Section 504 defines a person with a *disability* as one (a) who has a physical or mental impairment that substantially limits one or more of the major life activities of the individual, (b) who has a record of such an impairment, or (c) who is regarded as having such an impairment. Because most public schools receive federal funds, they must comply with Section 504. While special education law only includes 13 specific disability categories, Section 504 includes all disabilities. For example, children with attention-deficit hyperactivity disorder (ADHD), diabetes, asthma, cancer, or AIDS may not qualify for special education services, but they are protected under Section 504. Schools must make appropriate accommodations to ensure that these students receive education opportunities.

**THE EDUCATION FOR ALL HANDICAPPED CHILDREN ACT.**    The *PARC* and *Mills* decisions laid the foundation for the passage of the Education for All Handicapped Children Act (PL 94–142) in 1975. The Education for All Handicapped Children Act provided federal funding to states that agreed to educate students with disabilities in the public schools. The act specified that students with disabilities had a right to a free and appropriate public education in the least restrictive environment. The schools were required to develop an individualized education plan for each child and due process procedures were established to protect the rights of the child.

**TABLE 1.1    Historical Events Relating to Children with Emotional and Behavior Disorders**

| Year | Event |
| --- | --- |
| 1578 | Pedro Ponce de León teaches sign language to deaf people. He is the first special education teacher. |
| 1620 | Jean Pablo Bonet publishes *Simplification of the Letters of the Alphabet and a Method Teaching Deaf-Mutes to Speak,* the first special education textbook. |
| 1799 | Jean-Marc Gaspard Itard publishes his report of the wild boy of Averyon. |
| 1841 | Dorothea Dix begins advocating for humanitarian reforms in mental institutions. |
| 1880 | Henry Maudsley published *Physiology and Pathology of the Mind.* |
| 1908 | Clifford Beers publishes *A Mind That Found Itself.* |
| 1910 | The first White House Conference on Children is held. |
| 1914 | Michigan establishes the first teacher training program in special education. |
| 1919 | Ohio passes a Law for the statewide care of children with disabilities. |
| 1922 | Council for Exceptional Children is founded. |
| 1924 | American Orthopsychiatric Association is founded. |
| 1935 | Bellevue Psychiatric Hospital is established. |
| 1943 | Leo Kanner describes early infantile autism. |
| 1946 | Pioneer House is opened. |
| 1954 | *Brown v. the Board of Education of Topeka* rules that segregation is unconstitutional. |
| 1960 | Eli Bower publishes *The Early Identification of Emotionally Handicapped Children in the School,* setting the definition for emotional and behavior disorders. |
| 1962 | Norris Haring and Lakin Phillips publish *Educating Emotionally Disturbed Children.* The Council for Children with Behavioral Disorders is established. |
| 1972 | *Pennsylvania Association for Retarded Citizens v. Pennsylvania* sets the foundation for a free public education for children with disabilities. |
| 1972 | *Mills v. Board of Education* provides a framework for special education legislation. |
| 1975 | The Education of All Handicapped Children Act (PL 94–142) is enacted. |
| 1990 | The Education of All Handicapped Children Act is reauthorized as the Individuals Disabilities Education Act (IDEA). |
| 1997 | IDEA is reauthorized. "Seriously emotionally disturbed" is changed to "emotionally disturbed." |
| 2001 | No Child Left Behind is enacted. |
| 2004 | IDEA is reauthorized. |

As defined by law, *free and appropriate public education* (FAPE) is an educational program that is provided at no charge to parents or guardians. An individualized education program (IEP) must be developed to ensure that a child with a disability receives an appropriate education. The IEP identifies special education and related services. The development of the IEP is a team process that includes the parent or guardian of the child, the general education teacher of the child, a special education teacher who is familiar with the area of disability, a representative of the school (usually a principal or an assistant principal), an individual who can interpret the instructional implication of the assessment results, and the child if appropriate (IDEA, 2004).

Federal law also stipulated that students with disabilities were to be educated in the least restrictive environment. This requirement means that, to the maximum extent appropriate, children with disabilities are to be educated together with children who are not disabled (IDEA, 2004). Thus, the first placement for a child with a disability is the general education classroom. A child with a disability should be removed from the classroom only when the nature or severity of the disability is such that education in the general education classroom cannot be achieved.

**THE INDIVIDUALS WITH DISABILITIES EDUCATION ACT.**    In 1990, the Education for All Handicapped Children Act was reauthorized and renamed the Individuals with Disabilities Education Act (IDEA). IDEA added traumatic brain injury and autism as new disability categories. Prior to that addition, many children with autism were treated under the category of emotional disturbance. The term *handicapped* was replaced with *disability*, and the language of IDEA was also changed to follow a "people first" format. It was no longer correct to describe a child as a "mentally retarded child"; rather, the correct term was "child with mental retardation." It was recognized that a disability did not define the individual but was merely a characteristic of the individual. The child came first. (See Table 1.2.)

IDEA was reauthorized in 1997, at which time several major provisions were added. Those provisions included positive behavior support plans and a manifestation determination by the IEP team that would be held if a school suspended or expelled a student with a disability for more than 10 days. Positive behavior support plans focus on reinforcing the

---

**TABLE 1.2    The Six Principles of IDEA**

| | |
|---|---|
| • Zero Reject | All children with disabilities will be educated. State education agencies are required to locate, indentify and evaluate all children from birth to 21 years who are suspected of having a disability. |
| • Nondiscriminatory Evaluation | Multifaceted, comprehensive evaluations are used to determine whether a child has a disability and whether the child needs special education services. |
| • Free and Appropriate Public Education (FAPE) | Education is provided at public expense. An individualized education program is developed and implemented. |
| • Least Restrictive Environment | Children with disabilities will be educated to the maximum extent appropriate with children who do not have disabilities. |
| • Due Process Safeguards | Protects the rights of children with disabilities and their parents. Provides for mediation. Provides for due process hearings. |
| • Parent Participation | Parents are involved in the development and implementation of special education services for their children. |

appropriate behavior of the student. (For more information, see Chapter 6.) The manifesta-tion determination is a hearing to determine whether a student's inappropriate behavior is related to the student's disability. If the team determines that the behavior is due to the dis-ability, the student cannot be expelled. (See Chapter 11.)

**THE NO CHILD LEFT BEHIND ACT AND IDEA.**    Another important legislative act, the No Child Left Behind Act of 2001 (NCLB), has affected not only the education of children with disabil-ities, but that of all children in the public schools. The primary goal of NCLB is to guarantee that all children in the public schools are proficient in important academic subjects by the 2013–2014 school year. NCLB also ensures that highly qualified teachers will teach all students by the 2005–2006 school year. Highly qualified teachers must have a bachelor's degree, must be fully certified for the area in which they teach, and must demonstrate com-petency in the subjects they teach (Yell, 2006). Accountability is a major component of NCLB; all public schools are required to assess 95% of their students, including students with disabilities. The purpose of these assessments is to measure the educational progress of stu-dents. However, NCLB has been criticized for providing inadequate funding and for forcing teachers to teach to the test rather than teaching broad mastery of the subject.

IDEA was reauthorized in 2004 as the Individuals with Disabilities Education Improvement Act, but it is still known as IDEA or IDEA 2004. The reauthorization of IDEA 2004 aligns IDEA with NCLB. IDEA 2004 defines highly qualified special education teachers in the same manner as NCLB defines highly qualified teachers. Special education teachers generally teach more than one core subject and are required to meet additional require-ments. IDEA 2004 no longer requires IEPs to include short-term objectives (with the excep-tion of plans for students who have moderate/profound mental retardation). In addition, a student with a disability who brings drugs or weapons to school or who causes serious bod-ily injury to another individual may be removed to an alternative setting for up to 45 days without a manifestation determination.

## DEFINITION OF EMOTIONAL AND BEHAVIOR DISORDERS

Identifying students who have emotional and behavior disorders is difficult due to several factors. The current federal definition is vague and subjective. Professionals in the field do not agree on a definition. Terminology varies among professionals and among school dis-tricts in different states. _Emotional disturbance_ as defined in IDEA 2004 is a social construct that is perceived according to societal rules. This definition is so vague that it may be inter-preted in a variety of ways. It is understandable that general education teachers, special edu-cation teachers, and school administrators have a difficult time identifying students who have emotional and behavior disorders.

In order to understand the nature of emotional and behavior disorders, teachers and administrators must understand the operational definition of these disorders. However, the current federal definition has been widely criticized as impractical and illogical (Kauffman, 2005; Merrell & Walker, 2004).

### Federal Definition

During the 1950s, Eli Bower conducted research involving a thousand students in California. In his book _The Early Identification of Emotionally Handicapped Children in the School_

(1960/1981), Bower proposed the definition of emotional disturbance that was adopted by the U.S. Department of Education and included in PL 94–142 and IDEA 2004. These laws define emotional disturbance as follows:

**(i)** Emotional disturbance means a condition exhibiting one or more of the following characteristics over a long period of time and to a marked degree that adversely affects educational performance:

　**(a)** an inability to learn which cannot be explained by intellectual, sensory, or health factors;

　**(b)** an inability to build or maintain satisfactory interpersonal relationships with peers and teachers;

　**(c)** inappropriate types of behavior or feelings under normal circumstances;

　**(d)** a general pervasive mood of unhappiness or depression;

　**(e)** a tendency to develop physical symptoms or fears associated with personal or school problems.

**(ii)** Emotional disturbance includes schizophrenia. The term does not apply to children who are socially maladjusted, unless it is determined that they have an emotional disturbance. (IDEA, 2004, p. 46756)

The first part of the definition contains three important components: a condition that exists *over a long period of time*, that exhibits symptoms *to a marked degree*, and that *adversely affects educational performance*. These are crucial elements of defining emotional and behavior disorders. As Bower (1982) pointed out himself, one or more of the characteristics of emotional disturbance could be observed in all children (or even adults) at different points in their lives. The crucial difference that distinguishes students with emotional and behavior disorders is that they experience these characteristics over a long period of time and to a marked degree.

Unfortunately, these terms are problematic because they are subjective. How long is a long period of time, and how severe is a marked degree? Guidelines have not been established for these criteria, so they are subject to the tolerance level and expectations of the teacher. For example, one teacher may view a student who cannot remain in his seat as having disruptive and unacceptable behavior; another teacher views the same student as simply being fidgety and ignores the behavior. One teacher might view a student as depressed because she sits in the corner of the classroom and does not interact with peers; another teacher might view this student as shy.

Another difficulty in defining behavioral expectations by societal norms is the presence of ethnic and cultural differences among students. Many teachers receive little, if any, training in multicultural and diversity issues, and frequently, without being cognizant of it, define inappropriate behavior on the basis of their own cultural experiences. Often, students with different behavioral and learning styles are inappropriately identified as having academic problems (Obiakor & Utley, 2004). Another point of contention with the definition is that it states that the emotional disturbance must adversely affect a child's educational performance, yet once again, guidelines have not been established to clarify what is meant by *educational performance*. Does it mean academic achievement? Can educational performance include social skills, since the ability to get along with others and comply with the expectations of teachers could affect one's academic achievement? It can be argued that social skills are part of the educational performance of students with emotional and behavior disorders, since IDEA 2004 requires school professionals to consider academic achievement *and* functional performance in the development of IEPs.

The five characteristics in the definition are evaluated according to the subjective judgment of the individual. For example, how do you define *satisfactory interpersonal relationship* or *pervasive mood of unhappiness?* If a student is shy and does not interact well with her peers, does she have an emotional and behavior disorder? Because there is no consensus in operational definitions, identification of students with emotional and behavior disorders varies from state to state. As a result, a number of students may be inappropriately identified as having emotional and behavior disorders, and a number of students who have emotional and behavior disorders may not be identified. Failure to be identified is especially common among students who exhibit a pervasive mood of unhappiness or depression. Often, these students do not display overt behaviors, and because they are not disruptive influences in the classroom, they may not be readily identified. As a result, they may not receive the interventions they need.

Another difficulty in identifying students with emotional and behavior disorders is the fact that different states use different terminology. Some of the terms commonly used include *emotional disturbance, socially and emotionally maladjusted, emotionally handicapped, behaviorally disordered*, and *emotionally and behaviorally disordered* (Kidder-Ashley, Deni, Azar, & Anderson, 2000). Because the terminology and operational definitions are different, a child conceivably could be identified in one state but not another.

**SOCIAL MALADJUSTMENT EXCLUSION.**    Another criticism of the federal definition is that it does not include students who are socially maladjusted. In fact, Bower has stated that the five characteristics of his definition are indicators of social maladjustment (Bower, 1982), and it is difficult to imagine a child who has a social maladjustment who does not meet any of the five characteristics in IDEA.

Some professionals equate social maladjustment with delinquency. They argue that these children are psychologically normal and able to follow rules and meet expectations, but that they choose to violate the norms for acceptable behavior (Costenbader & Buntaine, 1999; Stein & Merrell, 1992). Because social maladjustment has not been defined in federal law, some states and school districts associate it with delinquency, antisocial behavior, conduct disorder, and behavior disorder. These states use the exclusionary clause to avoid identifying these students as emotionally disturbed under the federal definition (Cohen, 1994; Costenbader & Buntaine, 1999; Merrell & Walker, 2004; Quinn, Rutherford, Leone, Osher, & Poirier, 2005). As a result, many school districts are not serving children who have behavioral problems, and this has added to the criticism of the federal definition (Kauffman, 2005).

## The Council for Children with Behavioral Disorders Definition

The Council for Children with Behavioral Disorders (CCBD, 1989) adopted an alternative definition of emotional and behavior disorder. This definition was developed by a group of professionals and advocates assigned by the National Mental Health and Special Education Coalition. The CCBD definition includes terminology used by professionals and is more representative of the wide spectrum of students who have emotional and behavior disorders. More importantly, it does not distinguish between social maladjustment and emotional disturbance.

The CCBD definition states,

1. The term "emotional or behavioral disorder" means a disability that is characterized by emotional or behavioral responses in school programs so different from appropriate age,

cultural, or ethnic norms that the responses adversely affect educational performance, including academic, social, vocational or personal skills, more than a temporary, expected response to stressful events in the environment; consistently exhibited in two different settings, at least one of which is school related; and unresponsive to direct intervention in general education, or the condition of the child is such that general education interventions would be insufficient.

2. The term includes such a disability that co-exists with other disabilities.
3. The term includes a schizophrenic disorder, affective disorder, anxiety disorder, or other sustained disorder of conduct or adjustment, affecting a child if the disorder affects educational performance as described in paragraph (1). (Executive Committee of the Council for Children with Behavioral Disorders, 1989; Forness & Knitzer, 1992)

The CCBD definition was submitted to the U.S. Congress as a proposed replacement for the current federal definition of emotional disturbance. While this definition seemed to have support in the field, it was not adopted for IDEA 2004, and Bower's 1960 definition for emotional disturbance has been left virtually unchanged in the federal legislation.

## THE SOCIAL CONSTRUCTION OF EMOTIONAL AND BEHAVIOR DISORDERS

### Perceptions of Social Construction

Individuals with disabilities also are affected by the social construction of the society in which they live. *Social construction* includes cultural expectations, societal norms, and the political response to these expectations. In 1841, when Dorothea Dix asked why the women inmates confined to the East Cambridge Jail were housed in unheated and foul-smelling quarters, she was informed that insane people *do not feel the heat or cold* (Viney & Zorich, 1982). A Massachusetts court ruled that students exhibiting behavior due to *imbecility* could be expelled, a ruling that prevented a number of children with mental retardation from attending public schools (*Watson v. City of Cambridge*, 1893). In 1919, a Wisconsin court ruled that a student with a disability could be excluded from public school if his or her disability had a *depressing and nauseating effect on the teachers and other students* (*Beattie v. Board of Education*, 1919).

Social construction also influences how individuals or groups are perceived. For example, a woman wearing a swimsuit to church on Sunday morning would violate the societal expectation of most groups. Even if the temperature were over 100°, wearing a swimsuit to church would simply be unacceptable; however, if the same woman wore a swimsuit to a church function at the beach, societal norms would not have been breached.

### Perception of Emotional and Behavior Disorders

Unlike students with Down syndrome or physical disabilities, who have observable disabilities, students with emotional and behavior disorders appear normal. As a result, the students are usually not perceived to have disabilities, and when they behave inappropriately, these students are viewed as troublemakers or believed to come from dysfunctional families in which societal expectations were not taught. In these cases, emotional and behavior disorders are simply not acknowledged as a disability.

## Case Study 1.2

### Johnny

Jennifer Garcia has been a kindergarten teacher at Franklin Pierce Elementary School for nearly 25 years. She has taught a number of children over the years with different behaviors and temperaments. This year, her challenging student is Johnny.

Johnny is a 6-year-old student who refuses to comply with any classroom expectations. He refuses to sit at his desk. When he is redirected, he throws his pencil at Mrs. Garcia, yelling, "You're not my mother!" He intimidates the other children by threatening to hit them, but has yet to carry through on his threat.

Mrs. Garcia has tried a number of behavior management techniques with Johnny. When she told him that he could play with his favorite toy if he would sit at his desk, Johnny threw the toy out the window. When she told Johnny to stay inside during recess, he refused and went outside anyway until the principal, Mr. Price, took him to his office.

Mrs. Gloria has talked to Johnny's mother several times, but she was informed that Johnny was just as noncompliant at home.

After Johnny had shown inappropriate behavior for several months and had stolen 5 dollars from her purse, Mrs. Garcia felt that Johnny qualified as needing special educational services due to emotional disturbance. Johnny was "*unable to build or maintain satisfactory interpersonal relationships with peers and teachers,*" and he "*displayed inappropriate types of behavior under normal circumstances.*"

Mrs. Garcia turned in a referral form to the guidance counselor, Mrs. Wickert. Mrs. Wickert felt Johnny did not qualify for special education at this time. His behaviors had not interfered with his grades, and she felt that the recent death of his father could be the cause of his inappropriate behaviors. Mrs. Wickert suggested that Mrs. Garcia meet with the grade-level Student Assistance Team for suggestions on helping Johnny succeed in the classroom. She agreed to meet with Johnny once a week for counseling.

Mrs. Garcia was concerned. She felt that Johnny needed special education services. She wondered what it would take before he could be placed in a special education classroom.

Conversely, others believe that if a student's behavior is a problem in the classroom, then he or she has an emotional and behavior disorder and should be taught in a special education classroom. In many instances, teachers and other educational professionals define students with emotional and behavior disorders as those who exhibit disruptive behaviors in school. Yet emotional and behavior disorders are not identifiable solely on the basis of the students' disruptive behaviors. Students who are suffering from depression and are not exhibiting behaviors that are disruptive to the class are generally not referred for special education because they do not threaten the classroom archetype. They fail quietly. These students do not fit the perception of children who have emotional and behavior disorders. The ambiguity of the definition and the subjective nature of emotional and behavior disorders can be confusing, especially to individuals who are responsible for identifying students with emotional and behavior disorders.

For example, consider a student invited to a team meeting with his teachers to discuss his poor progress in school. The teachers calmly discuss their expectations of him. The boy listens intently, intimidated by the eight teachers surrounding him. When the teachers finish, they ask him what he needs to do. The student replies honestly that he needs to tell them what they want to hear in order to return to class. One teacher, feeling that the boy's reply was disrespectful, responds angrily that this is not some kind of game. The boy bristles as the discussion continues heatedly for a few more minutes. Finally, he is dismissed. The boy leaves the room, slamming the door behind him. Outraged, several teachers remark that the boy exhibits mood swings and has a behavior problem. They recommend that he be referred for evaluation for special education services. From the perspective of the student, the teachers were harassing him and had no right to do so. He feels that he was being honest in his replies and that he became angry only when provoked.

Consider some additional examples:

- A student rocks constantly in her seat. Does she have an emotional and behavior disorder?
- A student beats up a peer because he was singing a song from a popular movie at lunch. Does the aggressor have an emotional and behavior disorder?
- A student threatens to commit suicide because her parents are getting a divorce. Does she have an emotional and behavior disorder?

Many of these students do not have emotional and behavior disorders. Because the definition of emotional disturbance is subjective, the identification of students who have emotional and behavior disorders is based on the observer's perspective and affected by social construction.

## Culturally Responsive Teaching

Another factor affecting the identification of students with emotional and behavior disorders is the impact of culture and language on the education process. The number of teachers from diverse backgrounds is not keeping pace with the increasing number of culturally and linguistically diverse learners. The majority of these students are taught by female European American teachers (Aaroe & Nelson, 2000; Nieto, 2002; Trent & Artiles, 2007), and it is difficult for these teachers to be culturally responsive to students whose cultural characteristics are different (Brown, 2007).

Culture influences the way in which a student behaves and learns. Teachers need to be aware that while the behavior of a student might not be acceptable according to the norms of the dominant culture, it may reflect the child's own cultural background. Given the increasing number of culturally and linguistically diverse learners in public schools, it is crucial for educators to·determine whether students who have behavior problems have disabilities or whether the perceived disabilities are due to cultural and language differences (Gollnick & Chinn, 2001; Obiakor, 2003).

Unfortunately, many teachers lack the pedagogical skills, knowledge, and attitudes to teach culturally and linguistically diverse learners (Brown, 2007; McSwain, 2002; Trent, Kea, & Oh, 2008). The teachers' lack of understanding of different cultures and the effects that culture can have on behavior sometimes cause teachers to misidentify students as having disabilities (Ochoa, Robles-Pina, Garcia, & Breunig, 1999) and to inappropriately identify ethnically diverse learners as having emotional and behavior disorders (Aaroe & Nelson,

Index Open

Culturally responsive teachers understand their culture and incorporate it with the values, mores, beliefs, and traditions of cultures of their students.

2000; Nieto, 2002). Teachers need to understand the cultures of their students, and the impacts that culture has on the educational process.

Teachers also need to promote appreciation, acceptance, and understanding of the different students' cultures in the school environment. Cultural understanding requires teachers first to understand their own cultures and to recognize how culture affects the way they view their students, but many teachers do not take the time to examine their own cultures. Teachers need to recognize aspects of their own cultures and the cultures of their students, particularly when they make judgments about social skills and behaviors (Cartledge & Kourea, 2008). Culturally responsive teachers understand their own cultures and incorporate their own values, mores, beliefs, and traditions with those of their students' cultures (Grant & Sleeter, 2006; Morrier, Irving, Dandy, Dmitriyev, & Ukeje, 2007; Saifer & Barton, 2007). Not only does this practice reduce the overrepresentation of culturally and linguistically diverse students in special education classes, but it allows culturally and linguistically diverse students to improve their academic achievement (Gay, 2002).

## Emotional Disturbance Versus Social Maladjustment

The debate regarding the exclusion of social maladjustment from the federal definition of emotional disturbance has been raging since the passage of the Education for All Handicapped Children Act in 1975. Social maladjustment has not been clearly defined, and it is interesting that Congress has chosen to exclude something it has not defined (Kehle, Bray, Theodore, Zhou, & McCoach, 2004). Some have stated that social maladjustment was excluded from the definition of emotional disturbance in the Education for All Handicapped Children Act of 1975 because of poor legislative oversight and concerns over providing special education services to juvenile delinquents who are under court supervision (Skiba & Grizzle, 1991).

Some experts believe that a difference exists between children who are socially maladjusted and children who have emotional disturbances. Children who are socially maladjusted and who have elevated levels of psychopathy may cause considerable harm to others, violate major age-appropriate societal norms, and violate the rights of others. Some professionals feel that combining the two categories would lead to the victimization of children who are truly emotionally disturbed by students who are socially maladjusted (Gacono & Hughes, 2004).

Other professionals believe that children who are socially maladjusted are able to follow rules and meet expectations, but they choose to violate societal norms (Costenbader & Buntaine, 1999; Stein & Merrell, 1992). Seen in this light, social maladjustment is not a disability and such students should not be considered for special educational services. Common interpretations of social maladjustment include delinquency, antisocial behavior, externalizing behavior disorders, and social deviance. Many states and school districts use the exclusionary clause to avoid identifying these children as having emotional and behavior disorders and thus to exclude them from special education services (Costenbader & Buntaine, 1999; Kehle et al., 2004; Merrell & Walker, 2004).

Several basic assumptions regarding social maladjustment have been used to justify the exclusion of socially maladjusted children from the emotional disturbance classification:

1. Social maladjustment is equivalent to the psychiatric diagnoses of conduct disorder and oppositional defiant disorder.
2. Socially maladjusted children make *conscious decisions* to behave negatively, whereas children with serious emotional disturbances act without forethought.
3. Socially maladjusted children *understand* the consequences or impacts of their behavior, whereas children with serious emotional disturbances fail to appreciate the consequences of their behavior.
4. Socially maladjusted children have the ability to *control* their behavior, whereas children with serious emotional disturbances lack the ability to regulate or inhibit their behavior.
5. Socially maladjusted children exhibit *no guilt or remorse* for their negative behavior.
6. Socially maladjusted children exhibit *externalizing* behaviors, whereas seriously emotionally disturbed children exhibit internalizing behaviors.
7. Socially maladjusted children are *nondisabled*, whereas seriously emotionally disturbed children have disabilities (Olympia et al., 2004, p. 837).

Other experts contend that these assumptions are not supported by research (Olympia et al., 2004; Walker, Ramsey, & Gresham, 2004). Because the definition of emotional disturbance is vague, some experts recommend that the two groups should not be distinguished from each other for special education services (Forness & Knitzer, 1992; Olympia et al., 2004). The exclusionary clause is considered incomprehensible (Kauffman, 2005). This viewpoint holds that a child who is socially maladjusted is also emotionally disturbed and that it is hard to conceive of a child who is socially maladjusted who does not possess any of the five characteristics listed in the federal definition of emotional disturbance (Bower, 1982). The American Psychological Association (APA) and the CCBD have proposed that children with conduct disorder, oppositional defiant disorder, and ADHD should receive special education services (APA, 1989; CCBD, 1990).

The debate about emotional disturbance and social maladjustment is far from over. The lack of clear operational definitions of emotional and behavior disorders and social maladjustment has prevented a number of students from receiving needed services.

## The Social Meaning of Labels

For centuries, labels were designed to exclude people. Groups of people were labeled on the basis of race, ability, gender, and class, a practice that continues to this day. Assessment of different attributes is used to distinguish between individuals who represent the norm and those who do not meet the norm, even if the definition of normal is societal and not based on fact. For example, those who wear glasses are considered "different." Note that children with glasses are often teased and called names like "four eyes" and that many people wear contacts or have laser surgery performed on their eyes to avoid being different. Yet a majority of people are nearsighted or farsighted, so individuals who need glasses are the norm; however, societal expectations contradict this fact.

Disability has been called "a pocket of social arrangement" (McDermott & Varenne, 1996) that is supported by societal norms and officially propagated by educators. Because a majority of students with disabilities live in poverty and are culturally and linguistically diverse learners, the identification of students with disabilities may be discriminatory (Brantlinger, 2001).

As soon as a student has been identified as having an emotional and behavior disorder, he is often viewed differently by teachers and administrators. Even before he steps inside the classroom, this student is seen as someone who will disrupt the classroom, who is a troublemaker, and who belongs in an alternative setting. The expectations placed on the student often become a self-fulfilling prophecy.

Students with emotional and behavior disorders are often placed in specialized, separated classrooms that may not meet the definition of the least restrictive environment. These placements are morally, ethically, and professionally wrong; the determination of special education services is supposed to be based on the individual needs of the student. Unfortunately, students with emotional and behavior disorders are reassigned to new schools by their school districts at a higher rate than students with other disabilities or students without disabilities (Wagner, Kutash, Duchnowski, Epstein, & Sumi, 2005).

Yet labels are necessary for communication among teachers, administrators, and other professionals. Labels provide the information that teams need to develop appropriate programs for students with emotional and behavior disorders. Teachers and administrators need to understand the meaning of labels and at the same time to recognize that, regardless of labels, each student is an individual with unique needs.

## The Labeling Process

In order for students to receive special education services, they must be identified as having a disability and classified into one of the 13 disability categories specified by IDEA. Not only does classification involves scientific and fiscal interests, it also involves political and ethical considerations (Luckasson & Reeve, 2001). Some educators and professionals believe that labeling a student with a disability stigmatizes that student. Others argue that labeling is necessary in order to provide specific educational services for students with disabilities. The benefits and disadvantages of labeling have not changed in the past 20 years.

Some of the possible advantages of special education labeling include the following:

1. Federal and local funding for research and special education programs are tied to specific categories of disabilities.
2. Labeling enables teachers, administrators, and professionals to communicate with one another and conveys general characteristics of specific disabilities.
3. Labels allow advocacy groups to promote specific programs and prompt legislative action.
4. Labeling may improve the understanding and tolerance of children with disabilities by children without disabilities.

Some of the disadvantages of labeling are as follows:

1. Labels shape teacher expectations. This is especially true for students with emotional and behavior disorders. Their teachers expect inappropriate behaviors.
2. Labels may stigmatize students.
3. Labels may affect students' self-esteem.
4. Labels suggest that the learning problem is with the students, and they can be an excuse for ineffective instruction.
5. Students cannot receive special education services until they are labeled.
6. The use of labels causes a disproportionate number of culturally and linguistically diverse learners to be identified as having disabilities.
7. Special education labels can persist for the entire academic career of the student.

Alternative methods to labels have been discussed, but none has been widely accepted. Even if the current method of identifying and labeling students with emotional and behavior disorders did change, another method of labeling would take its place (Hallahan & Kauffman, 2003). As long as schools continue to provide interventions and programs for students with disabilities, labels will be an unavoidable part of the process.

## The Social Organization of Schools

Since the era of one-room schools, the image of the ideal classroom has involved a teacher providing the lesson and maintaining control, while the students sit dutifully at their desks and meet the behavioral and academic expectations of the teacher, school district, and community. Even now, this view of the classroom persists in the minds of people who are not familiar with the day-to-day operation of public schools. Teachers are still expected to teach the lesson. They are still expected to maintain control of the classroom environment. Students are expected to learn, and they are expected to behave. State and federal governments expect teachers to be highly qualified and expect all students to learn core subjects at age-appropriate levels.

Unfortunately, the reality of public education is a different picture. Not all students behave. Not all students learn at age-appropriate levels, and some students will never be at grade level. Many educators teach to state-mandated tests rather than teaching a more varied curriculum for fear of being stigmatized with an unacceptability rating. Good schools help learners become more heterogeneous, and good special education programs help children with disabilities achieve more than they could have otherwise (Kauffman, 2004), but schools and special education programs cannot help *all* students achieve at the same level. The unrealistic and impossible expectations placed on schools affect the types of services provided to students with disabilities, especially students with emotional and behavior disorders. The requirements of No Child Left Behind and IDEA 2004 are adding to these issues and concerns.

Students with emotional and behavior disorders have difficulty meeting school standards, and the current system sets them up to fail. These students are the proverbial square pegs being forced into round holes. The expectations of schools often force these students into failure. Students with emotional and behavior disorders are unlikely to meet classroom expectations and often are not liked by teachers or accepted by peers. Teachers are sometimes less tolerant of the behaviors of students who have been identified as having emotional and behavior disorders. Understanding students with emotional and behavior disorders is a prerequisite to providing the interventions and services these children need (Wagner, Kutash, et al., 2005).

## IDENTIFYING CHILDREN WITH EMOTIONAL AND BEHAVIOR DISORDERS

Considering that the federal definition of *emotional and behavior disorders* is subjective, how can teachers, special educators, school psychologists, and administrators identify students who have these disorders? This task becomes even more problematic when experts in the field disagree with the definition of emotional disturbance. Despite this debate, it is possible to extrapolate some general guidelines from the federal definition.

To qualify as having an emotional disturbance, a student must exhibit one or more of the five characteristics over a long period of time. To borrow from the definition of ADHD in the *Diagnostic and Statistical Manual of Mental Disorders, Fourth Edition–Text Revision* (*DSM-IV-TR*, American Psychiatric Association, 2000), this period of time should be at least 6 months. The student's teacher should check grades and disciplinary referrals from the previous year to determine whether the student had academic and social difficulties in earlier grades. If the student did not have any difficulties in previous years, then the teacher needs to ask why the student is having problems now.

The severity of the student's grades and the number of absences should be examined. When examining grades, the teacher should look for a drop in grades, such as a drop from a C average to a D- average with failing grades for several classes. The absence rate must be extreme in order to indicate an emotional and behavior disorder. The absence rate might increase from 1 or 2 days a month to 5 or 6 days a month. Alternatively, some students with emotional and behavior disorders have few absences because school tends to be their most stable environment.

In general, students with emotional and behavior disorders display more maladaptive behaviors than students without emotional and behavior disorders (Cullinan & Sabornie, 2004; Wagner, Kutash, et al., 2005). But it is difficult to operationalize, or define in a measurable manner, the five characteristics of emotional disturbance. That is why it is important to use systematic screening for students who are at risk for developing emotional and behavior disorders (Sprague & Walker, 2000). Behavior checklists are generally used to screen children who are at risk for these disorders. The student's teacher and a parent or guardian need to complete a behavior checklist that assesses maladaptive behaviors across multiple environments (Toffalo & Pedersen, 2005).

It is important to note that one person alone cannot make the determination that a student has an emotional and behavior disorder. If a teacher suspects that a student has an emotional and behavior disorder, the teacher needs to follow the assessment process prescribed by IDEA for identifying a child with a disability. (See Chapter 4.) This process not only provides a method for identifying a student with an emotional and behavior disorder, but also provides assistance for the teacher who has the student in his or her classroom. Thus, the teacher does not stand alone in his or her efforts to educate students with emotional and behavior disorders.

However, the role of the teacher in identifying students with emotional and behavior disorders cannot be underestimated. Teachers are often the first to suspect that students may have disabilities, and they are also the first ones to initiate the process that may provide needed services for their students. When they understand the nature and characteristics of emotional and behavior disorders, teachers can provide the interventions and strategies that allow students with emotional and behavior disorders to be successful in school.

## Summary

Identifying a student with emotional and behavior disorders is a complex and difficult process because the federal definition is subjective in nature. Once a student has been identified and labeled as having an emotional and behavior disorder, the child's entire school experience is altered forever. It is extremely important that the student be appropriately identified as early as possible to provide interventions that may prevent escalation of the inappropriate behaviors. It is important for educators to remember the following factors regarding emotional and behavior disorders:

1. The definition of *emotional disturbance* is vague and subjective.
2. Operational definitions differ from state to state.
3. Many students with emotional and behavior disorders are never identified.
4. Students with emotional and behavior disorders are more likely to be serviced in self-contained classrooms or alternative settings.

General education teachers can expect to have at least one student in the classroom each year who has some type of emotional and behavior disorder. In fact, teachers have reported an average of 3 children with some type of behavior problem in their classrooms each year (Henry, Gordon, Mashburn, & Ponder, 2001).

Without some type of appropriate intervention, these students will have limited success in school and after they leave school. Fifty-one percent of students with emotional and behavior disorders drop out of school (U.S. Department of Education, 2002). Over 50% of students with emotional and behavior disorders were unemployed for the first 5 years after leaving school (D'Amico & Blackorby, 1992; D'Amico & Marder, 1991; Wagner, Newman, Cameto, Garza, & Levine, 2005; Zigmond, 2006). Fifty percent of students with emotional and behavior disorders have had at least one arrest within 3 years of leaving school (Bullis & Cheney, 1999).

Public schools are the only child-serving institutions mandated to serve children and youths with emotional and behavior disorders (Wagner, Kutash, et al., 2005). Teachers are generally the first ones to recognize that a child may have emotional and behavior disorders, and they are often the child's only hope of receiving the necessary intervention and services needed to have a productive life. Understanding the nature and severity of emotional and behavior disorders is just the first step for educators.

## Review Questions

1. How has the identification and treatment of individuals with emotional and behavior disorders changed over the years?
2. Compare and contrast Section 504 of the Rehabilitation Act, the Education for All Handicapped Children Act, IDEA, and NCLB. Explain how each piece of legislation relates to emotional and behavior disorders.
3. Give the definition of emotional disturbance stated by IDEA. How does it differ from the CCBD definition of emotional and behavior disorders?
4. Should social maladjustment be considered to be part of the definition of emotional and behavior disorders? Why or why not?
5. What are the advantages and disadvantages of labeling children with emotional and behavior disorders?
6. As a teacher or school administrator, examine your own cultural and societal expectations. How could these expectations affect the way you view a child with emotional and behavior disorders?
7. What are some of the difficulties that educators face in identifying children with emotional and behavior disorders?

# CHAPTER 2

# Characteristics of Emotional and Behavior Disorders

**After reading this chapter, you should be able to**

- Discuss the factors that affect the prevalence of emotional and behavior disorders.
- Describe the factors that hinder the identification of young children displaying

emotional and behavior disorders and how this identification problem affects efforts to provide early intervention.

- Explain the differences between internalizing and externalizing disorders.

## PREVALENCE OF EMOTIONAL AND BEHAVIOR DISORDERS

Because the federal definition of emotional disturbance is subjective and vague, it is extremely difficult to estimate the prevalence of this condition or the number of students with emotional and behavior disorders who attend public schools, but the estimates are staggering. The World Health Organization has estimated that neuropsychiatric disorders will rise by over 50% internationally by 2020, and the National Institute of Mental Health (2001) has reported that between 5% and 7% of children used some type of mental health service between 1996 and 1998. Some experts estimate the prevalence of students with emotional and behavior disorders to be between 16% and 22% (U.S. Public Health Service, 2000). Yet, during the 2000–2001 school year, the number of students between ages 6 and 21 years who received special education services under IDEA due to having emotional and behavior disorders was less than 1% (.72%) (U.S. Department of Education, 2002). This number is below the 2% estimate the federal government used for providing services for students with emotional and behavior disorders, and far below the estimate of experts, which means that thousands of students with emotional and behavior disorders are not receiving special education services.

## Gender

Boys tend to be identified more often as having emotional and behavior disorders than girls. Compared with European American female students, European American male students are four times as likely to be identified as having emotional and behavior disorders. Hispanic males are three times as likely, and African American males are six times as likely, as European American males to be identified as having emotional and behavior disorders (Billingsley, Fall, & Williams, 2006; Coutinho, Oswald, Best, & Forness, 2002). Boys are more likely than girls to have externalizing problems and to display conduct problems, immaturity, antisocial behavior, and aggressive behaviors (Talbott & Lloyd, 1997; Talbott & Thiede, 1999). Girls are more likely than boys to have internalizing problems and to display depression and social withdrawal, and they are less likely to cause disruptions in the classroom. Because teachers see boys' behavioral problems as more disturbing, boys are more often identified as having emotional and behavior disorders.

## Cultural and Linguistic Diversity

Culturally and linguistically diverse students are disproportionately identified as having emotional and behavior disorders (Coutinho et al., 2002). In this context, disproportionate identification means that some culturally and linguistically diverse groups are overidentified, while others are underidentified. This phenomenon suggests that some students in the overidentified group probably should not have been identified as having emotional and behavior disorders, whereas some students in the underidentified groups have emotional and behavior disorders but have not been identified.

Federal government data indicate that African American students historically have been overrepresented in many of the disability categories. They are twice as likely as other racial groups to be identified as having emotional and behavior disorders. Hispanics, American Indians or Alaskan Natives, and Asian or Pacific Islanders historically have been underidentified. (See Figure 2.1.) The racial/ethnic composition of students in public schools in 2000 was as follows: 16.6% African American; 16.6% Hispanic; 61.3% European American; and 5.4% all other races (U.S. Department of Education, National Center for Education Statistics, 2002). The racial/ethnic composition of students identified as having an emotional disturbance during the 2000–2001 school year was 1.23% American Indian or Alaskan Native; 1.26% Asian or Pacific Islander; 26.68% African American; 8.12% Hispanic; and 62.71% European American. (See Figure 2.2.) (U.S. Department of Education, 2002).

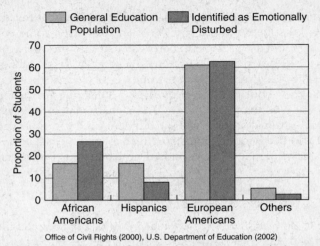

Office of Civil Rights (2000), U.S. Department of Education (2002)

**FIGURE 2.1**   Racial/Ethnic Comparison of General Education Population and Emotional Disturbance

## Factors Affecting Disproportionate Representation

A number of factors may be responsible for the disproportionate identification of some students as having emotional and behavior disorders. These factors include teacher bias, a lack of effective prereferral interventions, use of inappropriate and/or inequitable assessment procedures, assignment of certain students to low-ability groups/tracking, and teacher expectations (Wilder et al., 2007).

Poverty is associated with higher identification rates of emotional and behavior disorders (Coutinho et al., 2002). Children who live in poverty experience poor health and have

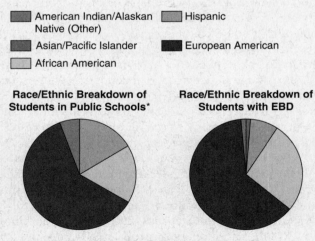

*American Indian/Alaskan Native, Asian/Pacific Islander are listed as Other
Department of Education, 2002

**FIGURE 2.2**   Race/Ethnicity Breakdown of Children Served Under IDEA During the 2000–2001 School Year

public insurance or no health insurance, poor education, and poor social outcome (Duncan & Brooks-Gunn, 1997; Mark & Buck, 2006).

Minority status is another factor that increases identification rates of emotional and behavior disorders. Many minorities are disproportionately poor. They are more likely than European Americans to be identified as having mental retardation or learning disabilities, and African Americans in particular are more likely to be identified as having emotional and behavior disorders (Wagner, Kutash, et al., 2005). As the mean income of a community increases, the identification rate for African Americans increases and rates for European American and Hispanics decrease (Yeh, Forness, Ho, McCabe, & Hough, 2004). The disproportionate representation of minorities in special education settings has been viewed as a sociopolitical problem caused by conflicts between family culture and school culture (Yeh et al., 2004).

## EMOTIONAL AND BEHAVIOR DISORDERS IN EARLY CHILDHOOD

There is a relationship between children who develop emotional and behavior disorders and their environments (Conroy & Brown, 2004; Kaiser, Cai, Hancock, & Foster, 2002; Qi & Kaiser, 2003). Nearly 21% of children under the age of 5 years live in poverty (The Annie E. Casey Foundation, 2004). As many as 10 million children live in situations where they are exposed to domestic violence and parental drug and alcohol abuse (National Center for Children Exposed to Violence, 2003). Nearly 1,400 children died from abuse or neglect in 2001, and 76% of those were under the age of 4 years (U.S. Department of Health and Human Services, 2002). Children from these environments demonstrate severe and chronic behavior problems by the time they are of school age, and these children seldom receive any type of early intervention.

Several barriers make it difficult to identify young children displaying emotional and behavioral problems and provide intervention. As mentioned previously, the vague wording of the federal definition of emotional disturbance makes identifying young children problematic. Young children display a broad range of behaviors. In the absence of a clearly defined operational definition, it is difficult to determine whether a particular behavior is within the parameters of developmental norms or the result of an emotional and behavior disorder.

Furthermore, from birth to age 5 years, a child's behavior is influenced by temperament and parental interaction, and early behavior may not be predictive of later behavior. Because young children are not in school, it is difficult to ascertain whether their behaviors have persisted over a long period of time or whether they are displaying behaviors that affect academic performance (Convoy & Brown, 2004).

In addition, coordination and collaboration between services is limited or practically nonexistent, which means that the identification process for children with emotional and behavior disorders does not begin until after they enter school.

Finally, many educators, pediatricians, and other practitioners are reluctant to identify young children with emotional and behavior disorders because they are unsure that the child has the disorder or they erroneously attribute the child's school problems to learning problems (Drotar, 2004; Forness, 2003).

Despite evidence that children might avoid being placed in special education if they receive effective early intervention (Perry, 2007), students with emotional and behavior disorders are typically identified later in life. They seldom receive early intervention when it could have had a substantive impact.

## Identification and Intervention

Early identification and prevention is crucial in serving young children who are at risk for emotional and behavior disorders (Serna, Lamros, Nielsen, & Forness, 2002; Serna, Nielsen, Lamros, & Forness, 2000). It is critical that young children who are at risk for emotional or behavior problems be accurately identified and that early intervention programs be provided to prevent or delay the development of emotional and behavior disorders. Early identification typically involves screening children in preschool or day-care settings.

A primary intervention program should include several different strategies and typically targets large groups of young children (Serna, Nielsen, Mattern, & Forness, 2003). Universal interventions entail providing rules and instructions with appropriate consequences and reinforcers. Effective components of early interventions for children who are at risk for developing emotional and behavior disorders include social skills instruction, parent training, and related skill building (Lopez, Tarullo, Forness, & Boyce, 2000).

Despite the effectiveness of early intervention, many students at risk for emotional and behavior disorders are not identified until much later. By this time, the student's behavior has exceeded the tolerance level of many teachers. Until adequate resources have been committed to early identification and intervention, students who are at risk for developing emotional and behavior disorders will not receive services when these services could do the most good.

## TYPES AND CHARACTERISTICS OF EMOTIONAL AND BEHAVIOR DISORDERS

So how can teachers, special educators, and administrators identify students who have emotional and behavior disorders? Unfortunately, no single set of characteristics exists, although researchers have postulated marked dimensions to childhood behavioral problems. Some symptomatic behaviors include those found in conduct disorders, oppositional defiant disorders, anxiety disorders, mood disorders, depression, and schizophrenia. Experts have grouped emotional and behavioral problems into *internalizing* and *externalizing* dimensions (Achenbach & Edelbrock, 1981, 1983; Kauffman, 2005; Lambros, Ward, Bocian, MacMillan, & Gresham, 1998).

Internalizing behavioral disorders are characterized by anxiety, withdrawal, depression, and overcontrolled behaviors. Internalizing behaviors are directed inward and are covert. Externalizing behavioral disorders are characterized by aggressive, disruptive, and undercontrolled behaviors. These behaviors include conduct disorder, oppositional defiant disorder, and ADHD. Girls tend to have more internalizing conditions, whereas boys tend to have more externalizing conditions (Bailey, Zauszniewski, Heinzer, & Hemstrom-Krainess, 2007; Vierhaus & Lohaus, 2008).

Students who have internalizing behaviors frequently do not present discipline or behavioral problems in the classroom. Because they do not challenge the teacher's authority or disrupt the classroom, they are often under identified. Without identification, these students seldom receive direct interventions and are at risk for having social adjustment difficulties later in life.

As might be expected, externalizing behaviors are more problematic, because they often disrupt the classroom. In order for students to be successful in the classroom, they must respect the authority of the teacher. The teacher generally has control of the seating arrangements, the curriculum, the pedagogical method for delivering the instruction, and the social and emotional climate of the classroom. This arrangement is generally successful because the majority of students and parents accept the teacher's role in their children's education. However, a student who has an emotional and behavior disorder who displays externalizing behaviors tends to directly challenge the teacher's authority, interfere with instruction, and affect classmates (Lambros et al., 1998). Such a student is quickly referred for special education services.

Teachers are likely to have students with comorbid disorders—more than one coexisting disorders or disabilities. It is not uncommon to have a student with emotional and behavior disorders and either ADHD or some type of learning disability. For example, a student may have posttraumatic stress disorder as a result of physical or sexual abuse or depression due to a feeling of worthlessness.

It is prudent to have some understanding of the various types of disorders in order to identify a student who may have emotional and behavior disorders.

## Internalizing Conditions

Teachers of students with emotional and behavior disorders will encounter children and adolescents with internalizing conditions. These conditions are not always obvious, and teachers need to be vigilant in recognizing the subtle symptoms. Most students with internalizing conditions exhibit depression and anxiety disorders.

**DEPRESSION.**   Categorized as a mood disorder in the *Diagnostic and Statistical Manual of Mental Disorders* (*DSM-IV-TR*, American Psychiatric Association, 2000), depression interferes with the ability to work, study, sleep, eat, and enjoy once pleasurable activities. Whereas it is not unusual for an individual to suffer from depression only once in the course of a lifetime, depression generally occurs several times (National Institute of Mental Health, 2002).

Depression among children and adolescents was once considered a part of normal development. Behaviors differ from one developmental stage to another, which makes it difficult to determine whether a child is going through a phase or suffering from depression (National Institute of Mental Health, 2007). Unfortunately, depression among children and adolescents is a growing problem (Kaslow, Morris, & Rehm, 1997), and it has only recently been taken seriously. A young child who is suffering from depression may pretend to feel sick or refuse to go to school. Older children may be irritable or angry and have behavioral problems at school. Adolescent depression may affect the student's interpersonal relationships and academic performance and may lead to suicide (McCarthy, Downes, & Sherman, 2008).

High rates of childhood depression may be associated with being the recipient of abuse, teasing, or bullying; having a parent with mental illness; having a genetic predisposition to depression; and having other health problems. Children and adolescents who live in neighborhoods that have drugs, gangs, and high crime rates may also be subject to depression (Woolley & Curtis, 2007).

Major depression may include emotional, cognitive, motivational, and physical symptoms. A child with emotional symptoms may have feelings of worthlessness, hopelessness,

---

**TABLE 2.1   Symptoms of Depression**

---

- Persistent sad, anxious, or "empty" mood
- Feelings of hopelessness
- Feelings of guilt, worthlessness, helplessness
- Losing interest in play, friends, and schoolwork, or loss of interest in activities that were once enjoyed
- Loss of energy or fatigue
- Loss of concentration
- Insomnia or oversleeping
- Change In appetite; weight loss or overeating and weight gain
- Thoughts of death or suicide; suicide attempts
- Restlessness, irritability, anger

---

*Source: DSM-IV-TR;* American Psychiatric Association, 2000; National Institute of Mental Health. 2000

and guilt. He may feel rejected by peers and act sad or lonely. He may feel that nothing in his life is going right and that these events are not likely to change. Children with cognitive symptoms of depression may be unable to concentrate on academics or may feel that they are unable to do anything right. Often they avoid tasks and social interactions. They may not be motivated and may have suicidal ideation. Some physical symptoms of depression include a change in appetite or weight, insomnia, or too much sleep. Some related conditions include eating disorders, substance abuse, anxiety disorders, and juvenile delinquency. (See Table 2.1.) A less severe form of depression is *dysthymia.* By definition this disorder lasts for at least 2 years, but the symptoms are not as severe as those of major depression. Many children with dysthymia are not diagnosed and do not receive the needed intervention. Some of the symptoms include poor school performance, social withdrawal, shyness, irritability, and sleep irregularities.

*Bipolar disorder* is another mood disorder, but it is in a separate category from depression. Once known as manic–depressive illness, bipolar disorder often begins in late adolescence. A child with bipolar disorder experiences extreme mood swings. He or she may experience times of heightened activity and may be extremely energetic and productive for several days. Then there are times when the child experiences severe depression with symptoms similar to those who suffer from major depression. Generally, bipolar disorder can be treated with medication, but many individuals may not seek treatment, especially when they are feeling "up." Also, medication is not always effective for children and may exacerbate symptoms.

Most cases of depression have unknown causes. Some types of depression run in families. Children of parents suffering from depression are more likely to display physical symptoms of depression. Yet depression can also occur in children who have no family history of depression.

Generally, a psychiatrist or psychologist diagnoses depression in children and adolescents. He or she should complete a multifaceted evaluation that includes the perspective of the child's teacher as an integral part. Teachers' observations of children can play a crucial role in identifying children with depression and providing the needed intervention, which usually includes medications and/or psychotherapies. Unfortunately, only half or fewer than half of children and adolescents with depression receive the needed mental health services (McCarty et al., 2008).

**ANXIETY DISORDERS.** *Anxiety disorders* are characterized by excessive fear, worry, and uneasiness that prevent an individual from functioning in daily life. As with depression, anxiety disorders in children have only recently been taken seriously as a clinical syndrome requiring treatment. Three intervention approaches have been successful in resolving anxieties and fears in children: desensitization, modeling, and self-control training (Brown, 2005; Coleman & Webber, 2002; Dadds & Barrett, 2001). Some children respond when these methods are incorporated into their school environment, but others need more intensive interventions that span school and home environments. The different anxiety disorders that affect children and adolescents include separation anxiety disorder, generalized anxiety disorder, specific phobias, social anxiety disorder, obsessive–compulsive disorder, posttraumatic stress disorder, panic disorder, and eating disorders.

**SEPARATION ANXIETY DISORDER.** Separation anxiety disorder is one of the few anxiety disorders listed under "Disorders Usually First Diagnosed in Infancy, Childhood, or Adolescence" in the *DSM-IV-TR*. The others are listed under "Anxiety Disorders" and the entries describe adult symptomatology rather than childhood illness.

The onset of separation anxiety disorder can occur before the age of 6 years. As the name implies, a child has *separation anxiety disorder* when he or she has excessive anxiety concerning separation from the home or from those to whom the child is attached. A child with separation anxiety disorder has an overwhelming fear that something will happen to his or her parents. Children with separation anxiety may cry, complain of headaches or stomachaches, frequently call home to see if their parents are all right, refuse to sleep alone, or refuse to leave the house (Jurbergs & Ledley, 2005). They may refuse to go to school because they worry that something will happen while they are away from home. Several intervention techniques, namely, systematic desensitization, modeling, and shaping, are used to treat separation anxiety disorder.

Systematic desensitization is used to treat a number of anxiety disorders (Piacentini & Roblek, 2002; Reisner, 2005). Using counterconditioning to alleviate anxiety, systematic desensitization follows three basic steps:

1. Establishing a hierarchy of fear-inducing stimuli.
2. Learning deep-muscle relaxation exercises.
3. Pairing the relaxation state with each of the stimuli on the hierarchy (Coleman & Webber, 2002).

As a treatment for separation anxiety disorder, systematic desensitization involves activities that result in separation from the parent. These activities occur one step at a time and range from playing outside the house to spending the night with a friend.

Another treatment for separation anxiety disorder is modeling. A counselor or therapist will model an anxious situation and demonstrate strategies to overcome the situation.

Shaping involves taking gradual steps to eliminate an anxiety. For example, if the goal for the child is to attend school without the fear of being away from home, the first step may be taking the child to a public library for a short time. A subsequent step could be attending school for half a day. The final step would then be attending school all day.

**GENERALIZED ANXIETY DISORDER.**    Generalized anxiety disorder involves excessive anxiety and worry that is not caused by any recent events or activities. Worries are accompanied by physical symptoms, especially fatigue, headaches, muscle tension, muscle aches, difficulty with concentration, irritability, and sleeping difficulties. Children and adolescents with generalized anxiety disorder often worry about their school performance or competence in sporting events. They may be overly fervent in seeking approval and reassurance.

**SPECIFIC PHOBIAS.**    A *specific phobia* is an intense fear of objects or situations that pose little or no threat to the person, to which the person responds by actively avoiding the objects or situations. Some of the more common specific phobias are fear of closed-in places such as elevators and crowded malls (claustrophobia), fear of heights (acrophobia), fear of spiders (arachnophobia), fear of water (hydrophobia), fear of blood (hemophobia), and a fear of flying (aviophobia). More than 350 phobias have been identified. Many of these phobias are irrational fears of an object or situation. Such phobias are not just extreme fear; they are irrational fear of a particular thing. When confronted with a feared object or situation, many individuals have an immediate anxiety reaction (sweating, difficulty breathing, crying, clinging, and feeling panicky). Most individuals who have phobias simply avoid the object or situation they fear, and most children with phobias are not detected unless the phobic stimulus is in the school or the classroom.

**SOCIAL ANXIETY DISORDER.**    Children with *social anxiety disorder* have a persistent and excessive fear of social situations, interpersonal scrutiny, and the associated potential for embarrassment or humiliation (Mancini, van Ameringen, Bennett, Patterson, & Watson, 2005). Children may appear extremely timid and cling to familiar persons. They may cry or throw tantrums. Adolescents with social phobia have poor peer relationships, are rejected by peers, have fewer quality friendships, and have higher rates of peer victimization (Erath, Flanagan, & Bierman, 2007; Storch, Brassard, & Masia-Warner, 2003).

Students with social anxiety disorder are shy, quiet, or withdrawn when meeting new people or in unfamiliar social settings. They might show obvious evidence of uneasiness (for example, blushing, keeping their heads down, or looking away). Many children and adolescents experience intense emotional or physical symptoms such as fear, a racing heart, sweating, and trembling (Stein & Stein, 2008). Many individuals with social anxiety disorders try to avoid social situations, but children, who are required to attend school, often do not have this option.

**SCHOOL REFUSAL.**    *School refusal* is defined as all attempts by a child or adolescent to miss school. It is usually the result of an emotional disorder, such as generalized anxiety disorder, separation anxiety disorder, or depression, or the result of school and family factors (Wimmer, 2008). School refusal may include harboring fear of the school environment due to tests (an increasing problem as the number of state- and federally mandated tests increases), public bathrooms, or teachers; escaping aversive social situations due to difficulties with peers (bullying, gang activities) and with teachers (lack of support or criticism); or attention-seeking behaviors such as crying or difficulties sleeping (Fremont, 2003). School refusal is more common among young children than adolescents (Kearney & Bates, 2005).

A number of interventions could increase student attendance in schools. Cognitive behavioral strategies that include relaxation and cognitive restructuring could be used. Social skills training, school-wide positive behavior support, medication, and parent training may also help reduce absenteeism due to school refusal (Wimmer, 2008).

**OBSESSIVE–COMPULSIVE DISORDER.** A child who has *obsessive–compulsive disorder* has recurrent, persistent thoughts that cause distress and displays repetitive behaviors that reduce anxiety. The behaviors for children with obsessive–compulsive disorder are similar to those behaviors exhibited by adults with the disorder. The most common obsessions, or persistent distressful thoughts, are fear of contamination, fear of harming others, or inappropriate impulses such as thoughts of violence and aggression. The most common compulsive behaviors in children include hand washing (cleaning), checking to make sure that the doors are locked (checking), making sure that toys are placed in a certain order (ritual ordering), and making sure that everything is in its right place (straightening). The goal of compulsive behaviors is to reduce anxiety. Boys are more likely to develop obsessive–compulsive disorder as children, while girls are more likely to develop the disorder as young adults. Medication and cognitive behavioral therapy are the treatment options for obsessive–compulsive disorder. Medication may help reduce the anxiety, while cognitive behavioral therapy may help students understand and cope with the disorder (Paige, 2007).

**POSTTRAUMATIC STRESS DISORDER.** Children with *posttraumatic stress disorder* (PTSD) experience intense fear or display agitated behavior following exposure to a traumatic event that involves real or perceived death, injury, or threat to their physical well-being. Other events that could result in PTSD include witnessing a violent act, experiencing the death of a close relative, or experiencing sexual or physical abuse. The three clusters of PTSD symptoms include (1) reexperiencing the traumatic event, (2) persistently avoiding anything associated with the trauma and experiencing numbing of general responsiveness, and (3) having persistent symptoms of increased arousal (Brown, 2005). Some of the symptoms can include repetitive play involving the traumatic event, nightmares, social detachment, sleep difficulties, and hyper-vigilance. Ordinary events that remind the child of the traumatic event can trigger flashbacks.

A number of children and adolescents are exposed to traumatic events that include physical and/or sexual abuse, domestic violence in the household, and community violence. Child sexual abuse has been reported to affect nearly 50% of physically abused children and adolescents (Paolucci, Genuis, & Violato, 2001). Children who have been sexually abused are at increased risk of PTSD (Brown, 2005; Negrao, Bonanno, Noll, Putnam, & Trickett, 2005), and indeed, a high frequency of sexually abused children have PTSD (Kaplow, Dodge, Amaya-Jackson, & Saxe, 2005). Children who experience or witness violent events, such as the Columbine High School shootings or the 9/11 terrorist attacks, are also at risk for developing PTSD. (See Case Study 2.1.) One form of intervention is the reexposure approach, in which the traumatic event is reviewed and reprocessed in a safe environment.

**PANIC DISORDER.** Children who have a panic disorder have sudden and repeated panic attacks or a period of intense, overwhelming fear. A person experiencing a panic attack may feel that his or her heart is pounding and may feel weak and dizzy. The person may feel nauseated and afraid that something bad is going to happen. Unfortunately, many children and adolescents who have panic attacks attribute them to external stimuli, and this disorder is rarely identified in children. As a result, there has been limited research regarding interventions in children.

**EATING DISORDERS.** Eating disorders are characterized by severe disturbances in eating behavior. The two most common eating disorders are anorexia nervosa and bulimia nervosa.

## Case Study 2.1

### Mary: Posttraumatic: Stress Disorder

David Poteet was a high school teacher for students with emotional and behavior disorders at Franklin Pierce High School. He had recently been perplexed by the behavior of a new student, Mary. Mary was a thirteen-year-old who displayed agitated and aggressive behavior. Every day, a bus would bring Mary from her high school, which was located a few miles away, to Franklin Pierce without incident. However, as Mary approached Mr. Poteet's classroom, she would "freak out." She would become highly agitated and would refuse to enter the classroom. Eventually she would be sent home. This was unusual behavior for her. Truancy had not been a problem at her home school. Although Mr. Poteet and the counselor at Franklin Pierce tried a number of interventions, Mary still refused to enter Mr. Poteet's classroom.

One day, Mr. Poteet was ill and unable to go to school. A substitute teacher took his place, and on that day, Mary entered the classroom without incident. When Mr. Poteet returned the next day, Mary once again became agitated and refused to enter the classroom.

Realizing that something about Mr. Poteet was triggering Mary's behavior, the school counselor met with Mary's, parents. The parents told the psychologist that Mary was being seen weekly about her behavior at school. Through the course of the sessions with Mary, the psychologist discovered that Mary has been sexually abused by a farmhand when she was 10 years old. Both the farmhand and Mr. Poteet had beards. Once Mr. Poteet shaved his beard, Mary was able to enter his classroom without incident. Over the following months, Mary grew more comfortable with her teacher and Mr. Poteet regrew his beard. Although Mary occasionally felt anxious when she saw Mr. Poteet with a beard, she was able to enter the classroom and function adequately.

*Anorexia nervosa* is characterized by a refusal to maintain a minimally normal body weight, an attitude that results in severe weight loss. Often children and adolescents with anorexia nervosa see themselves as being overweight even though they are thin. They avoid food or eat small quantities. They may engage in excessive exercising and may induce vomiting or misuse laxatives as a method of controlling their weight. Individuals with anorexia nervosa frequently come from overcontrolled homes. Individuals with anorexia nervosa have a mortality rate that is about 12 times higher than that of other females ages 15–24 years (Sullivan, 1995).

A child with *bulimia nervosa* eats an abnormally large amount of food and then self-induces vomiting or misuses laxatives to control weight. Because these individuals "binge and purge," their weight is usually normal for their age and height. Individuals with bulimia nervosa are aware that their eating habits are abnormal, and they keep their behaviors secret. As a result they feel anxiety and guilt when they binge, but relief when they purge.

The majority of individuals with anorexia nervosa or bulimia nervosa are females. The estimated rate of females suffering from anorexia nervosa is 0.5%–3.7%, whereas the estimated rate of bulimia nervosa is 1.1%–4.2% of females (American Psychiatric Association Work Group on Eating Disorders, 2000). The treatment of eating disorders can be complicated. Some strategies include behavioral interventions focusing on realistic weight expectations, psychosocial interventions, shaping dietary behavior, and medication management.

## Externalizing Conditions

**CONDUCT DISORDER.**    Individuals with *conduct disorder* show a repetitive and persistent pattern of behavior in which they violate the basic rights of others or major age-appropriate societal norms or rules at home, in school, and in the community (*DSM-IV-TR*, American Psychiatric Association, 2000). These antisocial behaviors include fighting, assaulting others, destroying property, stealing, lying, and being physically cruel to people or animals. Conduct disorder is a disorder that can affect the school environment in a number of ways. Children with the condition can disrupt the classroom, hindering other students from learning (Frick, 2004). Children with conduct disorders are often referred to the principal's office for school suspensions (Walker & Severson, 2002). Children with conduct disorder tend to be academic underachievers and experience peer rejection (Gresham, Lane, & Beebe-Frankenberger, 2005). The prevalence of children with conduct disorders ranges from 3.92%–16%, and the prevalence rate for boys is higher (Kaufmann, 2005; Waschbusch, 2002).

Conduct disorder is associated with early age of onset, certain dispositional characteristics within the child, and an unfavorable social context (Frick, 2004; Kauffman, 2005). The difference between children who begin showing conduct problems in childhood and those who begin showing antisocial behavior at the beginning of adolescence was integrated into the *DMS-IV-TR*. Children with conduct problems tend to show covert behaviors, such as lying, stealing, and truancy, at an early age, and their inappropriate behaviors tend to increase in intensity and severity as they get older (Frick, 2004; Walker et al., 2004). Children who display overt conduct disorders are oppositional, aggressive, inattentive, and impulsive. They tend to develop delinquent, antisocial behaviors at the beginning of adolescence. These children with undersocialized conduct disorders are at risk for criminal behaviors in adolescence and adulthood (Eddy, Reid, & Curry, 2002; Frick, 2004; Gresham et al., 2005).

Dispositional risk factors include child temperament, neuropsychological deficits and difficulties, and poor academic performance. Temperament generally refers to the behavioral style of the child and how he or she acts in different environmental settings (Chess & Thomas, 1996). The three components of temperament are sociability, activity, and emotionality (Houck & Spegman, 1999), which include nine temperament dimensions. (See Table 2.2.) Children may be described as having *easy, slow to warm up*, and *difficult* temperaments. Although a child with any type of temperament could develop emotional and behavior disorders, a child with a difficult temperament has an increased chance of developing difficult behaviors (Keogh, 2003). *Temperament* also is affected by the child's social environment. A number of social factors can place a child at risk for developing conduct disorder. These include the relationship the child has with the family, the child's culture, the socioeconomic status of the child's environment, his or her acceptance by peers, and the quality of the school setting. Children tend to model the behavior they observe in family and friends. If family and friends model aggressive and inappropriate behavior, the child is more likely to display similar behavior. Many children with behavioral disorders are from dysfunctional homes. Family risk variables include a large family, a single parent, inadequate parent involvement and discipline, low education level of a parent, and parental involvement in

**TABLE 2.2    Temperament Dimensions**

| Dimension | Definition |
| --- | --- |
| Activity Level | How much a child moves during active and inactive periods. |
| Rhythmicity | The regularity, or predictability and/or unpredictability with which the child eats, sleeps, and eliminates. |
| Approach/Withdrawal | The initial response of a child to new stimulus, such as new food, a new toy, or a new person. |
| Adaptability | How quickly a child responds to new or altered situations. |
| Intensity of Reaction | The energy level of a positive or negative response. |
| Mood | The amount of pleasant, joyful, and friendly behavior, as compared with unpleasant, crying, and unfriendly behavior. |
| Distractibility | The effectiveness with which stimuli interferes with the direction of the child's behavior. |
| Persistence | The continuation of an activity despite interruptions. |
| Threshold of Responsiveness | The intensity level of stimulation need to obtain a response from the child. |

*Source:* Chess & Thomas, 1999

criminal activity and substance abuse (Frick, 2004; Keogh, 2000). Children from families with low socioeconomic status are more likely to do poor in school and are at risk for developing behavioral disorders (Frick, 2004; Keogh, 2000). Unfortunately, many ethnically diverse learners live in low socioeconomic environments and are at risk for behavioral disorders.

**ADHD.**    While ADHD is not necessarily an external characteristic of emotional and behavior disorders, it has been estimated that nearly 60%–70% of children with learning disabilities and behavior disorders have ADHD (Kube, Petersen, & Palmer, 2002). ADHD is generally characterized by symptoms of inattention, hyperactivity, and/or impulsivity that are developmentally inappropriate and not the result of other conditions. Children must exhibit these symptoms before 7 years of age, in at least two settings, usually at home and school. Also, the symptoms of ADHD must interfere with the child's developmentally appropriate social, academic, or occupational functioning (American Psychiatric Association, 2000).

Three types of ADHD exist. The first type of ADHD is referred to as attention-deficit disorder (ADD). This is the predominantly inattentive type. Students with this disorder are often observed daydreaming or occupied with internal thoughts. They produce careless work, have poor organizational skills, and are forgetful. They often seem to be apathetic or confused.

The second type of ADHD is predominantly the hyperactive–impulsive type. These students talk excessively, play loudly, fidget, are restless, and have a tendency to interrupt. These characteristics can also be symptoms of autism and conduct disorder. Bedwetting, sleep problems, temper tantrums, and stubbornness are common problems for students with ADHD.

The third type of ADHD is a combined type of ADHD. ADHD is the typology with characteristics of inattention and hyperactivity–impulsivity. Yet many teachers do not understand that there are three types of ADHD and tend to identify children as having ADHD only if they show inappropriate hyperactive behaviors. Few teachers associate ADHD with children who have characteristics of the inattentive type. Whereas a small number of teachers recognize that ADHD is a medical condition that must be diagnosed by a physician, more teachers criticize these children as being lazy or unwilling to behave.

Often ADHD overlaps with emotional and behavior disorders, conduct disorders, and oppositional defiant disorders (Gresham et al., 2005). Children with conduct disorder and ADHD, especially those with hyperactivity and/or impulsivity, are at risk for antisocial and criminal behavior (Barkley, Fischer, Smallish, & Fletcher, 2004; Miller, Lynam, & Leukefeld, 2003).

Between 3% and 6% of children in school have ADHD (American Psychiatric Association, 2000; Goldman, Genel, Bezman, & Slanetz, 1998), which means that probably every classroom has at least one child who has ADHD (Barkley, 2000). More boys are identified as having ADHD than girls due to their disruptive behavior (Gingerich, Turnock, Liftin, & Rosen, 1998); however, that is changing. From 1990 to 1998, the male–female ratio of documented children with ADHD has narrowed from 5.4 : 1 to 2.3 : 1 (Robison, Skaer, Sclar, & Galin, 2002).

The most common treatment for ADHD is medication. Ritalin, Adderall, Dexedrine, and Cylert are frequently prescribed psychostimulant medications for ADHD, and in 2000 more than 3 million children were receiving medication for ADHD (Jensen, 2000). Many people wonder how a stimulant can calm a child who has ADHD, but medication stimulates the brain and enables the person to filter out extraneous stimuli. For example, suppose you are with a friend at the food court in the mall on a Saturday afternoon. The noise level is extremely loud, yet you are able to have a conversation with your friend because you are able to filter out the irrelevant conversations of others. A person with ADHD is unable to filter out the noise. He is cueing in on every conversation, trying desperately to quiet his mind, and becoming hyperactive in the process. Psychostimulants help him filter out the extraneous noise, allowing him to focus on his companion's conversation, and thus they have a calming effect.

Teachers are actively involved in the identification and remediation of ADHD. They are usually the first to suspect that a child has ADHD, due to his or her inappropriate behaviors. They usually maintain some type of anecdotal records or complete surveys that assess the child for ADHD. Once a child has been identified, the teacher is usually involved in behavioral management plans or provides feedback to the doctor or parent that can be used to adjust the dosage of medication.

**SUICIDE.**    Completed suicide is the third leading cause of death of young people between the ages of 15 and 24 years (Anderson & Smith, 2003; Centers for Disease and Prevention, 2002; Heron, 2007). Approximately 1,600 adolescents complete suicide every year (Anderson, 2002), and the incidence of completed suicide and attempted suicide has increased over the past 20 years (Miller & Taylor, 2005; Spirito & Overholser, 2003). Females engage in parasuicide, or attempted suicide, more often than males; however, males successfully complete suicide more often than females (Ash, 2008; Gould, Greenberg, Velting, & Shaffer, 2003). Nearly 90% of adolescents who completed suicide had psychiatric problems (U.S. Public Health Service, 1999) such as depression, anxiety disorders, and posttraumatic stress (Miller & Taylor, 2005). Students with emotional and behavior disorders are at increased risk for suicide.

Other factors affecting suicidal ideation in adolescents are a dysfunctional family, life stressors (Miller & Taylor, 2005), and a history of family suicidal behavior. Risk factors that may predict suicidal behavior in adolescents include substance abuse, exposure to suicide, loss of a family member or friend, chronic illness, and access to lethal means, generally firearms. Exposure to suicide has a contagion effect; an adolescent who has been exposed to a parasuicide or completed suicide may consider suicide. Suicide among adolescents increases with the amount, duration, and prominence of media coverage (Gould et al., 2003). Suicide is rare in children under 10 years old, but it is increasing.

Feelings of extreme loneliness and hopelessness appear to be among the best predictors of suicidal thoughts and intentions (Spirito & Overholser, 2003). Often, these children have chronic depression. They feel that things will not get better and that no one cares. This sense of hopelessness is so overwhelming that the individual feels that the only reasonable option is suicide.

Teachers can help prevent suicide if they recognize the risk factors and respond appropriately. Some of the risk factors include sudden change in usual behavior, problems in school, family and peer problems, giving away possessions, and talk of suicide. Teachers need to take all suicide threats seriously. They should not try to second-guess the child. They should provide emotional support for the child, listen and talk to the child, and refer the child to appropriate professionals.

## Childhood-Onset Schizophrenia

*Schizophrenia* is included in the federal definition of emotional disturbance but is difficult to define in children. The *DSM-IV-TR* does not include a specific category for childhood-onset schizophrenia because the characteristics of adult schizophrenia and childhood-onset schizophrenia are similar. These characteristics include delusions and hallucinations, disorders in speech, disorganized or catatonic behavior, and inappropriate expression of emotions (*DSM-IV-TR*, 2000; NIMH, National Institute of Mental Health, 2006).

Unlike adult schizophrenia, which begins abruptly, childhood-onset schizophrenia begins gradually, often with speech and language disorders. These children develop mutism (not speaking) or use a private language that others do not understand. Often, children with schizophrenia are identified as having autism. Children with schizophrenia believe that people can read their minds or that they receive special messages from the radio. They see things that are not there or laugh at sad events (American Academy of Child and Adolescent Psychiatry Official Action, 2001; NIMH, 2006).

Evidence suggests that genetics is the cause of childhood-onset schizophrenia. Children who have a first-degree relative with schizophrenia have an increased chance of developing the illness, and those with an identical twin with schizophrenia have a 50% chance of developing schizophrenia (NIMH, 2006). Fortunately, childhood-onset schizophrenia is rare: Only 1 in 40,000 children develops schizophrenia (Nicolson & Rapoport, 1999).

## Cultural and Racial Factors

Race, culture, and ethnicity may play a role in the prevalence of internalizing and externalizing conditions and in the identification of students with emotional and behavior disorders. It is important to understand these factors in order to identify students who are at risk for depression, aggressive behavior, anxiety disorders, and suicide. Identification can lead to interventions that may prevent or delay emotional and behavioral problems.

Hispanic adolescents display more symptoms of depression than youths of other ethnicities. This is especially true of Hispanic females (Li & Prevatt, 2007; McLaughlin, Hilt, & Nolen-Hoeksema, 2007). Hispanic females are expected to be submissive and place the concerns of the family above themselves. American culture emphasizes independence and individuation from family during adolescence. This conflict between cultural values and gender roles places Hispanic females at increased risk for depression (Ash, 2008).

African American males engage in higher levels of aggression and overt aggression than males of other groups. African Americans were 1.7 times more likely to be identified as having emotional and behavior disorders and were likely to be in more restrictive settings (Skiba, Poloni-Staudinger, Gallini, Simmons, & Feggins-Azziz, 2006). African Americans were also more likely to be suspended or expelled than other students (Krezmien, Leone, & Achilles, 2006). It is possible that the learning styles of African Americans are more relational and the absence of a familiar relationship between the teacher and student can be detrimental to these students' academic and behavioral performances (Townsend, 2000).

Hispanic female adolescents and African American male adolescents display higher levels of anxiety than others of their age (McLaughlin et al., 2007; Varela, Weems, Berman, Hensley, & de Bernal, 2007). Hispanic females may feel anxiety for the same reasons that they feel depression: conflicting gender roles. African American males display more separation anxiety symptoms than do non-African American males.

European American children and adolescents display higher rates of suicide than do African American youths (Ash, 2008), although the suicide rate for African American adolescent males has increased dramatically within the last 20 years (Day-Vines, 2007). Factors contributing to suicide risk include a sense of hopelessness, poverty, exposure to violence, and family problems.

## Summary

Many factors affect the prevalence of students with emotional and behavior disorders. Because the federal definition of emotional disturbance is subjective and vague, it is extremely difficult to estimate the prevalence of emotional and behavior disorders (the number of students with these disorders) in the public schools. Students with emotional and behavior disorders are predominantly male and disproportionately African Americans. Teacher bias, a lack of effective prereferral interventions, inappropriate assessment procedures, lack of tracking, and weighted teacher expectations contribute to the disproportionate identification of male and African American students with emotional and behavior disorders.

Many professionals are reluctant to identify young children with emotional and behavior disorders. The vagueness of the federal definition makes it difficult to identify young children. It is also difficult to determine whether the behavior is inappropriate because a child's behavior is influenced by temperament and parental interaction and may not be predictive of later behavior. As a result, students with emotional and behavior disorders are typically identified later in life and seldom receive early intervention.

Behaviors associated with emotional and behavior disorders are generally grouped into internalizing and externalizing behaviors. Internalizing behavioral disorders are characterized by anxiety, withdrawal, depression, and overcontrolled behaviors, whereas externalizing behavioral disorders are characterized by aggressive, disruptive, and undercontrolled behaviors.

Other characteristics of children with emotional and behavior disorders include suicidal ideation and childhood-onset schizophrenia. Students with emotional and behavior disorders are at increased risk for suicide. Nearly all adolescents who complete suicide suffered from depression, anxiety disorders, posttraumatic stress, or other psychiatric problems. Although childhood-onset schizophrenia is rare, it does exist; children with this disorder have delusions and hallucinations, disorders in speech, disorganized or catatonic behavior, and inappropriate expression of emotions.

Race, culture, and ethnicity may play a role in internalizing and externalizing conditions. It is important to understand these factors in order to identify students who are at risk for depression, aggressive behavior, anxiety disorders, and suicide.

Teachers, administrators, and other education professionals need to understand the characteristics associated with emotional and behavior disorders. Internalizing conditions, externalizing conditions, and cultural and racial factors affect the way a child behaves. Understanding these characteristics is an important first step in identifying a student who may have emotional and behavior disorders.

## Review Questions

1. Why are more children of certain racial or cultural backgrounds identified as having emotional and behavior disorders more often than children of other racial or cultural backgrounds?
2. Why is there a marked difference between estimates of the prevalence of children with emotional and behavior disorders and the number of children actually receiving interventions for these disorders in the public schools?
3. What are the characteristics of children with emotional and behavior disorders?
4. Compare and contrast internalizing and externalizing behaviors. Give examples of each. In your opinion, which condition is more problematic in the classroom? Why?

# CHAPTER 3

# Theories and Causation

**After reading this chapter, you should be able to**

- Explain the differences among congenital theory, biochemical theory, and acquired theory.
- Describe the differences between the psychodynamic theories of Freud and Erikson.
- Identify and explain the differences among the three basic types of behavior theories.
- Identify the two principles of social learning theory.
- Describe Bronfenbrenner's five components of the ecological systems theory.

- Compare and contrast the moral development theories of Piaget, Kohlberg, and Gilligan.
- Identify and describe the three principles of the dynamic systems approach to child development.
- Recognize some of the socioeconomic factors that may influence the development of a child.
- Explain how child abuse may affect the development stages of a child.
- Explain how the national culture may conflict with microcultures and influence the development of a child.

Teachers, administrators, and educational professionals who work with students with emotional and behavior disorders need to know about interventions and programs that can help these students to be successful in the classroom. They may cast theories and causation aside in favor of focusing on the more practical applications of treatment. While it is understandable that teachers want to master the practical applications of teaching students with emotional and behavior disorders, there are two important reasons that they should understand developmental theories. First, the nature of development affects how children are treated and how childhood is interpreted (Thelen, 2005). Theories provide an understanding of the development of children and adolescents, and theoretical approaches have guided compilation of the factors that may cause emotional and behavior disorders. Second, because therapeutic intervention is a developmental process (Thelen, 2005), theories provide the basis for practical applications to improve the behavioral, social, academic, and emotional characteristics of students and adolescents with emotional and behavior disorders.

Diverse and frequently contentious theories are used to explain emotional and behavior disorders. These theories examine physical, psychosocial, and environmental causes of emotional and behavior disorders.

## PSYCHONEUROLOGICAL THEORY

Psychoneurological theory examines biological factors as a causal explanation of emotional and behavior disorders. Emotional and behavioral disturbances in children are caused by physical and brain-related factors and are divided into three different categories explained by congenital, biochemical, and acquired theories.

## Congenital Theory

*Congenital theory* states that certain prenatal and perinatal events cause emotional disturbances. These events include genetic disorders, exposure to toxins, and infections. Genetic conditions have been used to explain schizophrenia, autism spectrum disorder, attention-deficit hyperactivity disorder, and other psychiatric disorders.

Family, twin, and adoption studies have provided compelling evidence of a genetic connection for a spectrum of schizophrenic disorders (Stone, Faraone, Seidman, Olson, & Tsuang, 2005). Schizophrenia occurs in 1% of the general population, but the risk of having it increases to 10% in individuals who have a first-degree relative, such as a parent, brother, or sister, who has schizophrenia (National Institute of Mental Health, 2005; Seidman et al., 2003). The identical twin of an individual with schizophrenia has a 40%–65% chance of developing schizophrenia (National Institute of Mental Health, 2005).

On the basis of numerous twin studies, some experts suspect that autism spectrum disorder has some genetic foundation (Bartlett, Goedken, & Vieland, 2005; Segurado, Conroy, Meally, Fitzgerald, Gill, & Gallagher, 2005; Yonan et al., 2003), but environmental factors are also known to trigger autism.

Similar studies suggest that attention-deficit hyperactivity disorder also has a hereditary basis. Studies have suggested that ADHD is common among biological relatives of children who have it, and the condition appears especially in twins (Larsson, Larsson, & Lichtenstein, 2004; Rasmussen, Neuman, Heath, Levy, Hay, & Todd, 2004). Children with ADHD are more likely to have adult relatives with ADHD than children who do not have ADHD, but this discovery has not been widely accepted, due to poor methodology and design involved in research (Barkley, 1998; Joseph, 2000).

The genetic explanation of aggression and other inappropriate behaviors in children with emotional and behavior disorders has not been widely accepted. Some studies have indicated that physical aggression has some genetic component (Beatty, Heisel, Hall, Levine, & La France, 2002; Rhee & Waldman, 2002) while social aggression has a weak relationship to heredity (Brendgen, Dionne, Girard, Boivin, Vitaro, & Pérusse, 2005).

## Biochemical Theory

According to *biochemical theory*, biochemistry affects the behavior of children with emotional and behavior disorders. Some children with autism have an overproduction of serotonin and dopamine, neurotransmitters that relay impulses to receptors in brain cells (Keltner, Hogan, & Guy, 2001; Spiker, 1999). Children with autism who took medication to regulate these neurotransmitters showed some improvement in behavior (Barnard, Young, Pearson, Geddes, & O'Brien, 2002).

Many parents and practitioners believe that diet affects behavior. For example, many individuals believe that sugar will make a child hyperactive (Sachs, 2004), and anecdotal records from parents show adverse behaviors in children with autism spectrum disorder after they consumed sugar and other sweeteners (Kidd, 2003). But no hard evidence exists to support the contention that sugar causes hyperactivity (Sachs, 2004).

The Feingold diet is based on the assumption that salicylates contained in artificial food colorings and flavorings cause or contribute to symptoms of hyperactivity, aggression, and impulsivity (Feingold, 1975). Little methodologically sound support exists for the effectiveness of the diet (Lilienfeld, 2005). Dietary modifications that have been helpful are the elimination of casein, which is found in dairy products, and of glutens, found in wheat products. These changes have had positive effects on behavior, especially in children with autism spectrum disorder (Kidd, 2003). However, removing all dairy and wheat products from a child's diet can be extremely challenging, and while some children with autism have shown improvement on elimination diets, in most studies these diets have been less than successful in reducing hyperactivity and behavioral problems.

## Acquired Theory

*Acquired theory* stresses the arrest or regression of normal development due to an identifiable event such as traumatic brain injury. A traumatic brain injury is an acquired injury to the brain caused by an external physical force and is the leading cause of death in children (Centers for Disease Control and Prevention, 2002). Brain injuries can cause physical changes, cognitive impairments, and social, emotional, and behavior difficulties. These children may display poor judgment, impulsiveness, aggression, and socially unacceptable behaviors. Children who have traumatic brain injuries have an increased risk of developing ADHD, depression, and conduct disorder (Max et al., 2005).

Environmental factors often interact with psychoneurological variables and contribute to certain behavior disorders. Many children have predispositions for developing certain disorders, but it is not clear why some children develop the disorder and why some do not, even when they share the same familial environment. As a result, many treatment options should include modification of the child's environment.

Generally, drug therapy is the most common form of intervention for children with behavior problems due to biophysical factors. The teacher of such a child needs to develop a good partnership with the child's doctor through the child's parent. The teacher should be able to describe the child's behavior prior to identification of the disorder, observe the child's response to medication, and assist the parents and doctor in adjusting the dosage of medication for optimal effect. Other interventions could include diet therapy, exercise, vitamins, and biofeedback.

## PSYCHODYNAMIC THEORY

*Psychodynamic theory* explains human behavior and psychopathology in a comprehensive framework by bridging normality and the study of psychiatric disorders (Kerbeshian & Burd, 2005). Psychodynamic theory emphasizes the child's autonomy and sense of self, the child's perception of the world, and the forces that affect development. Psychodynamic theory draws from a number of theories that include those of Freud, Erikson, Redl, Wineman, and others.

### Freud

In the late 19th and early 20th centuries, Sigmund Freud began to develop psychoanalytic theory, the best known of the psychodynamic models. Freud believed that normal children have intense bodily needs and wishes. His psychosexual theory viewed infants and young children as sexual beings and suggested that the way parents managed their child's sexual and aggressive drives was crucial for healthy personality development. Freud expanded his views to include three psychological structures that describe personality: the id, ego, and superego (Freud, 1923/1962; 1923/1975).

**ID, EGO, AND SUPEREGO.**    The id is the most primitive and largest aspect of the personality. The id is the part of the personality that seeks immediate satisfaction of biological needs and desires and avoids pain (Steuer, 1994). For example, an infant who is hungry will cry until he is fed. The id is the primary aspect of the personality of an infant, and it includes sexual and aggressive sentiments.

As the infant matures and perceives the world more fully, the ego develops. The ego is the rational part of the personality that redirects the id's impulses so that the child behaves according to the expectations of the parents and society at the appropriate time and place. The ego often acts as a mediator between reality, the id, and the superego. This aspect of the personality urges the individual to delay gratification until a more opportune time. For example, a child who is hungry will stop crying when he sees his mother warming up a bottle of milk.

Between 3 and 6 years of age, the superego develops from the interaction between the child and the parents. The superego is the part of the personality that contains the moral standards and values of society that guide the individual throughout life. It is the child's conscience. For example, a child who is hungry and who sees another child eating snack crackers may have an impulse to hit the child and take the crackers to meet his needs. But his superego tells him that it is wrong to hit the child and steal the crackers. His id may reconcile the differences between the two personalities and prompt the child to ask the other child for a cracker instead. The relationship between the id, ego, and superego during these early years will determine the individual's basic personality.

**TABLE 3.1    Freud's Psychosexual Stages**

| Stage | Age | Description |
|---|---|---|
| Oral Stage: | Birth–1 Year | Sucking is the primary source of pleasure for the infant and is directed toward the breast or the bottle. If the infant's needs are met, he can move to the next stage. If the infant's needs are not met, he becomes mistrustful, or if the infant is indulged, he will find it hard to cope with a world that does not meet all of his demands. |
| Anal Stage: | 1–3 Years | The child is expected to develop bowel control. The anus is the primary source of pleasure. Conflicts about anus control could result in extreme orderliness or disorderliness. The child learns control with regard not only to toilent training, but to urges and behaviors in general. |
| Phallic Stage: | 3–6 Years | The child's focus is on the genitals, and he finds pleasure in genital stimulation. Children develop an Oedipus conflict or Electra conflict and have sexual desires for the opposite-sex parent. Emotional conflicts are resolved by identifying with characteristics and values of the same-sex parent. |
| Latency Stage: | 6–11 Years | The sexual and aggressive drives are less active and psychosexual conflict is diminished. The child acquires values from adults such as teachers and from same-sex friends. The superego develops further. |
| Genital Stage: | Adolescence | Sexual impulses reappear. If the child has successfully completed earlier stages, he is psychologically well adjusted and balanced. |

**FREUD'S FIVE STAGES.**    According to Freud, the child must go through five distinct stages in order to develop into a well-adjusted adult. (See Table 3.1.) These include the oral, anal, phallic, latency, and genital psychosexual stages (Freud, 1938/1989). During each of these stages, parents must strike a balance between too much and too little gratification. If a balance is maintained, the child grows up to be psychologically well-adjusted. Freud's psychosexual development theory emphasizes the importance of family relationships.

## Erikson

Erik Erikson, a follower of Freud's, expanded the psychoanalytic theory to include the child's social world in his or her psychological development. This psychosocial theory has eight stages. (See Table 3.2.) The first five stages are similar to Freud's psychosexual stages, but Erikson did not believe development was restricted to early childhood and added four adult stages. Although psychosocial theory is no longer the predominant theory, it is still instructive to review its components.

**PSYCHOSOCIAL THEORY.**    A major principle of Erikson's psychosocial theory is epigenesis (Erikson, 1959; Russell, 1999), which means that a child must successfully complete each developmental stage before going on to the next stage. If a developmental stage is hindered, then the child has a difficult time reaching and completing ensuing stages. Unlike Freud, Erikson included the influence of society and culture, not just sexuality, on the development of personality.

Erikson's first stage, the *basic trust versus basic distrust* stage, is much like Freud's oral stage. In this stage, an infant will develop a lasting sense of trust if the mother or primary

**TABLE 3.2    Erikson's Psychosocial Stages**

| | | |
|---|---|---|
| Basic Trust Versus Mistrust (Freud: Oral Stage) | Birth–1 Year | The infant learns to trust or mistrust, depending on the quality of maternal care. |
| Autonomy Versus Shame and Doubt (Freud: Anal Stage) | 1–3 Years | The child learns to make his own decisions or becomes doubtful. When parents allow the child to make reasonable choices, the child becomes autonomous. |
| Initiative Versus Guilt (Freud: Phallic Stage) | 3–6 Years | The child develops a sense of ambition and responsibility. Without the parents' support of the child's new sense of purpose and direction, the child could develop guilt, which may cause repression of purpose or abrogation of the child's ego. The Oedipal conflict occurs at this stage. |
| Industry Versus Inferiority Diffusion (Freud: Latency Stage) | 6–11 Years | The child becomes productive and learns to get along with others. Without encouragement and acceptance from adults and peers, the child feels inferior. |
| Identity Versus Identity Confusion (Freud: Genital Stage) | Adolescence | The adolescent tries to understand his role in life. He is concerned with the way that others view him and develops values independent of others. Confusion about identity could lead to difficulties as an adult. |
| Intimacy Versus Isolation | Young Adult | The young adults establishes intimate relationships with others. Because of earlier experiences, the individual may avoid relationships, which could lead to isolation and self-absorption. |
| Generativity Versus Stagnation | Middle Adulthood | Generativity means establishing and guiding the next generation through child rearing, caring for others, or doing productive work. The successful individual feels a sense of accomplishment. |
| Ego Integrity Versus Despair | Old Age | The individual who feels that he has accomplished something with his life develops integrity. Despair occurs when the individual feels he has wasted his life. He fears death and loss of control over his life. |

caretaker is comforting and the child's basic needs are met (Erikson, 1959; Steuer, 1994). If the infant does not achieve this trust or does not bond with his or her mother, the child could suffer detrimental effects throughout the early developmental stages (Erikson & Erikson, 1997). For example, if an infant cries and his mother consistently fails to pick him up, the child may conclude that any effort he makes to communicate to his mother will be ignored. As a result, the infant may develop a sense of mistrust. If this mistrust is reinforced, the child may have difficulties interacting with others and may develop low self-esteem. A child must acquire basic trust in his parents and his world in order to progress to the next stage.

The child at the *autonomy versus shame and doubt* stage of development, which is similar to Freud's anal stage, recognizes himself as an individual separate from those around him. During this stage, the child's ego develops; the child also learns to respect the word "no" and learns bladder and bowel control. Toilet training is a central issue of the autonomous stage (Erikson & Erikson, 1997; Freud, 1923/1962). With the parents' encouragement and support,

## Case Study 3.1

### Johnny

When he was 5 years old, Johnny witnessed the death of his father. As was his custom, he was sitting on his front porch waiting for his father to come home after work. His father was devoted to Johnny and often brought him a "s'prise" when he came home. Recently, Johnny had begun pulling away from his father and spending more time with his mother, but he still waited for his father on the porch every afternoon. That day, Johnny saw his father's car heading down the street when a truck, running a stop sign, smashed into the driver's side of the car. Johnny's father was killed instantly.

Johnny's mother was devastated by the loss of her husband and was unable to provide any emotional support for Johnny. Without the steady income that Johnny's father had provided, Johnny and his mother had to move to a smaller home. The mother had to take on two jobs just to make ends meet. Johnny was often left by himself and seldom had any parameters imposed on him. He became increasingly defiant in interactions with his mother, who was generally too tired to discipline Johnny.

Johnny's defiance continued when he began kindergarten. His teacher noted that Johnny refused to follow any redirections, often challenging the teacher to "make him" follow classroom rules. During play time, Johnny was aggressive toward other children, often taking toys and games away from them. Many of the children avoided him. In the following years, Johnny became increasingly aggressive at home and at school. He seldom followed the directions of teachers, although he was more responsive to male teachers. He started fights with his peers. By second grade, school personnel were concerned about Johnny's progress. Although they had tried several behavior modification plans, none had made any significant improvement in his behavior, and he was failing many of his classes.

The At-Risk Team recommended counseling for Johnny, and sessions were arranged at a local counseling center with a male therapist. After several months, the counselor was able to ascertain that Johnny had feelings of overwhelming sadness about his father's death. He had wanted to spend more time with his mother and felt that his life had changed for the worse.

the child learns self-control. If the child is constantly criticized for toileting accidents and receives little or no encouragement, the child feels a loss of self-control and a sense of shame due to his inability to control his environment. His self-doubt about the ability to be independent is likely to extend beyond the toilet-training stage.

The child's inner psyche also develops during this stage. The child realizes that he is an individual and starts making his own decisions. He also believes that thought equals the deed in some magical manner. If a parent dies or the parents get a divorce, the child may blame himself for having had hostile thoughts or bad behavior that somehow made it happen. For this reason, losing a parent between the ages of 2 and 3 years creates a high risk for future behavioral complications (Keith, 1991). *Initiative versus guilt* is the third stage of development according to Erikson and parallels Freud's phallic stage. During this stage, the child develops a sense of ambition and responsibility and learns that he or she is a sexual being. The theory posits that boys at this age experience sexual desire for their mothers (Oedipus complex) and girls experience sexual desire for their fathers (Electra complex). The normal child resolves these conflicts through the development of the superego and adopts the characteristics and values of the same-sex parent.

The next stage is *industry versus inferiority diffusion* and is similar to Freud's latency stage. During this stage, sexual interests enter a latency period and do not reemerge until adolescence. The child becomes interested in rules and routines. He or she enjoys a sense of industry, takes an interest in achieving in school, and learns to work and cooperate with others.

The final stage of childhood is *identify versus identify confusion.* At this time sexual interests reappear and the adolescent begins questioning his or her place in the world. He or she begins thinking about the future, vocational goals, and plans for marriage and children. Individuals at this stage develop their own values based on their experiences. Those who do not successfully complete this developmental stage become confused about their roles as adults.

The final three stages of Erikson's psychosocial theory—*intimacy versus isolation, generativity versus stagnation,* and *ego integrity versus despair*—take place in adulthood and will not be covered in this text. In 1997, Erikson's wife Joan added a ninth stage to the psychosocial theory that goes beyond old age. In the *gerotranscendance stage,* the individual has had healthy resolutions of earlier stage conflicts, which has led to a deepening appreciation of the past while recognizing the limitations and constraints of old age (Erikson & Erikson, 1997).

According to psychodynamic theory, when a child's normal psychosexual development is hindered, the child develops an emotional and behavior disorder. Disruptions at each developmental stage can produce delinquent behavior. Twenty-two functions of a healthy ego have been described. A child with a deficient ego has not learned to control the impulses of the id. He expresses inappropriate behavior without remorse. He generally rationalizes his behavior and displaces any superego controls. These deficiencies of the ego can cause the child to get easily frustrated or become unable to resist temptation. A child with a deficient superego has not learned self-control at the *autonomy versus shame and doubt* stage. He may have trouble controlling his aggressive behavior at a later stage (Redl & Wineman, 1957).

Psychodynamic theory is no longer widely accepted. Many of the concepts are vague and open to interpretation, and many of these psychoanalytic ideas are difficult to test empirically. However, like Erikson's outline of psychosocial change, it is still therapeutically useful (Kerbeshian & Burd, 2005).

## BEHAVIORAL THEORY

Behavioral theory stresses that individuals learn and maintain inappropriate behavior in the same manner as they do normal behavior. Behavior is the result of a person's interaction with the environment. According to behaviorists, children with emotional and behavior disorders learn socially unacceptable behaviors from their interactions with other people in their environment (that is, family, friends, neighbors). These inappropriate behaviors are consistently reinforced, and as a result the child is unable to function along expected norms (Schroeder & Riddle, 1991). The three basic types of behavior theories are classical conditioning, operant conditioning, and social cognitive theory.

### Classical Conditioning

**PAVLOV.**   In the early 1900s, Russian physiologist Ivan Pavlov was studying the physiology of digestion through dogs. He noticed that the dogs started salivating whenever the trainer brought their food. He began to wonder whether a neutral stimulus (the trainer) could cause a reflexive response (salivation). He began pairing the sound of a bell with the presentation of food (the stimulus) and successfully taught the dogs to salivate at the sound of the bell. This was the beginning of *classical conditioning*. Classical conditioning takes advantage of the relationship between an unconditioned stimulus and an unconditioned response. When a neutral stimulus is paired repeatedly with the unconditioned stimulus, it may elicit the unconditioned response. When this occurs, the neutral stimulus becomes a conditioned stimulus and the reflective response becomes a conditioned response.

**WATSON.**    One of the first behaviorists was John B. Watson. He viewed conditioning as the basis for most human learning and advocated adopting a behaviorist approach to psychology by measuring only observable phenomena: stimuli and responses. In a classic study, 9-month-old Albert was conditioned to fear a soft, white rat (the neutral stimuli). Initially, the child eagerly played with the animal, but researchers paired a loud clang (the unconditioned stimulus), a sound that frightened Albert, with the rat. The loud clang was repeated each time the child touched the rat, and after several pairings, Albert began to cry (the reflective response) when he saw the rat. This fear became generalized to other white, furry objects, such as a white rabbit and Santa Claus (Watson & Raynor, 1920). Watson believed that the development of the child's personality was through conditioning, also called habit training.

## Operant Conditioning

**SKINNER.**    Classical conditioning, which dealt specifically with reflexes, was actually a forerunner to operant conditioning. B.F. Skinner pioneered operant conditioning by examining how the environment and environmental events affected behavior. Operant conditioning is the second aspect of Skinner's selection by consequences, a theory involving the survival of the species. The first is natural selection and the third aspect is social behavior (Skinner, 1994).

*Operant conditioning* governs the way that the response of the individual is conditioned. Consequences following a behavior can either strengthen the response (reinforcing stimulus) or weaken the response (punishment). Behavior may lead to one of four possible consequences: positive reinforcement, negative reinforcement, extinction, and punishment.

**BEHAVIORAL CONSEQUENCES.**    Reinforcements increase the probability that a behavior will be repeated. Two types of reinforcements increase behavior: positive reinforcement and negative reinforcement. A positive reinforcement strengthens a behavior by adding an incentive, a pleasant and desired stimulus. Positive reinforcements could include praise for getting a good grade on a paper, a candy bar as a reward for putting away books, or classroom tokens for appropriate behavior. A negative reinforcement also increases the probability that a behavior will be repeated by taking away an unpleasant or unwanted stimulus (Skinner, 1953; Skinner, 1994). Negative reinforcements could include cold weather that inspires a person to put on a warm coat, the fading of headache pain after taking an aspirin, and the cessation of nagging reminders from a parent after a child cleans up his or her room.

For example, consider a mother and her 4-year-old daughter going to a toy store to buy a birthday present for one of the daughter's friends. The daughter sees a doll that she wants and asks her mother for it. The mother gently reminds the daughter that they are there to find a birthday present. Not satisfied with the mother's response, the child begins screaming that she wants the doll. The mother firmly tells the child that she cannot have the doll, but this does not curtail the child's tantrum. In frustration, the mother takes the coveted doll from the shelf and gives it to the daughter. The child's inappropriate behavior has been strengthened through positive reinforcement (receiving a reward for her tantrum), and the incident has increased the probability that the behavior will be repeated.

Teachers also need to be careful not to use reinforcements to increase inappropriate behavior. For example, Miguel, a third grader in Mrs. Smith's class, refuses to complete his math assignment during class. Mrs. Smith warns Miguel that if he does not complete the assignment, he will have to stay in at lunch to complete it. Miguel refuses to comply and ends up eating lunch with Mrs. Smith who provides one-on-one instruction for the math assignment. The next day, Miguel once again refuses to complete his assignment, and once again Mrs. Smith keeps him in at lunch. Because Miguel enjoyed the individual attention he received at lunch, Mrs. Smith's attempt to punish him by giving him lunch detention actually increases Miguel's behavior through positive reinforcement.

Extinction decreases the behavior by withholding reinforcement. Mrs. Smith decides to change her approach and ignores Miguel's refusal to complete his math assignment, thereby not giving him any reinforcement for his behavior. Planned ignoring can be a successful behavior management technique for mild student behaviors, but it must be used properly. Ignoring inappropriate behavior must be used in conjunction with praising appropriate behavior (Obenchain & Taylor, 2005).

Punishment decreases the behavior by presenting an aversive consequence. Placing a child in timeout is often an effective form of punishment, but the effectiveness of most other forms of punishment has been debated. (See Chapter 6.)

The behavioral theorist is interested only in behavior that can be observed. Both environmental factors and the response of the child to the environment are identifiable and measurable. Opponents maintain that weaknesses of behavior theory are that it ignores internal determinants of development and that it provides intervention for the symptoms but not the causes of the inappropriate behavior.

## Functional Behavioral Analysis

Once a behavior has been identified, it can be predicted by observing the environment and controlled by making changes to the environment. Intervention is based on rearranging antecedent events and consequences. A common intervention method is known as the ABCs (Antecedent, Behavior, and Consequence) of functional behavioral analysis. The antecedent is the event that occurs before the behavior, and the consequence is the response to the behavior. For example, Marty takes Roberto's toy (antecedent), Roberto punches Marty (behavior), and Marty gives the toy back to Roberto (consequence).

The advantage of behavioral theory is that it provides a method for identifying the behavior and the variables that may trigger the behavior. It is possible to record the intensity and frequency of the behavior and measure the effectiveness of the intervention.

## SOCIAL LEARNING THEORY

### Bandura

*Social learning theory*, championed by Albert Bandura, blends the principles of operant conditioning and social interaction. The theory developed to address the criticism that behaviorism did not explain all behavior. According to social learning theory, a child does not have to elicit or directly experience a response in order to learn a behavior. He or she can learn the behavior vicariously and through self-reinforcement. Most human behavior is learned from watching others (Bandura, 1986), including parents, siblings, peers, and media figures.

In a famous study, three groups of children aged 3 and 4 years were shown a man, woman, and a cartoon cat hitting and yelling at an inflatable clown. The fourth group was shown no aggressive model. When placed in a room with the clown, the children who had been shown the aggressive films hit and yelled at the clown, while the children who were not exposed to aggressive behavior did not hit or yell at the clown (Bandura, Ross, & Ross, 1963).

Modeling promotes the attainment of new behaviors and cognitive skills. Children also learn from observing the consequences of the behavior of others. For example, if a child refuses to eat his vegetables, he is not allowed to watch a favorite television show after dinner. The child's sister learns through observation that if she does not eat her vegetables, she will not be able to watch television. Modeling teaches children to refrain from inappropriate behaviors and reinforces the memory of previously learned behavior. This abstract modeling occurs when children learn rules from observing another's behaviors.

A final aspect of social learning theory is *self-efficacy*. Self-efficacy is a person's belief in his or her own competence to carry out certain actions and persist at certain activities despite difficulties and initial failures (Bandura, 1997). Self-efficacy is the most important variable in understanding how an individual's perceived abilities and situation influence his or her behavior (Briones, Tabernero, & Arenas, 2007). For example, a student who does not believe in his ability to do well in school will most likely not do well in school.

One barrier to self-efficacy is cultural expectations. For example, Hispanic females may be discouraged from considering certain occupations or pursuing higher education degrees due to conflicting familial expectations. Hispanic female students may not be expected to do well in school, and these expectations may actually discourage their academic performances. Perceived barriers could influence the development of self-efficacy in these young women (Rivera, Chen, Flores, Blumberg, & Ponterotto, 2007).

## COGNITIVE DEVELOPMENTAL THEORY

### Piaget

One of the most influential individuals in the field of child development was Jean Piaget. His work involved the stages of cognitive development through which children pass. Children may progress through the stages at different rates, but must go through them in order. These developmental stages are defined by the acquisition of knowledge though assimilation and accommodation. *Assimilation* occurs when the child gains new knowledge and incorporates it into an existing knowledge structure known as a *schema*. For example, when a child who owns a plush duck sees another plush toy, she may call it a duck because that is the most suitable schema she has. As she sees more plush toys, she begins to notice that they are different. The process by which children change their schema is called *accommodation*.

Piaget identified four stages of cognitive development. These four stages include the sensorimotor stage, the preoperational stage, the concrete operational stage, and the formal operational stage. The rate at which an individual progresses through the stages may vary, especially among children from different cultures (Piaget, 2008).

**TABLE 3.3   Piaget's Stages of Cognitive Development**

| Stage | Approximate Age of Development | Description |
|---|---|---|
| Sensorimotor | Birth–2 Years | The infant uses senses and motor skills to gain knowledge about the world. Schemas involve activities. |
| Preoperational | 2–7 Years | The child acquires knowledge and organizes it using symbols. A prime example is the use of language. Schemas are instinctive rather than logical. |
| Concrete Operational | 7–11 Years | The child acquires knowledge and organizes it symbolically and logically. However, schemas are limited to concrete and present objects and events. The child cannot apply his knowledge to abstract events. |
| Formal Operational | 11 Years and Older | The adolescent acquires knowledge, organizes it symbolically and logically, and can apply his knowledge to abstract events. This ability allows the individual to reason using symbols that do not refer to objects and events in the real world. |

**THE SENSORIMOTOR STAGE.**   During the sensorimotor stage, the child gains knowledge through sensory perception and motor activities. The child goes through six substages as he or she gains more knowledge and experience. The Reflexes substage (birth to about 1 month) includes basic behaviors such as sucking. During the Primary Circular Reactions (about 1 to 4 months), the child explores sensations related to his or her own body. For example, the child may accidentally pull on his or her ear, find the sensation interesting, and purposely pull at it again. The Secondary Circular Reaction (about 4 to 8 months) involves objects in the environment. The child may accidentally roll a ball across the living room. The child then rolls the ball on purpose. The Coordination of Secondary Circular Reactions (8 to 12 months) involves the combination of two learned behaviors to achieve a goal. For example, a child may cry out and reach for his mother when he is hungry. Piaget believed that a child reaching this substage was displaying the first signs of intelligence. When the child becomes interested in experimenting to achieve results, he or she has entered the Tertiary Circular Reaction substage (about 12 to 18 months). The child may push cookie crumbs from his or her high chair one at a time and watch them fall to the floor. The final substage is Invention of New Means through Mental Combinations (about 18 to 24 months). The child now achieves goals by thinking, not by trial and error. He or she is capable of putting a round peg in a round hole. (See Table 3.3.)

The child also develops object permanence during the sensorimotor stage. If a mother hid a ball behind her back, a 4-month-old infant might think that the ball was gone or no longer existed, but a 1-year-old child would know that the ball still existed even if he could not see it.

**THE PREOPERATIONAL STAGE.**    The second stage of cognitive development is the preoperational stage. During this stage, the child acquires knowledge through symbols such as words, but some of the child's schemas may be illogical. Symbolic thought is an important function of this stage because it allows the development of language, which is symbolic, and creative play. Words are abstract representations of objects and actions. It is during the preoperational stage that a child begins to attach words to objects. Also during the preoperational stage, children begin to display the awareness that make-believe play is representative of their world. For example, a child may say to another, "I'll pretend that I am a doctor, and you pretend that you are the patient." These sociodramatic plays indicate that children are becoming aware of the mental processes of others.

Piaget believed that during this stage, children are egocentric, or unaware of any viewpoints except their own (Piaget, 1950/2001). In a kindergarten classroom, a child may look toward the front of the room at her teacher and chalkboard. This is the only viewpoint that exists for the child, who is completely unaware that the teacher, who is looking toward the children and the back of the classroom, has a totally different viewpoint.

Children at the preoperational stage are unable to *conserve*, or understand that rearranging the appearance of an object does not always change the physical reality of the object. For example, imagine you pour milk into a tall, thin glass. Then pour the milk from the tall glass into a short, fat glass, changing the appearance of the milk. A child would assume that the short glass contains less milk even though it contains the same amount of milk as was in the tall glass.

Children at the preoperational stage are also unable to classify objects. They assign attributes of the objects as they see them, rather than developing mental categories on the basis of traits they have previously noted. For example, given a number of manipulatives (objects the child can move around) that have different shapes and colors, a child may choose a blue triangle. Next, he may choose a yellow circle. The child is influenced by what he sees, rather than organizing objects based on a common characteristic such as color or shape.

**THE CONCRETE OPERATIONAL STAGE.**    The third stage of cognitive developmental theory is the concrete operational stage. During this stage, children become more logical in their thinking, but schemas are limited to tangible and present object and events. The child now understands that others can have a viewpoint or perspective that is different from his or her own. Children at this stage also are aware that the quantity of milk does not change when you pour milk from a tall, thin glass into a short, fat glass. Children, however, understand conservation problems in stages. First they become capable of understanding how to conserve numbers, then length, mass, and liquid, and finally area and weight. Children are able to classify objects, but only concrete ones, not abstract objects. For example, when a child is asked who is tallest if Johnny is taller than David and David is taller than Jimmy, the child may have difficulty answering the question.

Children at this stage are also able to process the feature of reversibility: They have the ability to understand that objects can be put back in their original forms. For example, a child now knows that he or she can take a ball of clay, break it into smaller pieces, and then roll the pieces back into the ball.

**THE FORMAL OPERATIONAL STAGE.**    The final stage is the formal operational stage. The individual is able to think logically about abstract issues and is capable of making assumptions without having any real evidence (Inhelder & Piaget, 1955/58). This hypothetico-deductive reasoning allows adolescents to consider alternatives and choose the best solution to a problem. An adolescent is also able to examine a statement and determine whether it is logical regardless of whether it makes sense in the real world. For example, an adolescent given the following propositional argument should be able to come up with the conclusion shown:

> *Premise 1:* All dogs have long hair.
>
> *Premise 2:* A Chihuahua does not have long hair.
>
> *Conclusion:* A Chihuahua is not a dog.

Knowing that in reality Chihuahuas are dogs, the adolescent would reason that just because the Chihuahua does not have long hair does not mean it is not a dog. Thus, the conclusion is false (even though the argument is valid) because the first premise is false. He does not have to see a Chihuahua to know that the conclusion is false. This mental exercise can take place without the adolescent's ever seeing an actual Chihuahua.

While many have questioned and refuted Piaget's findings (Bickhard, 1997), he still remains a major figure in the cognitive development of children and adolescents. He has inspired others to examine the intellectual capabilities of infants and children and has provided the foundation on which others have built.

## ECOLOGICAL SYSTEMS THEORY

The ecological model, which has been in existence since the 1960s, considers the child's environment as the cause of emotional and behavior disorders. When a match exists between the child's behavior and the environmental demands, then the child is considered normal. When a mismatch occurs, then the child has some type of emotional and behavior disorder.

The assumptions of the ecological model include the following:

1. The child is inseparable from the many complex social systems that surround him or her.
2. Disturbed behavior occurs when there is discordance between the reciprocal interactions of the child and the expectations of the child's social system.
3. Interventions are designed to make ecological systems work, and continue working in the future, without intervention.
4. Improvement in any part of the system benefits the entire system.
5. Intervention must involve the child, the environment, and the attitudes and expectations of all those in the ecosystem (Apter, 1977; Apter & Conoley, 1984).

### Bronfenbrenner

Ecological systems theory emphasizes the mutual dependence between the behavior of the child and the environment in which the behavior occurs. Urie Bronfenbrenner, one of the best known proponents of ecological psychology, developed a model for understanding a child's interaction with his environment. As the child develops, his ability to understand and influence the ecological environment increases. The environment is "a set of nested structures, each inside the next, like a set of Russian dolls" (Bronfenbrenner, 1979, p. 3). This ecological system includes five components: the microsystem, mesosystem, exosystem, macrosystem, and chronosystem (Bronfenbrenner, 1979; 2005). (See Figure 3.1.)

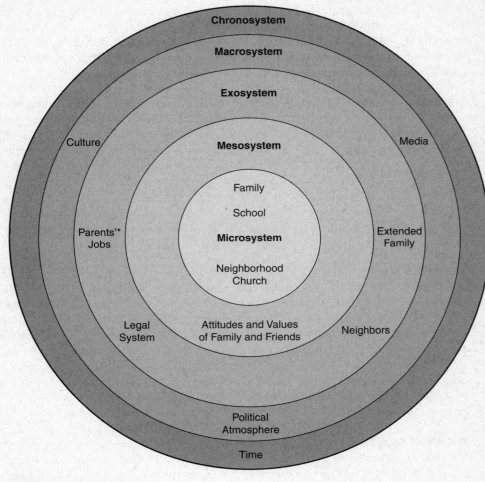

*Bronfenbrenner, 1979, 2005

**FIGURE 3.1** Bronfenbrenner's Ecological System

**THE MICROSYSTEM.** The child's immediate environment is known as the microsystem. The microsystem includes a key circle of influences that surround the child, such as parents and siblings, school, and peer groups (Brendtro, 2006). These relationships are bidirectional and reciprocal; parents and siblings affect the child's behavior, and the child affects the behavior of the parents and siblings. For example, if a boy is hyperactive, the parents may devote a lot of time to him and less time to his brother. The brother may exhibit jealousy toward the hyperactive child for occupying their parents' time. The parents may be exhausted at the end of each day of dealing with their hyperactive boy and may have little patience left. When the brother makes demands on their time and the parents rebuff him, he may feel that they do not love him as much as they love the child who is hyperactive. Through time, these reciprocal interactions become established and influence development (Bronfenbrenner, 1995).

The functioning level of the microsystem also influences the development of the child. Low socioeconomic status, a single-parent family, parental divorce, abuse, and other stress factors can have deleterious effects on the development of the child. An increase in the number of multiple family stressors experienced by the child increases the risk of psychological maladjustment (Gaylord, Kitzmann, & Lockwood, 2003).

**THE MESOSYSTEM.**    The microsystem can involve a number of environments such as home, playground, and school; the mesosystem is the interaction of these separate environments. The mesosystem is a system of microsystems (Bronfenbrenner, 2005a). It is the child's most intimate learning environment and is the reference point to the world (Swick & Williams, 2006). If the parents view the school as a hostile environment and do not value education, these attitudes will affect the child's behavior and academic performance at school. The atmosphere in the child's neighborhood also has been shown to affect his or her performance at school. Neighborhoods that have extreme poverty and crime have been shown to contribute to poor academic achievement (Nettles, Caughy, & O'Campo, 2008).

**THE EXOSYSTEM.**    While the child does not interact with exosystems, these elements may still have an influence on him or her. Elements of the exosystem could include parents' jobs, the parents' friends, the teacher's home life, the local school board, the zoning board, and the church policy-making body. For example, the state school board has established that children need to be in school for a specified number of days. Although children have no direct involvement with the state school board, this law directly influences their lives.

For parents, the greatest stressor in raising children is finances, followed by the parents' work environments (Bronfenbrenner, 2005b). The parents' work environments affect how they interact with their children at home, especially if these environments are unsatisfying or stressful.

**THE MACROSYSTEM.**    The fourth component of the ecological model is the macrosystem. The macrosystem consists of the surrounding culture's beliefs, values, laws, and ideologies, as well as global events and phenomena such as the terrorist attack on September 11, war, poverty, and racism (Abrams, Theberge, & Karan, 2005). Under the ecological model, a multilayered social environment influences the development of the child. The macrosystem "may be thought of as a societal blueprint for a particular culture or subculture" (Bronfenbrenner, 2005a, p. 81).

**THE CHRONOSYSTEM.**    The final component of the ecological system model is the chronosystem. The individual's environments change through time as he or she grows and develops. The normal events that each of us experiences through time include puberty, the transition from school to work, marriage, and retirement. Other events could include death in the family, divorce, parenthood, and moving. These events occur throughout life and can have a profound impact on personal development.

According to the ecological theory, a child is not born disturbed. A child develops an emotional and behavior disorder when societal expectations and values view the child's interactions with the environment as inappropriate. Disturbance is a result of dissension in the mutual interactions of the child with components of the child's social system. When a child's interactions are appropriate and compatible with the environment, the child and the ecosystem are balanced. When the interaction is harmonious or balanced, ecological theory suggests that the child's behavior is acceptable by societal norms. Whenever the child and ecosystem are out of balance, unacceptable behavior will occur (Johnson, 1994). This social system is very complex.

As children get older and interact with the ecosystem at different points of their lives, they create and modify their own environments on the basis of past experiences. Children become both products of and producers of their environment.

## SOCIOLOGICAL THEORIES

### Vygotsky

Lev Semenovich Vygotsky believed that a child's cognitive development was acquired through social interactions with adults. According to Vygotsky's sociocultural theory, social interaction between a child and his or her immediate learning environment was necessary for the child to be *enculturated* into the learning community (Liu & Matthews, 2005). Over the course of repeated interactions, the child acquires the values, knowledge, beliefs, and traditions of the cultural community. Since social interaction is crucial for the cognitive development of the child, language is an important aspect of the child's development. Without language, the transferral of knowledge about the social and cultural community cannot take place. Vygotsky believed that human consciousness was not possible without language.

According to Vygotsky, every function in the child's cultural development appears first on the social level between people and later on the individual level, inside the child (1978). For example, consider an infant who reaches for a ball but is unable to grasp it. The mother, understanding the child's interest in the ball, points to it. The mother then picks up the ball, identifies it verbally as a ball, and gives it to the child. Through this interaction, the infant gains knowledge and internalizes it as thought. This internalization of knowledge is the means by which the values and beliefs of culture are transferred from one generation to the next. This is especially true when the sociocultural identity is based on specific history, oral traditions, and language (Kawakami & Dudoit, 2000) and is prevalent among Hispanics, Native Americans, and Kanaka Maoli (Native Hawaiians). It is critical for teachers of ethnically and linguistically diverse learners to use a social context of learning.

A second aspect of Vygotsky's theory is the idea that the potential for cognitive development depends upon the *zone of proximal development,* "the distance between the actual development level as determined by independent problem solving and the level of potential development as determined through problem solving under adult guidance or in collaboration with more capable peers" (Vygotsky, 1978, p. 86). The zone of proximal development is the difference between what the child can do independently and what he can do when assisted by a more expert adult or peer. Since children do not acquire capabilities at exactly the same ages, their zone of proximal development needs to be considered in the classroom.

This consideration could be especially important for children with emotional and behavior disorders who lack social skills and so have difficulty acquiring knowledge about appropriate social interactions. The cultural community teaches societal expectations, and if that knowledge is not transferred to a particular child, the child's zone of proximal development will be different from that of another child who has learned those expectations. If a child is not taught to value education or hears from his parents that the public schools are failing to educate children, the child may talk back to the teacher because cultural expectations have not taught him to respect the teacher.

## MORAL DEVELOPMENT

Moral development involves a system of beliefs, values, and fundamental judgments about the rightness or wrongness of human acts (Zimbardo & Gerrig, 2004) and how these acts relate to societal expectations. Both Piaget and another influential psychologist, Lawrence Kohlberg, viewed the moral development of a child as a function of cognitive development and believed that the child must pass through each stage sequentially.

### Piaget's Theory of Moral Development

Piaget's theory of moral development had two stages (1932/1997). The first stage is *heteronomous morality* (ages 5 to 10 years). Children regard the rules handed down by authority figures as unchangeable. When judging the wrongness of an act, a child focuses on the amount of damage done, not whether the infraction was accidental or intentional. For example, a child who accidentally breaks seven cups believes that he has committed more of an offense than if he intentionally had broken one cup.

Around 9 to 12 years of age, children make the transition to *autonomous morality*. They now realize that the intentions and the outcomes of their acts should be taken into consideration. They understand that rules are determined by societal expectations and can be revised depending on the circumstances. Older children and adolescents become more democratic and mature in changing and following rules using a standard of fairness called *reciprocity*, or treating others as they want to be treated.

### Kohlberg

Kohlberg organized his theory of moral development into three levels known as preconventional, conventional, and postconventional. Each moral developmental level contained two stages. (See Table 3.4.)

The two stages at the preconventional level are *punishment and obedience orientation* (Stage 1) and *instrumental relativist orientation* (Stage 2). At Stage 1, the child follows the rules to avoid punishment. The morality of the child is based on his or her fear of the consequences of violating a rule. At Stage 2, the child complies with expectations because he or she expects to be rewarded for good behavior. A child at this stage believes that other individuals also act out of self-interest and that they will do something for him if he does something for them.

At the conventional level, the stages are the *good boy–good girl orientation*, or interpersonal concordance (Stage 3), and *social-order-maintaining orientation*, or law-and-order orientation (Stage 4). At Stage 3, the child behaves in a way that will gain approval and affection from others. She believes that if she is a "good girl," her parents will approve of her. She also begins to have the same concern for others' feelings and wishes as she has for her own. Understanding that others have needs and desires is the basic concept of morality (Minnameier, 2001). At Stage 4, the child believes societal laws have the utmost importance. Laws are fixed and cannot be disobeyed.

The final two stages of morality development, at the postconventional level, are the *social contract orientation* (Stage 5) and the *universal ethical-principle orientation* (Stage 6).

**TABLE 3.4  Kohlberg's Moral Development Stages**

| Level and Stage | Description |
|---|---|
| **PRECONVENTIONAL LEVEL** | |
| Punishment and Obedience Orientation | The child follows rules to avoid punishment. |
| Instrumental Relativist Orientation | The child follows rules in order to satisfy personal needs. He will do favors for others if they do something for him. |
| **CONVENTIONAL LEVEL** | |
| Good Boy—Good Girl Orientation | The child behaves in a way that will maintain the affection and approval of family and friends. |
| Social Order Maintaining Orientation | The child feels a duty to follow rules and laws for the sake of moral conformity. |
| **POSTCONVENTIONAL LEVEL** | |
| Social Contract Orientation | The individual values the rights of the individual and believes that laws are designed to protect those rights. |
| Universal Ethical Principle Orientation | The individual sees the equality of human rights and the dignity of humans as fundamental universal principles. |

At Stage 5, the rights of the individual are valued, and laws are to be followed as long as they are consistent with those rights. Laws are understood to be based on societal expectations, and individuals are willing to change the laws once they appear inconsistent with these expectations. At Stage 6, appropriate behavior is defined by the self-chosen principles of the conscious individuals involved. Equality of human rights and the dignity of human beings is a fundamental aspect of this stage.

While some research has supported the universality of Kohlberg's moral development (Gibbs, Basinger, Grime, & Snarey, 2007), other researchers have refuted Kohlberg's principles as biased in relation to culture and gender. Kohlberg's theory emphasizes the individual, and many cultures do not place value on individual rights.

## Gilligan

Carol Gilligan (1982) has argued that Kohlberg's theory does not represent the morality of women. Kohlberg's study included only white males. Gilligan believed that men subscribe to a morality of individual rights and societal order, while women subscribe to an ethic of care; men's morality is based on rules and justice while women are more inclined to think in terms of caring and relationships. Women and girls are taught very early by societal norms to care for other people and to expect others to care for them. As a result women's experience with morality does not focus on abstract rules or impartial societal norms. Women try to solve "moral dilemmas through negotiation and communication, through attempts to make the facts clear in a dilemma situation" (Driver, 2005, p. 184).

In Gilligan's theory of moral development, women develop through a sequence of three levels and two transitions. The levels are *orientation toward self-interest, goodness as self-sacrifice,* and the *morality of nonviolence.* These developmental stages show the progression from initial concern with survival to social or conventional morality and, finally, to postconventional or principled nonviolence as a means to settle moral conflicts.

Many researchers have been critical of Gilligan's theory. Gender differences in moral development do begin in early childhood and increase as children get older (Gilligan, 1982), but one study found that whereas boys used significantly more rules of justice than girls did, all the children were more justice oriented than care oriented (Tulviste & Koor, 2005). In other cultures, the differences between the moral development of men and women are not significant. Gilligan's ethic of care may be culture specific and not gender related (Vikan, Camino, & Biaggio, 2005).

Yet Gilligan's theory of moral development could account for the underrepresentation of girls identified with emotional and behavior disorders. One study found that boys' play produces more conflicts. Because conflicts are often caused by moral transgression, the study suggests that boys purposefully play more aggressively than girls do in order to explore their concept of morality. Conversely, girls seldom participated in play that created conflict (Tulviste & Koor, 2005). Boys are likely to display conduct problems, immaturity, antisocial behavior, and aggressive behaviors, whereas girls are more likely to display depression and social withdrawal. Because the societal community expects girls to follow a morality of caring and not to display aggressive behavior, they are less likely to cause disruptions in the classroom and are less likely to be identified as having emotional and behavior disorders.

## DYNAMIC SYSTEMS PERSPECTIVE

The current theory in developmental and general psychology is the dynamic systems approach (Sergiyenko, 2005). Developed by Esther Thelen and Linda Smith (1994), this theory holds that all the different aspects of a child's world are integrated into a single system that guides the development of the child. Thelen compares child development to a mountain stream because a mountain stream is "moving all the time in a continuous flow and continuous change" (2005, p. 259). A child's development is constantly in motion, and any change, such as a traumatic brain injury, disrupts the relationship between the child and the environment. When this change occurs, the child reorganizes his or her behavior so that the system works together again.

All children develop pretty much the same way, reaching certain milestones at about the same time. However, behavior is variable; the way a child behaves depends not only on his current environment, but on his past behaviors and the biological constraints with which he was born (Thelen, 2005). As a result, children learn similar skills in different ways and at different times. For example, two children with similar biological characteristics may learn to walk at different times because the parents of one child may work more with the child on walking skills.

Children also react differently to specific events in their lives. Consider the example of two children who both live in homes where they are verbally abused. Each child is made to feel worthless. Yet one child becomes an overachiever to prove his worth. He goes to college, earns a master's degree, and is successful in his chosen occupation. The other child develops emotional and behavior disorders. He drops out of school and has difficulty maintaining a job. Some children are more resilient than others when faced with the same environmental challenge.

Every child walks a developmental path. Upon reaching a fork in the road, the child chooses which path to take on the basis of his or her physical and cognitive abilities, social environments, and experiences. Since these qualities are different in each child, the decisions that children make are different even though the paths they take are similar.

## Complexity, Continuity, and Stability

*Complexity, continuity in time,* and *dynamic stability* are the three principles of the dynamic systems approach.

Human development is a complex process. Everything in the child's life contributes to his or her development: the child's physical and mental abilities, the surrounding environment, and every minute event in the child's life. Each thread contributes to a complex and unique tapestry. As a result, the dynamic systems approach does not assign the child's behavior to a single cause but examines interactions as nonlinear—differing from one child to another due to individual factors.

The second principle is continuity in time. The child's behavior is affected by the experiences of the past, and these experiences, in combination with those of the present, affect the child's behavior in the future. The development of the child is a response to the accumulated experiences of every moment of the child's life.

Dynamic stability is almost a contradiction in terms. A dynamic system is constantly in motion, while a stable system remains consistent. However, some human behavior is extremely stable and predictable. For example, a child without any cognitive or physical impediments will learn to walk around 12 months and learn to talk around 18 months. However, when the child's environment changes, as it might if, for example, the parents divorced, then the child will reorganize his or her behavior so that the various factors of the environment become stable again. The child still interacts with both parents, but in a more complex and effective way.

The dynamic systems approach encompasses ethological, ecological, and sociocultural theories. Compared with previous developmental theories, the dynamic systems approach is fairly new and is still in its early stage. However, it offers a useful tool for practitioners and educators of children with emotional and behavior disorders; introducing new and stable systems into the child's life may help disrupt systems that are maladapted.

## SOCIOECONOMIC FACTORS

A number of factors may contribute to the emergence of emotional and behavior disorders in a child. Experience and opportunities, coupled with the biological characteristics of the child and the characteristics of the surrounding environment, affect a child's development.

Children with emotional and behavior disorders are more likely to come from households with low socioeconomic status (Coutinho et al., 2002; Wagner, Kutash, et al., 2005). Poverty is a critical problem that is associated with a heightened risk of disability, including emotional and behavioral disorders (Fujiura & Yamaki, 2000). It is easy to infer that poverty causes emotional and behavior disorders; however, many children from households of low socioeconomic status never develop emotional and behavior disorders. It is important to understand that poverty is a factor that merely increases the risk of developing emotional and behavior disorders.

More than a third of children identified with emotional and behavior disorders are from single-parent homes (Wagner, Kutash, et al., 2005). In homes without a father, boys may be at heightened risk for developing aggressive behaviors and girls may lack a role model for an appropriate relationship between a man and a woman (Kauffman, 2005). Unfortunately, additional risk variables are associated with single-parent homes. These risk factors include economic hardship, lack of parental involvement, inadequate discipline, and parental substance abuse (Frick, 2004; Keogh, 2000).

Family interaction is crucial to the development of the child. Depending on the type of interaction, it may offset risk factors such as low socioeconomic status and single-parent home, or it may intensify the risk of behavior problems. Children from dysfunctional families are at heightened risk for developing a number of emotional and behavior problems including depression, conduct disorder, and anxiety disorders. Children often learn aggressive behaviors from family members who are aggressive. Abusive and neglectful parents tend to be less responsive and less demanding than parents in functional families (Baumrind, 1994).

## CHILD ABUSE

Child abuse can also affect the development of a child. Not only is the developmental stage in which the abuse takes place important, but it may affect later developmental stages if the abuse continues (English, Graham, Litrownik, Everson, & Bangdiwala, 2005). Many of these children demonstrate severe and chronic behavior problems by the time they get to school.

In 2002, an estimated 896,000 children were victims of abuse and neglect. Nationally, 60.5% of children who were abused experienced neglect, 18.6% were physically abused, 9.9% were sexually abused, and 6.5% were emotionally abused. Nearly 1,400 children died from abuse (U.S. Department of Health and Human Services, 2002). Child sexual abuse has been reported to affect between 4% and 50% of children and adolescents (Paolucci et al., 2001). Child abuse and child sexual abuse traumatically affect development and also put children at heightened risk for developing posttraumatic stress disorder, depression, and sexual promiscuity. (See Case Study 3.2.) These children are also at risk for entering a victim–perpetrator cycle (the victim becomes a perpetrator), having poor academic achievement, and attempting or carrying out suicide (Brown, 2005; Negrao et al., 2005; Paolucci et al., 2001).

## CULTURAL INFLUENCES ON DEVELOPMENT

Culture also plays a role in child development. It influences children's interactions with their family and peers, their behavior, and their values. Many individuals are not even aware of aspects of their culture unless they experience the culture of others. Often, individuals do not realize that, along with our shared national culture, there are numerous microcultures. These microcultures have unique characteristics that are frequently different from, and sometimes in conflict with, those of the dominant culture.

One aspect of the national culture is the autonomous view of the family, a central component of American life. Americans tend to value independence, self-reliance, and privacy. Many developmental theories that are relevant to Americans emphasize the individual.

## Case Study 3.2

### Angelica

Angelica was 14 years old and pregnant for the third time. After she was placed in a residential treatment center, case workers discovered that she had been impregnated each time by her stepfather. Each times she gave birth, the baby was sold on the black market. Yet Angelica refused to discuss the abuse with authorities and was anxious to return home. She was convinced that she and her stepfather were in love and that this time they were going to keep their child. The chronic sexual abuse had distorted Angelica's view of the relationship between a man and a woman and had hindered her social development. Even if she received years of therapeutic counseling, her social worker feared that Angelica would not develop normal social and sexual relations.

Children are taught to value individual accomplishments and achievements and to be self-reliant and independent. American culture expects children to grow up, find their own ways, and move away from the family unit to begin their own families. The United States is largely an individualistic society in which people largely think of themselves as separate entities who will be successful or unsuccessful as a result of their own efforts. Individuals who are successful are viewed as role models, yet the media, which promotes many of these individuals, also glorifies violence and sexual encounters in the lives of celebrities. Such idolization of celebrities whose images promote violence and sex has an effect on culture and the development of children.

In contrast with this admiration of the individual, many microcultures in the United States emphasize cooperative structures. These cultural groups stress cooperation between individuals and the needs of the many over individualism. The tradition of extended families—which may include not just parents and child, but grandparents, aunts, and uncles—is a characteristic of many microcultures. These aspects of culture affect the development of the child.

Culture and diversity also play a role in behavior, but often that behavior is viewed as unacceptable by the societal norms of the dominant culture. For example, avoiding eye contact and maintaining silence when asked a question by a teacher is a cultural aspect of Hispanic and Asian American children that may be interpreted as disrespect or inadequate social skills by a European American female teacher (Lian, 1996; Shepherd, Linn, & Brown, 2005; Wilder, Dyches, Obiakor, & Algozzine, 2004). The teacher's lack of understanding of the child's culture could cause that teacher to misidentify a student as having a disability.

Cultural pluralism, or allowing microcultures to function separately without requiring them to be assimilated into the dominant culture, is not readily accepted by individualistic societies. Often, ethnically diverse groups develop societal structures within their communities. The expectations of the dominant culture and the microcultures differ, and when the societal expectations and values of the dominant culture view the child's interactions with the environment as inappropriate, the child may be deemed as having emotional and behavior disorders.

## Summary

Child development theories provide a way to understand the cognitive, emotional, and social growth of children and adolescents and suggest factors that may cause emotional and behavior disorders. It is valuable to understand development because it affects how childhood is interpreted and how children with emotional and behavior disorders are treated. Over the years, various theories have been embraced and then discarded by practitioners.

Interactions occur within and between several settings in a child's life, such as home and school. The key participants in childhood development are individuals who contribute and receive the transactions of the child's environment. Both contributors and receiving members have responsibility for altering any disturbing interaction patterns. If persons, behaviors, and environments interact deterministically, then it is important to assess and understand the contribution of each of these components (Gaughan, 1995).

## Review Questions

1. Why is it important for teachers and administrators of students with emotional and behavior disorders to understand developmental theories?
2. Of the development theories covered in this chapter, which would you embrace and why? Which theory would you reject and why?
3. What are some of the socioeconomic factors that can influence the development of a child?
4. Consider the case of Kami, a 7-year-old Kanaka Maoli (Native Hawaiian) boy who has grown up in a cooperative 'ohana (extended family) structure. How might his microculture conflict with the national culture and affect his development?

# Identifying Students with Emotional and Behavior Disorders

**After reading this chapter, you should be able to**

- Explain the three different steps of the assessment process and how they are important in identifying students with emotional and behavior disorders.

- Describe the seven steps for conducting a comprehensive evaluation.

- Describe the two types of tests for assessing academic skills.

- Describe three methods of assessing behavior.

- Explain two ways of assessing social skills.

- Describe how the Eligibility Team determines whether a student has emotional and behavior disorders.

The identification of students with emotional and behavior disorders is an important first step in meeting their behavioral, social, academic, and emotional needs. Unfortunately, because the federal definition is subjective, it is difficult to identify students with emotional and behavior disorders. Students who exhibit behavioral difficulties in the classroom, but who do not have emotional and behavior disorders, frequently are referred for special education services. Conversely, students who exhibit internalizing behaviors such as depression and who do not display inappropriate behaviors in the classroom often are not referred for services even though they have emotional and behavior disorders. Finally, many teachers and professionals are reluctant to identify students with emotional and behavior disorders (Drotar, 2004; Forness, 2003). These students do not receive the necessary interventions that would help them take advantage of the educational opportunities afforded to them by the public schools.

Identifying students with emotional and behavior disorders is contingent on the *assessment process,* a three-tiered process that culminates in a comprehensive, multifaceted assessment and the development of an Individualized Education Program (IEP). The assessment process incorporates procedures for screening, prereferral interventions, and special education referrals (Kea, Campbell-Whatley, & Bratton, 2003). If the student is identified as having emotional and behavior disorders at the completion of the assessment process and needs special education services, then school personnel and others work together to develop an IEP. Because the IEP is based on the information obtained from the comprehensive assessment, the assessment process itself is the initial intervention for students who are struggling in the education setting.

## THE ASSESSMENT PROCESS

*Assessment* is the process of gathering information about the student's academic, behavioral, emotional, and social performances in school. An improperly conducted assessment could result in erroneous placement decisions, inappropriate reactive program development, and ineffective instructional delivery. It is important for school personnel to follow the assessment process to reduce improper placement and inappropriate eligibility decisions.

The three steps of the assessment process include screening, prereferral interventions, and referral (which includes the comprehensive evaluation). Each successive component of the assessment process builds on the previous step and ultimately leads to decisions about eligibility for special services, individual educational program planning, and appropriate educational placement in the least restrictive environment.

### Screening

The first step of the assessment process is *screening.* The purpose of screening is to gather information which indicates that the student has a potential for academic and behavioral difficulties. Almost all students in public schools receive some type of screening. For example, many elementary school students have their vision or hearing examined.

The screening process looks for students who may have the potential for learning, behavioral, and sensory problems that might interfere with their academic performances. It also may provide the information that educators need to develop an intervention to correct the problem. For example, if the student is not completing her homework, a vision screening may determine that the student is nearsighted and unable to clearly see the assignment written on the chalkboard. Interventions could include moving the student to the front of the classroom and/or providing the student with glasses to correct her vision.

Screening can be targeted for students who appear to be at risk for academic and behavioral difficulties. Screening should begin in preschool and kindergarten and continue in the primary and secondary school years (Lane, Gresham, & O'Shaughnessy, 2002). Early identification and prevention is crucial in serving young children who are at risk for emotional and behavior disorders (Serna et al., 2002; Serna et al., 2000). Screening children in preschool and kindergarten has the potential to identify a greater proportion of children who are at risk for emotional and behavior disorders, and it can provide the needed strategies and interventions to reduce the severity and long-term impact of the disorder (DiStefano & Kamphaus, 2007).

Screening instruments are quick, inexpensive assessments that can be given easily to large groups of students (Heward, 2006). Screening instruments provides a thoughtful way to investigate whether students need a more comprehensive assessment.

Several checklists and procedures have been recommended for identifying emotional and behavior disorders in young children. The *Child Behavior Checklist for Ages 2–3* (Achenbach & Rescorla, 2000) is one of the more widely used measures of behavior in young children, although there is some concern that it may not adequately interpret the results of screenings of ethnically diverse children (Konold, Hamre, & Pianta, 2003). The *Systematic Screening for Behavioral Disorders* (Walker & Severson, 1990) is another promising instrument that can help identify young children with emotional and behavior disorders (Serna et al., 2000). The *Early Screening Profile* (Walker, Severson, & Feil, 1995) is founded on a multistaged screening approach for identifying children who display externalizing and internalizing problem behaviors and who are at risk for emotional or behavioral problems (Conroy & Brown, 2004; DiStefano & Kamphaus, 2007; Hester et al., 2004). The *Social Skills Rating Scale* (Gresham & Elliot, 1990) focuses on social skills and examines deficits in social and behavioral skills. These instruments are useful tools for identifying young children who may be at risk for developing emotional and behavior disorders.

When the results of screening indicate that a disorder exists, school personnel can make plans for early intervention. Additionally, screening can identify students who may respond well to intervention and instruction, and who may not need special education (Fuchs, Fuchs, & Speece, 2002). Thus, screening can also lead to academic and behavioral intervention prior to any consideration of special education services.

For example, consider Johnny, the subject of case studies throughout the text. When he was in third grade, Johnny's vision and hearing were tested and were within normal ranges. The state-mandated assessment given to all students in the third grade also screened students for academic ability. This examination showed that Johnny was not functioning at grade level. The information obtained from the screening was used at the next step of the assessment process.

It is important to remember that the information gathered from screening should not be used by itself to determine whether a student is eligible for special education services. Many testing instruments used for screening are not technically sound and would not provide enough information to make a determination about the student's eligibility. In order to make a determination that a student is eligible for special education, the public school would need to conduct a full and individualized evaluation [20 U.S.C. § 300.301(a)].

## Prereferral Interventions

The next step in the assessment process is prereferral interventions. The prereferral process is considered to be a more specific method than the general screenings that will lead to interventions and strategies promoting academic success. By definition, *prereferral* interventions are considerations, plans, and efforts to improve the child's functioning that are attempted prior to any formal referral for special education assessment and intervention. Prereferral intervention has two main purposes: providing accommodations and gathering information.

The first purpose is to provide accommodations for students who are having difficulties in their academic programs. The intent is to develop interventions that provide students with the opportunities to be successful academically without qualifying them for special education services.

Teachers are now required in most states to demonstrate and document that appropriate interventions have been attempted before any student is referred to special education (Salvia & Ysseldyke, 2004). When a student is struggling in class, the teacher should provide some basic accommodations. These accommodations need not be elaborate and should not change the curriculum. Accommodations can be as simple as moving the student to the front of the room, giving the student more time to complete assignments, or shortening assignments for that particular student. If these initial accommodations are not successful, the teacher should present this student to the school's At-Risk Team or Grade Level Team, where the teachers in attendance should brainstorm strategies to help the student in the classroom.

Designing interventions for culturally and linguistically diverse students poses a challenge for the At-Risk Team. The team needs to ascertain whether the inappropriate behavior displayed by the student is the norm for the student's culture or whether it is influenced by cultural expectations. Parental participation is crucial in assessing the cultural influences on a student's behavior. The At-Risk Team also should assess the student's level of language proficiency in both his or her native language and English. Understanding the student's relative proficiency in the native language and in English is an important step in distinguishing the differences between language problems and learning problems (Hardin, Roach-Scott, & Peisner-Feinberg, 2007). In some areas of the United States, especially along the Mexican border, some students are not proficient in their native language or in English, making it difficult for educators to accurately measure their academic skills. This problem is compounded when the native language has evolved to include words that are meaningless beyond a particular region. For example, a *mariachi* is a musical group comprising singers and musicians who play guitars, horns, and violins, but in one specific region of southern Texas, "mariachi" also means "breakfast taco" (Shepherd et al., 2005).

At-Risk Teams can provide needed interventions for culturally and linguistically diverse students. To be effective, the team needs to (1) include teachers with expertise in teaching English language learners, (2) involve the student's parents in order to determine the influence of the student's language and culture on his or her behavior, and (3) design interventions that take into consideration cultural and linguistic factors (Ortiz, Wilkinson, Roberton-Courtney, & Kushner, 2006).

Some teachers are under the impression that they cannot provide accommodations unless the student is already receiving special education services, but IDEA 2004 actually encourages the provision of early intervention services to students who have not been identified as needing special education services. Under IDEA, schools can provide educational and behavioral evaluations, services, and support for students and professional development for teachers. Schools also can use up to 15% of their federal special education funds to develop early intervention services for students who need additional academic and behavioral support (20 U.S.C. § 300.226).

**RESPONSE-TO-INTERVENTIONS.**    Another aspect of prereferral interventions is a tool called response-to-interventions (RTI) that provides various levels of interventions *prior to referral for special education services*. RTI has been used to identify students with learning disabilities (Gresham, 2005; Gresham et al., 2005; Linan-Thompson, Vaughn, Prater, & Cirino, 2006), but it also can be used to identify students with emotional and behavior disorders (Fairbanks, Sugai, Guardino, & Lathrop, 2007; Gresham, 2005).

Much like Positive Behavioral Support (see Chapter 6), RTI has been conceptualized as a three-tier prevention model with primary, secondary, and tertiary interventions. Primary, or universal, intervention is a school-wide intervention involving all students. Secondary, or individualized, intervention provides specialized support for individual students or classrooms with identified needs. Tertiary, or comprehensive, intervention provides extensive, individualized support (Bradley, Danielson, & Doolittle, 2005; Marston, 2005; Walker, Cheney, Stage, & Blurn, 2005).

In order to use RTI, school personnel must develop effective interventions at each level. School personnel need to appropriately define the student's academic or behavioral problem, develop an intervention that is likely to be effective, implement the intervention, and monitor the effects of the intervention. If the student shows adequate response to interventions at the primary stage, then he or she is expected to continue to make progress in the general education classroom. If the student does not meet benchmarks after receiving primary interventions, then the student is provided with secondary interventions. These are more specialized interventions or group interventions in which students receive similar and intensive interventions. If the student does not show an adequate response to interventions at this stage, he or she proceeds to tertiary interventions. This stage could involve functional behavioral analysis, behavioral intervention plans, or specialized help from special education teachers. If the student's academic or behavioral problems continue to be unacceptable, then the student should be referred for special education evaluations (Bradley et al., 2005; Linan-Thompson et al., 2006; VanDerHeyden, Witt, & Gilbertson, 2007).

A crucial and often excluded component of RTI is an analysis of general education classrooms. Teachers and administrators need to determine whether a student with academic and behavioral difficulties is receiving adequate instruction in the general education classroom prior to making referrals and eligibility decisions (Klinger & Edwards, 2006). This is especially relevant for culturally and linguistically diverse students whose learning styles may not match the teaching styles of the classroom.

As with the prereferral process, general education teachers have the primary responsibility for conducting instruction, monitoring functioning, and implementing interventions at the primary and secondary level. Special education teachers may provide consultation at these levels and may be more involved at the tertiary level (Mastropieri & Scruggs, 2005).

If students with academic, emotional, and behavioral difficulties experience success after receiving interventions, further assessment and evaluation may not be necessary. Thus, prereferral interventions will avoid placing students in special education programs who do not have an eligible disability (Fuchs et al., 2002). However, students who continue to have problems should be referred for comprehensive evaluations. All of the interventions developed for the prereferral interventions should be documented and included in the comprehensive evaluation. The documented information becomes the initial information source about students who will be referred for evaluation consideration in special education.

## Comprehensive Evaluation

IDEA provides specific steps for planning and conducting comprehensive evaluations of students who are suspected of having emotional and behavior disorders. The legislation clearly delineates the following steps for conducting evaluations (see Figure 4.1):

1. Documentation of Prereferral Interventions
2. Parental Permission
3. Selection of the Evaluation Team
4. Reviewing Existing Information
5. Plan for Evaluation
6. Conducting Evaluations
7. Compiling Results

**DOCUMENTATION OF PREREFERRAL INTERVENTIONS.**    Prior to performing a comprehensive evaluation, educators should attempt prereferral interventions to avoid inappropriately identifying a student as having emotional and behavior disorders. The type of interventions and the duration of the interventions should be carefully documented. In addition, the file

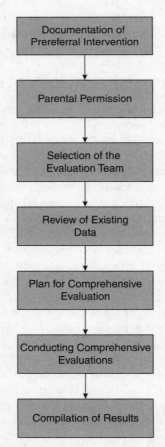

**FIGURE 4.1**  Steps for Conducting Evaluations

should contain evidence that the presumed disability has adversely affected the student's educational and functional performances. If the student's educational performance has not been severely affected (for example, he or she is not failing classes), considering that student for special education services might be premature. Also, if prereferral documentation does not exist, consideration for a comprehensive evaluation should be postponed until the documentation is provided.

**PARENTAL PERMISSION.**    Parents are guaranteed the right to participate in decisions involving their child's education. School personnel must make every effort to involve parents during the screening, prereferral, referral, evaluation, educational program planning, implementation of programs, review of educational programs, and any future reevaluations. As a part of this process, educators must obtain parental permission before conducting any assessment or evaluation of a student suspected of having emotional and behavior disorders. School personnel must make reasonable efforts to obtain written permission from the parents for an initial evaluation to determine whether the child has a disability; a verbal agreement is not sufficient (20 U.S.C. § 300.300). Under IDEA 2004, if the parent refuses to give permission for the initial evaluation or does not respond to a request for permission, the public school does not have to pursue the evaluation. However, if the student is clearly not doing well in the general education classroom and needs services, it would be in the best interest of the child if the school pursued special education placement through mediation and/or due process.

**SELECTION OF THE EVALUATION TEAM.**    The selection of the Evaluation Team is a critical aspect of the comprehensive evaluation and is determined in part by the suspected disability of the student being considered for evaluation. The Evaluation Team, which is similar to the IEP Team (see Chapter 5), should include qualified personnel who conduct and review evaluations. Members of this team could include regular classroom teachers, special education teachers, the school psychologist, school counselors, parents, and others who may be necessary and helpful to the assessment process.

**REVIEWING EXISTING INFORMATION.**    The first step the Evaluation Team should take is to review existing information. This information includes the results of screening and prereferral interventions; evaluations and information provided by the parents, such as social and developmental histories; results of current assessments, including state assessments or academic records; and observations by teachers and other school personnel, including disciplinary documents. Parental consent is not required for the team to review existing information or for the student to receive an evaluation that is given to all students (vision and hearing screening, state-mandated examinations, etc.).

**PLAN FOR EVALUATION.**    After reviewing the existing information about a student suspected of having a disability, the evaluation team develops a comprehensive evaluation plan on the basis of two questions. First, what additional information is needed to complete the comprehensive evaluation? Generally, formal assessments of aptitude, achievement, behavioral, and social functioning are needed. Second, how can the Evaluation Team obtain the additional information needed? The responses to these questions form the plan for evaluation. The plan should determine what assessment activities will be conducted and who will conduct them. In addition, the plan should describe how the information will be compiled and summarized.

**CONDUCTING EVALUATIONS.**    Prior to identifying a student with emotional and behavior disorders and providing special education services to that student, educators should conduct a comprehensive evaluation in all areas of suspected disability. This evaluation will be an assessment of vision, hearing, social, emotional and behavioral status, general intelligence, current academic performance and any other area that the evaluation team deems pertinent. Screening and prereferral documents also should be included in the file. The evaluation must consist of multiple procedures with a variety of assessment instruments and tools to gather the needed information in the functional, developmental, and academic areas, and it must be completed within 60 days of receiving permission from the parents to conduct the evaluation.

The evaluation team must use more than one assessment instrument. For example, the evaluation should include results from aptitude, achievement, and behavioral assessments. If the student is an English language learner, the assessment should use the child's dominant language. The team also should employ nonverbal aptitude assessment to avoid identifying a student as having a disability on the basis of nonnative language acquisition. Additionally, assessments should not be culturally or racially biased.

All assessments should use valid and reliable techniques of measurement and should be administered by trained personnel. Teachers, school psychologists, and others who hold professional certification are often qualified to conduct assessments (34 CFR § 300.301; 34 CFR § 300.304).

**COMPILING RESULTS.**    After all tests and assessments have been completed, the evaluation team compiles the results in a written report. The report should be concise, but should contain enough detail that the child's teachers and other involved individuals can understand the information and act on it. The summary report should contain information obtained prior to the evaluation, a description of the assessment tools that were utilized to gain further information, specific results gathered by the evaluation process, and evaluation team member assumptions generated from the assessment results.

## Confidentiality

Education professionals who deal with personal information during the assessment process, eligibility consideration, individual education program development, and program delivery must hold this information in the strictest confidence. They should not share the information with anyone who is not directly involved with the student's education. In other words, individuals who are involved with the education of a student who is eligible for special education services may need access to confidential information. But individuals who do not deal with that student in an education setting do not need or merit access to confidential information (34 CFR § 300.610-300.626).

Personal information includes the student's name; the names of the student's parents or other family members; the address of the student or student's family members; any personal identifier, such as a student ID number, driver's license number, or social security number; and any description of characteristics of the student that could easily identify him or her to individuals not associated with the student's education. All of this information should be kept absolutely in confidence and shared only with those who need the information to provide appropriate services to the student.

Additional rights for parents and students are described in the Family Education Rights and Privacy Act of 1974 (FERPA) (20 U.S.C. § 1232g; 34 CFR Part 99). Each school district is directed to train personnel on keeping student information confidential. In addition, school personnel deliver the information about confidentiality to parents, students, and the community. Confidentiality is a shared responsibility.

## ASSESSING ACADEMIC SKILLS

An important component of assessing students suspected of having emotional and behavior disorders is examining the present levels of the students' academic performance. Multiple studies indicate that students with emotional and behavior disorders experience moderate to severe academic difficulties (Hinshaw, 1992; Lloyd, Kauffman, Landrum, & Roe, 1991; Rapport, Scanlan, & Denny, 1999). Because the assessment process is designed both to establish eligibility for special education and to determine appropriate intervention strategies, it is essential to evaluate academic skill. A thorough understanding of the individual student's current academic functioning and general intelligence provides the information necessary to develop strategies, interventions, and programs that will address the student's academic needs.

A number of academic and intelligence assessments are available to educators. Most have high levels of validity and reliability. Many commonly used academic evaluation tools are designed so that teachers or other educational professionals can administer them without further training. Other instruments can be used only by professionals who have been trained on the evaluation tool itself. Finally, only professionals who have received specific training and certification or credentials as a school psychologist or educational diagnostician can administer certain assessment tools.

Evaluation teams usually choose standardized intelligence tests and academic achievement tests because the results of these tests may be compared with results earned by other students in the same age range. It is important to remember that although there have been efforts to make assessments as impartial as possible, the tests are not always sensitive to socioeconomic, cultural, and ethnic issues. Some of the most widely used assessments do not reflect the cultural experiences of minority students and can fail to accurately measure ability (Hagie, Gallipo, & Svien, 2003). It is important to remember that there is no such thing as an unbiased assessment because of the multitude of culturally and linguistically diverse students in the public schools.

Standardized tests are not perfect indicators of ability because so many variables may affect the outcome of a test. These variables are usually specific to the student being tested or the environment where the testing is conducted. A student's score may be affected by the time of day the testing takes place, whether the student had breakfast, whether the student is feeling sick, and many other issues. The student may not be comfortable with the test administrator, may be uneasy because the test is given in an unfamiliar room, or may have trouble concentrating because of external noise. All these factors can influence the results of the tests. The true or real score is a hypothetical value that probably falls within a range of possible scores above and below the actual score the student earned; this range is known as the *standard error of measurement*. An instrument that has a lower error of measurement will be more reliable. Therefore, all scores from standardized tests are suspect and should be considered only as general indicators of the student's ability or academic performance.

## Standardized Intelligence Tests

### WECHSLER INTELLIGENCE SCALE FOR CHILDREN (4TH EDITION).    One of the most widely used tests for special education eligibility consideration is the Wechsler Intelligence Scale for Children–Fourth Edition (WISC-IV) (Wechsler, 2003). David Wechsler developed the

Wechsler Intelligence Scale for Children in 1949 and standardized the instrument in 1974 (Wechsler, 1974). The WISC is the standard to which all other assessments are compared. The WISC was revised recently, and the present version is substantially different from the WISC-III.

The WISC-IV is divided into four indexes: Verbal Comprehension, Perceptual Reasoning, Working Memory, and Processing Speed. Each category contains several subtests.

The Verbal Comprehension Index (VCI) includes Similarities, Vocabulary, and Comprehension subtests that were retained from the WISC-III. The Information subtest is now optional and is no longer included in the VCI or Full Scale IQ (FSIQ). The Similarities subtest measures the ability to identify likenesses between words and concepts. The Vocabulary subtest simply measures word recognition, definition, and understanding. The Comprehension subtest measures understanding of verbal statements and commands. Finally, the optional Information subtest measures knowledge by asking fact-based questions. The questions are about topics that are considered common knowledge gained in educational settings, as well as knowledge gained outside of the classroom.

The Perceptual Reasoning Index (PRI) is composed of three subtests: Picture Concepts, Matrix Reasoning, and Block Design. The first two subtests are untimed, motor-free, visual reasoning tests that replace the Picture Completion, Picture Arrangement, and Object Assembly subtests from the WISC-III. These changes to the PRI are the most significant differences between the WISC-III and the WISC-IV. Students who are strong in visual reasoning will have an advantage on the Picture Concepts and Matrix Reasoning visual subtests (Mayes & Calhoun, 2008).

The Working Memory Index (WMI) consists of Digit Span and Letter–Number Sequencing, replacing the Digit Span and Arithmetic on the Freedom from Distractibility Index from WISC-III.

Only the Processing Speed Index (PSI) has not been changed from the version in the WISC-III and still consists of the Coding and Symbol Search subtests. The Coding subtest measures the ability to correlate symbols and then write them on paper. Symbol Search examines the ability to scan groups of symbols and determine whether targeted symbols are present in the group.

All four indexes are used to calculate the FSIQ. For students with neurological disorders, the General Ability Index (which is calculated using just the VCI and PRI) may be a more valid measure of intelligence than the FSIQ (Mayes & Calhoun, 2008; Saklofske, Prifitera, Weiss, Rolfhus, & Zhu, 2005).

**WOODCOCK–JOHNSON PSYCHOEDUCATIONAL BATTERY-III.** The Woodcock–Johnson Psychoeducational Battery-III: Tests of Cognitive Abilities (WJ-III-COG) is another frequently used assessment instrument that measures the cognitive abilities of students (Woodcock, McGrew, & Mather, 2001a). The popularity of the WJ-III-COG is due, in part, to the fact that it is designed to be administered with the companion **Woodcock–Johnson-III NU Tests of Achievement** (WJ-III-NU). The combined tests assess both IQ and academic achievement (Woodcock et al., 2001a). The WJ-III-COG is founded on the Cattell–Horn–Carroll three-stratum theory of cognitive abilities (Carroll, 1993), which may be grouped into eight broader constructs of ability underlying a general factor of intelligence (Lohman, 2003).

The WJ-III-COG consists of 20 subtests that are grouped into seven broad cognitive categories. The broad categories include comprehension–knowledge, long-term retrieval, visual–spatial thinking, auditory processing, fluid reasoning, processing speed, and short-term memory. School psychologists or educational diagnosticians should carefully examine the subtests in each category to note whether any significant differences exist between scores from subtests in each of the indices. Any extreme score differences between subtests may provide useful information in interpreting results (Woodcock et al., 2001a).

The comprehension–knowledge category contains two subtests and examines both knowledge and the ability to explain that knowledge. The three subtests in the long-term retrieval category measure the capability to accurately recall information stored in memory. The visual–spatial thinking category contains three subtests designed to measure thinking in terms of visual patterns. The two subtests in the auditory processing category determine level of skill in analyzing and synthesizing verbal communications and other sounds. The fluid reasoning category contains three subtests that measure problem-solving skills when an individual is presented with previously unknown information. The processing speed category includes two tests that measure automatic cognitive task performance. The final broad category, short-term memory, contains two subtests that measure recall of newly presented information (Salvia & Ysseldyke, 2004). The Supplemental Tests contain additional subtests, which are used to assess specific clinical clusters.

The WJ-III is scored by an easily operated computer program provided by the test developer. Scores are reported according to age and grade norms, percentile ranks, standard scores, and discrepancy scores. In addition, the results include confidence bands of 95%, 90%, and 68%, making it possible to discuss the real accuracy of generated scores during reporting (Woodcock et al., 2001a).

**STANFORD–BINET INTELLIGENCE SCALE (5ᵀᴴ EDITION).**   Originally developed as the Binet–Simon Intelligence Test (Binet & Simon, 1905), the Stanford–Binet Intelligence Scale is the oldest test of cognitive abilities. The most recent incarnation is the Stanford–Binet Intelligence Scale–Fifth Edition (SB5) (Roid, 2003). The SB5 is a test of general intellectual ability and provides a Full Scale IQ, a Nonverbal IQ, a Verbal IQ, and an Abbreviated Battery IQ (Coolican, Bryson, & Zwaigenbaum, 2008). The SB5 allows a comparison of verbal and nonverbal performance (Becker, 2003) and places a higher priority on vocabulary than on reasoning skills (Oetting, Cleveland, & Cope III, 2008).

The current version of the test includes five different areas: fluid reasoning, knowledge, quantitative reasoning, visual–spatial processing, and working memory. The five areas are evaluated by 15 subtests: object series/matrices, early reasoning, verbal absurdities, verbal analogies, procedural knowledge, picture absurdities, vocabulary, quantitative reasoning, form board, form patterns, position and direction, delayed response, block span, memory for sentences, and last word. The vocabulary and object series/matrices subtests are initial routing tests that determine the number and level of subtests that will be administered. Each subtest takes about 5 minutes to administer and the total testing time is 45–90 minutes. The number of items answered correctly determines raw scores. These scores are converted into a standard score corresponding to the student's age group. The resulting score is comparable to an IQ measure. The SB5 has a mean of 100 and a standard deviation of 15.

**NONVERBAL INTELLIGENCE TESTS.**   Intelligence tests are often used to determine a student's academic aptitude and special education eligibility. It is important for these tests to measure actual cognitive abilities that are not affected by culture or language (Hooper & Bell, 2006). Nonverbal intelligence refers to cognitive abilities that exist independently of language. Because increasing numbers of culturally and linguistically diverse students are entering the public schools, more nonverbal assessments of intelligence are being developed and implemented. These tests may effectively assess the cognitive strengths of culturally and linguistically diverse students (Ford, Grantham, & Whiting, 2008). The Comprehensive Test of Nonverbal Intelligence and the Universal Nonverbal Intelligence Test are two commonly used nonverbal intelligence tests.

The Comprehensive Test of Nonverbal Intelligence (CTONI) was constructed to minimize the effects of language, extended education, and acculturation (Hammill, Pearson, & Wiederholt, 1997; Lassiter, Matthews, & Feeback, 2007). The CTONI includes three pictorial and three geometric subtests. These subtests measure analogical reasoning, categorical classification, and sequential reasoning abilities. The six subtests combine to produce a Full Scale Nonverbal IQ.

The CTONI instructions to the student may be verbal or nonverbal, but the required response is always nonverbal. Nonverbal assessments do not always take different cultural backgrounds into consideration. For example, the CTONI instructs the examiner to administer the test using pantomime directions for individuals who speak a language other than English. In order to understand, students must make eye contact with the examiner. Some cultures may consider this rude and unacceptable behavior. Students belonging to these cultures may avoid eye contact, which could corrupt the testing procedure and invalidates the results (Shepherd et al., 2005).

According to the testing manual, the CTONI Nonverbal IQ scores significantly correlate with the WISC-III Full Scale IQ (Hammill et al., 1997), but few validity studies have been reported. Compared with the WJ-III-COG, the CTONI Nonverbal IQ score might not accurately measure the intellectual functioning of individuals who are either gifted or of low average intelligence (Lassiter et al., 2007).

Another nonverbal measure of general intelligence and cognitive abilities is the Universal Nonverbal Intelligence Test (UNIT) (Bracken & McCallum, 1998). The UNIT consists of six subtests: Symbolic Memory, Spatial Memory, Object Memory, Cube Design, Analogic Reasoning, and Mazes.

The UNIT is a multidimensional intelligence test intended to assess the intelligence of students who have speech, language, or hearing impairments, different cultural or language backgrounds, and emotional problems (Wilhoit & McCallum, 2002). The examiner must use nonverbal directions, adhere to the directions and time limitations, and score accurately. A criticism of the UNIT is that test administrators may require additional time to become proficient in its use (Fives & Flanagan, 2002).

## Standardized Achievement Tests

Evaluation teams use several measures to gather information on a student's current academic performance. Group intelligence tests like the California Achievement Tests, Iowa Test of Basic Skills, and the Metropolitan Achievement Tests are given to students in many school districts. The results can provide accurate measures of general achievement. In addition, most teachers maintain a consistent testing schedule within their classrooms. This information can provide additional measures of academic achievement that indicate skills and weaknesses. Most teachers, diagnosticians, school psychologists, and evaluation teams prefer to rely on results generated by individually administered norm-referenced tests such as the WJ-III-NU and the Peabody Individual Achievement Test (Taylor, 2003).

**WOODCOCK–JOHNSON-III NU TEST OF ACHIEVEMENT.**   The WJ-III-NU is an evaluation instrument that is frequently used to determine variations between learning abilities and achievement (Woodcock, McGrew, & Mather, 2001).

The WJ-III-NU includes seven clusters of skills: oral expression, listening comprehension, basic reading skills, reading comprehension, math calculation skills, math reasoning, and written expression. These clusters are measured by subtests that are divided into the Standard Battery of tests and the Extended Battery of tests. Subtests 1 through 12 of the Standard Battery are combined into the broad areas of reading, mathematics, and writing. The 10 subtests of the Extended Battery provide in-depth diagnostic information on specific academic strengths and weaknesses.

Oral expression is assessed with two subtests that focus on linguistic competency, listening ability, and comprehension. Listening comprehension also is measured using two subtests. Basic reading skills measures come from two subtests that address sight vocabulary and phonological skills. Reading comprehension uses two subtests to measure reading comprehension, vocabulary, and reasoning. Math calculation skills are determined using two subtests that address math conceptual skills and understanding of basic math facts. Math reasoning is assessed with two subtests that examine math vocabulary and problem-solving skills. Finally, written expression is measured with two subtests focused on fluency and writing skills (Salvia & Ysseldyke, 2004).

As with the WJ-III-COG, an easily operated computer program provided by the test developer scores the WJ-III-NU. Like its companion test, scores are reported according to age and grade norms, percentile ranks, standard scores, and discrepancy scores. In addition, the computed results include confidence bands of 95%, 90%, and 68% (Woodcock et al., 2001).

**PEABODY INDIVIDUAL ACHIEVEMENT TEST-REVISED.**   The Peabody Individual Achievement Test-Revised-Normative Update (PIAT-R/NU) retains the same content as when it was introduced in 1989 (Markwardt, 1998). However, the norms were updated in 1998 to improve the test's accuracy. The PIAT-R/NU is designed to assess academic skills in general information, reading recognition, reading comprehension, written expression, mathematics, and spelling. The PIAT-R/NU appears to be an efficient assessment instrument requiring 60 minutes or less for administration. The only questions administered are those which fall within the student's range of difficulty. This reduces the time needed for administration.

The subtests are designed to measure expected academic skills. In the area of general information, up to 100 items are presented, depending on the student's ability. The reading recognition subtest contains 100 items to measure recognition of printed letters and the ability to read. In reading comprehension, 82 questions each present a sentence with four pictures and ask the student to choose the picture that best illustrates the sentence. For the written expression subtest, students write a story about a presented picture. Math skills are measured through 100 multiple-choice questions that assess knowledge and application of math concepts and facts. Finally, spelling is measured with 100 multiple-choice items that measure recognition of correctly spelled words (Markwardt, 1998).

Test scores for the PIAT-R/NU are presented with a mean of 100 and standard deviation of 15, except for written expression scores, which are reported as grade-based scores and shown in percentile ranks. This common presentation of scores makes it easy for most teachers and parents to compare students. The only concern that experts have

# Case Study 4.1

## Johnny

In fifth grade, Johnny's academic performance and behavior continued to deteriorate. He was failing a majority of his classes, and he was constantly getting into fights with other students. His counseling sessions had been discontinued because Johnny refused to attend the sessions. After a number of attempts at accommodations, adaptations, and behavioral plans, the At-Risk Team decided to refer Johnny for special education evaluation. Almost immediately, Johnny's mother consented to the evaluation.

Within 60 calendar days of the initial referral, the comprehensive evaluation was completed. Johnny's mother and fifth grade teacher completed the Vineland Adaptive Behavior Scale, a behavior rating scale. The school psychologist administered the WISC-IV and the WJ-III-NU. The school counselor gathered information from Johnny's mother for the sociodevelopmental component of the evaluation, and a teacher certified in emotional and behavior disorders completed several classroom observations of Johnny.

Within 90 calendar days of the initial referral, the Evaluation Team met to review the results of the comprehensive evaluation.

The sociodevelopmental history reviewed the fact that Johnny had witnessed the death of his father when he was 5 years old and that he had somehow blamed himself for his father's death. Counseling had been recommended and initiated in second grade, but it had been discontinued by third grade because Johnny refused to attend the sessions. Both Johnny's mother and the fifth grade teacher reported that Johnny was noncompliant, was aggressive, and showed a lack of respect for females in authority.

According to the Vineland, Johnny had a standard score of 78 on the Communication Domain, 88 on Daily Living Skills, and 68 on the Socialization Domain. He had an Adaptive Behavior Composite of 72. Areas of concern were listening and attending, following instructions, responding to others, expressing and recognizing emotions, and belonging to groups.

The school psychologist reported that Johnny's aptitude and achievement abilities ranged from low average to below average. On the WISC-IV, Johnny had a Verbal Score of 83, a Performance Score of 86, and a Full Scale IQ of 85. On the WJ-III-NU, Johnny had a Broad Reading Score of 86 and a Broad Mathematics Score of 88. The school psychologist noted that Johnny did not appear to have any type of learning or mental disability.

The special education teacher who observed Johnny noted that he did not interact well with peers and teachers. In fact, Johnny tended to stay to himself, and while Johnny maintained that he had friends, the children he named were more like acquaintances than real friends. During recess, Johnny tried to intimidate peers and threatened to "beat them up" if he did not get his way. On one occasion, while the students were quietly working on a worksheet, the special education teacher observed that Johnny was sitting at his desk, crying softly. There was no apparent reason for this behavior.

On the basis of the information obtained from the comprehensive evaluation and input from all the members of the Eligibility Team (which included Johnny's mother), the team determined that Johnny qualified as a student with emotional and behavior disorders. The team agreed that he would benefit greatly from special education and related services.

about the test is whether the PIAT-R/NU correlates with the curriculum presented to students.

**WECHSLER INDIVIDUAL ACHIEVEMENT TEST (SECOND EDITION).**    The Wechsler Individual Achievement Test–Second Edition (WIAT-II) is designed to determine discrepancies between a student's cognitive and academic abilities (Wechsler, 2002). It is empirically linked with the WISC-IV. The nine subtests are word reading, numerical operations, reading comprehension, spelling, pseudoword decoding, math reasoning, written expression, listening comprehension, and oral expression.

Word reading includes visual memory and discrimination, letter recognition, and phonological skills. Number recognition, counting, and solving computations are involved in numerical operations. In the reading comprehension section, students must match words to pictures, read sentences out loud, and answer questions about reading passages. In the spelling subtest, students respond in writing to letters, sounds, or words that are dictated and read in sentences. Pseudoword decoding is a new subtest in the WIAT-II that asks students to read nonsense words aloud from cards. Students count, identify shapes, and solve word problems in the math reasoning subtest. For the written expression subtest, students write letters and words quickly and also write sentences and paragraphs, all of which are scored for mechanics and vocabulary. Listening comprehension and oral expression usually are not included in achievement tests, but they may provide needed information for interventions. In listening comprehension, students are orally presented with questions to which they must respond, and in oral expression, students repeat sentences and describe pictures, scenes, and activities.

## ASSESSING BEHAVIOR PROBLEMS

### Behavior Rating Scales

It is becoming increasingly common to use rating scales to assess the behaviors of children suspected of having emotional and behavior disorders, because these scales are easy to administer. They have been used to assess behavior, social skills, depression, anxiety, and ADHD. Behavior rating scales provide quantifiable and systemically organized information, are relatively easy to complete and score, include normative data for comparing a child's score with the average score of children without disabilities, and can be used to compare ratings of different children (McConaughy & Ritter, 2002). Many behavior rating scales take approximately 10 to 20 minutes to complete and may be completed by a teacher, a parent, or the child. They are usually checklists that ask the responder whether a specific behavior has been observed at any time (see Table 4.1).

**CHILD BEHAVIOR CHECKLIST.**    The most widely used behavior rating scale is the Child Behavior Checklist (CBCL) (Achenbach & Edelbrock, 1983; Konold et al., 2003; Konold, Walthall, & Pianta, 2004). The CBCL has a parent version with 118 questions, a teacher version with 113 questions, and a Youth Self-Report form with 112 questions. It uses a 3-point scale (0 = not true, 1 = sometimes true, 2 = often true).

The CBCL assesses two broad domains of child and adolescent behavior, an externalizing factor and an internalizing factor. These factors measure behavior problems relating to aggression, delinquency, hyperactivity, depression, social withdrawal, and obsessive–compulsive behaviors. In addition, the CBCL includes 20 items assessing social

---

### TABLE 4.1    Behavior Rating Scales

Behavior Assessment System for Children (Reynolds & Kamphaus, 1992)
Behavioral Objective Sequence (Braaten, 1998)
Behavior Rating Scale-2 (McCarney & Leigh, 1990)
Child Behavior Checklist (Achenbach & Edelbrock, 1983)
Conners Parent Rating Scale (Conners, 1985)
Conners Teacher Rating Scale (Conners, 1985)
Devereux Adolescent Behavior Rating Scale (Spivack, Spotts, & Haimes, 1967)
Devereux Child Behavior Rating Scale (Spivack & Spotts, 1966)
Revised Behavior Problem Checklist (Quay & Peterson, 1987)
Systematic Screening for Behavior Disorders (Walker & Severson, 1990)
Social Skills Rating System (Gresham & Elliott, 1990)
Student Self-Concept Scale (Gresham, Elliott, & Evans-Fernandez, 1992)
Walker–McConnell Scale of Social Competence and School Adjustment (Walker & McConnell, 1995)
Walker Problem Behavior Identification Checklist (Walker, 1983)

---

competence, social relations, and quality of the child's involvement in activities. (See Table 4.2.)

**THE SYSTEMATIC SCREENING FOR BEHAVIOR DISORDERS.**    The Systematic Screening for Behavior Disorders (SSBD) is a multigated procedure for identifying children who are at risk for emotional and behavior disorders. The SSBD uses a combination of teacher nominations, teacher rating scales, and direct observations of the child's behavior. Students have to pass through three stages, or gates, before being referred for special education services. (See Figure 4.2.) This three-stage system assesses the externalizing or internalizing behavior problems of students (Walker & Severson, 1994).

At the first gate of the SSBD, the general education teacher considers the externalizing behaviors (aggression, disruption, and other undercontrolled behaviors) and the internalizing behaviors (anxiety, withdrawal, depression, and other overcontrolled behaviors) of all children in the classroom. At the second gate, the teacher uses the Critical Events Checklist

---

### TABLE 4.2    Sample questions from the *Child Behavior Checklist-Teacher's Report Form*

|  | Often | Somewhat | Not at All |
|---|---|---|---|
| 1. Argues a lot. | 2 | 1 | 0 |
| 2. Defiant, talks back to staff. | 2 | 1 | 0 |
| 3. Can't sit still, restless, or hyperactive. | 2 | 1 | 0 |
| 4. Feels he/she has to be perfect. | 2 | 1 | 0 |
| 5. Impulsive or acts without thinking. | 2 | 1 | 0 |

*Source:* Information from Achenback & Edelbrock, 1980

to rate the top three children in the class who display externalizing behaviors and the top three children who display internalizing behaviors. The CEC rates student behavior according to 33 items that measure externalizing and internalizing behaviors, which the teacher reports on the Critical Events Index. Also at this juncture, the teacher rates students using the Combined Frequency Index, which measures the intensity of a behavior (how often the child displays it). Children

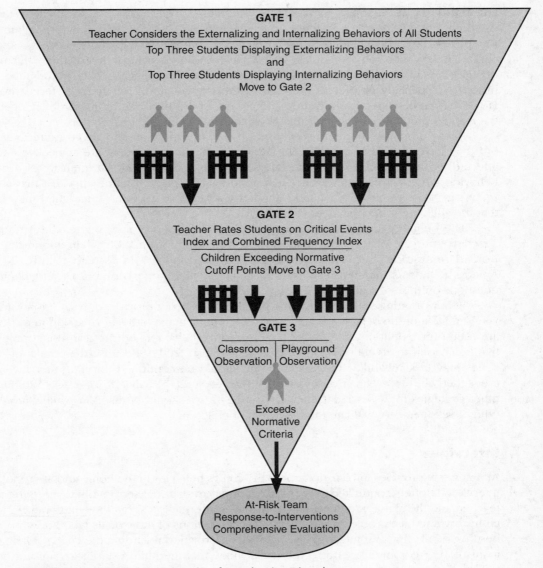

**FIGURE 4.2**   Systematic Screening for Behavior Disorders

*Source:* From H. M. Walker et al. (1988). Systematic screening of pupils in the elementary age range at risk for behavior disorders: Development and trial testing of a multiple gating model. *Remedial and Special Education, 9*(3), 8-14. Adapted/reprinted by permission.

who exceed the normative cutoff points for adaptive and maladaptive behaviors are assessed in the third gate. At this stage, children are observed in a general education classroom setting and in a playground setting on two separate occasions by a school professional. Children who exceed the normative cutoff points are referred to the school's at-risk team for further intervention or referred for more formal assessments (Walker & Severson, 1990).

**THE BEHAVIOR ASSESSMENT SYSTEM FOR CHILDREN.**    The Behavior Assessment System for Children (BASC) tries to provide a comprehensive assessment of behavior (Reynolds & Kamphaus, 1992). It includes rating forms to be completed by parents, teachers, and the child. Unlike other behavior rating scales, the BASC also includes a structured behavioral observation and requires examiners to record the developmental history of the child. This history is especially helpful as the team gathers information for the prereferral process. However, the behavioral observation component of the BASC may pose problems because the manual provides little technical support for conducting the observation.

Behavior rating scales and checklists are easy to administer and are cost-effective tools, but they have several disadvantages. The results of the assessment are subjective and are affected by the expectations of the rater. Raters may overreport the intensity of a child's behavior. For example, one teacher may report on a behavior rating checklist that a child *always* gets out of his seat, whereas another teacher observing the same child may report that the child *sometimes* gets out of his seat.

The behavior rating scales may be culturally biased. For example, the Attitude to Teachers subscale of the BASC may not provide valid information when administered to Korean Americans. Because teachers are highly respected in Korean culture, Korean American students may not respond the same way as European American students to the questions on this subscale (Cho, Hudley, & Back, 2003).

Behavior rating scales identify the problem but do not provide a prescription for intervention. Most of the behavior scales have a high percentage of negative action items, which are useful for monitoring the frequency of negative behaviors but not for monitoring positive behavioral interventions (Hosp, Howell, & Hosp, 2003). Because the results of rating scales may lack reliability and validity, they should be confirmed through interviews with the student and from direct observations (Hosp et al., 2003; Salvia & Ysseldyke, 2001). Like other strategies for assessment, behavior rating scales should be used in combination with other assessments to evaluate the behaviors of children.

## Interviews

An interview provides information about the child's behavior in the home and at school. The interview is often conducted prior to any formal evaluation and involves the parent, the teacher, and the child. Interviewing also provides information about the child's developmental history and past problems and reveals the perceptions of individuals who know the child best. An eco-behavioral interview can provide information regarding the child's relationship to his or her community and to the social networks the child establishes among home, school, and community (Witt, Elliott, Daly, Gresham, & Kramer, 1998).

It is important to generate questions prior to the interview to increase the reliability of the information that will be gathered. The more structured the interview, the more accurate the information obtained will be. However, sometimes it is necessary to deviate from an anticipated plan in response to developments that may occur during an interview. The parent or student may answer a predetermined question in such a way that it would be prudent for the interviewer to ask follow-up questions.

In an interview, parents can describe the behavior and the daily routines of the child at home. The teacher can provide information regarding the child's school activities and interactions with peers and school staff. The child can provide insight into his perceptions of school and home. It is important to remember that parents typically underreport behavior problems while teachers tend to overreport behavior problems. Children, especially those who have emotional and behavior disorders, generally have limited insight into their problems and tend to underreport their behaviors. An interview should be only one component of the assessment process, which also should include behavior rating scales and direct observation of the child's behavior.

## Behavioral Observations

An accurate and reliable way to identify behaviors to be targeted in an intervention plan is through direct observations (Hintze et al., 2002). This direct assessment of behavior occurs at the time and place the behavior is exhibited. A number of recording methods can be used to measure behavior, depending on the behavior that is being observed. The four dimensions of behavior that can be observed are frequency, duration, latency, and intensity. *Frequency* refers to how often the behavior occurs in a period of time. *Duration* refers to how long the behavior lasts. *Latency* refers to the amount of time that elapses between a prompt and the initiation of the appropriate behavior. *Intensity* denotes the amount of force used in performance of the behavior. The three basic methods for recording observations are (1) event-based methods, (2) interval-based methods, and (3) time-based methods.

**EVENT-BASED RECORDING METHODS.**　Event-based recording measures the frequency of a behavior, or how often it occurs, in the classroom. This method is relatively easy, but it is best used with behaviors that are *discrete* (that are well-defined with a definite beginning and end). Behaviors such as talking, raising one's hand, and getting out of one's seat are examples of discrete behaviors. The teacher first identifies the behavior that is to be measured, then records the number of times it occurs in a given period. For example, the teacher records how many times the student talks without raising her hand. At the end of the observation period, the rate of the behavior is determined by dividing the number of times the behavior occurred by the amount of time the behavior was observed. For example, if the student talked without raising her hand nine times during a 20-minute observation period, the rate of behavior would be 45% (9 ÷ 20 = .45), or 0.45 such behaviors per minute. (See Figure 4.3.)

**INTERVAL-BASED RECORDING METHODS.**　The interval-based method measures whether or not particular behaviors occur during specified time intervals, to provide a sample of the child's behavior during a classroom period. A 10-minute academic period might be divided into ten 1-minute intervals. Three types of interval-based recording methods are (1) whole-interval recording, (2) partial-interval recording, and (3) point–time sampling.

A teacher using whole-interval recording records the behavior only if the child exhibits it during the entire interval. For example, the teacher records the student talking only if the

Child's Name: <u>Marta</u>  Week of: <u>January 21</u>

Observer: <u>Mrs. Smart</u>  Teacher: <u>Mrs. Garza</u>

Behavioral Definition: <u>Talking without permission (permission is granted when the child raises a hand and receives verbal permission from teacher).</u>

| Day | Observation Time | Frequency | Total | Rate |
|---|---|---|---|---|
| Monday | 8:30-8:50 (20 minutes) | | 9 | 9/20 = .45 |
| Tuesday | 8:30-8:50 (20 minutes) | | 7 | 7/20 = .35 |
| Wednesday | 8:30-8:50 (20 minutes) | | 10 | 10/20 = .50 |
| Thursday | 8:30-8:50 (20 minutes) | | 4 | 4/20 = .20 |
| Friday | 8:30-8:50 (20 minutes) | | 6 | 6/20 = .30 |
| **TOTAL** | | | 36 | 36/100 = .36 |

**FIGURE 4.3** Example of Event-Based Recording

child talks throughout the entire 1-minute interval. If the child quits talking at any time during the interval, then the teacher would score the behavior as not occurring.

With partial-interval recording, the behavior is recorded when it occurs at any time during the 1-minute interval. For example, if the student talks during the first 10 seconds of the 1-minute interval, the teacher records the event as occurring during the interval. If the child talks several times during the 1-minute interval, it is recorded as having occurred once during the interval. (See Figure 4.4.)

A teacher using point–time sampling records the behavior as occurring if it is happening at the moment the interval ends. For example, an external system, such as a stopwatch or egg timer, would signal the end of an interval. When the timer goes off, if the student is talking without permission, the teacher records the behavior as occurring during the entire interval. If the student talks at the beginning of the interval, but is not talking at the end of the interval, the teacher does not score the behavior as occurring. Point–time sampling is a good method to use when the teacher does not have much time to observe a specific student's behavior.

Child's Name: <u>Marta</u>  Week of: <u>January 21</u>

Observer: <u>Mrs. Smart</u>  Teacher: <u>Mrs. Garza</u>

Behavioral Definition: <u>Talking without permission, which includes raising hand and receiving verbal permission from teacher.</u>

| 1 min. | 2 mins. | 3 mins. | 4 mins. | 5 mins. | 6 mins. | 7 mins. | 8 mins. | 9 mins. | 10 mins. |
|---|---|---|---|---|---|---|---|---|---|
| O | X | X | X | O | O | X | X | X | O |

X = Behavior Occurred
O = Behavior Did Not Occur
% = 60%

**FIGURE 4.4** Example of Interval-Based Recording

Interval-based recording does not provide a measure of frequency the way event-based recording does, and it cannot report the number of times the behavior occurs. It does indicate the percentage of the intervals in which the observed behavior occurs. The percentage can by calculated by using the following formula:

$$\frac{\text{Number of Behaviors Recorded}}{\text{Total Number of Intervals}} \times 100$$

**TIME-BASED RECORDING METHODS.**   Time-based recording methods are convenient if the teacher does not have a block of time to devote to observing and recording the student's behavior. Using this method, a teacher records the amount of time that the behavior occurs, not the frequency. Two types of time-based recordings are duration recording and latency recording.

With duration recording, the teacher simply times how long a behavior occurs within the chosen period. For example, if the student begins talking at 8:30 and stops talking at 8:40, the duration of the behavior is 10 minutes. If the student begins talking again in the same academic period, the teacher adds that time to the previous time. Thus, if the student begins talking again at 8:55 and stops talking at 9:00, 5 minutes is added to the previous amount of 10 minutes. As a result, the duration of the behavior is 15 minutes.

To use latency recording, the teacher records the time that elapses between a specific event and the start of the target behavior. For example, if the student is asked to stop talking, the teacher records how long it takes for the student to comply with the request.

Direct observations are generally cost efficient and easy to implement. However, like all assessment methods, they are more valuable when observers are trained to measure behaviors reliably. School districts cannot afford to train observers, so teachers usually end up recording behaviors, but they often do not have the time to do direct observations because they have responsibilities to fulfill to other students, administrators, parents, and state legislators.

## ASSESSING SOCIAL SKILLS

### Naturalistic Observation

Many children with emotional and behavior disorders have deficits in social skills. *Social skills* are specific behaviors that a student uses to perform appropriately on a given social task (Gresham, 2002). These skills could include raising a hand to be called on before speaking, saying "please" and "thank you," and participating in group activities. Generally, parents, teachers, and peers evaluate a student's social skills. They may do so by systematically recording observable behaviors of children in a natural setting—a technique often called *observation-based assessment.*

One method for assessing social skills through observation is frequency recording. This relatively easy-to-use technique involves tallying the number of times a behavior occurs during a specified period. The teacher first identifies which social-skills behavior is to be measured, then records the number of times it occurs in a given period. For example, the teacher records how many times the student says "thank you" or "please" to other students. At the end of the observation period, the rate of the behavior is determined by dividing the number of times the behavior occurred by the amount of time the behavior was observed.

For example, if the student said "thank you" and "please" eight times during a 20-minute observation period, the rate of behavior would be 40% (8 ÷ 20 = .40). Frequency recording is more appropriate when applied to specific and brief behaviors that can be counted. Because social interactions tend to be continuous, gaining an overall understanding of the student's social skills with this technique might be difficult.

A time-based recording method is another approach for assessing the social interaction of children. Again, the teacher identifies the social skills behavior that is to be observed. One example is participating in a board game with other students. The teacher starts a stopwatch or digital timer whenever the student engages in appropriately playing the board game with peers. When the student stops participating in the game or when the student's behavior becomes inappropriate, the teacher stops the stopwatch. When the student resumes playing the game, the teacher turns the watch on again without resetting it. This way, the teacher records the cumulative time of the behavior. At the end of the observation period, the teacher can determine the amount of time the child was engaged in the appropriate behavior by dividing the number of minutes on task by the total number of minutes in the observation period. For example, if the child participated in the board game for 16 minutes during a 20-minute observation period, the child was engaged in appropriate social participation 80% of the time (16 ÷ 20 = .80). At the conclusion of a 20-minute observation period, if the stopwatch totals 11 minutes, the child has been engaged in appropriate social participation 55% of the time (11 ÷ 20 = .55).

## Sociometric Measures

A *sociometric measure* is a primary tool for assessing the social skills of a student by asking the child's peer group (Cillessen & Bukowski, 2000). The result indicates the estimated level of acceptance among peers. The two types of sociometric measures are peer nomination and peer rating.

Using peer nomination, the teacher would ask students to nominate peers who match specific descriptions (DeRosier & Thomas, 2003). Students might be asked to name their best friends, or the other students with whom they like to play. A comparison of scores across the peer group will allow educators to estimate a child's social competence in a particular area.

Using peer rating, each student in a class rates the other students on items related to peer acceptance and social competence. After positive and negative nominations have been tallied, students are assigned to one of four extreme sociometric status groups: popular, controversial, rejected, and neglected. Students with many positives and few negatives are assigned to the popular sociometric status group. Those with many positive and many negative nominations are assigned to the controversial group. Those with few positives and many negative nominations are in the rejected group, and those who receive few positive and few negative nominations are in the neglected group (Coie, Dodge, and Coppotelli, 1982; DeRosier & Thomas, 2003). Children who are rejected by their peers tend to display poor social skills (Miller-Johnson, Coie, Maumary-Gremaud, & Bierman, 2002).

When evaluators use sociometric measures, it is important for them to consider whether social acceptance is best determined by the number of friends a student has. It is a good idea to combine sociometric measures, which measure friendship status, with teacher rating scales, which measure overall acceptance. Understanding whether or not peers accept a child is important for a number of reasons. However, it is important that the results of sociometric measures be kept confidential and that the negative nominations of peers not be shared.

## DETERMINING ELIGIBILITY FOR SPECIAL EDUCATION

The final step in the evaluation process is the determination of eligibility for special education services. This decision is the most important one in the process. It has a far-reaching impact on programs and, more importantly, on individuals. This one decision can change the course of a child's life. It may bring lasting relief for a student who has struggled for years to navigate the educational process. The decision has the potential to set the course for a student to achieve in the academic setting and eventually to prosper in post-secondary education and adult life. It can bring hope for the future for many students and parents who have been lost in the jungle of modern educational systems.

On the other hand, if the decision-making process fails, students needing valuable assistance could be left to suffer. It is well known that even students who are appropriately placed in special education have extremely low rates of graduation and educational success (U.S. Department of Education, 2002), especially students with emotional and behavior disorders (Cameto, 2003). It is easy to surmise that students who never receive appropriate educational intervention will suffer even higher rates of school failure.

Another consequence of an incorrect eligibility decision is the assignment of a student to special education who does not qualify for these services. In such cases, the student faces the stigma of labeling and receives educational services that fail to meet the student's needs. Furthermore, providing special education services to students who are not legitimately qualified overwhelms special educational systems that are significantly underfunded and understaffed.

Whereas the process of determining eligibility is incredibly important, it is also relatively simple. Eligibility criteria for students with emotional and behavior disorders are specifically stated in IDEA and the accompanying regulations. The eligibility team simply compares the comprehensive evaluation results with the mandated eligibility criteria and answers the following question: Does this student qualify for special education intervention and special education services?

## The Eligibility Team Process

Determining whether a student has a disability is a team decision. No individual should make that decision alone. The Eligibility Team makes decisions that are based on the results of completed assessments and evaluations. The Eligibility Team is similar to the Evaluation Team and the IEP Team and includes general education teachers, special education teachers, school administrators, individuals who can interpret assessment results, the child and his or her parents, and professionals who are knowledgeable about the suspected disability and who have the expertise to assist in making decisions about the student. This team considers all the information gathered during the evaluation process, including information obtained from the screening and prereferral process. The team ensures that the information comes from a variety of sources, including aptitude tests, achievement tests, parent input, teacher recommendations, assessments of physical condition, a consideration of the child's social and cultural background, and records of behavior. The team examines the findings from the comprehensive evaluation and makes an eligibility decision using the federal definition of emotional disturbance.

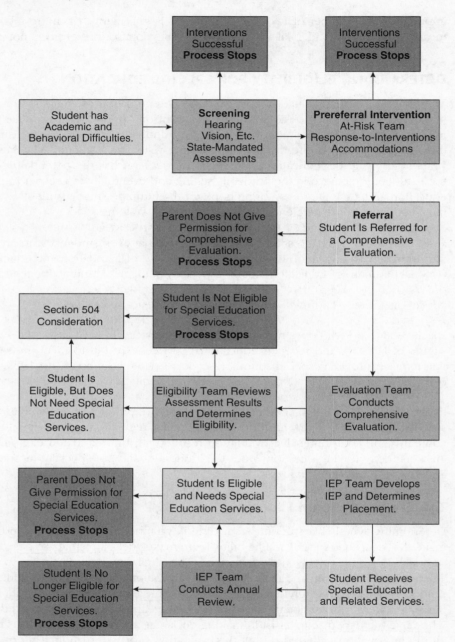

**FIGURE 4.5**   Assessment, Identification, and Placement Process

To determine whether a student is eligible for special education services under IDEA, the team should answer two questions: *Does the student have a disability?* and *Does the student need special education services?* Just because the answer to the first question is "yes" does not mean that the answer to the second question is also "yes." For example, a student with ADHD has a disability, but he or she may not need special education services. The student may simply need accommodations in the general education classroom. The student's right to receive these accommodations is protected under Section 504 of the Rehabilitation Act (1973).

One other qualifying criterion is considered in the determination process: The definition of *emotional disturbance* includes students who have characteristics that adversely affect their educational performance. This particular criterion is the benchmark for eligibility in the category of emotional disturbance. If a student who is being considered for eligibility in the category of emotional disturbance is satisfactorily competing in the academic arena, he or she does not qualify for special education services. This does not mean that there are no resources for this student or for his or her teachers. It simply means that the services and resources available to the student and teachers will be something other than special education. In this case, the Evaluation Team will provide suggestions and possible resources to assist the student in the educational setting. If the Eligibility Team determines that the student does have a disability and needs special education services, the next step is to develop the IEP and provide special education and related services. (See Figure 4.5 on p. 86.)

## Summary

The identification of students with emotional and behavior disorders is an important step in providing needed services to these students, but it is problematic because the federal definition of emotional disturbance is subjective. Identification involves a three-tiered assessment process that includes procedures for screening, prereferral interventions, and special education referrals.

Screening is the first step of the assessment process. Its purpose is to gather information about students who may have learning, behavioral, and sensory problems that might interfere with their academic performances. Screening should begin in preschool and kindergarten and continue in primary and secondary school years.

The next step in the assessment process is prereferral interventions. These interventions can provide accommodations for students who are having difficulties in their academic programs. Response-to-interventions is one method of providing various levels of interventions prior to referring a student for special education services. The second purpose of the prereferral process is to gather information about students' academic and functional difficulties in the general education classrooms.

The next step of the assessment process is completion by the Evaluation Team of a multifaceted, comprehensive evaluation. The comprehensive evaluation can include assessments of vision, hearing, social skills, emotional and behavioral status, general intelligence, current academic performance, and any other area that the evaluation team deems pertinent. It also includes screening and prereferral documents. Several assessments are available to establish eligibility for special education and determine appropriate intervention strategies. These assessments include standardized intelligence and achievement tests, behavior rating scales and observations, and sociometric measures.

The final step in the assessment process is the determination of eligibility. The Eligibility Team considers all the information gathered during the evaluation process and makes a decision based on the federal definition of emotional disturbance. Once the Eligibility Team determines that the student does have a disability and needs special education services, the next step is to develop the individualized education program and provide special education and related services for the student.

## Review Questions

1. Briefly describe each of the three steps of the assessment process.
2. If you are planning to conduct a multifaceted evaluation for a student suspected of having emotional and behavior disorders, what areas would you assess and how would you measure those areas?
3. Because of Anna's inappropriate behavior in the classroom, Anna's teacher suspects her of having emotional and behavior disorders. Anna's scores on assessments of intelligence, achievement, and behavior in a comprehensive evaluation were very low. Do her scores preclude her from being identified as having emotional and behavior disorders? Why?
4. Is it acceptable for an educational diagnostician or a school psychologist to inform the IEP team members at a meeting that, on the basis of the comprehensive evaluations, the student has an emotional and behavior disorder? Why or why not?
5. What two questions should the Eligibility Team ask before providing a student with special education services?

# CHAPTER 5

# The Individualized Education Program

**After reading this chapter, you should be able to**

- Recognize the required seven components of the Individualized Education Program (IEP).
- Describe the roles and the responsibilities of the IEP Team.
- Describe and explain the seven informative sections included in the development of the IEP.
- Identify the steps schools need to take to ensure that the parents have the opportu-

nity to participate in the development of the IEP.
- Explain the importance of student participation in the development of transition plans.
- Describe the four issues that may trigger a due process hearing, and explain how school districts can reduce the occurrence of a due process hearing.

## THE IEP COMPONENTS

Once an Eligibility Team has determined that a student has a disability and needs special education services, an Individualized Education Program (IEP) must be developed for the student. The IEP is a written plan that is developed with input from the school, parents, and student and is designed to meet the unique academic, behavioral, social, and emotional needs of the student. Although IEPs for different students might be similar, no two IEPs should be exactly the same. Schools need to exercise caution when employing IEPs that consist of a checklist of goals or when using computer-generated IEP programs because it is too easy to replicate identical IEPs for different students.

IEPs vary in appearance from school district to school district and from state to state, but all IEPs must contain seven components specified by IDEA:

1. A statement of the student's present levels of academic achievement and functional performance.
2. A statement of measurable annual goals, including academic and functional goals.
3. A description of how the student's progress toward meeting the annual goals will be measured.
4. A statement of the special education and related services and supplementary aids and services that will be offered to the student and that is based on peer-reviewed research to the extent practicable.
5. An explanation of the extent, if any, to which the student will not participate with nondisabled children in the regular classroom and will not participate in the general education curriculum, extracurricular activities, and other nonacademic activities of the school.
6. A statement of any accommodations that are necessary to measure the academic achievement and functional performance of the child on state- and district-wide assessments.
7. The projected date for the beginning of the services and modifications, and the anticipated frequency, location, and duration of those services and modifications (§ 300.320).

The IEP Team also should consider special factors when developing an IEP for a student with emotional and behavior disorders. The team might want to consider implementing a functional behavioral analysis and developing a behavioral intervention plan. (See Chapter 6.)

## THE IEP TEAM

In many instances, the IEP Team is composed of the same members as the Eligibility Team which determined that the student had a disability and needed special education and related services. The development of the IEP often follows an Eligibility Team meeting. It is important to remember that the Eligibility Team meets first to determine eligibility, and the IEP Team meets afterwards to develop the IEP on the basis of the student's needs as determined by the assessment process. If the IEP meeting does not follow directly after the Eligibility Team meeting, the IEP Team must meet to develop an IEP within 30 days of the determination that the student needs special education and related services.

The IEP Team includes a general education teacher, a special education teacher, a representative of the school (usually a principal or assistant principal), someone who can interpret evaluation results, the student's parents, and, when appropriate, the student. Sometimes specialists such as behavioral intervention specialists and therapists are part of the IEP Team. Other individuals who possess knowledge or special expertise regarding the student may be invited to attend the IEP Team meeting at the discretion of the parent or the school.

Chapter 5 • The Individualized Education Program

## The General and Special Education Teachers

In an initial IEP Team meeting, the general education teacher is usually a teacher who has the student in her class. In the case of Johnny, the student who was the subject of several case studies in earlier chapters, the general education teacher is Mrs. Smart, Johnny's math teacher. The special education teacher should be a teacher of the suspected disability category who is knowledgeable about the services and accommodations the student might need. Mr. Poteet, who teaches students with emotional and behavior disorders, is a member of Johnny's IEP Team.

## The School Representative

The school representative is usually the principal, the assistant principal, or the school counselor. In some school districts, the representative might be the director or assistant director of special education. This individual must be qualified to supervise or provide special education instruction, must understand the general education curriculum, and, most importantly, must know the resources of the school that are available. For example, if the IEP Team decides that the student needs a laptop computer to complete assignments, this representative needs to know whether the school has the resources to provide the student with a laptop computer. Limited funds or resources cannot be a rationale for withholding a resource the student needs, but the school is required to provide only an *appropriate* education, not an optimum education. The school representative can assist the team in focusing on what is appropriate.

The school representative member of the IEP Team should also serve as the facilitator who leads the meeting and makes sure that all the members of the team, including the student's parents, have an opportunity to voice their opinions and make recommendations. For example, Mr. Price, the principal at Franklin Pierce High School, takes the program for students with emotional and behavior disorders at his school very seriously and attends all meetings involving the program.

## Someone Who Interprets Evaluations

Ms. Salazar is the educational diagnostician who administered the assessment instruments to Johnny. Most states employ school psychologists, but a few use educational diagnosticians. These professionals have a responsibility to explain the results of the evaluations to the other members of the IEP Team. IDEA does not specify that this member must be a school psychologist or educational diagnostician; it may be any member of the team, as long as that person "can interpret the instructional implications of evaluation results." If the special education teacher is capable of explaining the implications of the evaluation results, the school psychologist or the educational diagnostician may not be required to attend the IEP Team meeting. In most cases, as in the implementation of the comprehensive evaluation, multiple individuals interpret the data obtained from the evaluation. However, it is best to include the school psychologist or the educational diagnostician at the student's initial IEP Team meeting. Their training and education may provide insight that will help the team develop the student's first IEP. It is also good practice for the school psychologist or educational diagnostician to attend any IEP meeting involving a reevaluation of the student's abilities.

## The Parent and Student

The IEP Team should include the parent and the student whenever possible. An IEP Team meeting is conducted without the parent only if the school is unable to convince the parent that he or she should attend, but the school must make all reasonable attempts to encourage the parent to attend. The school should keep detailed records of telephone calls its staff have made or have attempted to make to the parents, keep copies of all written attempts, and keep a record of any visits to the parent's home or place of employment. Sending two or three letters may not be considered a reasonable attempt to contact the parent and may be viewed later as denying parents their right to be involved. In Johnny's case, the school has contacted Mrs. Martin, Johnny's mother, by telephone, and she has agreed to attend the IEP Team meeting.

IDEA also recommends that the student be involved with the IEP process whenever possible. Participation in the development of the IEP provides the student with a sense of ownership of his own education. Participation by younger students is optional, but any student who is turning 16 years old or older that year must be involved in the development of the IEP. At this point, an Individualized Transition Plan (ITP) should be developed to meet the postsecondary goals of the student. The development of the ITP could occur sooner if the IEP Team determines that it would be beneficial for the student to have such a plan, and some states may require transition planning earlier than age 16 years. All students who are 17 or older the year that the IEP is developed must be informed of their rights regarding their education. In this case, Johnny is currently in eighth grade and has been included as a member of the IEP Team.

### Additional Individuals

The last member of the IEP Team is Mrs. Whasit, who has been Johnny's counselor for the past 3 years. Her special knowledge of Johnny may be helpful in developing an appropriate educational program for him. The school or the parents may also invite additional individuals who have relevant information about the student to attend the IEP Team meeting. If the school invites additional individuals, the school must mention those individuals on the notice of the IEP meeting that is sent to the parents. However, parents are not required to inform the school of any additional individuals they have invited to attend the IEP Team meeting. In some Hispanic communities, it is common for parents to include grandparents in the IEP process because extended families are a characteristic of that culture.

### Attendance

It is expected that the general education teacher, special education teacher, school representative, and the individual who can interpret the evaluation results will attend the IEP Team meeting. However, IDEA 2004 states that a team member is not required to attend if the member's area of the curriculum or related services is not modified or discussed and if the parent and the school agree in writing that the member's attendance is not necessary. Even when the modification of the curriculum or the discussion does affect the member's area of expertise, he or she may still be excused from attending if the parent and the school agree in writing to do so and if, prior to the meeting, the member submits to the IEP Team written input into the development of the IEP (§ 300.321[e]). It is conceivable that the general education teacher or the school psychologist may be excused from part of or the entire IEP meeting, but it is unlikely and is poor practice for the school representative or the special education teacher to be absent from the meeting. In the case of Johnny, this is the first team meeting to develop an IEP for him, and all of the members are expected to attend.

## DEVELOPING THE IEP

In order to develop Johnny's IEP, the IEP Team must consider his strengths, Mrs. Martin's concerns about her son's education, the results of Johnny's initial or most recent evaluation, and Johnny's academic, developmental, and functional needs. One of the changes in IDEA 2004 over the previous version of the legislation is the inclusion of functional performance in the development of the IEP, but IDEA 2004 does not define "functional performance," nor does it explain how this concept relates to the student's unique needs or affects the student's education. Functional performance might be similar to *adaptive behavior*—a set of abilities that includes interpersonal relationships, self-care skills, leisure skills, and functional academics.

The IEP Team should consider including positive behavior interventions and supports in plans for students with emotional and behavior disorders whose behavior impedes learning. Other strategies, such as a Behavioral Intervention Plan, may also be useful. (See Chapter 6.)

The IEP should include seven informative sections:

1. A description of the student.
2. A description of the student's present levels of academic achievement and functional performance.
3. A list of measurable annual academic and functional goals for the student.
4. A description of the special education and related services and supplementary aids and services that will be offered to the student on the basis of peer-reviewed research to the extent practicable.
5. A description of the extent, if any, to which the student will not participate with nondisabled children in the general education classroom or in the general education curriculum, extracurricular activities, and other nonacademic activities.
6. An explanation of the student's participation in statewide and district assessments.
7. A description of how the student's progress toward meeting the annual goals will be measured and reported to the parents on a regular basis (Gibb & Dyches, 2007).

Source: Patrick White/Merrill

Transition goals should be developed based on the student's interests and aspirations.

## Description of the Student

The first component of the IEP simply identifies and describes the student. This section includes identification data, reason for the referral, and relevant background.

The identification data comprise demographic information, including the student's name and date of birth, the parents' names and address, the school's name and address, the primary language of the student, and the student's disability classification. Inclusion of the primary language informs administrators and teachers who read the IEP that the student's language may affect the student's educational progress.

The next section provides the reasons for the referral and information regarding the events leading up to the student's identification and placement in special education. For example, Johnny's referral indicates that his failing grades and difficulties interacting with others were interfering with his education.

Finally, the background information may provide some insight into the student's disability. It includes medical information, socioemotional information, or information regarding the student's developmental milestones. The background information in Johnny's file states how he witnessed the automobile accident that killed his father, how it has affected his emotional well-being, and possibly why his academic and behavioral performances are better with a male teacher. (See Figure 5.1.)

## Present Level of Academic and Functional Performances

IDEA 2004 changes *educational performance* in the previous version of the legislation to *academic achievement and functional performance*. This change clarifies and expands the focus of the student's IEP (Gartin & Murdick, 2005).

---

**Individualized Education Program**
**Benjamin Franklin Pierce Middle School**
**1701 Enterprise Lane**
**Laredo, TX 78049**

Student's Name: __Jonathan T. Martin__   Date of Birth: __5-19-1996__ Age/Grade: __13/8th__

Parent/Guardian: __Kathleen Martin__   Address: __76 Whitehead Lane, Laredo, Tx 78049__

Student's Primary Language: __English__   Secondary Language: __None__

Primary Disability: __Emotional Disturbance__   Secondary Disability: __ADHD__

*Reason for Referral*

Johnny is failing all his classes with the exception of physical education. He has had extreme difficulties interacting with peers and adults. He has threatened and intimidated peers on several occasions.

*Relevant Background*

Johnny's developmental milestones were age-appropriate. Vision and hearing are normal. He has been diagnosed as having ADHD (predominantly inattentive type). When Johnny was 5 years old, he witnessed the automobile accident that caused the death of his father. His counselor has reported that this has affected his academic and behavioral performance at school, and that he may do better with a male teacher.

---

**FIGURE 5.1** Johnny's IEP: Identification

Information about the student's present level of academic and functional performance usually can be obtained from the formal and informal assessments that are performed prior to the IEP meeting. This information can include results of standardized academic and achievement assessments, results of behavioral scales, observations, current academic grades, and information from other sources. (See Chapter 4.) The description of the student's present level of academic and functional performance includes information about how the student's disability affects his involvement and progress in the general education curriculum. For example, *Johnny's disability affects his ability to complete assignments in many of his classes, so he is receiving failing grades.* (See Figure 5.2.)

---

**Individualized Education Program**
**Benjamin Franklin Pierce Middle School**
**1701 Enterprise Lane**
**Laredo, TX 78049**

---

Student's Name:   Jonathan T. Martin        Date of Birth:  5-19-1996  Age/Grade   13/8th

Parent/Guardian:   Kathleen Martin        Address: 76 Whitehead Lane, Laredo, Tx 78049

Student's Primary Language:  English    Secondary Language:   None

Primary Disability:  Emotional Disturbance  Secondary Disability:   ADHD

*Reason for Referral*

Johnny is failing all his classes with the exception of physical education. He has had extreme difficulties interacting with peers and adults. He has threatened and intimidated peers on several occasions.

*Relevant Background*

Johnny's developmental milestones were age-appropriate. Vision and hearing are normal. He has been diagnosed as having ADHD (predominantly inattentive type). When Johnny was 5 years old, he witnessed the automobile accident that caused the death of his father. His counselor has reported that this has affected his academic and behavioral performance at school, and that he may do better with a male teacher.

*Present Level of Academic and Functional Performances*

| | | |
|---|---|---|
| WISC-IV: | Verbal Score: | 83 |
| | Performance Score: | 86 |
| | Full IQ Scale Score: | 85 |
| WJ-III | Broad Reading: | 86 |
| | Broad Math: | 88 |
| Vineland: | Communications: | 78 |
| | Daily Living Skills: | 88 |
| | Socialization: | 68 |
| | Adaptive Behavior Composite: | 72 |

Johnny's academic and functional performances are within the below-average range, with the exception of the socialization domain of the Vineland. He is functioning at the 6th grade level in reading and math. He is currently failing all academic courses with the exception of physical education. He has deficits in listening and attending, following instructions, responding to others, and belonging to groups. Johnny's disabilities affect his ability to complete assignments, which results in failing grades. Johnny also has difficulties developing and maintaining relationships with peers and adults.

---

**FIGURE 5.2**  Johnny's IEP: Present Level of Academic and Functional Performances

## Measurable Annual Goals

Measurable annual goals are designed to enable the student to participate and make progress in the general education curriculum; the goals also should meet the other educational needs of the student that result from his or her disability. For example, an annual goal for Johnny might be that *Johnny will complete assignments in all his classes with a minimal grade of 70%.*

IDEA 2004 eliminated short-term objectives from the IEP unless the student is scheduled to take an alternative assessment, although individual states could decide to continue requiring all students to complete short-term objectives. If the IEP Team decides that the student will take an alternative assessment that is not aligned to meet alternative achievement standards, the IEP must include a description of benchmarks or short-term objectives (20 U.S.C. § 300.320 [a][2][ii]). In Johnny's case, the IEP Team has determined that he will take the statewide assessment, so benchmarks or short-term objectives are not required in his IEP. (See Figure 5.3.)

## Special Education and Related Services

IDEA 2004 requires the IEP to describe the special education and related services and supplementary aids and services that will be prescribed for the student with emotional and behavior disorders. The team should include in the IEP interventions that are proven effective in peer-reviewed studies.

Special education services are specific academic and related instructions provided by the special education teacher, usually in the resource room or a self-contained classroom that is separate from the general education classroom. The special education curriculum may cover social skills, self-management instructions, and study strategies. The special education teacher may also provide instruction in an inclusionary classroom with all students—those who have emotional and behavior disorders and those who do not.

Related services help the student to achieve success in special education. They may include transportation, a common need for students with emotional and behavior disorders who receive special education services at a location other than in their home school. Other related services include psychological services, counseling, and job-related training.

---

**Individualized Education Program**                                          2

Student:  __Jonathan T. Martin__

---

*Measurable Annual Goals*

1. Johnny will complete 90% of the assignments in all his classes. Johnny's progress toward this goal will be measured by direct observation and work sample.

2. Johnny will reduce his verbally abusive behavior toward peers by 80%. Johnny's progress toward this goal will be measured by direct observation.

---

**FIGURE 5.3**  Johnny's IEP: Measurable Annual Goals

Supplementary aids and services help the student participate in the general education classroom. These services may include assistive technology, behavioral intervention plans, social skills training, peer tutoring, classroom support from the paraprofessional (a classroom assistant trained in special education), and modifications to the academic curriculum (McLeskey & Waldron, 2007; Yell & Katsiyannis, 2004).

## Participation

Students with emotional and behavior disorders should be educated in the least restrictive environment. IDEA specifically states that, to the maximum extent appropriate, students with disabilities should be educated in the same setting as students without disabilities. Special education placement decisions must be made on the basis of the student's needs and not according to the type of disability, severity of disability, availability of educational or related services, availability of space, or administrative convenience (Yell & Katsiyannis, 2004). The student cannot be placed automatically in a self-contained classroom for students with emotional and behavior disorders simply because he or she was identified as having emotional and behavior disorders, because there was no other classroom available, or because that is the school principal's preference. The student's placement is determined by the IEP Team and should meet the needs of the student and the goals of the IEP. The first educational placement consideration is the general education setting; other placement options may be considered only if the IEP Team decides that the student's needs cannot be appropriately met in the general education setting, even with supplementary aids and services.

If the student is not going to participate alongside students without disabilities in the general education classroom or in the general education curriculum, extracurricular activities, or other nonacademic curricula, then the extent to which the student will not participate must be described in the student's IEP for each area. There are a number of ways to write this statement into the IEP. For example, the statement in Johnny's file might be *Johnny will receive mathematics instruction in the resource room* or *Johnny will not participate in mathematics instruction in the general education setting.*

Other methods of writing nonparticipation descriptions for the general education curriculum include the following:

- *Johnny will participate in the general education curriculum 40% of the time* or *Johnny will not participate in the general education curriculum 60% of the time.*
- *Johnny will participate in the general education curriculum 100 minutes per day* or *Johnny will not participate in the general education curriculum 380 minutes per day.*
- *Johnny will participate in the general education curriculum for a total of 8 hours and 20 minutes per week* or *Johnny will not participate in the general education curriculum for a total of 31 hours and 40 minutes per week.*

Nonparticipation descriptions must also be written for extracurricular activities and nonacademic activities. For example, Johnny's file might contain the description *Johnny will not participate in any extracurricular activities after school* or *Johnny will not eat lunch at the same time as students without disabilities.*

There should be some legitimate reason that the student will not participate in each activity. For example, Johnny will receive mathematics instruction in the resource room because his academic needs cannot be met in the general education setting, even with

---

**Individualized Education Program**                                    2

Student:  Jonathan T. Martin

---

*Measurable Annual Goals*

1.  Johnny will complete 90% of the assignments in all his classes. Johnny's progress toward this goal will be measured by direct observation and work sample.

2.  Johnny will reduce his verbally abusive behavior toward peers by 80%.  Johnny's progress toward this goal will be measured by direct observation.

*Special Education and Related Services*              Beginning Date:  9/01/2009

Special Education Services:  Johnny will receive specially designed instruction in the resource classroom 60% of the time. The special education teacher will be responsible for implementation.

Johnny will participate in the general education curriculum 40% of the time. The special education teacher and general education teachers will be responsible for implementation.

Related Services:  Johnny will meet with his counselor 50 minutes per week. The counselor from the Beer Mental Health Center will be responsible for implementation.

Supplementary Aids and Services:  Johnny will receive social skills training 50 minutes per week. The special education teacher will be responsible for implementation.

Extracurricular and Non-Academic Activities:  Johnny will not eat lunch at the same time as students without disabilities. The special education teacher will be responsible for implementation.

---

**FIGURE 5.4**   Johnny's IEP: Special Education and Related Services and Participation

---

supplementary aids and services. Johnny will not have lunch at the same time as students without disabilities because he does not have the interpersonal skills to be successful in that particular nonacademic setting. (However, his goals should include social skills training that would eventually lead to his participation in the regular lunch schedule.) (See Figure 5.4.)

The goal of the IEP Team should be to develop an IEP that will allow the student to participate as much as is appropriate in the general education setting, extracurricular activities, and nonacademic activities. To meet that goal, the IEP and the student's subsequent placement should be oriented around meeting the student's unique needs.

## State- and District-Wide Assessments

Students with disabilities are expected to take the same state- and districtwide assessments mandated by the No Child Left Behind Act as students without disabilities. The IEP Team can determine whether the student needs accommodations in order for the student's academic achievement and functional performance to be measured on statewide and district assessments. Accommodations do not change the content of the assessment, but they may affect the manner in which the assessment is presented to the student, the way that the student responds to questions, the amount of time the student is given to complete the assessment, or the setting in which the assessment is given. Appropriate accommodations could include providing more time, having a teacher read the test questions orally to the student, using assistive technology (such as a word processing document or PowerPoint file on a computer) to administer the test, using a large-print version of the test, and providing color overlays to enhance the contrast of test materials (Rieck & Wadsworth, 2005).

If the IEP Team determines that, even with accommodations, the regular state- and district-wide assessments cannot measure the academic achievement and functional performance of the student, the student can take an alternative assessment. The IEP must explain why the regular assessment is not appropriate and what alternative assessment will be used. Alternative assessments could include portfolios of school assignments, assessments of functional living skills or adaptive behavior skills, and/or curriculum-based assessment procedures. Some states have even developed statewide alternative assessments for students with disabilities who are unable to take the regular statewide assessments.

The IEP Team has determined that Johnny will participate in the statewide assessment with accommodations. The accommodations include taking the test in the resource room and receiving an extended period of time in which to take the test. (See Figure 5.5.)

---

**Individualized Education Program**        2

Student: __Jonathan T. Martin__

*Measurable Annual Goals*

1. Johnny will complete 90% of the assignments in all his classes. Johnny's progress toward this goal will be measured by direct observation and work sample.

2. Johnny will reduce his verbally abusive behavior toward peers by 80%. Johnny's progress toward this goal will be measured by direct observation.

*Special Education and Related Services*        Beginning Date: 9/01/2009

Special Education Services: Johnny will receive specially designed instruction in the resource classroom 60% of the time. The special education teacher will be responsible for implementation.

Johnny will participate in the general education curriculum 40% of the time. The special education teacher and general education teachers will be responsible for implementation.

Related Services: Johnny will meet with his counselor 50 minutes per week. The counselor from the Beer Mental Health Center will be responsible for implementation.

Supplementary Aids and Services: Johnny will receive social skills training 50 minutes per week. The special education teacher will be responsible for implementation.

Extracurricular and Non-Academic Activities: Johnny will not eat lunch at the same time as students without disabilities. The special education teacher will be responsible for implementation.

*State- and District-wide Assessments*

Johnny will participate in the state-wide assessment with modifications. Modifications include taking the state-wide assessment in the special education resource room, and having an extended period of time to complete the assessment.

---

**FIGURE 5.5** Johnny's IEP: State- and District-wide Assessments

## Measuring and Reporting Student Progress

The IEP must describe how the student's progress toward meeting the annual goals will be measured and how that progress will be reported to the parents on a regular basis. The student's progress may be measured by the number of annual goals he or she has met, the results of classroom quizzes or tests, progress charts, and results of state- and district-wide assessments.

The parents may be informed of the student's progress through the same methods as the parents of students without disabilities: report cards, parent–teacher conferences, weekly progress reports, and phone calls. The report cards should note the progress the student has made toward completing his or her annual goals.

The IEP Team has determined that Johnny's mother will be informed of his progress toward annual goals through report cards, parent–teacher conferences, and weekly progress reports. (See Figure 5.6.)

## IEP Considerations

Development of the IEP is a team effort. Each member of the team should be encouraged to contribute to the process. It is important for the school representative to ensure that all members have a voice by asking for their input at the meeting.

Once the IEP has been developed, the IEP Team needs to determine the student's placement using the IEP, the student's annual goals, and the student's individual needs. The student should be placed in the least restrictive environment, and unless otherwise specified in the IEP, the student should be educated in the school that he or she would attend if the student did not have a disability.

The IEP Team should determine the date on which services and accommodations will begin. The student needs to receive special education and related services as soon as possible after the IEP has been developed; however, this decision needs to be tempered by reasonable judgment. For example, changing the student's current placement a couple of days prior to a vacation or one week before summer break will probably not be beneficial for the student and may have detrimental consequences. If the IEP Team determines that a student has a disability and needs special education services 2 weeks before the end of the academic year, it would be prudent to begin services at the beginning of the next academic year.

Once the IEP has been developed, it must be accessible to the teachers and other service providers who are responsible for its implementation. This does not mean that multiple copies of the IEP are distributed to teachers. Instead, the IEP should be in a secure filing cabinet that is accessible to the teachers. Schools also need to ensure that privacy issues under the Family Education Rights and Privacy Act (FERPA; 20 U.S.C. § 1232g; 34 CFR Part 99) and IDEA are followed. (See Chapter 11.)

Teachers need to be aware of their responsibilities in implementing the IEP and to be informed of the specific accommodations, modifications, and supports that the student should receive. Many schools provide teachers and service providers with accommodations checklists that contain the student's specific accommodations. Accommodations checklists are generally issued at the beginning of the academic year or immediately after the student's IEP has been developed.

---

**Individualized Education Program** 2

Student:  Jonathan T. Martin

---

*Measurable Annual Goals*

1. Johnny will complete 90% of the assignments in all his classes. Johnny's progress toward this goal will be measured by direct observation and work sample.

2. Johnny will reduce his verbally abusive behavior toward peers by 80%. Johnny's progress toward this goal will be measured by direct observation.

*Special Education and Related Services*          Beginning Date:  9/01/2009

Special Education Services: Johnny will receive specially designed instruction in the resource classroom 60% of the time. The special education teacher will be responsible for implementation.

Johnny will participate in the general education curriculum 40% of the time. The special education teacher and general education teachers will be responsible for implementation.

Related Services: Johnny will meet with his counselor 50 minutes per week. The counselor from the Beer Mental Health Center will be responsible for implementation.

Supplementary Aids and Services: Johnny will receive social skills training 50 minutes per week. The special education teacher will be responsible for implementation.

Extracurricular and Non-Academic Activities: Johnny will not eat lunch at the same time as students without disabilities. The special education teacher will be responsible for implementation.

*State- and District-wide Assessments*

Johnny will participate in the state-wide assessment with modifications. Modifications include taking the state-wide assessment in the special education resource room, and having an extended period of time to complete the assessment.

*Reporting Student Progress*

          X  Report Cards          X  Parent/Teacher Conferences  X  Weekly Progress Reports

          ___ Weekly Phone Calls ___ Home Notes

IEP Team Participants

Parent: _____     Administrator:  David Price

General Education Teacher:  Letty Smart     Student:  **Johnny Martin**

Special Education Teacher:  David Poteet     Diagnostician:  Maria Salazar

Addtional Members:  **Bessie Whatsit**     Addtional Members: _____

**FIGURE 5.6**  Johnny's IEP: Reporting Student Progress

Finally, the IEP has to be reviewed and revised annually if not more often. The IEP Team must determine whether the student is meeting the annual goals that were prescribed in the IEP. If the student is not meeting the annual goals, then the IEP Team must revise the IEP to address the student's lack of progress.

## PARENTS AND THE IEP PROCESS

Parents' participation in their child's education is a fundamental component of IDEA. Schools must ensure that the parents have the opportunity to participate in the development of the IEP. Parents need to receive enough notice of an IEP Team meeting in order to attend, and the meeting needs to be scheduled at a time and place to which all participants agree. For example, some parents cannot attend a meeting during the day due to their jobs or other obligations. In such cases, the school should schedule the IEP Team meeting in the evening. Parents may feel uncomfortable meeting at the school. Meetings then could be held in conference rooms at a public library or at some other place upon which all participants agree.

If the parent does not understand English well or has a hearing impairment, the school should provide an interpreter. The school needs to take whatever actions are necessary to ensure that the parent understands the proceedings.

Because parental involvement in a child's education is so important, IDEA mandates that parents receive "a document explaining their rights and responsibilities any time their child is referred for an evaluation, and at other times throughout the special education process" (FitzGerald & Watkins, 2006, p. 497). This document, called a *Procedural Safeguard*, must be written in a language understandable to the general population and presented in the parents' native language or other mode of communication.

According to IDEA 2004, the Procedural Safeguard document should include information about

- the student's independent educational evaluations,
- prior written notice to the parent(s) when the school proposes to evaluate a student,
- parental consent to evaluate the student for special education eligibility,
- access to education records,
- due process procedures,
- mediation,
- the student's placement while awaiting the outcome of any due process complaint,
- interim alternative educational settings,
- placement in private schools,
- state-level appeals,
- civil actions,
- and attorney fees (§ 300.504[c]).

Unfortunately, parents often receive their Procedural Safeguard document without further explanation from the special education teacher or other school personnel, and they often do not understand the information it contains. Many of the Procedural Safeguard components (92% to 96%) are written at a ninth-grade level or higher, with nearly 50% written at a college level. A majority of Americans read at an eighth-grade reading level, so Procedural Safeguard documents are too difficult for nearly 90% of the parents to understand (FitzGerald & Watkins, 2006).

Even if they do understand their rights and responsibilities, parents typically have low levels of participation in the IEP process. They are often intimidated by the educational experts at the IEP table and may be hesitant to challenge the school's authority or jeopardize their relationship with school personnel. Parents who have low socioeconomic status, whose native language is not English, or who belong to a different culture are less likely to participate in IEP Team meetings (Leiter & Krauss, 2004).

Increasing parents' knowledge and understanding of their rights and responsibilities under IDEA can increase their participation in IEP Team meetings. A good first step is to provide them with a Procedural Safeguard document that is written in an easily understandable manner. It should be assessed according to a readability measure to make sure that the reading level is not above the eighth-grade level, and it should be revised if it is above the eighth-grade level. The document should be brief. Parents are less likely to read through long Procedural Safeguard documents. The print should be no smaller than 12-point font so that parents with visual limitations can read it (FitzGerald & Watkins, 2006).

Special education teachers or other school personnel should take the time to explain the Procedural Safeguard document to the parents and to inform parents of their roles and responsibilities at the IEP Team meeting. School districts could even provide in-services for parents, designed to provide the information about their rights and responsibilities.

Finally, parents need to be encouraged to participate at IEP Team meetings. The school administrator or other facilitator of the meeting should consistently solicit parents' input and ask them whether they have any questions regarding their child's education. The student's teacher should sit by the parent and offer support. Making parents feel comfortable and making them feel that their contributions to the process are valued will increase their participation in the IEP process, and their involvement will translate to greater benefits for the student.

## INDIVIDUALIZED TRANSITION PLANS

The employment rate of young adults with disabilities is much lower than that of young adults without disabilities. Individuals with emotional and behavior disorders are more likely to drop out of school, are more likely to be unemployed 2 years after leaving school, and are more likely to have at least one arrest on their record 3 years after leaving school (Bullis & Cheney, 1999; Koyanagi & Gaines, 1993; U.S. Department of Education, 2002; Wagner, Newman, et al., 2005). Transition services focus on improving the academic and functional achievement of the student to help him or her move from school to postschool activities, which could include postsecondary education (college, vocational, and adult education), integrated employment, or independent living. IDEA requires these services to be well planned and to consist of specific activities that are included in the student's IEP (Savage, 2005).

According to IDEA 2004, transition services should be selected and implemented during the development of the IEP that would be in effect when the student turns 16 years old, or earlier if it is considered appropriate by the IEP Team or by individual states. The IEP must include appropriate measurable postsecondary goals on the basis of age-appropriate transition assessments related to training, education, employment, and independent living skills. These goals inform the creation of an *Individualized Transition Plan* (ITP), which is a part of the IEP and guides the development of the IEP. The ITP also includes the student's current levels of academic and functional performance, the student's interests and aptitude, transition activities (vocational and career education, work experience, functional skills instruction, and community-based instructions), and the individuals who will be responsible for implementing the ITP. Like the IEP, the ITP should be reviewed annually.

The ITP focuses on the student's course of study. For example, if the student is interested in becoming an auto mechanic, the IEP should include coursework in industrial technology or auto shop. Through transition planning, the IEP reflects the student's goals

---

**Individualized Transition Plan**

Student: _Jonathan T. Martin_          Disability: _Emotional Disturbance_

Goal: _Vocational Education: Auto Mechanics_

---

Grade: _8th_

    IEP Team Develops ITP

Grade: _9th_

    Build Career Awareness
    Complete Vocational Assessment
    IEP Team Reviews IEP/ITP
    Contact Vocational Rehabilitation Office (provide them with student's name, etc.)

Grade: _10th_

    Explore Vocational Choices
    Review Information Describing Auto Mechanics
    Visit Businesses Employing Workers in Auto Mechanics
    IEP Team Reviews IEP/ITP
    Invite Vocational Rehabilitation (VR) Counselor for Next IEP/ITP

Grade: _11th_

    Begin Vocational Training
    Enroll in Chosen High School Vocational Programs
        Industrial Technology, Computer Technology, Health & Safety
    Apply for Adult Services Programs
    Explore Post-Secondary Vocational Program (Technical Schools for Auto Mechanics)
    IEP Team Reviews IEP/ITP
    Discuss Options with VR Counselor

Grade: _12th_

    Continue Vocational Training
    Continue in Chosen High School Vocational Programs
    Apply for Post-Secondary Vocational Program
    IEP Team Conducts Exit Procedures

---

**FIGURE 5.7**  Johnny's ITP

and aspirations, and it is crucial that the student be actively involved in the transition process. (See Figure 5.7.)

Despite the importance of student participation in the development of their IEPs/ITPs, one study found that students attending IEP Team meetings often did not know the reason for the meeting, did not know what their role should be in the meeting, and did not understand what was being discussed (Martin, Marshall, & Sale, 2004). Another study found that the atmosphere of the IEP Team meeting was intimidating to the student (Arndt, Konrad, & Test, 2006). As a result, students' participation in the process was extremely limited.

Students with emotional and behavior disorders need to develop the skills to actively participate in the transition process at IEP Team meetings. To increase their participation at their IEP meetings, students can be taught skills in goal setting, planning, self-evaluation, mediation, public speaking, and self-advocacy (Martin, Marshall, Maxson, & Jerman, 1997). Modeling, student assignments, and role-playing can be used to teach students the skills they need to actively participate in IEP Team meetings (Martin, Van Dycke, Christensen, Greene, Gardner, & Lovett, 2006). When the students actively participate in their IEP Team meetings and have a voice in developing their transition goals, they feel invested in the process and are more likely to pursue those goals (Arndt et al., 2006).

The student needs to discuss his or her postsecondary interests with the IEP Team, so that the team can develop appropriate goals. For example, if Johnny is interested in fixing cars, then his goals should be geared toward a vocation in automobile mechanics. Goals could include *knowing safety principles and practices, knowing the proper care and use of tools,* and *developing skills to maintain, service, and repair different types of transportation vehicles.*

After developing a set of goals, the IEP Team, including the student, plans a course of study that will help the student reach his or her transition goals. The course of study will include classes for each grade level and vocational experiences that will help the student achieve the transition goals (Martin, 2002). For example, Johnny may take several classes in industrial technology, driver's education, and mechanics. He may also participate in a job release program at a garage as part of his course of study.

Providing students who have emotional and behavior disorders with self-determination skills will help them to actively participate in the IEP Team meetings and transition process. Participation gives students a sense of ownership of their future and makes them more likely to pursue the goals developed by the IEP Team. When they feel invested in their futures, students are more likely to complete high school and to be employed 2 years after leaving school, and they are less likely to be involved in activities that could result in an arrest.

## PREVENTING DUE PROCESS HEARINGS

The likelihood that a disagreement between the school and the parents of a student with emotional and behavior disorders will result in a due process hearing is higher than that associated with other disabilities. The four common disagreements between the school and parents that lead to a due process hearing are evaluation, identification, placement, and free and appropriate public education. If school districts follow the procedures set forth by IDEA, the probability that a parent will initiate a due process procedure is lower, and if the parent does initiate a due process procedure, the hearing officer is more likely to side with the school.

As stated previously, IDEA requires that the parents participate in all meetings and decisions regarding their child's evaluation, identification, and placement. The school must obtain informed parental consent prior to conducting an initial evaluation of a student suspected of having a disability. In addition, the school should take the time to explain the evaluation process to the parents in their native language. The parents should be given the name and telephone number of a school official they can call if they have further questions or concerns regarding the evaluation. Parents also should be informed that the consent for the evaluation is voluntary and can be revoked in writing at any time.

School officials must give parents specific notice before they make a decision regarding the student's disability, change the student's IEP, or change the student's placement. The notice must be provided in a timely fashion that allows the parents the opportunity to participate in decisions and meetings. IDEA does not define "timely fashion," but many school districts provide parents with a notice of 5 school days or more before any decisions or meetings occur. School districts should make reasonable attempts to notify parents of meetings by sending them written notices, calling them, or informing them through face-to-face contacts.

## Case Study 5.1

### Johnny

Johnny sat in the small conference room at Roddenberry Middle School. Sitting beside him was Mr. Poteet, the special education teacher at Franklin Pierce High School. Johnny was going to be attending an IEP Team meeting tomorrow, and since he was attending the high school next year, Mr. Poteet wanted to meet with him prior to the meeting.

"Good morning, Johnny," said Mr. Poteet. "How are you today?"

Johnny shrugged his shoulders. "Okay, I guess," he said a little reservedly. He did not trust people readily. They were always yelling at him or leaving him.

"I wanted to meet with you to talk to you about the meeting tomorrow." Mr. Poteet continued, "Do you know what an IEP Team meeting is?"

"Some meeting where everyone is going to talk about what to do with me," said Johnny.

"They are going to talk about what we can do to help you be successful in school,"

corrected Mr. Poteet, "but it is important that you also be involved. We want you to have a say in your education."

"Why?"

"Who knows you better than you?" replied Mr. Poteet. "It is your education we are talking about."

Johnny asked, "Who would listen to me?"

"All of us." Mr. Poteet nameed the members of the IEP Team, explained their roles, and described the procedures of the IEP Team meeting.

"So, Johnny," continued Mr. Poteet, "whenever you have a question or want to say something, you need to speak up."

"I, I don't know if I can do that, Mr. Poteet," Johnny responded nervously.

"I'll tell you what," smiled Mr. Poteet. "I will sit beside you at the meeting, and I will ask you if you have any questions. Will that help?"

"Yeah, I think so."

IDEA requires the school to schedule IEP Team meetings at a time and place to which all participants agree. This process should accommodate the parents' work schedule to ensure that one or both parents have the opportunity to participate in IEP Team meetings. If the parents cannot attend the IEP Team meeting in person, then the team should consider involving them through an alternative means of meeting participation. This alternative means of participation could be a video conference (an increasingly viable method with the increasing popularity of computer programs such as iChat) or a conference call.

Once the student has been evaluated and identified as having a disability, the school should provide an appropriate education for the student without cost to the parent. Under IDEA 2004, the parent must agree to the placement of the student. If the parent does not agree to special education and related services, the school will not place the student in special education and will not be held accountable for providing special education services.

When the school and the parents disagree on the evaluation, identification, or placement of the student, the parents may initiate a due process hearing. An impartial hearing officer will listen to both parties and make a determination regarding the disagreement. The officer must make a final decision within 45 days after the parent has requested a hearing. The decision is binding on both parties, but either may appeal.

If parents are actively involved in the initial evaluation process, IEP Team meetings, and placement decisions, the chance that they will initiate a due process hearing diminishes. It is up to the facilitator of the IEP Team meeting to make sure that parents have the opportunity to participate by giving them chances to make comments and ask questions regarding their child's education. Schools need to regularly inform parents of their student's progress and of any changes in the student's program.

## Summary

The Individualized Education Program (IEP) is a written plan designed to meet the academic, behavioral, social, and emotional needs of a student with emotional and behavior disorders. All IEPs must contain specific components specified by IDEA.

The IEP Team includes a general education teacher, a special education teacher, a representative of the school, someone who can interpret evaluation results, the parents, and, when appropriate, the student. The IEP Team designs the IEP to meet the academic and functional needs of the student.

An IEP has seven components. The first component consists of student demographic information, reason for the referral, and relevant background information. The next component is the student's present level of academic achievement and functional performance, obtained from the comprehensive assessment conducted prior to the IEP Team meeting. The student's annual measurable goals and the special education and related services that the student will receive are also included. If the student is not going to participate in the general education setting alongside students without disabilities, then the extent in which the student will not participate must be described in the IEP. The IEP must also state whether the student will take the same state- and district-wide assessments as students without disabilities or whether the student will complete an alternative assessment. The IEP needs to include a description of how the student will be assessed and what accommodations, if any, the student may need. Finally, the IEP needs to include an expla-

nation of how the student's progress toward meeting the annual goals will be measured and how that progress will be reported to the parents.

Schools must take steps to ensure that parents have the opportunity to participate in the development of the IEP. Parents need to receive enough notice of an IEP Team meeting so that they can attend, and the meeting needs to be scheduled at a time and place to which all participants agree. If a parent does not understand English well or has a hearing impairment, an interpreter needs to be provided to ensure that the parent understands the proceedings. The parents also should receive a Procedural Safeguard document that explains their rights and responsibilities. Parents who understand their rights and responsibilities under IDEA are more likely to actively participate in the IEP Team meeting. Unfortunately, parents often do not understand the content of the Procedural Safeguard document, which hinders their ability to participate in their child's education.

An Individualized Transition Plan (ITP) for postschool life should be developed and included in the IEP by the time the student is 16 years old. The ITP must include appropriate measurable postsecondary goals on the basis of age-appropriate transition assessments related to training, education, employment, and independent living skills. Students with emotional and behavior disorders should be taught the skills they need to actively participate in the transition process at IEP Team meetings.

The IEP is a crucial component of a student's special education program. A well-developed

IEP not only will ensure that the student with emotional and behavior disorders benefits from special education services, but also will reduce conflicts between the school district and the student's parents. A due process procedure occurs when the parent and the school disagree over the evaluation, identification, placement, or free and appropriate public education of the student. Tailoring the IEP to meet the individual needs of the student, following procedures set forth by IDEA, and ensuring that parents participate in all meetings and decisions regarding their child's education will reduce the types of difficulties that could trigger a due process hearing.

## Review Questions

1. What information should be included in the IEP? What information in the IEP is essential for general education teachers of students with emotional and behavior disorders?
2. Why is it important to include information about a student's goals when developing an IEP for a student with emotional and behavior disorders?
3. Imagine that you are the special education teacher at an IEP Team meeting. How would you ensure that the parent of the student has an opportunity to participate in the meeting? Why is the parent's participation important?
4. Anna is a student with emotional and behavior disorders whose cognitive functioning is at the lower end of the range for average intelligence, but who does not meet the eligibility requirements for mild mental retardation. Anna states that she wants to be a nurse, but on the basis of her abilities, it is unlikely that she could reach this goal. As Anna's special education teacher, what should you do?
5. What could be the results of a poorly developed ITP?
6. The IEP Team has determined that Mary is a student with emotional and behavior disorders, but Mary's mother believes that her daughter's academic and behavioral difficulties in school are due to ADHD. What are the implications of this disagreement, and what could be the outcome?

# CHAPTER 6

# Managing Behavior

**After reading this chapter, you should be able to**

- Explain the significance of Positive Behavior Support compared with traditional behavior interventions and describe the three intervention levels of Positive Behavior Support.
- Name and describe the six basic steps in conducting a functional behavioral assessment.

- Name and describe the eight components of a behavior intervention plan.
- Name and describe the different classroom behavior management plans that can be used in the general and special education classrooms.
- Identify some concerns associated with behavior intervention strategies.

## GOALS OF MANAGING BEHAVIOR

Classroom behavior management is a crucial aspect of teaching students with emotional and behavior disorders. Teachers need to realize that they do not really control the behavior of students. If students behave well in the classroom and comply with the directions of teachers, it is because they choose to do so. Fortunately, in most classrooms, the majority of students choose to demonstrate appropriate behavior. Only a small percentage of students choose to demonstrate inappropriate behavior, and these students often take up most of the teacher's time. Students with emotional and behavior disorders have a harder time complying with the expectations of the school and the classrooms because they have more difficulty controlling their behaviors. The key to managing the behavior of any student is consistency.

For example, a middle-school student named David is talking to his friend in a social studies class about last night's television show instead of working on his assignment. His teacher, Mrs. Cantu, walks over to him and tells him to work on his assignment, but David does not comply. She then tells him that if he continues to talk, she will put his name on the chalkboard for talking. This step is the first consequence for violating classroom rules. David focuses on his assignment momentarily, but continues talking a few minutes later. Mrs. Cantu warns him again that she will put his name on the chalkboard. At this point, she should already have written his name on the chalkboard and put a checkmark by his name (the second consequence). David ignores her request and continues to talk. Frustrated, Mrs. Cantu stands in front of David's desk. She tells him that this is the last time she is going to warn him and that she really will put his name on the chalkboard. Another student mutters under her breath that David should have had three checkmarks after his name by now. Because she does not consistently follow her classroom behavior management plan, Mrs. Cantu's rules and consequences mean nothing to her students. David knows this, and the other students know this. As a result, Mrs. Cantu will probably spend most of her academic time trying unsuccessfully to control the behaviors of certain students.

There are three basic goals of managing behaviors in the general and special education classroom:

1. Provide a safe and secure environment in which learning can take place.
2. Provide opportunities for students to learn reasonable rules and consequences and to understand the reasons for them.
3. Assist students in managing their behaviors and help them to develop self-discipline and self-control (Laursen, 2003).

In simpler terms, a good behavior management plan allows teachers to teach and students to learn.

Many classroom management plans are founded on principles of behavior theory and include rules, consequences, and rewards similar to the Assertive Discipline classroom management plan (Canter & Canter, 2001). *Assertive Discipline* is a systematic behavior management plan that helps teachers maintain consistent expectations about behavior and provides appropriate consequences for poor student behavior. Assertive Discipline has four main components: a set of rules, a set of consequences, a set of rewards, and a plan for implementation (Malmgren, Trezek, & Paul, 2005). Teachers should have a short list of rules (usually around five) that are stated positively and in terms of specific behaviors. For example, it is difficult to enforce the common rule, "Respect Others," because it can be interpreted in different ways. However, "Keep hands, feet, and objects to yourself" is written in a positive manner and stated in terms of behavior.

A number of behavior management plans, techniques, and strategies are available for use by teachers and administrators. These interventions are effective for managing the behavior of students with severe behavior problems and students with emotional and behavior disorders. They include positive behavior support, functional behavioral assessments, behavior intervention plans, and other classroom management plans.

## POSITIVE BEHAVIOR SUPPORT

Traditionally, the behaviors of children with emotional and behavior disorders have been managed by providing consequences for their inappropriate behaviors. For example, if Johnny throws a pencil at Mike, then, as a result of this behavior, Johnny misses recess. The premise of this intervention is that knowledge of the consequence will prevent the behavior from occurring again. But reactive and punitive measures may actually exacerbate the situation and increase the inappropriate behavior (Safran, 2006; Turnbull et al., 2002).

IDEA 2004 requires that functional behavioral assessments and behavior intervention plans for students with disabilities be addressed only after their unacceptable behaviors result in a change of placement. A *change of placement* may occur when the student has been suspended for more than 10 days, when the student's behavior has been so disruptive that his or her needs cannot be met in the current placement, or if he or she brings drugs or weapons to school.

An alternative approach to the reactive, traditional types of behavior interventions is *Positive Behavior Support* (PBS). PBS is a proactive, positive behavior intervention designed to promote socially acceptable behavior for all students (Safran, 2006; Scott & Barrett, 2004; Sugai et al., 2000; Walker et al., 2005). Through PBS, students are instructed to exhibit socially acceptable behavior and the school environment is rearranged to prevent the unacceptable behavior.

There are six components of a PBS program that every school should have:

1. A brief statement of purpose that encompasses all students, staff, and settings and that describes academic and behavioral outcomes.
2. A clearly stated list of behaviors that students are expected to exhibit; these include "replacement" behaviors, or alternative and appropriate behaviors, for each problem behavior.
3. Procedures for teaching expected behaviors.
4. Procedures for reinforcing expected behavior using tangible and intangible incentives.
5. Procedures for discouraging inappropriate behavior using appropriate consequences.
6. Procedures for keeping records for assessing the effectiveness of the program (Lewis & Sugai, 1999).

PBS has three stages of intervention with increasing levels of support: primary, secondary, and tertiary. (See Figure 6.1.) Primary, or universal, intervention is a school-wide intervention involving all students. Secondary, or individualized, intervention provides specialized support for individual students or classrooms with identified needs. Tertiary, or comprehensive, intervention provides extensive, individualized supports (Walker et al., 2005). Many students with emotional and behavior disorders require tertiary interventions, as do some students with serious behavioral problems who may not have been identified for special educational services. Implementing all intervention levels in a systematic, school-wide approach may prevent some students with emotional and behavior disorders from engaging in inappropriate behaviors to the point of needing tertiary interventions.

### PBS Analysis

Before beginning a school-wide PBS program, a school-based PBS team should be created to analyze the behavioral environment of the school. This environment varies from school to school and from district to district. At a rural school in northern Indiana, one of the biggest behavior problems may be students talking back to teachers, whereas at an urban school in south Texas, teachers may be concerned about students flashing gang signs.

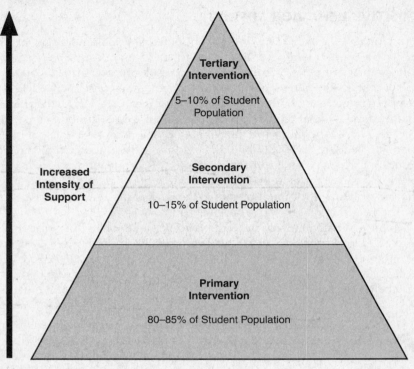

**FIGURE 6.1**    Positive Behavior Support Continuum

In districts with a culturally and linguistically diverse student population, the PBS Team should include members of the community who can represent these diverse backgrounds. Including input from community members in the development of the social expectations of the school is a good way to ensure that the school PBS program includes culturally responsive practices (Jones, Caravaca, Cizek, Horner, & Vincent, 2006).

The PBS team should first examine the administrative discipline contacts and principal's office referrals to identify areas and individuals in need of support. The team should look for patterns in the types of behavior and the times and places where the behavior occurs. (See Table 6.1.) For example, it is obvious from a review of office referrals that Johnny is displaying aggressive behavior during lunch and afternoon recess, so the team may want to consider several options to address this problem, including intensive support. It is less obvious that several students are having problems in math class. Further investigation reveals that all the office referrals are from Mrs. Barker's math class. The team may want to examine the environmental factors of Mrs. Barker's class. Another concern is Beverly, who is sleeping in class. If the office referrals had not been analyzed, Beverly's sleeping incidents in two classes might have gone unnoticed or might have been considered separate incidents. The team will check other office referrals to see if there is a pattern to Beverly's sleeping in class and to determine what level of support, if any, Beverly needs. The team also discovers that 73% of office referrals have occurred during the afternoon, and they may want to investigate this issue further.

Once the office referrals have been analyzed, the PBS team should complete further assessments. These additional assessments could include a survey of students and staff

**TABLE 6.1    Office Referrals**

| Student | Behavior | Place | Date | Time |
|---------|----------|-------|------|------|
| Johnny | Shoving student in line | Cafeteria | 11/13 | 12:01 |
| Mayra | Being disrespectful to teacher | Math Class | 11/13 | 1:30 |
| Johnny | Fighting | Recess | 11/13 | 2:20 |
| Johnny | Threatening student | Cafeteria | 11/15 | 12:07 |
| Jimmy | Cheating on exam | Science Class | 11/15 | 1:00 |
| Beverly | Sleeping in class | Math Class | 11/16 | 8:30 |
| Mayra | Threatening student | Hallway/Between Class | 11/16 | 11:15 |
| Johnny | Fighting | Cafeteria | 11/16 | 12:30 |
| Ted | Refusing to follow directions | Math Class | 11/16 | 2:05 |
| Roberto | Making spit wads | Social Studies Class | 11/17 | 10:43 |
| Mayra | Calling student names | Art Class | 11/17 | 12:55 |
| Johnny | Shoving student | Recess | 11/17 | 2:23 |
| Beverly | Sleeping in class | Social Studies Class | 11/20 | 8:55 |
| Ana | Stealing magazine | Library | 11/20 | 9:15 |
| Johnny | Threatening student | Lunch | 11/20 | 12:30 |
| Sammy | Being disrespectful to teacher | Math Class | 11/20 | 1:20 |
| Johnny | Fighting | Recess | 11/20 | 2:21 |
| Erica | Stealing money | Recess | 11/20 | 2:23 |

about the school environment, to add validity to the process (Safran, 2006). A school-wide screening process along with the analysis of office referrals may increase the number and types of students identified as at-risk. The behaviors of these students could be monitored, and increasing levels of interventions could be provided to them (Walker et al., 2005).

**PRIMARY INTERVENTION** *Primary intervention*, the first level of support, involves all students, staff, and areas (Lewis & Sugai, 1999; Safran, 2006; Walker et al., 2005). One primary intervention would be to adopt a school-wide behavior management system that would make the expectations, consequences, and rewards similar in all classes. It is important for all teachers to accept ownership of a school-wide behavior management plan. Any inconsistencies between classrooms could have negative results and foster inappropriate behavior.

Another primary intervention would be to develop strategies for managing nonacademic areas in the school. The PBS team has noted that a number of office referrals come from recess and the cafeteria. Supervision could be increased in these areas to assist in preventing inappropriate behaviors. Maybe too many students are in the cafeteria at lunch, or maybe the lunch period is too long, allowing students to become restless. The lunch schedule could be redesigned to make optimal use of time and space.

After primary intervention has been implemented school-wide, approximately 80% of the school's student population shows appropriate behavior (Horner & Sugai, 2002; Scott, 2003; Walker et al., 2005). However, a number of students continue to display inappropriate behavior. These students are at risk for developing further emotional and behavior problems that could significantly affect their academic performances. Students at this level may need more intensive interventions.

**TABLE 6.2    Skillstreaming Skill: Avoiding Trouble with Others**

| | |
|---|---|
| 1. Stop and think about the possible consequences of an action. | List and discuss the possible consequences of particular actions with the students. |
| 2. Decide whether you want to stay out of trouble. | Discuss how to decide wether it is important to avoid these consequences. |
| 3. Decide what to tell the other person. | |
| 4. Tell the person. | Discuss how to say no in a friendly but firm way. |

*Source:* From *The Prepare Curriculum* (p. 67) by Goldstein, (1999), Champaign, IL: Research Press. Copyright 1999 by Goldstein. Adapted/reprinted by permission.

**SECONDARY INTERVENTION**    *Secondary intervention* provides specialized support for individual students or classrooms with identified needs. Interventions at this level could include social skills training, school counseling programs, and peer tutoring (Horner & Sugai, 2002; Walker et al., 2005). Strategies for nonacademic areas could be generated from the results of the survey distributed by the PBS Team.

If teachers indicated, for example, that peer pressure is an area of concern, class time could be allocated to teach students the skills they need to resist peer pressure. Effective components of teaching these skills include introduction and instruction of the skill, modeling, role-playing, feedback, and reinforcement of desired behaviors (Miller, Lane, & Wehby, 2005; Turnbull et al., 2002). The teacher begins by introducing the lesson (avoiding being pressured by others) and providing a rationale for learning the skill. The teacher demonstrates the steps (see Table 6.2) by modeling appropriate social behaviors to students in a small group. Once the teacher has modeled the designated behavior, students are given the opportunity to practice behavior through role-playing. During role-playing, the teacher provides feedback on the performance of expected behavior. Once students have learned the desired behavior, teachers should give them tangible and intangible reinforcements (praise, stickers, certificates of recognition, etc.) to help generalize the skill.

Learning environments can also be addressed at the secondary intervention level. According to theories about behavior and ecological systems, appropriate and inappropriate behavior is learned, and behavior is affected by social and environmental factors. The behaviors of students can be traced to the exchanges between peers and teachers. Peer acceptance or rejection, appropriate or inappropriate teacher expectations, consistency of classroom management, and relevancy of academic skills may affect the occurrence of inappropriate student behavior. Identifying these factors is especially important if there are a high number of office referrals from a particular classroom. Over the course of the semester, Mrs. Barker has had a number of referrals from her math class. The number of office referrals from Mrs. Barker could be due to the nonoptimal learning environment she has unintentionally created. Mrs. Barker may be a novice teacher whose lecture-type format is not suitable for the type of students she is teaching. A mentor could be assigned to her to help her develop lessons that are based on real-world applications, manipulatives, or different learning strategies.

Approximately 10% to 15% of the typical school's student population needs secondary intervention (Horner & Sugai, 2002; Scott, 2003; Walker et al., 2005). Students who continue to have chronic and severe behavior problems many need more intensive interventions.

**TERTIARY INTERVENTION**  The final level of Positive Behavior Support is *tertiary intervention*. Students at this level need intensive and comprehensive support and interventions. Although many students needing this level of support do not qualify for special educational services, students with emotional and behavior disorders generally do need the intensive and individualized interventions provided at this level. Interventions at this level could include wraparound services (see Chapter 9), functional behavioral assessments, and contingency contracts (Walker et al., 2005).

## FUNCTIONAL BEHAVIORAL ASSESSMENTS AND BEHAVIOR INTERVENTION PLANS

Since IDEA was reauthorized in 2004, school districts have been required to conduct functional behavioral assessments (FBAs) and to implement behavior intervention plans (BIPs) to address severe, inappropriate behaviors that may result in a change of placement for students with disabilities. Unfortunately, the scope of these requirements is limited. First, school districts are compelled to meet these requirements only if the behavior of the student was caused by or had a direct, substantial relationship to his disability. If the student's behavior was not related to his disability, the school is not required to implement an FBA and BIP. But whether or not the behavior was related to the student's disability, it is judicious for school districts to conduct an FBA and implement a BIP. Taking these actions reflects evidence-based practices and ensures that the student receives a free and appropriate public education (Maag & Katsiyannis, 2006). Second, conducting an FBA and implementing a BIP generally are not required unless the school district is considering removing or changing the placement of a student with a disability. Not requiring these actions until this late point seems contrary to any type of meaningful intervention for students with behavioral problems. Because behavioral issues are a major concern among students with emotional and behavior disorders, it could be argued that conducting an FBA and implementing a BIP should be necessary components of students' IEPs. Finally, whereas IDEA may require FBAs and BIPs under specific circumstances, the federal government does not provide any guidelines for their implementation and development.

Because IDEA 2004 requires BIPs to be based on FBAs, an FBA should take place prior to the implementation of a BIP. FBAs are an evidence-based approach for making environmental and curricular modifications and accommodations for students with emotional and behavior disorders (Maag, 2005).

## CONDUCTING AN FBA

The purposes of FBAs are to clearly identify the problem behavior, determine the antecedent that prompts the behavior, and recognize the reinforcing consequences that maintain the behavior (Erickson, Stage, & Nelson, 2006; Sugai & Horner, 2003). Simply put, an FBA should identify the cause and effect of the inappropriate behavior.

As always in special education, the best practice for implementing an FBA, and subsequently, developing a BIP, is a team-based approach in order to share the work, consider multiple perspectives, and generate a variety of suggestions. The Behavior Intervention Team should include both special and general education teachers, administrators, school counselors, other professionals such as school psychologists or educational diagnosticians, behavioral specialists, and the student's parents. The team's responsibilities include collecting the data for the FBA and developing, implementing, and evaluating the BIP (Maag & Katsiyannis, 2006).

A typical FBA has six basic steps:

1. Clearly define the target behavior.
2. Collect observable data related to the target behavior.
3. Develop a behavioral hypothesis.
4. Develop replacement or alternative behaviors.
5. Generate a BIP.
6. Implement the BIP and evaluate its effectiveness (Barton-Arwood, Wehby, Gunter, & Lane, 2003; Sugai, Lewis-Palmer, & Hagan, 1998).

## Defining Target Behavior

The first step in conducting an FBA is to define the target behavior. Many teachers, professionals, and parents describe behavior in general terms. For example, *Johnny displays aggressive behavior toward others* is a vague definition of behavior. Aggressive behavior could mean different things to different individuals. How is Johnny aggressive? To whom is he aggressive, and when or where does he exhibit this behavior? It is critical that the target behavior is defined in concise, precise, and measurable terms. An inaccurate definition of behavior could result in interventions that are less effective or that even exacerbate the inappropriate behavior (Borgmeiser & Horner, 2006). A better way of defining Johnny's aggressive behavior might be as follows: *Johnny is verbally abusive to his peers at the beginning of mathematics class. Examples of his verbally abusive behavior include calling peers "stupid,"*

## Case Study 6.1

### Johnny

Johnny enters his mathematics classroom. The other students are getting their books and materials from the bookshelf and slowly making their way to their desks. Johnny walks over to Mike, a short, skinny boy who seldom says anything in class.

Johnny looks Mike in the eye, and says, "You are so ugly, Mike, I should rearrange your face after school."

Intimidated, Mike backs away, but Johnny follows him to his desk. "You're so ugly, you're stupid," Johnny tells him.

Mrs. Smart, the math teacher, observes what's going on. She instructs Johnny to get his math book and go to his seat, but Johnny doesn't move.

"Johnny," Mrs. Smart says more sternly, "you need to get to your seat or I'm going to have to send you to the office."

Johnny grudgingly goes to the bookshelf and retrieves his math book. He then goes to his desk in the back of the room, but not before giving Mike another contemptuous glare.

Mrs. Smart shakes her head in frustration. While Johnny has never followed through on any threats, he has been increasingly verbally aggressive toward the other students in her class. She has talked to the school counselor and Johnny's special education teacher. Both have talked to Johnny about his behavior, but it hasn't had any effect. Mrs. Smart wonders what else she could do to reduce and eliminate Johnny's inappropriate behavior.

*telling them they are ugly, and threatening to punch them.* In this statement, Johnny's aggressive behavior has been redefined as being verbally abusive toward peers, and verbally abusive has been further defined in examples of observable behavior.

## Collecting Data

Because FBAs and BIPs are rooted in applied behavior analysis (Safran & Oswald, 2003), it is important to collect information regarding the setting, antecedents, and consequences of the target behavior (Sugai & Horner, 2003). This information is important because in most cases behavior is affected by the events (antecedents) that occur prior to the behavior and by the consequences that follow the behavior. A common method of assessing behavior is the ABC approach. The "A" or antecedent occurs before the "B" or the behavior, and is followed by "C" or the consequence. An ABC Observation Form can be used to record and collect information needed to develop a BIP. (See Figure 6.2.)

*Antecedents* can include the time and place of the behavior, the people involved, and any events that may have occurred just prior to the inappropriate behavior (Mueller, Jenson, Reavis, & Andrews, 2002). For example, *Johnny is verbally abusive to his peers at the beginning of mathematics class.* The time and place of Johnny's behavior is at the beginning of mathematics class, but are there any other antecedents? Through direct observation of Johnny's behavior, Mrs. Smart, the mathematics teacher, has noted that Johnny is only verbally abusive toward male students. She also wonders if the unstructured time during

| Student's Name _____ Observer _____ | | |
| Dates of Observation _____ | | |
| **Antecedents Prior to Behavior** | **Behavior** | **Consequences Following Behavior** |
| --- | --- | --- |
| Time | Operational Definition | Reinforcements |
| Place | | |
| People | Frequency | |
| | Duration | |
| Events | Intensity | Permanent Products |
| Additional Comments | | |

**FIGURE 6.2** ABC Observation Form

Students's Name _Johnny Martin_          Observer _Mrs. I. M. Smart_

Dates of Observation _March 17-21, 2008_

| Antecedents Prior to Behavior | Behavior | Consequences Following Behavior |
|---|---|---|
| Time    _9:45 am_ _Beginning_ _of class_ | Operational Definition | Reinforcements |
| Place _Math Class_ | | |
| People _Male peers_ | Frequency | |
| | Duration | |
| Events _Students coming_ _into class._ _Students getting_ _their materials_  . | Intensity | Permanent Products |

Additional Comments

**FIGURE 6.3**   ABC Observation Form: Antecedents

which students are arriving at class and getting their materials prior to sitting at their desks could be a factor in Johnny's behavior. Mrs. Smart records this information on the ABC Observation Form. (See Figure 6.3.)

Behavior can be described by three attributes. These attributes are frequency, intensity, and duration, and each can be measured using simple direct observations. _Frequency_ refers to how often the behavior occurs in a specific time. Frequency recording or event-based recording includes the length of the observation, the number of times the target behavior occurs, and the rate of the behavior, which can be calculated by dividing the number of times the behavior occurs by the length of the observation. For example, Johnny was verbally abusive to male peers five times in a 30-minute period on Monday. The rate of the behavior is 5/30, or .17 times per minute. (See Figure 6.4.) Frequency recording is the easiest of the three behavior attributes for teachers to score because they only have to record the behavior when it occurs.

_Intensity_ refers to the amount of force used when the behavior is displayed. This attribute of behavior is pertinent because it is aligned with the federal definition of _emotional disturbance_, which states that the inappropriate behavior is present to a "marked" degree. However, intensity is very difficult to measure and is often subjective. If Johnny came into the classroom and began calling a peer names, intensity could describe how loud Johnny was. Was it only loud enough for the peer to hear? Was it loud enough for the teacher to hear or loud enough to reach the classroom next door?

Student's Name _Johnny Martin_          Observer _Mrs. I. M. Smart_

Week _March 17-21, 2008_          Place _Math Class_

Description of Target Behavior _Verbally abusive to peers, which includes calling peers "stupid", telling them they are ugly, and threatening to punch them._

| Day | Length of Observation | Frequency of Target Behavior | Total | Rate of Behavior |
|---|---|---|---|---|
| Monday | 9:45–10:15 30 minutes | ⁤ꜰ 5 | 5 | 5/30 = .17 |
| Tuesday | 9:45–10:00 15 minutes | ⁤ꜰ 4 | 4 | 4/15 = .27 |
| Wednesday | 9:45–10:05 20 minutes | ⁤ꜰ 3 | 3 | 3/20 = .15 |
| Thursday | 9:45–10:10 25 minutes | ⁤ꜰ 7 | 7 | 7/25 = .28 |
| Friday | 9:50–10:00 10 minutes | ⁤ꜰ 3 | 3 | 3/10 = .3 |
| **Total** | | | 22 | 22/100 = .22 |

**FIGURE 6.4**  Frequency Recording: Johnny

*Duration* refers to the period of time that the behavior continues. This method of assessment is difficult for a teacher because he or she has to notice and record each time the behavior begins and when it ends. In a classroom of 25 students, duration recording would be difficult and impractical. In a special education classroom, this type of assessment might be practical only if the number of students in the classroom was small enough for the teacher to conduct the assessment. If Johnny was verbally abusive to a peer beginning at 9:45 and ending at 9:50, the duration of the behavior would be 5 minutes. (See Figure 6.5.) Duration recording might be cumbersome for Johnny's target behavior, but might be more appropriate for measuring how long a student stayed on task or how long it took a student to comply with directions.

Other methods of collecting data could include using interviews and completing behavioral rating scales. (See Chapter 4.) The difficulties in collecting these types of data are that teachers generally are not trained to do such assessments and they lack the time to implement multifaceted and lengthy assessment procedures (Barton-Arwood et al., 2003). The description of the behavior also may be too narrowly defined. For example, if the teacher is recording instances in which Johnny threatens to punch peers, and one day Johnny threatens to slap a peer, it would constitute a case of inappropriate behavior. But if he takes a pencil from a peer and breaks it in front of the peer in an intimidating manner, the behavior cannot be recorded because it does not meet the parameters of the behavior the teacher is recording.

Once the data on behavior have been collected, it should be recorded on the ABC Observation Form. (See Figure 6.6.)

Consequences that follow the behavior are either positive or negative reinforcers. Positive reinforcement increases the probability the behavior will occur again. For example, Mary receives a gold star on any assignment in which she earns 90% or better. If Mary likes

| Student's Name | Johnny Martin | | Observer | Mrs. I. M. Smart |

Student's Name _Johnny Martin_    Observer _Mrs. I. M. Smart_
Week _March 17-21, 2008_    Place _Math Class_

Description of Target Behavior _Verbally abusive to peers, which includes calling peers "stupid", telling them they are ugly, and threatening to punch them._

| Day | Behavior Began | Behavior Ended | Duration |
|---|---|---|---|
| Monday 9:45-10:15 30 minutes | 9:45 9:54 9:58 10:07 10:14 | 9:50 9:57 10:00 10:11 10:15 | 5 minutes 3 minutes 2 minutes 4 minutes 1 minute |
| Tuesday 9:45-10:00 15 minutes | 9:46 9:49 9:54 9:57 | 9:47 9:51 9:56 10:00 | 1 minute 2 minutes 2 minutes 3 minutes |
| Wednesday 9:45-10:00 20 minutes | 9:47 9:55 10:02 | 9:50 9:59 10:04 | 3 minutes 4 minutes 2 minutes |
| Total | | | 32 minutes |

**FIGURE 6.5**  Duration Recording: Johnny

Student's Name _Johnny Martin_    Observer _Mrs. I. M. Smart_

Dates of Observation _March 17-21, 2008_

| Antecedents Prior to Behavior | Behavior | Consequences Following Behavior |
|---|---|---|
| Time    9:45 am Beginning of class Place   Math Class People   Male peers | Operational Definition Calling peers "stupid", telling them they are ugly, and threatening to punch them. Frequency 22% of time observed. Duration 32 mins. out of 65 mins. | Reinforcements |
| Events Students coming into class. Students getting their materials. | Intensity Loud enough for the teacher and other peers to hear. | Permanent Products |
| Additional Comments | | |

**FIGURE 6.6**  ABC Observation Form: Behavior

receiving gold stars, she will probably try to do well on other assignments. Negative reinforcement also increases the probability that the behavior will occur again by removing an aversive response to the behavior. For example, Johnny is consistently late to his math class. When he is late, he does not have to spend the few minutes at the beginning of class interacting with peers whom he does not like. He is likely to continue to be late so that he can continue to avoid this unpleasant interaction. Teachers need to be careful about using positive or negative reinforcement. Positive and negative reinforcement can increase appropriate behavior, but these techniques also can inadvertently increase inappropriate behavior.

The consequences of the target behavior are recorded on the ABC Observation Form. (See Figure 6.7.) The teacher needs to describe any positive or negative behaviors that occurred after the behavior and any possible motives for the student's behavior (such as gaining attention) (Mueller et al., 2002).

*Permanent products* are the results of behavior. These measures can be an important aspect of an FBA. For example, a permanent product of a behavior could be the number of assignments completed or the number of pencils the student has broken in frustration. Permanent products are generally physical by-products of behavior. These also should be recorded on the ABC Observation Form.

## Developing a Behavioral Hypothesis

The next step is developing a *behavioral hypothesis*, a prediction of the factors that elicit the inappropriate behavior. These factors could include a desire to avoid an activity or situation, a desire to seek attention, reinforcement of the target behavior, or other causes. This is an important step of conducting an FBA because the BIP will be formulated on the basis of the behavioral hypothesis.

The Behavior Intervention Team needs to analyze all available data regarding the student's behavior and then create a summary emphasizing the factors that cause and maintain the target behavior (Sugar & Horner, 2003). The team should determine the most plausible and testable explanation for the occurrence of the behavior (Curtiss, Mathur, & Rutherford, 2002). In Johnny's case, they should ask *Why is Johnny verbally abusive toward peers?* and *What is the function of the target behavior?*

The team knows that Johnny is verbally abusive toward male peers at the beginning of math class. Using the ABC Observation Form and direct observations from other members of the team, the team can develop several plausible explanations for his behavior. First, during the first several minutes of math class, students are arriving at class, getting their books from the bookshelf, going to their seats, and receiving materials that the teacher is passing out. It is possible that Johnny cannot handle unstructured time. Second, maybe the reaction that Johnny receives from peers reinforces his behavior. Third, maybe the function of his behavior is to elicit attention from the teacher. The Behavior Intervention Team could choose one or all of the plausible explanations for Johnny's behavior as the core of a behavioral hypothesis.

The team develops the following behavioral hypothesis for Johnny:

*There is a relationship between Johnny's verbally abusive behavior toward male peers and*

  **a.**  *the unstructured time at the beginning of mathematics class,*
  **b.**  *the response he receives from peers, and*
  **c.**  *the attention he receives from the mathematics teacher.*

Student's Name   _Johnny Martin_          Observer   _Mrs. I. M. Smart_

Dates of Observation   _March 17-21, 2008_

| Antecedents Prior to Behavior | Behavior | Consequences Following Behavior |
|---|---|---|
| Time   9:45 am Beginning of class Place   Math Class People   Male peers | Operational Definition   Calling peers "stupid", telling them they are ugly, and threatening to punch them. Frequency   22% of time observed. Duration   32 mins. out of 65 mins. | Reinforcements   Students back away from Johnny. Facial expressions show fear, hurt feelings. They leave him alone. Teacher reprimands Johnny – maybe he is seeking teacher's attention. |
| Events   Students coming into class. Students getting their materials. | Intensity   Loud enough for the teacher and other peers to hear. | Permanent Products   None |
| Additional Comments | | |

**FIGURE 6.7**   ABC Observation Form: Consequences

## Developing Replacement or Alternative Behaviors

Once the Behavior Intervention Team has developed the behavioral hypothesis, it needs to develop alternative and replacement behaviors. The BIP is based on manipulating the antecedents and consequences of behavior in an attempt to reduce and replace the target behavior. Four interventions that are useful for developing alternative and replacement behaviors are environmental modifications, instructional strategies, consequent intervention, and future alternative/replacement behavior.

*Environmental modifications* affect the antecedents that occur in the setting in which the behavior occurs. Antecedent modifications should be developed to prevent or decrease the occurrence of the target behavior and to increase the probability of appropriate behavior. Environmental modifications may include rearranging the physical layout of the classroom, managing transition times, and altering the routes that students take to and from the bathroom, playground, or cafeteria (Curtiss et al., 2002; Maag & Katsiyannis, 2006). To decrease Johnny's target behavior, the teacher may need to provide more structure during the first 15 minutes of class. She may need to have all mathematics books and materials on students' desks before the beginning of class to diminish the time that students spend off-task. She may need to engage students in the lesson sooner.

*Instructional strategies* alter the method and manner in which academic material is presented. Students with emotional or behavior disorders often are not motivated by traditional teaching methods. These students find academic tasks to be aversive, and their inappropriate behaviors and poor academic performances are an attempt to avoid completing academic assignments (Maag, 2004; Penno, Frank, & Wacker, 2000). To implement new instructional strategies, the teacher may change the delivery of instruction or make changes to the curriculum, instructional objectives, and methodology. (See Chapter 8.)

*Consequent intervention* alters behavior by changing the consequences of the behavior. The two types of consequent interventions that should be included in the BIP are positive reinforcement and differential reinforcement. Positive reinforcements include token economies, behavioral contracts, and group contingencies that are applied to a group of students or to the entire class (Hansen & Lignugaris/Kraft, 2005; Maag & Katsiyannis, 2006). Differential reinforcement includes reinforcement of other behavior (DRO), low rates of behavior (DRL), and incompatible behavior (DRI).

Differential reinforcement of other behavior (DRO) includes reinforcement of any appropriate behavior that is not the target behavior. For example, Johnny's target behavior is calling peers inappropriate names. If Johnny is sitting in his seat and completing his assignment, the teacher could reinforce this other behavior by commenting positively on how he is working on his assignment.

The frequency of inappropriate behavior can be reduced by reinforcing the target behavior only when it occurs at a lower rate of frequency by applying differential reinforcement of low rates of behavior (DRL). The reinforcement of the target behavior is gradually reduced over a period of time until the frequency rate is at a tolerably low level or until the behavior is eliminated completely. The appropriate behavior, which is occurring at a lower rate of frequency, is reinforced when it occurs at an increasingly higher rate. For example, the teacher could provide Johnny with student-preferred reinforcement such as computer time if he does not verbally abuse peers more than three times in a class period. At the same time, the teacher provides reinforcement whenever Johnny interacts appropriately with peers. Later, the teacher may change the frequency criteria for a reward to two times per class period, while increasing reinforcement of the appropriate behavior. The goal is to decrease the inappropriate behavior to zero times per class period.

Differential reinforcement of incompatible behavior (DRI) is reinforcing an appropriate behavior that is incompatible with the target behavior in an effort to reduce and eliminate the target behavior. For example, if Johnny is being verbally abusive toward peers to get the teacher's attention, then the teacher will provide attention to Johnny only when his behavior is appropriate.

The last type of intervention for developing alternative behaviors is *future alternative/ replacement behaviors*, which are appropriate behaviors that serve the same function as the inappropriate behavior. The reduction and elimination of the target behavior is more likely if the student develops a repertoire of alternative responses to situations that involve social skills, anger management, self-management, and problem-solving strategies (Curtiss et al., 2002). These alternative responses can be taught through replacement behavior training. Replacement behavior training teaches students appropriate alternative/replacement behaviors that serve the same purpose as the target behavior. Reinforcing the alternative/replacement behavior will decrease the frequency of the target behavior (Maag & Katsiyannis, 2006).

Replacement behavior training begins by making a list of alternative/replacement behaviors that are in the same response class as the target behavior and that serve the same function as the target behavior (for example, attention-seeking). The student is asked to rank the alternative/replacement behavior from this list that he would be most willing to perform.

The student is taught the alternative/replacement behavior using social skills intervention. (See Chapter 7.) Finally, a powerful reinforcement is provided to increase the probability that the student will perform the alternative/replacement behavior (Maag & Kemp, 2003).

Once the Behavior Intervention Team has developed some replacement or alternative behaviors, the team needs to generate a BIP. The BIP should include information obtained from the FBA, specific behavior goals, intervention strategies, and a method to assess the effectiveness of the plan.

## DEVELOPING A BIP

The purpose of a BIP is to implement strategies that will reduce or eliminate inappropriate behavior. BIPs are individualized plans that must be developed if the behavior is interfering with the student's learning. They should include positive behavior strategies that are based on the FBA. After the BIP has been implemented, its effects should be monitored (Etscheidt, 2006).

### Generating a BIP

Although there are no federal guidelines to help the Behavior Intervention Team develop a plan, Curtiss et al. (2002) have identified the following eight components of a BIP (see Figure 6.8) :

1. Definition of Target Behavior
2. Summary of Functional Behavior Analysis
3. Behavioral Hypothesis
4. Behavioral Goal 1 (Reduction of Behavior)
5. Objectives to Meet Goal 1
6. Behavioral Goal 2 (Replacement or Alternative Behavior)
7. Objectives to Meet Goal 2
8. Monitoring Plan

© Royalty Free/CORBIS

Student-preferred reinforcements, like computer time, can help reduce the frequency of the target behavior.

**Behavioral Intervention Plan (BIP)**

Student _____    Date _____

Team Members _____    Age _____

_____

_____

Start Date _____    Review Date _____

**Definition of Target Behavior**

**Summary of Functional Behavioral Analysis**
1. Frequency, intensity, and duration of target behavior
2. Setting of target behavior
3. Antecedents of target behavior
4. Consequences of target behavior

**Behavioral Hypothesis**
1. Avoidance of an activity
2. Attention-seeking
3. Reinforcement of target behavior
4. Other functions

**Behavioral Goal 1 (Reduction of Behavior)**
1. Specific definition of behavior to reduce
2. Timeline for implementation and review

**Objectives to Meet Goal 1**
1. Identify intervention strategies
2. Designate persons to implement strategies
3. Monitor the effectiveness of strategies

**Behavioral Goal 2 (Replacement or Alternative Behavior)**
1. Specific definition of behavior to promote
2. Timeline for implementation and review

**Objectives to Meet Goal 2**
1. Identify intervention strategies
2. Designate persons to implement strategies
3. Monitor the effectiveness of strategies

**Monitoring Plan**
1. List the strategies for monitoring the effectiveness of the Behavioral Intervention Plan

**FIGURE 6.8**  Behavioral Intervention Plan

*Source:* Curtiss, Mathur, & Rutherford, 2002.
Adapted/reprinted by permission.

Most of the information needed to complete the BIP can be provided by the FBA. The definition of the target behavior and the summary of the FBA can be obtained from the ABC Observation Form that was completed during the FBA. The Behavior Intervention Team has already developed the behavioral hypothesis. Next, they must identify behavioral goals and develop intervention strategies to reduce behaviors or reinforce replacement and alternative behaviors. The strategies to meet the behavioral goals need to include the intervention strategies, the individuals who will implement the strategies, and the method of monitoring the effectiveness of the intervention strategies. For example, the Behavior Intervention Team has decided that one of Johnny's goals is to reduce his verbally abusive behavior toward peers. The intervention strategies include environmental modification by making the first 15 minutes of class more structured and initiating a DRO procedure. Johnny's teachers will be responsible for implementing the plan, and the effectiveness of the interventions will be monitored through observations. (See Figure 6.9.)

## Implementing and Evaluating the Effectiveness of the BIP

After the behavior intervention plan has been implemented, the effectiveness of the plan needs to be monitored on a continuous basis (Curtiss et al., 2002; Etscheidt, 2006; Maag & Katsiyannis, 2006). The Behavior Intervention Team should determine whether the plan is having any effect on the target behavior and whether it needs to be revised. This task can be completed through direct observation and the completion of an ABC Observation Form. If the target behavior has not been reduced or eliminated, or if it has been exacerbated, the Behavior Intervention Team needs to reconvene and develop new behavioral goals and intervention strategies.

## Implications of BIPs

The implementation of FBAs and BIPs are mandated by IDEA when school districts seek a change in a student's placement due to behavior caused by his or her disability. Yet these mandates pose many difficulties for teachers, administrators, and school districts. Many teachers are not adequately trained to perform lengthy or complex assessments, and due to the increasing demands placed on teachers by administrators, parents, and government agencies, teachers do not have the time they need to implement assessment procedures (Killu, Weber, Derby, & Barretto, 2006; Sugai, Horner, & Sprague, 1999).

Another problem involving FBAs and BIPs is that the process is reactive. A school is not required to perform the procedures unless the school is seeking to change a student's current placement due to severe behavior or if the school is considering expelling the student. Yet FBAs and BIPs could be valuable proactive measures, not just reactive ones. Using them as positive and proactive interventions may reduce or eliminate behaviors that, if unchecked, could lead to a change of placement or expulsion.

Using FBAs and BIPs as positive and proactive interventions may also prevent and reduce the unwarranted referrals of minority students. Compared with European American or Hispanic males, African American males are 2–3 times more likely to be suspended, and 2–5 times more likely to be identified as having emotional and behavior disorders (Coutinho et al., 2002; Mendez & Knoff, 2003). Implementing FBAs and BIPs prior to and during placement may reduce the number of referrals and suspensions of African American males (Lo & Cartledge, 2006).

FBAs and BIPs can assist teachers, administrators, and paraprofessionals in reducing and replacing the inappropriate behaviors of students with emotional and behavior disorders.

## Behavioral Intervention Plan (BIP)

Student _Johnny Martin_                     Date _March 21, 2008_

Team Members _Mrs. I. M. Smart_            Age _12 years, 8 months_

        _Mrs. B. Whasit_

        _Mr. E. Bower_

Start Date _March 24, 2010_                 Review Date _May 23, 2010_

### Definition of Target Behavior

Johnny is verbally abusive to his peers at the beginning of mathematics class. Examples of his verbally abusive behavior include calling peers "stupid," telling them they are ugly, and threatening to punch them.

### Summary of Functional Behavioral Analysis

An applied behavioral analysis was conducted, and the results show that Johnny is verbally abusive 22% of the time during the first 30 minutes of math class.

### Behavioral Hypothesis

Johnny may not be able to handle the unstructured time at the beginning of math class. Johnny may be seeking attention from the teacher.

### Behavioral Goal 1 (Reduction of Behavior)

Johnny will reduce his verbally abusive behavior toward peers in math class.

### Objectives to Meet Goal 1

The teacher will implement environmental modification by increasing structured time during the first 15 minutes of math class by having books and materials on students' desks prior to class and by the beginning the lesson immediately. The teacher will initiate a differential reinforcement of other behavior (DRO) procedure by reinforcing any appropriate behaviors Johnny displays when he is not engaging in the target behavior. The effectiveness of the interventions will be monitored through observations.

### Behavioral Goal 2 (Replacement or Alternative Behavior)

Johnny will engage with male peers in an appropriate manner in math class.

### Objectives to Meet Goal 2

Johnny will receive replacement behavior training and social skills training from the school counselor. The effectiveness of this training will be monitored through observations.

### Monitoring Plan

The effectiveness of the BIP will be monitored through classroom observations and applied behavior analysis (ABC Observation Form). If Johnny does not show significant improvement, the team will meet prior to the review date. The effectiveness of the BIP will be assessed, and if necessary, a new plan will be developed.

**FIGURE 6.9**  Behavioral Intervention Plan: Johnny

*Source:* Curtiss, Mathur, & Rutherford, 2002.
Adapted/reprinted by permission.

To be effective, school personnel need the time, training, and administrative support to develop and implement these interventions.

## CLASSROOM BEHAVIOR MANAGEMENT

A number of classroom behavior management plans that can be implemented in the general and special education classrooms are effective for students with emotional and behavior disorders. Many of these strategies are based on Skinner's theory of operant conditioning (1994), in which the consequences following the behavior can either strengthen or weaken the undesired behavior or the desired behavior. These strategies are relatively easy to implement. They include classroom behavior strategies, positive and negative reinforcements, shaping, punishment, contingency contracts, token economies, and level systems.

## Classroom Behavior Strategies

*Classroom behavior strategies* are teacher-mediated strategies and are the simplest available interventions (Scott, 2003). These strategies generally involve an immediate response from the teacher to the student's inappropriate behavior. Classroom behavior strategies are not difficult to implement and do not require a large amount of time, which makes them more acceptable to classroom teachers. Many of these strategies are effective in reducing inappropriate behavior, but their effectiveness is often contingent on the rapport the teacher has with the students. Such strategies include planned ignoring, proximity control, signal interference, redirection, tension reduction, and removal of seductive objects.

*Planned ignoring* is withdrawing the reinforcement (usually attention) of the inappropriate behavior. The teacher simply does not respond to the inappropriate behavior. The behavior is usually relatively minor and is not likely to affect other students. For example, the teacher asks the class a question, and Johnny blurts out the answer. By ignoring Johnny's behavior, the teacher reduces the chance that he will continue to respond to questions without raising his hand. When Johnny does raise his hand in response to the teacher's question, the teacher should immediately call on him. This "catch 'em being good" strategy increases the probability that the appropriate behavior will be repeated. Planned ignoring can be an effective means of extinction of minor behaviors if it is used properly. However, if the behavior escalates and the teacher eventually responds to it, the teacher has reinforced the inappropriate behavior at a more intense level (Obenchain & Taylor, 2005). For example, when the teacher does not respond to Johnny's behavior, he continues to call out the answer without raising his hand and his outbursts grow louder. Finally, the teacher responds to Johnny's behavior and acknowledges the answer that he has called out, increasing the chance that next time he will call out the answer at this louder level. For planned ignoring to work effectively, the teacher needs to ignore the behavior completely even if it escalates.

*Proximity control* involves the teacher moving close to or standing beside the student who is behaving inappropriately. By being near the student, the teacher exerts a calming influence that helps the student to redirect his or her attention to the task at hand. For example, the teacher observes that Johnny is whispering to another student while the rest of the class is working on their math assignments. She quietly walks over to his desk and stands beside him. Johnny immediately quits whispering and refocuses on his assignment. Sometimes the teacher may place her hand on the student's desk or on the student's shoulder to emphasize her presence, but care should be taken. The teacher should make sure that she knows her students well enough to judge their likely response to this technique. Some students do not like to be touched, especially students with emotional and behavior disorders who have been physically and sexually abused.

*Signal interference* uses nonverbal cues to convey the teacher's disapproval of the student's inappropriate behavior. These cues could include hand gestures, facial expressions (frowns), and eye contact. Hand gestures could include thumbs up (approval), thumbs down (disapproval), or the number of fingers held up that corresponds to the number of the classroom rule. For example, Johnny is blurting out answers instead of raising his hand. The teacher makes eye contact with Johnny and holds up two fingers, which correspond to rule number two, *raise your hand*.

*Redirection* is a simple request from the teacher that the student discontinue his inappropriate behavior. When redirecting the student, the teacher should make sure that he or she has the student's attention, usually by using the student's name prior to the request. The teacher should not insist on eye contact; this may violate the cultural norms of linguistically and ethnically diverse students. The teacher should not point her finger at the student nor insist on having the last word. The request should be made in a positive manner. For example, *Johnny, you need to focus on your work*, instead of *Johnny, quit being lazy and do your work*. Redirections work well if you follow the basic principles of guerilla tactics: Make your point quickly and withdraw. This method prevents any type of power struggle between the teacher and the student.

*Tension reduction* is accomplished by using humor in difficult situations. Humor alleviates tension and can be used effectively with students with emotional and behavior disorders. For example, when Jimmy was frustrated with his math assignment, he went up to Mr. Poteet's desk and shoved a stack of books onto the floor. Grading papers at his desk, Mr. Poteet looks up at Jimmy, and said, "Thank you, Jimmy. I needed my desk cleared off." Mr. Poteet goes back to grading his papers. Dumbfounded, Jimmy stares at Mr. Poteet for a moment, and then picks up the books. Maintaining a sense of humor is also essential for the teacher's mental health and may help reduce his or her personal stress.

All students bring distracting items to class at one time or another. The teacher should simply remove the seductive objects and inform the student that the item will be returned at the end of class. This strategy will help prevent escalation of the behavior.

## Positive and Negative Reinforcements

A positive reinforcement is a stimulus that increases the frequency or strength of a behavior by giving the student a reward. Positive reinforcements should be given immediately after the student displays appropriate behavior. Positive reinforcements could include praise, a pat on the back, stickers, or computer time. These reinforcements are easy to use, take little or no preparation time, and are effective for many students. The most underused and most effective form of positive reinforcement with students who have emotional and behavior disorders is teacher praise. Studies have shown that teacher praise has positive effects on the academic outcomes and classroom behavior of students with emotional and behavior disorders (Sutherland, Copeland, & Wehby, 2001; Sutherland, Wehby, & Yoder, 2002). Yet teachers often select more punitive interventions when they feel that a behavior threatens their needs as instructors or when behaviors are too difficult for them to handle (Ishii-Jordan, 2000).

Teacher praise should be used immediately after the student displays the appropriate behavior, should be stated with sincerity, and should include a statement of the behavior. For example, if Johnny is diligently working on his assignment during class time, the teacher could say, "I like the way that Johnny is working on his assignment." Teachers should try to avoid using the word "good" because it denotes that another behavior could be "bad," and students often assume that "good" or "bad" describes them, not the behavior.

As with all reinforcements, teachers need to be careful that a negative reinforcement does not inadvertently increase an inappropriate behavior. For example, if Johnny's math teacher is constantly criticizing Johnny for his poor grades, he may avoid the negative reinforcement by not attending class.

Negative reinforcements could include verbal reprimands, frowns, or stern looks, all to be used immediately after the student displays the inappropriate behavior. Like positive reinforcements, negative reinforcements should address the behavior rather than the student.

## Shaping

A student may not reduce or eliminate target behaviors immediately because it may be beyond his or her abilities to meet the teacher's behavioral expectation (Horner, Sugai, Todd, & Lewis-Palmer, 2005). In such cases, the teacher can resort to shaping to at least achieve an approximation of the desired outcome. *Shaping* is the process of reinforcing successive approximations of the desired behavior (Downing, 2007; Kauffman, 2005; Kerr & Nelson, 2006). For example, Araceli is a student with emotional and behavior disorders who also has ADHD. Her target behavior is not remaining in her seat, but she has difficulty meeting the desired or replacement behavior of staying in her seat because of her ADHD. Through shaping, Araceli's teacher reinforces increments of the desired behavior. At first, the teacher reinforces Araceli's desired behavior after she remains in her seat for 10 seconds. The teacher waits increasing amounts of time to provide reinforcement to Araceli for remaining in her seat.

It is important to remember that a student may never meet the teacher's ultimate expectation of desired behavior. The teacher may have to measure success by the improvement the student has made toward the desired behavior.

## Punishment

*Punishment* decreases the frequency or strength of a behavior by following the behavior with an aversive consequence. Punishment is different from reinforcement because punishment decreases the target behavior, whereas reinforcement increases the target behavior. A drawback of punishment is that it focuses on decreasing inappropriate behavior rather than on increasing appropriate behavior. Three types of punishment are response cost, time-outs, and overcorrection.

Response cost refers to a loss of a privilege or a loss of a reinforcer. Generally, students lose points, tokens, or privileges that they have already earned. For example, Johnny gets angry and throws his books across the classroom. As a result he will not go to McDonald's for lunch on Friday, a privilege he had previously earned.

*Time-out* is a behavior reduction procedure in which the student is denied access to all opportunities for reinforcement of the behavior or removed from class activities because of his or her behavior (Alberto & Troutman, 2006). Different levels of time-outs may be used: inclusion time-out, exclusion time-out, and seclusion time-out. *Inclusion time-out* is the least restrictive form of time-out. The student is allowed to remain in his or her seat and observe classroom instruction, but does not have any opportunities to participate or receive reinforcements (Ryan, Sanders, Katsiyannis, & Yell, 2007). Planned ignoring could be considered a form of inclusion time-out. Another form of inclusion time-out is contingent observation, in which the student moves to another location in the classroom such as a corner or a time-out chair. The student can still observe what is going on in the classroom and is near the work environment but is unable to participate or earn reinforcements.

An *exclusion time-out* involves seating the student away from the work environment, at the back of the room or in a corner. The student is not required to observe what is going on in the classroom. He or she could be placed in the corner facing the wall or in a study carrel.

In a *seclusion time-out*, the student is removed from the classroom. This is the most restrictive form of time-out. The student is generally removed to a specified area such as a time-out room. The time-out room should be well ventilated, well lighted, and quiet. The purpose of moving the student here is to remove a disruptive influence from the classroom setting so that learning can continue for the remaining students. It also offers the disruptive student an opportunity to calm down in a neutral setting.

*Overcorrection* is a procedure for reducing or eliminating inappropriate behavior by requiring the student to repeat a corrective behavior many times or to make restitution. Having a student write "I will not talk without permission" 50 times on the chalkboard is an example of overcorrection. The two types of overcorrection are positive practice and restitutional. Positive practice overcorrection requires the student who has displayed the inappropriate behavior to practice the appropriate behavior repeatedly. For example, a student who runs down the hallway is called back by the teacher and asked to appropriately walk down the hallway several times. Restitutional overcorrection requires the student to restore the effects of her behavior on the environment to a state that is better than before she disrupted the environment. For example, a student who writes on her desk may be required to clean all the desks in the classroom.

Punishment should be used with caution. Racial, ethnical, and socioeconomic factors influence the type of interventions that teachers use with students. Students from lower socioeconomic groups and African Americans, who often display externalizing behaviors, receive punishment more often than other students. Teachers need to recognize their own personal biases and be sensitive to the backgrounds of their students (Ishii-Jordan, 2000). Punishment should be used only when the student's behavior is dangerous to the student or others, when other interventions have failed, or when the behavior is so disruptive that it prevents learning from taking place (Quinn et al., 2000).

Punishment should be used in conjunction with other behavior management strategies. Research has shown that punishment alone does not reduce inappropriate behavior, and when it is applied without positive supports, punishment can exacerbate the inappropriate behavior. The Council for Children with Behavior Disorders (CCBD) has strongly encouraged school districts to move beyond punishment and instead to implement behavior interventions that increase appropriate behaviors (CCBD, 2002).

## Contingency Contracts

A *contingency contract* is a formal, written agreement between the student and teacher that can be used to address the behavioral, academic, and social goals of the student. This behavior strategy is based on the Premack Principle or Grandma's Law: "First you eat your supper" (low-probability behavior, one that the student is unlikely to do on his or her own), "and then you can have dessert" (high-probability behavior, one in which the student readily engages). Another way to state it is "First do what I want you to do; then you may do what you want to do" (Habel & Bernard, 1999). The high-probability behavior is used to reinforce the low-probability behavior (Coleman & Webber, 2002). Contingency contracts have been effective in decreasing a number of inappropriate behaviors and increasing appropriate behaviors (Garrick Duhaney, 2003; Walker et al., 2004).

One of the advantages of a contingency contract is that the student actively participates in developing the contract. The student and teacher determine what behavior will be targeted (either increasing a desired behavior, or decreasing an inappropriate behavior), and what consequences are to be administered if the student succeeds in following the agreement or fails to follow the agreement. A contingency contract should include reinforcements that either increase or decrease the behavior, such as praise and reprimands (Garrick Duhaney, 2003; Nelson, Martella, & Marchand-Martella, 2002).

For example, Johnny and Mrs. Smart, his teacher, negotiate a contingency contract designed to reduce his verbally aggressive behavior toward others. The contract states that if Johnny refrains from calling peers "stupid," telling them they are ugly, and threatening to punch them, he will be allowed to listen to his iPod for the last 5 minutes of class, read a *Hot Rod* magazine at the library, or have lunch with Mrs. Smart. These incentives were chosen on the basis of Johnny's interests. In addition to providing the incentives, Mrs. Smart would immediately praise Johnny's appropriate behavior or reprimand him for his inappropriate behavior. She would use calm, firm, and consistent reprimands stated in a positive manner.

## Token Economy

A *token economy* is a behavior management system that dispenses tokens which can be exchanged for selected reinforcers. Tokens can be play money, stickers, points, checkmarks, or any other inexpensive items. The tokens are systematically awarded to students for engaging in appropriate behaviors and are traded for selected reinforcers. Research has shown that token economy systems have been successful in reducing inappropriate behavior and improving academic performance.

To implement a token economy in the classroom, a teacher needs to follow some basic steps:

1. Identify the target behavior or rules to be reinforced.
2. With student input, identify the reinforcers (for example, being allowed to skip an assignment or receiving candy bars, pencils, compact discs, etc.).
3. Determine the price or number of tokens a student must earn in order to receive a reinforcer.
4. Introduce and explain the token system to the students.
5. Design a system for monitoring the tokens each student earns and spends.
6. Implement the system (Garrick Duhaney, 2003; Myles, Moran, Ormsbee, & Downing, 1992; Salend, 2001).

For example, Johnny earned a score of 100% on a recent math assignment. According to the token system, he can earn $100 in play money every time he earns 100% on an assignment. He has earned a total of $1,800 from following the classroom rules, completing assignments, and refraining from being verbally aggressive toward his peers. During the last 5 minutes of class, which have been set aside for students to redeem their money for reinforcers, Johnny purchases a compact disc from the classroom store.

Providing reinforcers can be problematic. Reinforcers are often not part of a classroom budget, so, as a result, the teacher may have to bear the cost of providing reinforcers. This could be difficult if the teacher is on a limited budget. Fortunately, some reinforcers are inexpensive (for example, computer time and eating lunch with the teacher).

## Level System

A *level system* is a hierarchy of expected behaviors based on a token economy. Each level has clearly defined behavioral expectations and reinforcements. Students can advance to the next hierarchical level when they have demonstrated the appropriate behavior on their current level for a specified period of time, usually 1 week. For example, expected behaviors for Level 1 are following directions and abiding by classroom rules. The student earns 10 points (tokens) each day for 5 days and earns 50 points for the week. As a result, the student moves to Level 2 the following week, where the student is expected to follow directions and rules and also to complete all assignments. The student must meet the behavioral expectations of this level before advancing to Level 3 (Farrell, Smith, & Brownell, 1998). The reinforcers are different at each level. For example, on Level 1, the student may earn 5 minutes of quiet time at her desk at the end of the class, while another student on Level 3 may earn 10 minutes of computer time at the end of the class.

The level system seems to provide the structure that teachers need to manage student behavior (Farrell et al., 1998). Used in conjunction with reinforcements and interventions that increase appropriate behavior, it can be a viable classroom management program. Level systems are often used at residential treatment facilities, institutions, and hospitals, but they can also effectively manage the behavior of students with emotional and behavior disorders in the public schools. Because it takes time and attention to implement and monitor level systems, they are generally used only by teachers in self-contained classrooms or alternative educational settings, not in less restrictive environments.

## CONCERNS ABOUT BEHAVIOR INTERVENTION STRATEGIES

Most teacher-mediated behavior intervention strategies can improve the academic and behavioral outcomes of students with emotional and behavior disorders (Pierce, Reid, & Epstein, 2004). It is important to meet the needs of individual students within the framework of classroom management programs. A reinforcement system applied to the whole classroom does not meet the individual needs of all the students and is not in compliance with IDEA (Jim Thorpe Area School District, 1998). In other words, any classroom management plan should be flexible enough to respond to the individual needs of students.

Teachers also need to recognize that their own personal and cultural biases may affect how they implement behavior interventions. The racial, ethnic, and socioeconomic identities of some students influence the types of interventions that teachers use with those students. For example, teachers tend to apply punishment more often to students from low socioeconomic backgrounds and African American students, who often display externalizing behaviors (Ishii-Jordan, 2000).

Finally, consistency and fairness are crucial components of any behavior management plan. It does not matter how carefully the intervention is constructed if it is not implemented in a consistent and fair manner. The intervention will have limited success in changing the behavior of students with emotional and behavior disorders and may even be detrimental.

An example of a behavior management system that is not always implemented fairly is the zero-tolerance policy that many schools have to protect students from weapons, drugs, and serious bodily injury. The policy is good in theory, but the consequences for students who violate the rules are prescribed without consideration of the circumstances. For example, Paul attacks Caleb. Instead of allowing himself to be seriously injured, Caleb defends himself by fighting back. As a result, both Caleb and Paul are placed in an alternative setting for 45 school days. Even in a court of law, the right to defend oneself against injury is recognized, but not in zero-tolerance schools.

In another example, Randy is a 17-year-old student with severe mental retardation. Randy's "buddies" ask him to keep their marijuana in his backpack. Randy obviously does not understand the implications of possessing drugs on school grounds, but when he is caught, he is placed in an alternative setting for 45 school days and is charged with possession of drugs. Although the legal charges against him will be dropped due to the circumstances, Randy will still have to serve his time at the alternative placement. The punishment serves no purpose for him. He would benefit more if the discipline at his school were individualized and responsive to the situation and the person (Laursen, 2003).

## Summary

Behavior management is an important component of teaching students with emotional and behavior disorders. Behavior management provides students with a safe and secure environment in which learning can take place, teaches students the necessity of having rules and consequences, and helps students to develop self-discipline and self-control. A number of behavior management plans, techniques, and strategies are available for teachers and administrators to use. Many of these interventions are easy to implement and can be used in the general education or the special education classroom. Interventions that include positive behavior support (PBS), functional behavioral assessments (FBAs), and behavior intervention plans (BIPs) are more complicated and may require school-wide support.

PBS is a proactive, positive behavior intervention and system designed to promote socially acceptable behavior for all students within the school. It includes three stages: primary, secondary, and tertiary interventions. Primary intervention is a school-wide intervention involving all students. Secondary intervention provides specialized support for individual students or classrooms with identified needs, and tertiary intervention provides extensive, individualized support. Before beginning a school-wide positive behavior support program, a school-based PBS team should analyze the behavioral environment of the school and design a program that meets the unique cultural needs of the school.

An FBA identifies the causes and effects of the inappropriate behavior. The first step in conducting an FBA is to clearly define the target behavior. Once the behavior is defined, the antecedent and consequence of the target behavior can be observed and recorded. Using this information, the team can predict the factors that cause the behavior and replace them with alternative behaviors. The FBA forms the foundation of the BIP. The BIP includes the intervention strategies that will be used to meet the behavioral goals, the individuals who will implement the plan, and the way that the plan will be monitored.

Classroom management strategies that are effective for students with emotional and behavior disorders include classroom behavior strategies, positive and negative reinforcements, shaping, punishment, contingency contracts, token economies, and level systems. Classroom behavior strategies are simple teacher-mediated interventions that effectively reduce minor behavioral disruptions. Positive and negative reinforcement increase the frequency or strength of a behavior by allowing a student either to obtain a reward or to avoid a consequence. Shaping is the reinforcement of the behavior through a series of steps, whereas punishment decreases the frequency or strength of a behavior by following it with an aversive consequence. A contingency contract is an agreement between the student and teacher that addresses the behavioral, academic, and social goals of the student and that describes reinforcements that can either increase or decrease the behavior. A token economy increases or decreases behavior by dispensing tokens that can be exchanged for reinforcers, and a level system reinforces expected behaviors at different hierarchical levels that provide increased reinforcements.

Any classroom management plan should be flexible enough to meet the needs of individual students. Teachers also need to be aware that racial, ethnic, and socioeconomic labels might influence the type of interventions they use with particular students. Teachers and administrators need to apply behavior interventions consistently and fairly.

## Review Questions

1. What are the goals of managing behavior, and why are these goals important? How do they apply to students with emotional and behavior disorders?
2. When is it appropriate to conduct an FBA, and how would you perform an applied behavioral analysis of a student's inappropriate behavior?
3. In addition to the information from the FBA, what information should be included in a BIP?
4. A student in your classroom is refusing to complete his assignment. What classroom behavior strategy would you use and why?
5. A teacher has accused you of bribing your students because you reinforce their appropriate behavior. How would you respond to this teacher?
6. Is the zero-tolerance policy of most school districts too stringent or a necessary evil? Explain.

# CHAPTER 7

# Teaching Social Skills

**After reading this chapter, you should be able to**

- Explain the goals of teaching social skills to children with emotional and behavior disorders.
- Name and describe the common components of effective social skills programs.
- Describe a number of social skills programs developed for children and adolescents.
- Explain the importance of teaching problem-solving strategies along with social skills.
- Explain the importance of developing a student's self-determination skills.

- Describe the Girls and Boys Town Education Model as a school-wide model for teaching social skills.
- Understand a few simple classroom strategies that can improve the social skills of students.
- Explain why it is important for teachers to understand the cultural backgrounds, beliefs, and traditions of their students.
- Understand the importance of teaching social skills in school.

# GOALS OF SOCIAL SKILLS

*Social skills* are specific behaviors that well-socialized individuals demonstrate appropriately when they complete social tasks (Gresham, 2002). Human beings are very social creatures, although different individuals have different degrees of involvement in social life. At one end of the spectrum are the social wallflowers, whose shyness or inability to find acceptance in the group limits their social interactions, and at the other end are the social butterflies, who interact willingly and successfully with others.

Students with emotional and behavior disorders often do not have good social skills (Gresham, Cook, Crews, & Kern, 2004). Their difficulties interacting with others often cause them to experience teacher and peer rejection, school failure, and limited social involvement (Lane, Menzies, Barton-Arwood, Doukas, & Munton, 2005). In spite of the research indicating that social skills are necessary for school success (Gresham, 2002), these skills are seldom taught in the classroom.

It is extraordinary that social skills have not been a major topic of study in many general and special education classrooms, especially considering that two of the criteria described in the federal definition of emotional disturbance relate to social competence: (1) an inability to build or maintain satisfactory interpersonal relationships with peers and teachers and (2) inappropriate types of behavior or feelings under normal circumstances (U.S. Department of Education, 2006, p. 46756). Teaching social skills to students with poor social skills will help improve and maintain their behavior. Research has shown that social skills interventions can provide the skills that are needed by children with emotional and behavior disorders and those who are at risk for developing behavioral problems (Kam, Greenberg, & Kusche, 2004). Social skills need to be taught, learned, and practiced until students can exhibit the behavior in different settings (Lane et al., 2005).

Children with age-appropriate social skills know what is expected in a social situation and are able to behave in an expected manner. Some of the expectations in the classroom are that students will follow directions, ask for help in an appropriate manner (usually by raising their hands), and interact appropriately with peers and adults (Lane, Wehby, & Cooley, 2006). Students with emotional and behavior disorders often have trouble complying with these expectations. They have difficulties understanding and interpreting social cues, responding effectively in social situations, displaying empathy, and initiating age-appropriate interactions with peers and adults. However, not all children who have deficits in social skills are identified as having emotional and behavior disorders. Some children may be at risk for developing emotional and behavior disorders, or they may have a disorder but never be identified. All children with antisocial behaviors should receive interventions that will prevent them from developing more problematic behaviors that would interfere with their academic and social performances at school (Lo, Loe, & Cartledge, 2002).

Social skills training includes primary and secondary interventions. Primary interventions are designed to prevent a disorder or problem from occurring. These types of interventions are especially valuable for children who are at risk for developing social and behavioral problems due to deficits in social skills. Secondary interventions are designed to prevent an existing disorder or behavior from getting worse. The goals for teaching social skills to students are divided into three domains: Peer and Adult Interaction, Classroom Survival Skills, and Coping Skills.

*Peer and Adult Interaction*
    Listening to others
    Initiating interaction

>        Accepting and giving compliments
>        Apologizing
>    *Classroom Survival Skills*
>        Following rules and instructions
>        Asking for help
>        Completing assignments
>        Ignoring distractions
>    *Coping Skills*
>        Expressing anger appropriately
>        Solving problems
>        Compromising

## The Teacher's Role in Social Skills

Many social skills programs are pull-out programs (programs that are taught by outside individuals), but general education teachers and special education teachers often play a crucial role in helping children and adolescents develop social skills. In one study, students who had positive and supportive relationships with teachers had fewer behavioral problems, showed greater social competence, and displayed better academic performances than students who did not have good relationships with their teachers (Murray & Greenberg, 2006). Research has shown that if social skills programs are taught and implemented by the classroom teacher, instead of someone with whom the students are not familiar, students' social skills improve more and their gains are maintained longer (Farmer-Dougan, Viechtbauer, & French, 1999).

Because the relationships that students form with their teachers are important, and because children spend a major portion of their day at school, it seems like a natural choice to have teachers instruct children in social skills. Unfortunately, many teachers are unfamiliar with social skills programs. They need a framework that will help them decide which social skills program to implement in their classrooms. Understanding the components of different social skills programs will help teachers provide effective social skills training.

Although classroom activities often emphasize altering the behavior of students rather than that of the teacher, the classroom is a system in which teacher and student behaviors interact and are interdependent on one another. It appears that providing instruction, modeling appropriate teaching behaviors, and reinforcing the teacher for her new behaviors are as important to the success of a social skills education program as is reinforcing the children (Farmer-Dougan et al., 1999).

There are several components of effective social skills instruction. Teachers should employ modeling and use various examples as they teach. Social skills training should occur as peer-inclusive activities. Also, social skills should be taught and reinforced throughout the school day (Lo et al., 2002). Many social skills programs follow the behavioral model of practice and can be easily implemented into the academic curricula in either the general or special education classroom.

## COMPONENTS OF SOCIAL SKILLS PROGRAMS

A number of social skills programs are available. The most effective programs use a generic direct model that include introduction and instruction of the skill, modeling, peer involvement, role-playing, feedback, and reinforcement of desired social behaviors (Miller et al., 2005; Morgan & Jenson, 1988; Williams & Reisberg, 2003).

## Direct Instruction of Social Skills

The first step in teaching social skills is the direct instruction of the specific skills. At the start of the lesson, the teacher should identify the specific skills that are going to be taught and explain how mastery of them will benefit the students. Typically, any social skills lesson will benefit students by improving their interaction with peers and adults. It is worthwhile repeating this each lesson because if students do not see the need for learning social skills, they are less likely to acquire and maintain the skill.

Sometimes the teacher selects the skill to be taught ahead of time; other times the skill to be taught is chosen after an assessment of the students' needs or from student input. The teacher begins the social skills lesson by telling the students which skills they will be learning. For example, the teacher may inform the class, "Today, we are going to learn how to say 'thank you.'" Next, the teacher explains the importance of this skill and provides examples that are relevant to the students' lives. The explanation of the social skill should be conducted succinctly, avoiding protracted discussion over trivial details.

## Modeling

*Modeling* is the demonstration or performance of the skills to be taught. Modeling is an established intervention technique for reducing inappropriate behavior and correcting social skills deficits (Bandura, 1986), and it is logical to include it in social skills programs. Students are introduced to examples of social skills through live, audio, or video modeling.

It is important that teachers guide the social skills program, but some researchers have cited the advantages of using student peers as trainers and facilitators for social skills programs (Blake, Wang, Cartledge, & Gardner, 2000; Lo et al., 2002). Peer-mediated

Modeling is an intervention technique for inappropriate behavior and social skills deficits.

interventions have been shown to (1) improve students' opportunities to respond, (2) increase on-task behaviors, (3) provide immediate feedback on correct and incorrect responses, and (4) facilitate academic achievement, and (5) help improve social behaviors (Gardner et al., 2001, p. 24).

**PEER-MEDIATED SOCIAL SKILLS INTERVENTIONS**   Four types of peer-mediated social skills interventions have been identified: peer imitation training, proximity intervention, peer prompting and reinforcement, and peer social initiation (Blake et al., 2000; Odom & Strain, 1984; Rosenberg, Wilson, Maheady, & Sindelar, 2004).

Peer imitation training uses a peer to teach lessons to a child who has deficits in social skills. The peer models selected skills for the child, who is expected to imitate this behavior. If the child successfully demonstrates the behavior, the teacher provides reinforcement. If the child does not successfully exhibit the behavior, the teacher provides prompts.

Proximity interventions put the focus on the natural interaction of a child who has social deficits and a peer. The child is paired with his or her peer and they are expected to play or interact with each other.

Peer prompting and reinforcement involves teaching students to use prompts and reinforcement to increase appropriate social behaviors in peers. Peers prompt children with poor social skills to interact with others and then provide reinforcement for appropriate interactions. The goal is to train children who are socially withdrawn to eventually interact with others without the prompts.

The final peer-mediated technique is peer social initiation. A peer is trained by the teacher to initiate social interactions with a student who is socially withdrawn. The peer carries the responsibility of initiating the social interaction with the peer. Adults do not prompt nor reinforce the child's behavior because peer social interaction is a more natural way to acquire social skills.

Peer-mediated interventions can be labor intensive because they require teachers to supervise students during the modeling segment or to train peers to teach social skills to children with social deficits.

Generally, peer-mediated interventions involve peers without disabilities teaching social skills to children with disabilities, but some studies have had success using peers with disabilities as trainers. In one study, seventh-grade students with learning disabilities were able to successfully teach the social skills they had learned from their teachers to other students with learning disabilities (Prater, Serna, & Nakamura, 1999). In another study, children with emotional and behavior disorders successfully taught social skills to other children with emotional and behavior disorders (Blake et al., 2000).

No matter who provides the demonstration of the behavior, modeling is an essential component of social skills programs. Behavioral theory stresses that behavior is learned and maintained through modeling—that is, from watching others demonstrate specific behaviors. After the initial modeling session, the child must receive further instruction and opportunities to practice in order to acquire and generalize social skills.

## Social Stories

Social stories are skill-specific narratives that portray appropriate responses to social situations through visual cues and text. They may describe skills such as following directions, sharing, and problem solving. For example, a social story might be written for a child who is being teased. The social story will address the *who, what, when, where*, and *why* of the social situation by describing the child who is being teased, the setting in which the teasing occurs, and the way that the child feels about being teased (Sansosti & Powell-Smith, 2006). Social stories generally use animal characters to illustrate the social situation (Kam et al., 2004; Nielsen, Lambros, & Forness, 2000) and the skills are taught through role-playing. Social stories are often presented in the following format:

1. The major character (an animal) is introduced.
2. The problem is identified.
3. The skill steps are outlined.
4. The problem is solved with the use of a particular skill (Serna et al., 2003).

An example of a social story might be the following: None of the other animals liked Rabbit because he always dominated their conversations. They did not want to play any games with him. The teacher, Mrs. Owl, helped Rabbit identify the problem and taught him the skills to appropriately engage in conversation. Once he started using the skills that he had learned, Rabbit's relationships with the other animals improved.

Several studies have documented the effectiveness of social stories (Lorimer, Simpson, Myles, & Ganz, 2002; Sansosti & Powell-Smith, 2006; Serna et al., 2003). Social stories can be presented by means of video, audio, and computer technology. Computer simulations, which are underutilized in social skills development, respond to the student's pace, skill level, and performance and confront the student with the consequences of his or her decisions (Smokowski, 2003). Several computer programs incorporate stories to teach social skills to young children. Two primary intervention programs adapted for young children that include social stories are *Purpose: A Life-Long Learning Approach to Self-Determination* (Serna & Lau-Smith, 1995) and *Promoting Alternative Thinking Strategies* (Kusche & Greenberg, 1994).

## Role-Playing

Role-playing allows students to rehearse or practice social skills in a "safe" environment, the classroom in which the skill is being taught. Role-playing also gives the teacher and peers the opportunity to provide helpful suggestions to the student practicing the skill. Role-playing activities can be scripted or they can be designed by the student or teacher. If they are scripted, each participant involved in the activity needs to understand his or her roles and responsibilities. In an unscripted activity, the role-playing activity is drawn from the students' real-life situations.

In small group settings, each participant, including the co-actor, should have the opportunity to play the main actor once. Because practice is an important component of learning any skill, the role-playing should continue until the students have acquired the skill.

## Feedback

Performance feedback lets the student who took the role of the main actor know how he or she performed during the role-playing activity. The first person to provide feedback should be the co-actor. Next, students in the group should provide feedback, and finally, after they have completed their remarks, the teacher should provide feedback. Feedback should be positive and should focus on the behavior; it may include praise, approval, and constructive criticism. Once everyone has commented on the role-playing activity, the main actor should make remarks about the activity and the comments made by the group.

This exercise will allow the main actor to evaluate the effectiveness of his skill enactment (Goldstein, 1999).

## Generalization

Another important component of social skills training is the ability to generalize and maintain the acquired skills in different settings and situations. Children with emotional and behavior disorders and children with social skills deficits often acquire and master social skills, but fail to generalize these skills to other settings (Coster & Haltiwanger, 2004). They are more likely to learn to generalize if they have the opportunity to practice the skills in various settings. Many social skills programs include "homework" in which students are assigned to practice their skills in a different setting, usually another classroom. This task involves collaboration with other teachers, who need to know that students will be attempting to practice social skills in their classrooms. The other teachers will need to be supportive of the students' attempts and may even need to provide a situation in which the students can practice their social skills. For example, if the social skill lesson for the week is learning to say "thank you," the collaborative teacher may comment to a student that she "looks nice today." This comment gives the student the opportunity to say "thank you" for the compliment. As students maintain the acquired skill and grow confident using it, teachers should encourage them to use their skill in settings outside school and to report these attempts to their primary social skills teacher. The key to generalizing new social skills across different settings is providing students with the opportunity to practice these skills.

## MODELS FOR TEACHING SOCIAL SKILLS

Numerous social skills programs are available. General education teachers, special education teachers, and administrators are encouraged to investigate these programs.

## Prosocial Skills

In 1979, Arnold Goldstein published *Skillstreaming the Adolescent* (Goldstein & McGinnis, 1997), which was one of the first curricula for teaching prosocial skills to adolescents (Braaten, 2003). Another curricula for teaching prosocial skills, *The Prepare Curriculum: Teaching Prosocial Competencies*, is a series of psychoeducational courses designed for youths who are deficient in prosocial competencies (Goldstein, 1999). *The Prepare Curriculum* covered the instruction of 50 skills divided into six categories. (See Table 7.1).

Teaching prosocial skills, or *skillstreaming*, is taught through components of direct instruction. (See Chapter 8.) Direct instruction of social skills is a basic principle of the behavioral approach. The emphasis is on changing the inappropriate behavior and replacing it with behavior that is more acceptable.

Direct social skills lessons are taught through a scripted social skills instruction that includes defining and modeling the skill, having students practice with peers, reviewing the student's performance and giving feedback on it, and providing the student with opportunities to practice the skill in different settings (Kamps, Ellis, Mancina, & Greene, 1995). Although *The Prepare Curriculum* does not address the teacher's role in social skills training, it is crucial that the teachers be directly involved. The burden for social skills assessment, change, and evaluation is on the teachers. They need the initial training to implement the program and the support to make the program successful (Farmer-Dougan et al., 1999).

## TABLE 7.1  Skillstreaming Skills for Adolescents

**Group I: Beginning Social Skills**

1. Listening
2. Starting a Conversation
3. Having a Conversation
4. Asking a Question
5. Saying Thank You
6. Introducing Yourself
7. Introducing Other People
8. Giving a Compliment

**Group II: Advance Social Skills**

9. Asking for Help
10. Joining In
11. Giving Instructions
12. Following Instructions
13. Apologizing
14. Convincing Others

**Group III: Skills for Dealing with Feelings**

15. Knowing Your Feelings
16. Expressing Your Feelings
17. Understanding the Feelings of Others
18. Dealing with Someone Else's Anger
19. Expressing Affection
20. Dealing with Fear
21. Rewarding Yourself

**Group IV: Skill Alternative to Aggression**

22. Asking Permission
23. Sharing Something
24. Helping Others

25. Negotiating
26. Using Self-Control
27. Standing Up for Your Rights
28. Responding to Teasing
29. Avoiding Trouble with Others
30. Keeping Out of Fights

**Group V: Skills for Dealing with Stress**

31. Making a Complaint
32. Answering a Complaint
33. Being a Good Sport
34. Dealing with Embarrassment
35. Dealing with Being Left Out
36. Standing Up for a Friend
37. Responding to Persuasion
38. Responding to Failure
39. Dealing with Contradictory Messages
40. Dealing with an Accusation
41. Getting Ready for a Difficult Conversation
42. Dealing with Group Pressure

**Group VI: Planning Skills**

43. Deciding on Something to Do
44. Deciding What Caused a Problem
45. Setting a Goal
46. Deciding on Your Abilities
47. Gathering Information
48. Arranging Problems by Importance
49. Making a Decision
50. Concentrating on a Task

*Source:* From *The Prepare Curriculum* (pp. 16–17) by Goldstein, (1999), Champaign, IL: Research Press. Copyright 1999 by Goldstein. Adapted/reprinted by permission.

**COMPONENTS OF SKILLSTREAMING**   The teacher begins by modeling appropriate social behaviors to students in a small group. These behaviors range from listening and starting a conversation to making a decision. Once the teacher has modeled the designated behavior, students are given the opportunity to practice and rehearse the behavior. This practice time is a crucial component of teaching social skills. The student not only must acquire the new skill, but also must replace a previous learned, inappropriate behavior with the new one. This process is the crux of the matter, because once a child learns something, whether it is appropriate or inappropriate, it is difficult for him to unlearn the concept and replace it with a new one. For example, if a child incorrectly learns that George Washington's vice president

| **TABLE 7.2  Skillstreaming Training Steps** |
| --- |

**Modeling the Skill**
1. Define the Skill
2. Model the Skill

**Role-Playing**
1. Select a Role-Player
2. Conduct the Role-Play

**Provide Feedback**
1. Co-Actor
2. Group Members
3. Teacher

**Unguided Practice**
1. Assign Skill Homework
2. Complete Homework Form

*Source:* From *The Prepare Curriculum* (p. 23) by Goldstein, (1999), Champaign, IL: Research Press. Copyright 1999 by Goldstein. Adapted/reprinted by permission.

was Thomas Jefferson, it may take extra effort for her to learn that John Adams was actually Washington's vice president (See Table 7.2).

During the role-playing component of the curriculum, the teacher provides praise and redirection (performance feedback). The teacher's comments regarding the student's performance are usually restricted to how well the steps were followed.

The final step is to assign unguided practice. Students are instructed to practice their acquired skills in different settings. Students should report their experiences by completing a Homework Report Form, which includes the skill they used, the name of the person with whom the student tried to interact, the day, and the place. (See Figure 7.1.) Eventually, the student will need to generalize the skill to use it outside the school with peers, at home, and in the community.

It is extremely important for students to generalize and maintain the social skills that they learn. The only way teachers can accomplish this is to provide students with the opportunities to practice these skills in a multitude of settings and with a multiplicity of individuals. The school setting is the perfect place to begin generalization and maintenance. The students learn social skills in one classroom with one teacher. Later they practice the skills in other classrooms with other teachers, at recess with peers, and in the lunchroom with adults and peers.

**EXAMPLE OF SOCIAL SKILLS TRAINING**  An example of advanced social skills training is apologizing (Goldstein, 1999), a skill that is difficult for individuals even with appropriate social skills. The teacher models and explains the four steps of apologizing to a group of students who have deficits in this area. (See Table 7.3.) The first step is to decide whether or not to apologize for something. This can be problematic for students who feel no remorse for their actions. The teacher may give examples of situations in which an apology is appropriate: breaking something, interrupting someone, or hurting someone's feelings.

| Homework Report |
| --- |

Name:_____ Date: _____

**Fill in During This Class**

1. What skill will you use?

2. What are the steps for the skill?

3. Where will you try the skill?

4. With whom will you try the skill?

5. When will you try the skill?

**Fill in After Doing Your Homework**

1. What happened when you did you homework?

2. What skill steps did you really follow?

3. How good a job did you do in using the skill? (circle one)

    excellent          good          fair          poor

4. What do you think your next homework assignment should be?

**FIGURE 7.1** Homework Report.

*Source:* From *The Prepare Curriculum* (p. 33) by Goldstein, (1999), Champaign, IL: Research Press. Copyright 1999 by Goldstein. Adapted/reprinted by permission.

**TABLE 7.3 Sample Skillstreaming Skill: Apologizing**

| | Apologizing |
|---|---|
| **Steps** | **Trainer Notes** |
| 1. Decide whether it would be best for you to apologize for something you did. | You might apologize for breaking something, making an error, interrupting someone, or hurting someone's feelings. |
| 2. Think of the different ways you could apologize. | Say something; do something; write something. |
| 3. Choose the best time and place to apologize. | Do it privately and as soon as possible after creating the problem. |
| 4. Make your apology. | This might include an offer to make up for what happened. |

*Source:* From *The Prepare Curriculum* (p. 51) by Goldstein (1999), Champaign, IL: Research Press. Copyright 1999 by Goldstein. Adapted/reprinted by permission.

The second step is to think of ways to apologize. The teacher might explain that two ways of apologizing are saying something and writing something. Students often assume that there is only one way to apologize: verbally. It may not occur to them to write an apology or buy an apology card.

The third step is to choose the best time and place to apologize. The teachers might tell students to do it privately and as quickly as possible after creating the problem. The final step is to make the apology.

Once the teacher has explained and modeled the lesson, students take turns role-playing. The role-playing usually involves the main actor, who demonstrates the steps, and a co-actor, who assists the actor in the role-playing. Once the student has completed the role-playing, the co-actor provides feedback, followed by the members of the group, and finally the teacher.

When the role-playing and feedback component are completed, the student is assigned homework. The student must decide where and when he or she will practice the newly acquired skill. It is a good idea to practice it initially in another classroom. Once the student has practiced the skill, he or she needs to complete the Homework Report Form and turn it in to the teacher–trainer. The student should be encouraged to practice the skill in different settings within the school and in the community.

## A Children's Curriculum for Effective Peer and Teacher Skills

*A Children's Curriculum for Effective Peer and Teacher Skills* (ACCEPTS) is a well-known social skills intervention program (Walker et al., 1983). ACCEPTS contains classroom and peer-to-peer components. The classroom component includes classroom survival skills such as listening to the teacher, following directions and rules, and doing one's best on classroom assignments. The peer-to-peer component has four major skill groups: (1) basic interaction skills (making eye contact, using an appropriate voice, listening, and taking turns talking); (2) getting along (using polite words, sharing, and assisting others), making friends (grooming, smiling, complimenting, and expressing anger appropriately); and (4) coping (reacting appropriately when someone says "no," when someone teases, when someone tries to inflict harm, or when things do not go right).

All social skills are taught through a direct instruction format and include a placement test, a 9-step instructional procedure, role-playing tests, and behavior management procedures.

| **TABLE 7.4** The 17 Skills for *Getting Along With Others* | |
|---|---|
| Introducing | Offering to Help |
| Following Directions | Compromising |
| Giving and Receiving Positive Feedback | Asking for Clear Directions |
| Sending an "I'm Interested" Message | Problem Solving |
| Sending an Ignoring Message | Using Positive Consequences |
| Interrupting a Conversation | Giving and Receiving a Suggestion for Improvement |
| Joining a Conversation | |
| Starting a Conversation and Keeping It Going | Handling Name-Calling and Teasing |
| Sharing | Saying "No" to Stay Our of Trouble |

*Source: Getting Along With Others,* Jackson, Jackson, & Monroe, 1983.

The 9-step instructional procedure is similar to *The Prepare Curriculum.* The teacher identifies and defines a skill and then models it or shows a videotape that depicts positive and negative examples. The students role-play and practice the skill, and the teacher provides a homework assignment.

The behavior management component of ACCEPTS uses a point system for the classroom and for playground behavior. Targeting the two most recently learned social skills, the teacher rates the child's participation during recess over the course of three equal time intervals. If the student interacted appropriately with peers for at least half of an interval, he or she is awarded a point. The student can exchange the points for free time (that is, time during which the student can choose the activity).

## Getting Along with Others

*Getting Along with Others: Teaching Social Effectiveness to Children* (Jackson, Jackson, & Monroe, 1983) provides training in 17 social skills. (See Table 7.4.) Each session includes a scripted dialogue and instructions. The components of this social skills curriculum include simply telling the student what to do in a problem situation (define the problem), modeling the skill, and having the student practice the skill prior to using it in real-life situations (role-playing and feedback). The core elements of the program are enhanced by optional activities such as relaxation training, snack time, activity time, Home Note, and Homework.

An interesting aspect of *Getting Along with Others* is the reality check. Sometimes, children who use acquired social skills appropriately in different settings are still rejected by peers. The reality check teaches them to cope with this situation by ignoring the rejection or walking away.

## The *Promoting Alternative Thinking Strategies* Curriculum

The *Promoting Alternative Thinking Strategies* (PATHS) curriculum is a preventive program founded on basic developmental research that emphasizes the developmental integration of affect, behavior, and cognitive understanding (Kam et al., 2004). The PATHS curriculum covers five domains of social and emotional development: (1) self control, (2) emotional understanding, (3) self-esteem, (4) peer relations, and (5) interpersonal problem-solving skills.

Elementary-school teachers apply the PATHS curriculum on a regular basis throughout the academic year. Researchers have reported that use of the PATHS curriculum significantly reduced aggression and disruptive behavior of children (Greenberg, Kam, Heinrichs, & Conduct Problems Prevention Research Group, 2003).

**THE CONCEPTUAL UNITS OF THE PATHS CURRICULUM**     The PATHS curriculum covers four conceptual units: (1) Readiness and Self-Control, (2) Feelings and Relationships, (3) Problem Solving, and (4) Supplementary Lessons (The Conduct Problems Prevention Research Group, 2002; Kam et al., 2004; U.S. Department of Health and Human Services, Substance Abuse and Mental Health Services Administration, n.d.). The content of the PATHS curriculum of each grade level builds on what the children learned in the previous grade and is developmentally appropriate.

The Readiness and Self-Control Unit focuses on teaching behavioral self-control and the identification of problems through the use of the Turtle Technique. Developed by Robin, Schneider, and Dolnick (1976), the Turtle Technique allows aggressive elementary school children to practice withdrawal, relaxation, and problem solving (Guetzloe & Rockwell, 1998). Children learn about a turtle who has social, behavioral, and academic problems because he does not stop and think:

> Little Turtle was very upset about going to school. When he was there he got into trouble because he fought with his mates. Other turtles teased, bumped, or hit him. He then became angry and started fights. The teacher then punished him. One day he met the big old tortoise, who told him that his shell was the secret answer to many problems. The tortoise told Little Turtle to withdraw into his shell whenever he felt angry, and rest until he felt better. Little Turtle tried it the next day and it worked. He no longer became angry or started fights, his teacher now smiled at him, and he began to like school (Morgan & Jenson, 1988, p. 179; Robin et al., 1976).

Students learn to "do the turtle" when they have a problem during the day by pulling their arms and legs close to their bodies, laying their heads on their desks, and covering their heads with their arms. Students are taught to do the turtle when (1) they believe a conflict is about to occur between them and other students, (2) they are angry and ready to exhibit inappropriate behavior, (3) when the teacher tells them to "turtle," and (4) when a peer tells them to "turtle." When students appropriately follow the technique, the teacher rewards them with "turtle stamps."

The Feelings and Relationships Unit focuses on developing skills for understanding and communicating emotions and for interacting with peers. Children learn to identify feelings by using Feelings Faces. The teacher introduces a feeling to the students through modeling. The teacher makes a happy facial expression and holds up a Happy Face. Some of the other Feelings Faces include sad, private, fine, excited, tired, mad, angry, scared, and safe faces. The children keep their Feelings Faces inside boxes. During the day, they pull out Feelings Faces and places them on their desks according to how they feel. For example, when Mary feels tired, she pulls her Tired Face from the Feelings Box and places it on her desk. Not only does this teach her to identify her feelings, but it also lets others know how she is feeling (see Figure 7.2.).

The development of self-control and awareness are incorporated into the Feelings and Relationships Unit with the Control Signals Poster (Kam et al., 2004). The Control Signals Poster should be introduced before the teacher presents any informal problem-solving skills. The Control Signals Poster is modeled after a stoplight. A red light means to "stop/calm down," a yellow light means, "go slow/think," and a green light means "go/try the plan." The children are taught skills to use with the different signals in this simple problem-solving model.

New let's talk about feeling tired. Point to the Tired Feeling Face in the Feelings Chart and write the word TIRED on the board or overhead. Tired is the way we feel when we feel wornout or when we feel like we don't have much energy left. We often feel tired when we don't get enough sleep, when we work or play very hard, or when we are sick. When we feel tired, we don't feel like being active. When we feel tired, we feel like resting. Can anyone think of a time when they they felt tired? Elcit discussion.

Take the Tired Feeling Face out of the Feelings Chart and show it to the class. This Feeling Face shows someone who is feeling tired. Do you think that tired feels comfortable or uncomfortable inside? Elicit responses (uncomfortable). Yes, when we feel tired, we feel uncomfortable inside, so I'll ask (name of a child) to put the Tired Feeling Face on the blue side of the Feelings Chart. Ask the child to replace the Tired Face in the blue side of Feeling Chart.

Show Photographs 9 and 10. Here are two photograp of people who feel tired.

Point out the features that indicate tiredness (e.g., the droopy eyes, the yawn, body postures, etc.). Model as needed for further clarification or demonstration. Here is a picture of a girl who feels tired. What makes us think that she feels tired? Elicit responses (e.g., she's yawning; her eyes are droopy; etc.). Here is a picture of a boy who feels tired. What make us think that he feels tired? Elicit responces as before. Does anyone have any guesses about why he feels tired? (E.g., he's been reading a long time; it's his bedtime; etc.) Praise your students for their participation. Now let's all look and feel TIRED and practice the word together.

Say/sign and spell/fingerspell the word TIRED two times: TIRED, T-I-R-E-D, TIRED, T-I-R-E-D. Say/sign the sentence: I FEEL TIRED. That was great! I really like the way you _____ (finish as appropriate, e.g., "all make such good expressions," "speak up so loudly," etc.). Now I will hand out your Tired Feeling Faces for you to keep in your Feelings Boxes. Remember to color the hair so that they look like you, and put your name on the back of each one.

After the children have finished, say: Now I want each of you to stop and think about how you feel inside right now. After yu decide, pick the faces that show those feelings. OK, now put the rest of your Feeling Faces away in your Feelings Pouches. Remember to change your faces during the day when your feelings change inside.

**FIGURE 7.2** Sample PATHS Lesson: Tired.

*Source:* Kusche & Greenberg, 1994. Adapted and reprinted by permission.

The Problem-Solving Unit teaches students to follow a series of steps to find solutions to problems. The teacher keeps a "problem box" on his or her desk, and when a student is experiencing a problem, the student writes it down and puts it in the box. These problems are used as the focus of problem-solving meetings that the teacher conducts twice a week.

The final component of the PATHS curriculum is the Supplementary Lessons Unit, which contains optional lessons, reviews, and extensions.

The PATHS curriculum has been shown to reduce inappropriate behavior in the general and special education settings. Although most of the training occurs in the classroom at school, the PATHS curriculum also includes activities and information for parents.

## PROBLEM-SOLVING SKILLS

Children often find themselves in social situations in which they need to decide between choices. They need to learn the skills to make choices and to recognize the outcome of their choices (Gallagher, 1997). Children should be taught to be effective social problem solvers as part of their social skills training. When student learn problem-solving skills, their rates of inappropriate and impulsive behavior can decrease.

Many problem-solving strategies are available, and most are similar in nature. These strategies usually involve identifying the problem and developing possible solutions. One such strategy is the following:

1. Recognize the problem.
2. Define the problem and the goal.
3. Generate possible solutions.
4. Select a solution.
5. Predict the outcome of the solution.

## Case Study 7.1

### Tiffany

Twelve-year-old Tiffany was at the local 7–11 convenience store with her friend, Mahala, to buy a soda. As they were going down the candy aisle, Mahala stopped and picked up a Snickers bar. Tiffany was shocked when Mahala stuffed the candy bar in the pocket of her jacket.

"Take one," Mahala whispered to Tiffany.

Tiffany shook her head, and Mahala sneered, "What's the matter? You afraid?"

Tiffany didn't want to be look down on by her friend. She hesitated and then reached for a candy bar. Using a problem-solving strategy she had learned at school, Tiffany realized that there was a problem. If she took the candy bar, she'd win her friend's approval, but if she got caught, then she would be in trouble with her mother and might even be in trouble with the law. If she refused to take the candy bar, Mahala might think she was a baby, but she would not be in trouble with her mother or the law. Also, even if Mahala thought she was a baby, Tiffany knew she would probably get over it. Tiffany also knew that stealing was wrong.

Tiffany decided not to take the candy bar. Instead, she and Mahala went to the back of the store to get sodas. After purchasing the sodas, Tiffany and Mahala sat outside the store drinking their sodas. Mahala also ate the candy bar she had stolen, taunting and teasing Tiffany while she ate it. Tiffany ignored her, and once Mahala had finished the candy bar, she no longer teased Tiffany. The two friends went on their way. Tiffany decided she would behave in the same manner in a similar situation.

**6.** Select an alternative solution if the predicted outcome is not positive.

**7.** Evaluate the solution after it is implemented.

**8.** Decide what to do in a similar situation (D'Zurilla & Goldfried, 1971; Elksnin & Elksnin, 2003; Gallagher, 1997).

Problem-solving skills training uses the same cognitive–behavioral approach as social skills training, in which behavior is learned from watching others (for example, Bandura, 1977). Problem-solving skills training can incorporate a behavioral approach through direct instruction, role-playing, practice, feedback, and positive reinforcement. (See Case Study 7.1.)

## SELF-DETERMINATION

A fundamental component of long-term social skills success is the development of self-determination skills (Carter & Lunsford, 2005). *Self-determination* is an individual's ability to identify and pursue goals without external influences. The acquisition and performance of self-determination skills are associated with more positive adult outcomes, such as higher rate of employment and higher wages (Carter & Lunsford, 2005; Wehmeyer & Schwartz, 1997).

Components of self-determination include decision making; choice making; problem solving; self-management; independent living; goal setting and attainment; self-observation, evaluation, and reinforcement; self-instruction; self-understanding; self-advocacy and leadership; positive self-efficacy and outcome expectancy; internal locus of control; and self-awareness (Carter & Lunsford, 2005; Wehmeyer, Agran, & Hughes, 1998). Teachers can encourage students to develop self-determination skills by (1) promoting generalization of self-determination skills, (2) respecting students' choices and decisions, and (3) supporting students' goals (Wood, Karvonen, Test, Browder, & Algozzine, 2004). Teachers need to allow students to fully participate in the planning process, and they need to teach students to manage their own behaviors and engage in self-advocacy. As long as they are in school, children with emotional and behavior disorders have parents, teachers, and others advocating for their rights and needs. But once they have finished school, advocating for their rights becomes their responsibility, so learning self-advocacy skills is particularly important for them.

It is also important to remember that self-determination can easily be confused with individualism, which is traditionally valued by European American culture. In the collective culture of Asian Americans, Native Americans, and Hispanics, an individual's sense of self is understood with relation to others within the community (Browder, Wood, Test, Karvonen, & Algozzine, 2001). For example, in Hispanic families, young adults typically live with their families for an extended period of time. Even when they have married, for young adults to move out of a parent's home is considered a breakdown in family ties (Turnbull & Turnbull, 1996).

Cultural influences notwithstanding, students with emotional and behavior disorders can be successful in the real world only if they are capable of making their own decisions, solving problems, and managing their own behaviors. If they do not acquire self-determination skills, they are unlikely to maintain the social skills they have acquired, and appropriate social skills can bring employment success, coworker acceptance, and job satisfaction (Carter & Lunsford, 2005).

## THE GIRLS AND BOYS TOWN EDUCATION MODEL

Another social skills and behavioral program is the Girls and Boys Town Education Model. Developed in 1979, this program has been adapted to train teachers, administrators, and staff in the public schools to manage student behavior. It includes three workshops designed to teach skills and strategies for addressing the social skill needs of all students.

The Girls and Boys Town Education Model is a school-wide social skills curriculum that is taught both formally (through, for example, a skill of the week) and informally (for instance, during interactions with students). It includes basic skills such as accepting feedback and disagreeing appropriately (Hoff, DuPaul, & Handwerk, 2003). The four components of the Girls and Boys Town Education Model include a life skills curriculum, teaching methods that support the life skills curriculum, a motivation system, and administrative intervention (Girls and Boys Town, n.d.). The life skills curriculum teaches specific skills designed to promote student success and generalization. Teaching methods that support the life skills curriculum provide methodology that promotes student self-control. The motivation system is a simple classroom management system using tokens (see Chapter 6) and focuses on self-determination. The administrative intervention component provides school principals with methods of teaching alternative, appropriate behaviors to students who have been referred from the classroom.

The Girls and Boys Town Education Model provides an impetus for changing the way teachers and administrators address the social skills and behaviors of all children in the school. Schools that have implemented the program have reported significant improvement in academic achievement, student behavior, and rates of student referral (Gulley, Burke, & Hensley, 2003; Mojica et al., 2005). Implementing any organizational change may meet with resistance at the organization level or at the individual level (Hanson, 1996). When school officials are considering implementing school-wide programs, those who will be involved in the implementation should be involved in the development of the program and have ownership of it.

## CLASSROOM STRATEGIES

A number of simple strategies can be used in the general and special education classrooms to develop the social skills of children. Activities promoting social skills should occur at dedicated times in the classroom, but should also be combined with interventions outside the classroom. These activities should involve real-life social activities such as board games, sports, and other recreational activities (Farmer, 2000). Board games can teach a number of social skills, including communication, sharing, taking turns, and interacting with others (Rosenfeld, 2005). Games like Monopoly, Payday, and Uno can teach mathematics skills. All games also teach a very valuable social lesson: Sometimes things do not go the way you would like. This is a very difficult lesson for many children (and some adults) to learn. One minute, a child may have a lot of Monopoly money, and the next minute, he may land on Boardwalk with a hotel and lose all of his money to a peer. Such a situation is a good opportunity to practice social skills, including following rules and coping with unpleasant feelings.

If possible, the teacher or a classroom paraprofessional should play the game with the students. Playing the game with students helps to develop a rapport between students and teacher and also provides the teacher with the opportunity to teach appropriate social skills.

## Case Study 7.2

### Johnny

Johnny dropped a Wild Card on top of the pile. Holding one card and smiling, he called out "Uno!"

Johnny's teacher, Mr. Poteet, sat to the left of Johnny. He watched in amusement as he asked Johnny, "What color?" The Wild Card allowed Johnny to call the color of the next card.

"Red," grinned Johnny, looking at the red 2 he held in his hand. Mr. Poteet groaned good-naturedly. He didn't have a red card and had to draw from the deck.

Mary, a student to Mr. Poteet's left, put down a red 9 on the top of the Wild Card. She called out, "Uno."

Johnny became anxious, but wasn't overly concerned. His turn should come before Mary had another chance. Michael's turn was next, and then his.

Michael laid down a red "Reverse," which reversed the direction of the play, so that it was Mary's turn again.

Mary grinned as she laid down a red 7. "I'm out," she said triumphantly.

Johnny threw his card down on the table, shoved his chair back, and walked away.

Mr. Poteet looked at Mary and Michael, and told them to deal a new game. He got up and followed Johnny to his desk. Mr. Poteet had been working with Johnny for a long time and felt that he could easily talk to him about his behavior.

"What was that all about?" Mr. Poteet asked.

Not looking at his teacher, Johnny replied bitterly, "I should have won."

"You can't win all the time."

Johnny complained, "But it is not fair. I had a red 9."

"Life isn't always fair," Mr. Poteet reminded Johnny. "You are not always going to get your way, and it is important for you to learn how to handle disappointments."

Johnny grunted, but did not reply.

Mr. Poteet asked, "How should you have handled losing?"

"I guess I shouldn't have lost my cool."

"That's probably true," Mr. Poteet agreed, "and how do you think it made Mary feel when you got mad? She won the hand, and should have felt good about winning."

Johnny took a deep breath, not realizing how Mary must have felt. "She probably felt bad."

"And what do you think you should do to rectify the situation?" asked Mr. Poteet.

"I probably should tell her I'm sorry," admitted Johnny.

"And what about the next time?" asked his teacher.

Johnny grinned mischievously, "Not lose!"

Mr. Poteet returned the smile, knowing that Johnny was kidding.

"No, really," said Johnny. "I should not get mad. It is just a game."

Other activities besides board games can be useful opportunities to teach social skills. For example, recreational sports such as basketball are a good venue for teaching social skills. In the special education classroom, the teacher could take students to the gym when it is available as part of a token economy system. (See Chapter 6.) The teacher should not only provide appropriate guidance in social skills and sportsmanship, but also model the behaviors by participating in the activity along with the students.

Special education teachers also should take students out in the community to practice the social skills they have acquired. Bowling alleys, roller skating rinks, and restaurants are appropriate places for students to practice social skills. Restaurants should include fast-food establishments like McDonald's and Burger King, but also family restaurants. The educational possibilities afforded by a trip to a fancy, posh restaurant are endless. Prior to the event, the teacher should teach social skills that include dining etiquette, manners, and proper computation of tips. Students should be taught how to dress appropriately for such a dinner with girls wearing dresses and boys wearing shirts and ties.

Unfortunately, as schools attempt to meet the accountability requirements ordained by No Child Left Behind, social skills training tends to be omitted from school programs, including special education. Playing games in the classroom is viewed as a waste of time and is often met with resistance by administrators. School officials who are concerned with test results seldom support taking students to bowling alleys or restaurants. It is a shame that school, which can be fun, exciting, and educational, has become boring and monotonous to today's students due to the emphasis on high-stakes testing. It is also unfortunate that social skills, which are necessary survival skills in today's society and can serve students throughout their lives, are neglected at school, a place that provides wonderful opportunities for children to learn appropriate interaction with peers and authority figures.

## CULTURALLY RESPONSIVE PRACTICES IN SOCIAL BEHAVIOR

As the number of ethnically diverse children increases in the public schools, it is important for teachers to understand that social behavior is affected by cultural diversity. Teachers who are unfamiliar with the diverse backgrounds of their students may not know what is culturally acceptable to their students (Wilder et al., 2007) and therefore may not understand their students' social behaviors. They may even violate the culture beliefs and traditions of their students. For example, many Hispanic cultures display *simpatía*, behavior that prompts pleasant social relationships and minimizes conflict with others (Marin & Marin, 1991; Shepherd et al., 2005). As a result of *simpatía*, students may avoid eye contact with teachers because looking directly at an authority figure is considered rude and unacceptable behavior. This behavior becomes problematic because some social skills programs require students to make eye contact when conversing with others.

As another example, when having conversations with others, many Native Americans prefer to stand 2 to 3 feet from the person to whom they are talking. Many European Americans are comfortable being closer to others while talking (Lee & Cartledge, 1996). This habit could cause problems for students who are conducting role-playing scenarios if the teacher is not aware of this aspect of Native American culture.

African American males often engage in "capping" or "woofing," a form of verbal sparring. These exchanges are conducted in an atmosphere of sport (Irvine, 1990). The cultural misunderstanding of this ritual has resulted in a number of referrals to the principal's office.

It is increasingly important that teachers and administrators be culturally in tune with their ethnically diverse students. Addressing this issue will take the commitment of all those involved in public education. Universities and colleges that prepare teachers will need to train them how to teach diverse populations. School districts will need to provide training specific to the cultural attributes of their student population.

The relatively small numbers of ethnic and racial minorities among teachers is also part of the problem. Few African Americans, Native Americans, Hispanics, or Asian Americans go into the teaching field. Some regions have a large number of teachers who are ethnic minorities (in south Texas, for example, many teachers are Hispanic), but these individuals seldom leave their communities, due to strong familial ties. As a result of minorities' reluctance to enter the teaching profession or to teach outside their communities, many minority students across the nation are taught by European American, female teachers (Aaroe & Nelson, 2000; Nieto, 2002).

## IMPORTANCE OF SOCIAL SKILLS

The importance of social skills cannot be underestimated. Children with deficits in social skills are at risk for unemployment, aggressive interactions in the community, juvenile delinquency, and adult mental health problems (Elksnin & Elksnin, 1998a; Elksnin & Elksnin, 1998b). Yet social skills training is seldom an integral part of the general or even the special education curriculum. In today's political climate, academics, accountability, and testing are the major components of public education. Teachers themselves tend to value academics, even when the lack of social skills exhibited by children with emotional and behavior disorders will obscure any academic abilities these children might have (Nickerson & Brosof, 2003).

It is important to teach social skills in the general and special education classrooms to children who have emotional and behavior disorders or who are at risk for developing these disorders (Nickerson & Brosof, 2003). Although academics remain the main focus in the general education classroom, time should be allotted for social skills training that will benefit all children. In the special education classroom, especially in a classroom for children with emotional and behavior disorders, behavior management and social skills training should often take precedence over academics. In many instances, once these skills are in place, the students' academic performances will improve. After all, these children are identified as having a disability because their inappropriate emotions and behavior have adversely affected their educational performances.

Critics of social skills training sometimes contend that the skills taught to children with emotional and behavior disorders are not useful to the students, are not valued by others, and do not increase peer acceptance. Because the skills are not helpful, children do not perform them (Meadows, Neel, Parker, & Timo, 1991). To address this criticism, teachers should ensure that the social skills they are teaching can be used by the student in other settings and will be accepted by teachers and peers.

This problem is further exacerbated by the perceptions that people hold about children with emotional and behavior disorders. Teachers and peers sometimes expect these children to behave inappropriately, and they display a lack of tolerance and acceptance. For example, Timothy is a popular third grade student. He blows a spitball at Matthew, a child who has been identified as having emotional and behavior disorders. The class laughs, and the teacher mildly admonishes Timothy. However, when Matthew blows a spitball back at Timothy, Timothy complains vociferously and the teacher threatens to refer Matthew to the principal. The behavior is the same; the child is different.

When a school is implementing social skills into the school curriculum, it is important for the social skills training to be regarded as equally important as academic instruction. All children will benefit from social skills training. Appropriate social skills will allow them to get along with peers in school and work well with others once they are in the labor market.

According to No Child Left Behind, teachers implementing social skills programs should be highly qualified and trained to efficiently provide social skills training. They should allot adequate time for social skills training throughout the year and should reinforce skills that have been taught during instructional times during the school day to promote generalization.

Social skills programs should involve everyone: teachers providing the social skills training, other teachers in classrooms where students will do their social skills homework, and peers who facilitate the learning of students with social skills deficits.

Finally, social skills programs should be monitored and evaluated for effectiveness. Observations, self-reports, and behavioral checklists can be used to assess and improve a school's social skills program.

If they do not receive appropriate interventions, many individuals with social skills deficits will experience teacher and peer rejection, school failure, limited social involvement, unemployment, and adult mental health problems. It is critical that social skills training be provided for all children, especially those who have emotional and behavior disorders or who are at risk for developing these disorders.

## Summary

Students with emotional and behavior disorders often do not have social skills; as a result, they experience teacher and peer rejection, school failure, and limited social involvement. They have difficulties understanding and interpreting social cues, responding effectively in social situations, displaying empathy, and initiating age-appropriate interactions with peers and adults. Important social skills that students need to master include peer and adult interactions, classroom survival skills, and coping skills.

A number of social skills programs are available for teachers. Many of them incorporate direct instruction of social skills. This model includes introduction and instruction of the skill, modeling, peer involvement, role-playing, feedback, and reinforcement of desired social behaviors. The teacher begins the social skills lesson by introducing the skill that the students are going to be learning. The teacher then models the skill by demonstrating or performing it. The lesson might use peer involvement, a method that has been shown to improve the social behaviors of children with emotional and behavior disorders. Role-playing allows the students to rehearse or practice social skills in the classroom in which the skill is being taught, and performance feedback lets the student know how they performed during the role-playing activity.

Children also need to learn decision-making and problem-solving strategies. Students with emotional and behavior disorders often react poorly in social situations in which they need to decide between choices. They should be provided with opportunities to practice making choices and to recognize the outcome of their choices. They also need to develop self-determination skills: the ability to identify and pursue goals without external influences. Mastery of these skills is associated with more positive adult outcomes.

School-wide programs have been developed to teach social skills to all students. The Girls and Boys Town Education Model has been adapted to train teachers, administrators, and staff the skills and strategies they need to address the social skills needs of all students.

A number of simple strategies in the general and special education classrooms can help develop the social skills of children. These strategies should involve real-life social activities such as board games, sports, and other recreational activities.

Many teachers do not understand that student behavior is affected by cultural beliefs and traditions. It is important for teachers to understand the backgrounds of their students so that they can better understand their students' social behavior. Unfortunately, although the number of ethnically diverse students in today's schools is increasing, most teachers are European American females with little or no multicultural training. Universities and colleges who have teaching programs need to provide more training and classes oriented toward teaching diverse populations. School districts need to provide training specific to the cultural diversity of their student population. Ethnic and racial minorities also need to see teaching as a viable and important profession.

There are many benefits to integrating social skills into the general education curriculum. Individuals with deficits in social skills are at risk for unemployment, aggressive interactions in the community, juvenile delinquency, and adult mental health problems. Learning appropriate social skills will allow them to function in school and in the labor market.

## Review Questions

1. Why should social skills training be a part of the school curriculum?
2. What are the common components of social skills training programs?
3. Why is it important for teachers to understand the cultures and traditions of ethnically diverse students who have emotional and behavior disorders?
4. What are some of the strategies classroom teachers can use to promote social skills among their students?
5. Why is it important to include problem-solving strategies and self-determination skills when teaching social skills?

# CHAPTER 8

# Teaching Academic Skills

**After reading this chapter, you should be able to**

- List the goals and assumptions of teaching academic skills to students with emotional and behavior disorders.
- Define teacher-mediated academic interventions and identify teacher-mediated teaching strategies that are utilized for students with emotional and behavior disorders.
- Define peer-mediated academic interventions and identify peer-mediated teaching strategies that are utilized for students with emotional and behavior disorders.
- Define child-mediated academic interventions and identify child-mediated teaching

strategies that are utilized for students with emotional and behavior disorders.
- Describe strategies that are used to teach basic academic skills.
- Describe the similarities and differences between the two approaches for adapting instruction and the curriculum to meet the needs of students with emotional and behavior disorders.
- Name and explain the four levels of instructional time.
- Describe the importance of academic performance and strategies for reinforcing it.

## GOALS OF ACADEMIC INSTRUCTION

One of the criteria that identifies a child with emotional and behavior disorders is an inability to learn that cannot be explained by other factors (U.S. Department of Education, 1999, p. 12422). Conversely, a child should not be referred for special education services or receive these services unless the child's disability adversely affects his or her academic performance.

Teaching students with emotional and behavior disorders is a complex and overwhelming task for general and special education teachers, administrators, and related services personnel (Smith & Coutinho, 1997). Students with emotional and behavior disorders generally perform 1 to 2 years below grade level. These students have large academic deficits and they experience deficits in all content areas (Nelson, Benner, Lane, & Smith, 2004). Deficits in basic reading, writing, mathematics, and other content subjects significantly impair a student's ability to function academically, socially, and emotionally across a variety of domains (Trout, Nordness, Pierce, & Epstein, 2003). Compared with other students who have disabilities, students with emotional and behavior disorders have a lower graduation rate (Kauffman, 2005); over half of them drop out of school (U.S. Department of Education, 2002). A majority of students with emotional and behavior disorders were unemployed 5 years after leaving school, and the majority had had at least one arrest (Bullis & Cheney, 1999; D'Amico & Blackorby, 1992; D'Amico & Marder, 1991).

The primary function of public schools is to educate children in academic subjects, but little research exists on specific techniques and interventions that may be used to teach academics to students with emotional and behavior disorders (Lane, 2004; Pierce et al., 2004). Often the attention is on the behavior problems that affect achievement, and the academic needs of students with emotional and behavior disorders are secondary. The prevailing belief is that the child's behavior must be controlled before academics can be taught (Wehby, Lane, & Falk, 2003). However, a viable program should meet the academic, behavioral, social, and emotional needs of children with emotional and behavior disorders equally. Academics should be taught in conjunction with teaching behavioral management skills and social skills.

### Teaching Academic Material

Teaching academic material to students with emotional and behavior disorders is based on several assumptions:

1. Children with emotional and behavior disorders want to be successful in school, but their behaviors get in the way. They often do not have the ability to regulate or inhibit behavior. (This may not be true for children with social maladjustment, whom many professionals believe are able to follow rules and expectations, but choose to violate them [Costenbader & Buntaine, 1999; Stein & Merrell, 1992].) Teaching students with emotional and behavior disorders will take more effort on the part of the teacher.
2. Students with emotional and behavior disorders can be successful in school if they have a structured learning environment. A consistent classroom management plan is crucial and needs to be implemented in conjunction with academics.
3. The pedagogy used in teaching students with emotional and behavior disorders is similar to that used to teach other students, except that it is more intensive (Morgan & Jenson, 1988), and equal emphasis is placed on academics and on the child's behavioral, emotional, and social needs.

Unfortunately, students with emotional and behavior disorders generally do not receive the instruction from qualified teachers that they need. Of the nation's school districts, 98% report a shortage of qualified special education teachers (Bergert & Burnett, 2001), and the demand for special education teachers in the area of emotional and behavior disorders is high (Henderson et al., 2005). Students with emotional and behavior disorders do not benefit from effective teachers in the general education classroom because they are often referred to resource rooms, self-contained classrooms, and alternative placements.

Providing effective interventions is one way to improve the problem of academic under-achievement (Mooney, Epstein, Reid, & Nelson, 2003). A number of strategies are available for teaching students with emotional and behavior disorders. Many of these strategies are effective not only for students with emotional and behavior disorders, but also for students who do not have disabilities. Many such strategies could be applied in a general education classroom; a few would be more practical in a special education classroom. However, it is important to remember that there is no single best strategy for teaching children. Whatever method is used, the teacher needs to feel comfortable with it and embrace it as part of the pedagogy. The methods and strategies presented in this chapter are best practices, but they are only pedagogical suggestions for general and special education teachers and may be modified as these teachers see fit.

Three types of academic interventions are available for students with emotional and behavior disorders: (1) teacher-mediated academic interventions, (2) peer-mediated academic interventions, and (3) child-mediated academic interventions. These interventions have been successful in improving the academic performance of students with emotional and behavior disorders (Mooney, Denny, & Gunter, 2004).

## TEACHER-MEDIATED ACADEMIC INTERVENTIONS

With *teacher-mediated academic interventions*, teachers or classroom paraprofessionals are responsible for implementing interventions through management of antecedents and/or consequences (Pierce et al., 2004). Token economies (see Chapter 6), structured instructional systems such as Direct Instruction, and story mapping (similar to graphic organizers; see later) are examples of teacher-mediated academic intervention.

### Direct Instruction

Direct Instruction is a teaching method that was developed after researchers analyzed teaching practices that resulted in successful student achievement (Rosenshine, 1976; Rosenshine & Stevens, 1986). It has been used successfully in many classrooms.

Direct instruction is a sequential method of instruction designed to teach an entire class the same lesson simultaneously. The teacher begins the lesson by reviewing the previous day's lesson or reviewing prior knowledge. This gives students an opportunity to reinforce their skills and reteaches problem areas. The teacher then models the lesson giving clear instructions. Effective teachers spend more time demonstrating new skills and give more examples than less effective teachers. The teacher finally leads students in practicing the skill until all students are responding correctly to teacher prompts.

The sequential components of direct instruction are as follows:

1. Review previous learning.
2. State the goals of today's lesson.

**3.** Model the lesson.
**4.** Give clear instructions and explanations.
**5.** Help the students practice.
**6.** Check for understanding.
**7.** Give guided practice.
**8.** Provide feedback and corrections.
**9.** Provide and monitor seatwork.

For example, in order to teach a mathematics lesson on double-digit multiplication, the teacher may first want to review the previous lesson on single-digit multiplication (Step 1). Reviewing the previous lesson will connect the skills students have already acquired to the new skills they are about to learn. Review also serves to check the students' understanding of the previous skills before they attempt the new skills. Thus, the math teacher, Mrs. Smart, may write the following mathematics problems on the board:

$$
\begin{array}{ccccc}
12 & 25 & 37 & 19 & 44 \\
\times 4 & \times 3 & \times 5 & \times 7 & \times 6
\end{array}
$$

Mrs. Smart may ask the students to complete the problems at their desks, or she may call for volunteers to come to the front of the room and complete the problems on the board. It is extremely important for the teacher to know the students' abilities and temperaments. Some students do not feel comfortable performing academic tasks in front of their peers. Many students with emotional and behavior disorders are already having difficulties with academic tasks and may behave inappropriately if called on to complete problems at the board. These students often feel unequal to the task, and their inappropriate behavior is an attempt to save face.

Once Mrs. Smart is certain that her students understand single-digit multiplication, she introduces today's lesson: double-digit multiplication (Step 2) and proceeds to model it (Step 3). Modeling the lesson should involve more than just writing examples on the board. Teaching double-digit or any multidigit multiplication involves teaching the multiplication algorithm, which is a multistep procedure that follows the rules of mathematics for single-digit multiplication to find the answer to a more complex multiplication problem. The five principles for teaching algorithms are the following:

**1.** Model the operation with manipulatives or pictorial models.
**2.** Explain the meaningful mathematical rules that apply in this case.
**3.** Emphasize the important generalizations that describe the procedures.
**4.** Use the written algorithm as a recording of what happens when the algorithm is modeled.
**5.** Have the students use language that describes what they see when the operation is modeled (Tucker, Singleton, & Weaver, 2002).

Mrs. Smart may model the lesson by using manipulatives and teaching multiplication by 10. For example, she could teach 14 × 10 with the use of building blocks. (See Figure 8.1.)

When the teacher models the lesson, it is extremely important for him or her to provide clear instructions and explanations (Step 4). Using manipulatives or relating the lesson to real-world situations makes it easier for students to grasp concepts and apply them. It also shows students that the lesson has value beyond the classroom.

Once the teacher has explained the value of the lesson, modeled it, and provided clear instructions, he or she should allow time for the students to practice the skill (Step 5). To do this, Mrs. Smart puts a double-digit multiplication problem on the board and allows students to work the problem at their desks using bundled sticks. The teacher checks on the progress of each child using the *tennis shoe method* of teaching. In essence, the teacher puts on her "tennis shoes," monitors student progress and behavior by circulating through the classroom, and seldom sits down at her desk. Not only does this method allow the teacher to effectively check on students' understanding of the lesson, but her presence exerts a steadying influence on students, helping them to remain focused on the task. This proximity control also allows teachers to move closer to students who are misbehaving, which is sometimes all that is needed to redirect the students to the task at hand.

As the students practice the skill, Mrs. Smart checks each student's work to ensure that the student understands the process for solving double-digit multiplication problems (Step 6), sometimes offering guided practice (Step 7) to students who are having difficulties. Mrs. Smart puts several more problems on the board and continues to monitor the students' progress. This time she provides feedback and corrections, but little guided practice (Step 8). Remember, feedback can be positive comments to students who are mastering the concept. For example, Mrs. Smart sees that Kenya is doing well, so she comments that Kenya "really has an understanding of double-digit multiplication." The teacher should avoid telling

Problem: 10 × 12

First, connect 10 building blocks together to represent 10.

Second, use connected building blocks and include 2 more building blocks to represent 12.

**FIGURE 8.1**   Multiplying by Tens Using Building Blocks.

Third, use 10 sets of the grouped building blocks to represent 12 a total of 10 times.
Write 10 × 12 on the board.

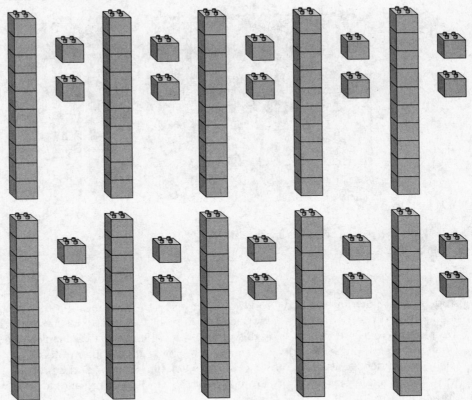

Fourth, put all the building blocks representing 'tens' together and all the building blocks
representing 'ones' together.

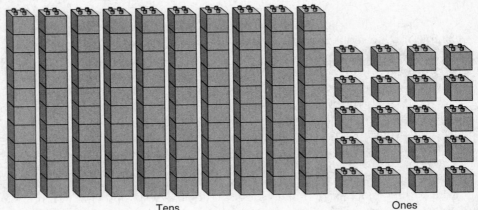

Tens

Ones

*Continued*

Finally, group the 'tens' building blocks together to make 100, and group the 'ones' building blocks together to make 20.

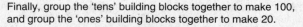

100                    +          20      = 120

Record the results on the board:                    10 × 12 = 120

**FIGURE 8.1**    *Continued*

students that they are doing a "good job" because of the implication that there must be a "bad job" and because the repetitive use of "good job" causes it to lose its value and become meaningless to the students. Using this phrase is a difficult habit for many teachers to break. Similarly, when Mrs. Smart observes a student doing the problem incorrectly, she avoids telling the student he is wrong. Instead, she may tell him to "look at the problem in a different way," once again staying away from the "right" and "wrong" allegations, which could discourage the student.

Finally, when the teacher feels confident that most of the students understand the lesson, she provides and monitors seatwork (Step 9). Mrs. Smart hands out a worksheet of double-digit multiplication problems and monitors the students' progress as they complete the assignment.

One of the major principles of direct instruction is that all children can be taught. Simple modifications and adaptations can be implemented to meet the needs of children with emotional and behavior disorders. These accommodations can also be used for children who are slow learners or who are at risk for developing emotional and behavior disorders. Accommodations include allowing the student more time to complete an assignment, having the student do a shortened version of the assignment, or having a peer help the student complete the assignment.

Direct instruction is an effective method of teaching in the general and special education classrooms, and it is a practical intervention to address the academic deficits of students with emotional and behavior disorders (Barton-Arwood, Wehby, & Falk, 2005). Even teachers who do not use direct instruction use some components of the method. However, students with severe emotional and behavior disorders may respond better to a more individualized approach to teaching. Individualized instruction is difficult to achieve in the general education classroom where the teacher has 20 to 30 students, but it may be more practical in a special education classroom.

## PEER-MEDIATED ACADEMIC INTERVENTIONS

*Peer-mediated academic interventions* involve students implementing teacher-selected instruction for their peers (Ryan, Reid, & Epstein, 2004). Some examples of these types of interventions are peer tutoring, class-wide peer tutoring (through programs such as Peer-Assisted Learning Strategies or Collaborative Strategic Reading), cross-age tutoring, peer modeling, and cooperative learning.

### Peer Tutoring

Teachers have informally been using certain students as peer tutors for a long time. Recently, structured peer tutoring programs have been developed to allow students to implement teacher-selected instruction to their peers. Peer tutoring strategies have been effective in improving the academic achievement, behavioral performance, and social relationships of the students who are tutored. In the academic setting, receiving peer tutoring can increase a student's time on task, provide more opportunity for the student to practice and to receive feedback, and accommodate the different ability levels of all students within the same classroom (Calhoon, 2005; Calhoon & Fuchs, 2003; Spencer, Scruggs, & Mastropieri, 2003; Wehby, Falk, Barton-Arwood, Lane, & Cooley, 2003), including English language learners (Fuchs & Fuchs, 2005). Peer-tutoring strategies can provide academic gains for both the tutor and the student who is being tutored (Falk & Wehby, 2001).

A peer tutoring strategy that provides instruction in small groups is class-wide peer tutoring (CWPT). Using this strategy, a teacher organizes all students in the classroom into tutor–tutee pairs (Greenwood & Delquadri, 1995). As with peer tutoring, CWPT is an effective method for increasing on-task behavior that provides students with increased practice time and feedback.

### Peer-Assisted Learning Strategies

A class-wide peer tutoring system that has been successful in teaching academic skills to students with learning disabilities and students with emotional and behavior disorders is the Peer-Assisted Learning Strategies, or PALS program (Falk & Wehby, 2001; Fuchs, Fuchs, Mathes, & Simmons, 1997). The PALS materials are structured and easy to use with explicit instructions on implementation (see Figure 8.2) and are used to supplement reading and math instructions in the classroom.

Using PALS, higher functioning students called "coaches" are paired with their lower performing classmates, or "players," to deliver academic instruction in either math or reading two to three times a week. The students take turns being coaches and players so that each can benefit from teaching and learning (Al Otaiba & Rivera, 2006; Falk & Wehby, 2001). Most students with emotional and behavior disorders have the ability to coach, but may need someone to model the behavior first.

**PALS READING PROGRAM**  In the PALS reading program, students complete three activities. The first activity is *partner reading*. First the coach, or higher functioning student, reads an assigned text. Then the player, or lower functioning student, rereads the same material, which is always written at the appropriate level for the player. When the player is finished reading the material, the player retells the text in his or her own words to the coach.

---

**Lesson 2: Outline**

**PARTNER READING**

**I. PREPARING MATERIALS FOR PEER-ASSISTED LEARNING STRATEGIES**
    A. The number of the first page of the day's story will be on the board.
    B. The second reader is responsible for turning to the correct page.
    C. The book is placed between partners.
    D. Pencils should be at the top of the desk.
    E. Question Cards should be placed at the top of desks.
    F. The Score Card should be ready for marking.

**II. BASIC PROCEDURES**
    A. Partner Reading will be conducted every day of Peer-Assisted Learning Strategies.
    B. The stronger reader reads aloud for 10 minutes.
    C. Students switch jobs and the weaker reader reads the same material for 10 minutes.
    D. Readers read carefully, quickly, and with expression.
    E. Coaches listen carefully for mistakes.
    F. Coaches pay attention to difficult words so they will know them when it is their turn to read.

**III. EARNING POINTS**
    A. One point is earned every time a sentence is read correctly.
    B. All mistakes must be corrected.
    C. It does not matter how many tries it takes to read the sentence correctly.

**IV. RECORDING POINTS**
    A. The coach marks points on the Score Card.
    B. After the reader reads a sentence correctly, the coach says, N1 point, Ó and records the point on the Score Card.
    C. While the coach is marking the points, the reader keeps track of where to begin reading again by pointing to where s/he stopped reading.

---

**FIGURE 8.2** PALS Explicit Instructions.

*Source:* From *Peer-Assisted Learning Strategies: Reading Methods for Grades 2–6 (1997),* by Fuchs, Mathes, & Fuchs. Copyrighted. Adapted/reprinted by permission.

The second PALS activity is *paragraph shrinking.* The player reads one paragraph at a time aloud. After reading each paragraph, the player identifies the main idea. The coach helps the player identify the main idea by asking who or what the paragraph is about. The player combines the information regarding the "who" or "what" of the paragraph to form main-idea statements of 10 words or less. After 5 minutes, the students switch roles.

The last activity is *prediction relay.* After reading half a page, the player predicts what will happen next. Then he or she reads the next half page aloud. While the player reads, the coach corrects any reading errors the player makes. After reading the half page, the player either confirms or refutes the prediction and states the main idea. After 5 minutes, the coach and player switch roles (Fuchs & Fuchs, 2005).

Students involved in the PALS reading program have made gains in reading fluency and reading comprehension (Calhoon, 2005; Fuchs & Fuchs, 2005). The program may be a promising approach to improving reading skills for English language learners (McMaster, Kung, Han, & Cao, 2008). It may also help to improve reading fluency and comprehension in students with emotional and behavior disorders, who often demonstrate significant reading difficulties. Correcting these deficits is very important; research has shown that a strong link exists between reading difficulties and conduct disorders and antisocial behavior in older students (Coleman & Vaughn, 2000).

**PALS MATHEMATICS PROGRAM**  The procedures for the PALS mathematics program are similar to those of the reading program. The stronger math student "coaches" the lower functioning "player." During each session, the coach and the player switch roles so that each student has the opportunity to tutor the other student. A structured question sheet guides the students through each step of the problem-solving algorithm. The coach provides immediate feedback as the player writes down the answer (Baker, Gersten, Dimino, & Griffiths, 2004).

During the coaching session, the coach tutors the player as he or she works through the problems on the first part of the Coaching Sheet. Then the coach and the player switch roles, and the lower functioning student tutors the higher functioning student as he or she works through the problems on the second part of the Coaching Sheet. (See Figure 8.3.)

---

**Math Samples**

This is a sample Coach Sheet from a third grade Computation lesson on adding. On this sheet, the Coach coaches the Player through the problems on the first two rows using the Coaching Question Sheet. The Coach and the Player then switch jobs and repeat the same procedure for the bottom two rows.

ADDING

Player's Name _____  Date _____

Coach's Name _____

| $34$ | $384$ | $954$ |
| $+83$ | $+328$ | $+72$ |

| $33$ | $294$ | $937$ |
| $+92$ | $+194$ | $+324$ |

| $734$ | $88$ | $29$ |
| $+83$ | $+26$ | $+22$ |

| $376$ | $93$ | $652$ |
| $+45$ | $+84$ | $+502$ |

---

**FIGURE 8.3**  PALS Math Samples.

*Source:* From *Peer-Mediated Mathematics Instruction: A Manual (1994),* by Fuchs, Fuchs, Karns, & Phillips. Copyrighted. Adapted/reprinted by permission.

The second part of the PALS mathematics program is independent practice. This exercise allows the students to practice newly acquired skills and previously attained skills. Students are awarded points at the end of each session. Points are awarded for cooperation and correct answers, and the dyad with the most points receives special recognition.

Mathematics lessons build upon previously taught skills in a particular sequence. Disruptions of this sequence can cause problem-solving difficulties for students with emotional and behavior disorders (Jolivette, Wehby, & Hirsch, 1999). Traditional mathematics lessons in the general education and special education classrooms have resulted in poor math performance among students with disabilities (Cawley, Parmar, Foley, Salmon, & Roy, 2001). Students with disabilities who participated in PALS mathematics programs achieved more than students in traditional programs (Calhoon & Fuchs, 2003).

Students with emotional or behavioral disorders often are not motivated by traditional teaching methods. These students find academic tasks aversive, and their inappropriate behaviors and poor academic performances are an attempt to avoid completing academic assignments (Maag, 2004; Penno et al., 2000). Class-wide peer tutoring programs like PALS actively engage students in the learning process and create a more positive learning environment. Peer tutoring increases the amount of time a student spends on task, provides more opportunities for students to practice and to receive immediate feedback, and accommodates different ability levels within the same classroom. In addition, students with emotional and behavior disorders also learn valuable social skills when they work cooperatively with other students. Peer tutoring and class-wide peer tutoring programs such as PALS have been shown to be an effective instructional strategy for students with emotional and behavior disorders at the elementary, middle, and high school levels (Spencer, 2006). As a result, peer tutoring can be a practical supplement to more traditional teaching strategies.

## Cooperative Learning Strategies

Teachers have used cooperative learning strategies for many years to facilitate learning. This method involves having students work together in small groups to complete an academic project. Like peer tutoring, cooperative learning increases student involvement in the lesson and promotes active learning (Jenkins, Antil, Wayne, & Vadasy, 2003). Cooperative learning encourages positive interaction in the general education classroom between students who have emotional and behavior disorders and students who do not have disabilities (Putnam, Markovchick, Johnson, & Johnson, 1996).

Cooperative learning strategies should be implemented with the following procedures:

1. Prior to the lesson, identify the academic objectives and the cooperative learning objectives that will be taught.
2. Decide on the size (generally no more than six students) and composition of the groups.
3. Assign roles to group members.
4. Explain the learning task and cooperative goals to the students.
5. Monitor the progress of the groups and intervene if necessary. Provide feedback on tasks.
6. Evaluate individual student learning, group products, and collaboration skills (Johnson & Johnson, 1986).

With cooperative learning strategies, students work together in small groups to complete an assigned academic project.

When students use cooperative learning strategies, they work together, help each other, and are evaluated together. Benefits of cooperative learning include improved self-esteem, opportunity to experience a safe learning environment, and increased academic performance (Jenkins et al., 2003).

## CHILD-MEDIATED ACADEMIC INTERVENTIONS

*Child-mediated academic interventions* give students the ultimate responsibility for implementing and managing their own academic interventions. This task includes self-instruction, goal setting, self-evaluation, and strategy instruction (Mooney et al., 2003). The Personalized System of Instruction (PSI) is a child-mediated academic intervention that places responsibility for the student's education on the student. It provides an alternative to traditional classroom pedagogy (Keller, 1968).

### Personalized System of Instruction

PSI is based on the operant psychology of Skinner (1953). Students are responsible for implementing and managing their own academic interventions. Individual students go through the elements or units of a course of study at their own pace, mastering each step before moving on to the next. Selected peers provide guidance and encouragement, and students earn maximal rewards when they complete their tasks (Keller, 1981). PSI focuses on meeting the needs and abilities of the learner, a fundamental component of IDEA.

PSI has five essential components:

1. Students proceed with lessons at their own pace.
2. Students must master each lesson before going on to the next lesson.
3. Teacher-mediated lectures and demonstrations are vehicles of motivation and are used infrequently.

4. The written word is the main format of teacher–student communications.
5. Student proctors are used to assist in the implementation of the program (Buskist, Cush, & DeGrandpre, 1991; Keller, 1968).

PSI places a special importance on active learning. Students learn to make decisions regarding lessons, solutions, and timetables for completion of the coursework. The teacher's role is facilitator and motivator. She suggests ways for students to complete the learning process (Peel & McCary, 1997; Saville, Zinn, & Elliott, 2005).

To implement PSI, the classroom teacher prepares individualized coursework that students can complete independently with little instruction from the teacher or paraprofessional. Students must master the first lesson in the coursework before going on to the next; if they do not master the first lesson, they must repeat it until they meet the criteria for mastery. Peer tutors help implement the program. Usually, higher functioning students are paired with their lower performing classmates.

A number of studies have demonstrated that PSI is a more powerful teaching method than traditional methods of classroom instruction (Callahan & Smith, 1990; Pear & Crone-Todd, 1999; Saville et al., 2005); however, very few teachers use PSI. Many teachers are hesitant to adopt a teaching methodology that is different from conventional pedagogical methods (Buskist et al., 1991). Because teachers have to prepare individualized units of instruction for students, PSI requires considerable preparation and resources, which may be a problem for many teachers (Boyce & Hineline, 2002). To overcome this problem, several computer-based versions of PSI have been developed. The Computer-Aided Personalized System of Instruction (CAPSI) is similar to PSI (Martin, Pear, & Martin, 2002; Pear & Crone-Todd, 1999). Students proceed with lessons at their own pace. They answer questions that are based on written material instead of attending lectures or demonstrations. The questions

## Case Study 8.1

### Johnny

Johnny walked into the special education resource class, ready to retake his math test. He had takn a test on least common denominators the week before, but had not earned 70% or better on it. Since Mr. Poteet, his special education teacher, expected him to get better than 70%, Johnny could not go on to the next unit until he passed this test.

During the last week, he had reviewed his work and practiced solving least common denominators using the method he had learned from the assignments and study guides Mr. Poteet had provided. Sometimes, Roger, a student in Mr. Poteet's class who was good at math, would help him out.

Johnny liked Mr. Poteet's class. He knew that if he did not do well on an assignment, he had a chance to go back and try to get a better score. It made him feel good about himself, especially because Mr. Poteet believed that he could do better.

Today, Johnny was retaking the math test on least common denominators. When he walked into the classroom he saw that Mr. Poteet had already put the test on his desk. Johnny sat down at his desk and pulled out his pencil. He felt ready for the test, but he knew that if he didn't do well, he would be able to try it again until he passed.

are grouped into small units, and a student must master each one before proceeding to the next unit. If a student does not master the unit, he or she may attempt a new test on the unit (Martin et al., 2002).

While many studies involving PSI have been at the college level, a few studies have been conducted in the public schools. Students identified as gifted and talented have benefited from PSI (Callahan & Smith, 1990). Students with emotional and behavior disorders have also increased their academic performance using PSI.

## ACADEMIC CONTENT

The basic academic skills are reading, writing, and mathematics. Mastery of these basic skills is needed to learn other skills and explore other content areas such as science, social studies, and fine arts. Students with emotional and behavior disorders often have deficits in the basic skills. The following sample strategies for teaching reading, writing, and mathematics are not exclusive. A number of other strategies are available, and it is the responsibility of general and special education teachers to keep abreast of the research occurring in the field. Journals such as *TEACHING Exceptional Children* and *Beyond Behavior* often provide practical teaching strategies for educators of students with emotional and behavior disorders.

### Reading

Students must be able to understand what they read in order to learn (Duke & Pearson, 2002), and students with emotional and behavior disorders have demonstrated significant difficulties in reading (Coleman & Vaughn, 2000). Some reading intervention programs have increased active responding, decreased reading errors, and reduced disruptive behavior of students with emotional and behavior disorders (Alber-Morgan, Ramp, Anderson & Martin, 2007; Sutherland & Snyder, 2007).

In addition to PALS, another peer-mediated intervention that aims to improve reading comprehension is Collaborative Strategic Reading (CSR). CSR is a multicomponent intervention that integrates several reading comprehension strategies for English language learners and students with reading, learning, and behavior problems (Klingner, Vaughn, Arguelles, Hughes, & Leftwich, 2004; Vaughn, Klingner, & Bryant, 2001). The first step in implementing CSR is to teach the four strategies to the entire class through modeling, role-playing, and thinking aloud. The four strategies of CSR are the following:

1. *Preview:* Students recall what they already know about the topic and predict what the passage might be about.
2. *Click and Clunk:* Students monitor comprehension by identifying difficult words in the passage and use fix-up strategies when the text does not make sense.
3. *Get the Gist:* Students restate the most important idea in a paragraph or section.
4. *Wrap-Up:* Students summarize key ideas and generate questions that a teacher might ask on a test (Klingner et al., 2004; Vaughn & Edmonds, 2006, p. 133).

These strategies can be expanded to increase students' comprehension. For example, prior to reading a passage, the teacher could preteach vocabulary that he or she knows will be difficult for the students. When they are working on Get the Gist, students could summarize the main idea by using the 5-finger strategy: Who, What, When, Where, and Why. Or students can summarize using the 10-finger strategy by stating the gist in 10 words or fewer (Levy, Coleman, & Alsman, 2002).

Once students have become proficient in using the strategies, the teacher should divide them into cooperative groups. Each group should include three to five students and should include at least one student who is a leader, at least one student who is a good reader, no more than one student who is a poor reader, and no more than one student who has a behavior problem. Each student should be assigned at least one role: group leader, clunk expert, gist expert, and note-taker/timekeeper. The group leader facilitates and manages the group, keeping the other students on task and guiding them through each strategy. The clunk expert makes sure that students have written their clunks, or words they do not understand, in the group's CSR Learning Log, and helps them resolve clunks. The gist expert helps students to determine the gist, or main idea of a paragraph or passage, and the note-taker/timekeeper makes sure that the CSR Learning Log is completed and that the assignment is completed within the allotted time. The CSR Learning Log (see Figure 8.4) is used to record either group or individual responses during CSR.

---

**Collaborative Strategic Reading Log**

Name (Group or Individual) _____ Date _____

Topic or Text Read _____

**Before Reading: Preview**

What do I already know about the topic?

What do I think I will learn?

**During Reading: Clunks and Gist**

*1st Section of the Passage*

What are my clunks?

What is my gist?

*2nd Section of the Passage*

What are my clunks?

What is my gist?

*3rd Section of the Passage*

What are my clunks?

What is my gist?

---

**FIGURE 8.4**   CSR Log.

*Source:* Vaughn & Edmonds, 2006. Adapted/reprinted by permission.

The CSR Learning Log may be maintained by the note-taker with input from the entire group (Vaughn & Edmonds, 2006).

Teachers who have used CSR in their classrooms have seen significant improvement in their students' reading comprehension, compared with the reading comprehension of students who did not use CSR in their classrooms. CSR is a fairly easy intervention to use and has benefited both English language learners and students with disabilities (Klingner et al., 2004).

## Language and Writing

Language skills are probably the most important academic skills that children need. Not only are these skills necessary for successful learning of math, reading, writing, science, and social studies (Nelson, Benner, & Cheney, 2005), but language skills are also necessary for social interactions and vocational endeavors. Students with emotional and behavior disorders were more likely to have deficits in language skills than students without behavior problems (Kaiser et al., 2002), and students who demonstrate deficits in receptive and expressive language functions in kindergarten are more likely to have behavioral problems by third grade (Hooper, Roberts, Zeisel, & Poe, 2003).

Writing ability depends on language and communication skills and is a neglected area for students with emotional and behavior disorders (Regan, Mastropieri, & Scruggs, 2005). Dialogue journals are a promising method for teaching writing to students with emotional and behavior disorders (Peyton & Staton, 1993). A *dialogue journal* is a written conversation between the student and the teacher.

In a journal, students can write as much as they want about areas of concern. The teacher regularly responds to the students' comments and questions. Rather than correcting the students' grammar and form, the teacher models correct English usage through a less obtrusive means by his or her written responses (Peyton, 1997; Regan et al., 2005). Dialogue journals can provide opportunities for social and language development that are consistent with Vygotsky's views on the role of language and social interactions in learning (Garmon, 1998; Vygotsky, 1978).

Students with emotional and behavior disorders also perceived that dialogue journals were useful as a forum for discussing issues. (See Figure 8.5.) Finally, dialogue journals are a strategy for increasing the students' self-awareness.

## Mathematics

In this increasingly technological society, it is important for all students, including those with emotional and behavior disorders, to understand mathematics. The National Council of Teachers of Mathematics Standards (NCTM) has stated that teachers are expected to teach higher level math skills to all students (NCTM, 2000).

A number of empirically validated approaches for teaching math are available. These approaches include the use of manipulatives to improve conceptual understanding, peer tutoring strategies such as PALS, and organizational strategies for retention such as cue cards of strategy steps, graphic organizers, mnemonics, and opportunities for additional practice (Maccini & Gagnon, 2006). Teachers can use activities to make mathematical concepts more concrete. For example, if the teacher was presenting a lesson on computing the area of a 4-inch by 6-inch rectangle, the students could cover the rectangle with 1-inch cubes and count how many cubes it took to cover the area. (See Figure 8.6.) Then students could

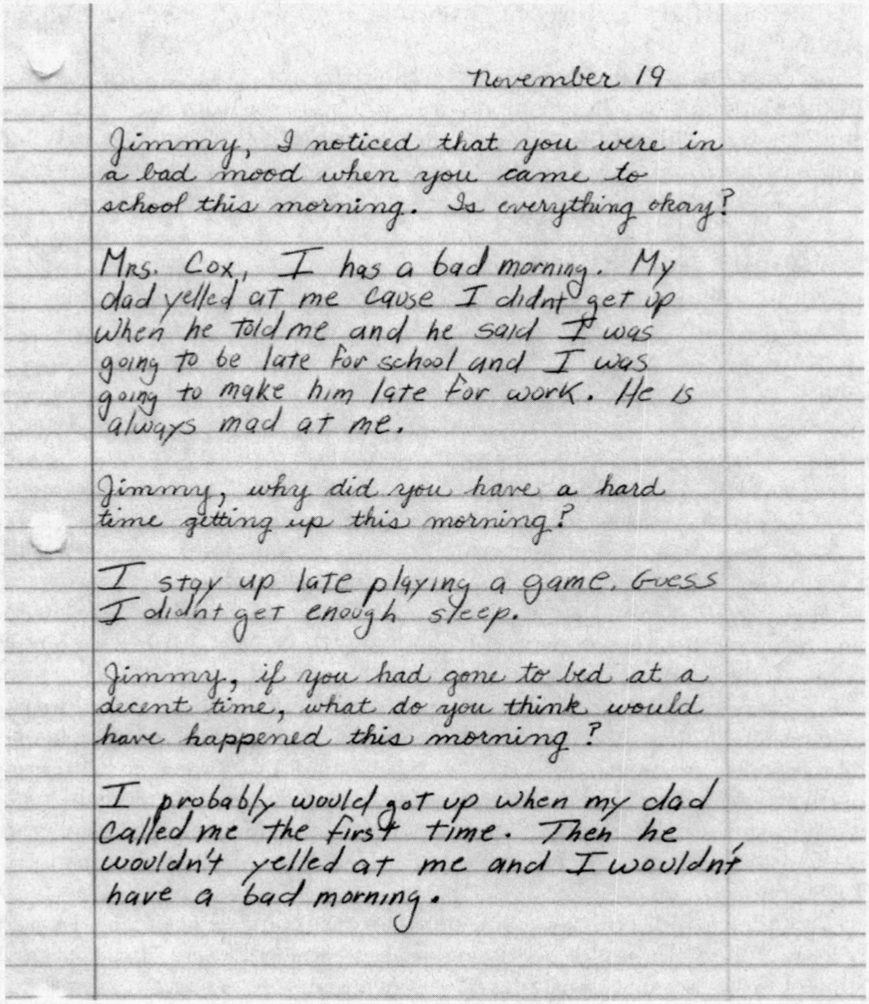

november 19

Jimmy, I noticed that you were in a bad mood when you came to school this morning. Is everything okay?

Mrs. Cox, I has a bad morning. My dad yelled at me cause I didnt get up when he told me and he said I was going to be late for school and I was going to make him late for work. He is always mad at me.

Jimmy, why did you have a hard time getting up this morning?

I stay up late playing a game. Guess I didnt get enough sleep.

Jimmy, if you had gone to bed at a decent time, what do you think would have happened this morning?

I probably would got up when my dad called me the first time. Then he wouldn't yelled at me and I wouldnt have a bad morning.

**FIGURE 8.5** Dialogue Journal Sample.

measure the length and width of the classroom or count the number of 12-inch by 12-inch tiles on the classroom floor to compute the area of the room.

Teachers should apply mathematics concepts to real-life situations. Teaching students how to write and balance checking accounts or how to figure the interest a student would pay on an automobile loan brings math into a realm that is meaningful to the students.

Another approach to teaching mathematics to students with emotional and behavior disorders is teaching strategies that promote retention. A 4-step process for solving math problems allows students to develop their own strategies:

1. Read and understand the math problem. Students may rewrite the problem in simpler terms if they wish.
2. Develop a strategy for solving the problem, and explain how this strategy was developed.

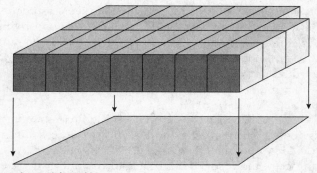

**FIGURE 8.6** Computing with Cubes.

**3.** Carry out the strategy and show all work.
**4.** Look back over the work and check the solution (Furner, Yahya, & Duffy, 2005; Polya, 2004).

Regardless of the content area, the No Child Left Behind Act sets high standards, demands accountability with regard to student learning, and mandates that highly qualified teachers be placed in classrooms. IDEA 2004 ensures that students with disabilities will be held to the same standards. Teachers are expected to effectively teach academic content areas to all students. General education teachers may have to adapt the curriculum and instruction for students with emotional and behavior disorders.

## ADAPTING THE CURRICULUM AND INSTRUCTION

As an increasing number of students with emotional and behavior disorders are educated in the general education setting, more teachers are being asked to meet the individual academic needs of a diverse population of students. Teachers are often required to make accommodations and modifications in the general education classroom to meet the needs of these students, but many teachers do not feel that they have the time, training, or resources to do so. When general education teachers do make accommodations, they usually make them for the entire class, rather than tailoring them to the needs of individual students (Rotter, 2004). Two approaches for adapting instruction and the curriculum to meet the needs of students with emotional and behavior disorders are the Universal Design for Learning and traditional accommodations and modifications.

### Universal Design for Learning

Universal Design for Learning (UDL) is a fairly new teaching paradigm that takes a proactive approach to developing curricula that meet the needs of students. In a traditional classroom, the teacher develops the curriculum to meet the academic needs of the whole class, viewing the students in the class as a single entity. When a student with a disability is placed in that classroom, the teacher allows accommodations and modifications as an afterthought to meet the individual needs of the student. A teacher using UDL would consider the needs of all students within the classroom before developing the curriculum. Such a teacher would consider the needs of students who have disabilities (including those who have emotional and behavior disorders), ethnically and linguistically diverse students, slow learners, and even gifted learners. Then the teacher would design a curriculum with materials, instructions, and sufficiently flexible learning environments that appropriately meets the needs of each student (Hitchcock, Meyer, Rose, & Jackson, 2002; Meo, 2008; Pisha & Coyne, 2001). The curriculum would be written at the learning level of the individual student, content would be presented in multiple ways, and creativity in student responses would be encouraged (Lieberman, Lytle, & Clarcq, 2008).

Flexible curricular materials are an essential component of UDL that is needed to support students' learning styles and ability to access information (Van Garderen & Whittaker, 2006). According to Vygotsky (1978), a student must employ three systems before learning can occur: the recognition, strategic, and affective systems (Rose & Meyer, 2002).

In order for students with emotional and behavior disorders to learn, they must be able to receive information from the teacher and understand it. They must *recognize* what they are learning. If a barrier prevents the student from recognizing what he or she is learning, then the teacher must remove the barrier. For example, if a student is upset because he had an argument with his father before school, the student is not going to learn. The teacher should implement a preconceived plan to remove the barrier. This plan could include assigning the student activities that will take his mind off the argument (such as passing out the textbooks or running an errand). Many barriers to learning can be overcome by providing a variety of modes of teaching (auditory, visual, kinesthetically, etc.). Teaching from a one-size-fits-all textbook will not be sufficient.

The strategic system allows students to use specific strategies to improve their learning. Students with emotional and behavior disorders might need to implement the social skills training they have received. A student who has reading difficulties might need the teacher to adapt the instruction by using an audiobook or a digital book. The advantages of a digital book are numerous. Students who cannot hold a book or turn its pages can turn the pages of a digital book by pressing a key on a computer keyboard, and if they are having problems reading a word, the computer can read it aloud. Unfortunately, digital text is not widely available (Pisha & Stahl, 2005).

The affective system addresses why students should learn. UDL must allow flexibility for the preferences and individual interest levels of the students. This philosophy is similar to that behind regular academic instruction, which focuses on what is meaningful for students. For example, Michael might be motivated to learn to compute the areas of squares, rectangles, and circles if he is shown how this knowledge applies to construction work, a vocation in which he has shown interest.

Many general education teachers currently individualize instruction by making accommodations and modifications for students with disabilities. But developing a universally designed curriculum by considering the needs of a diverse student population allows all students to benefit from a more flexible learning environment, not just students with disabilities (Meo, 2008). Unfortunately, UDL has not been widely accepted.

## Accommodations and Modifications

Because they lack proper training and preparation in using accommodations and modifications, teachers sometimes believe that such instruments are too elaborate to implement in the general education classroom. On the contrary, many accommodations are simple and easily employed.

The two types of adaptations made for students with emotional and behavior disorders in the general education classroom are accommodations and modifications.

**ACCOMMODATIONS**    *Accommodations* are changes to the delivery of instruction, method of student performance, or method of assessment. Accommodations do not significantly change the content or the difficulty level of the curriculum.

To change the delivery of instruction, the teacher might replace a standard lecture format with a series of short learning activities or incorporate graphic organizers, study guides, mnemonics, and the use of manipulatives into the lesson.

A *graphic organizer* is a visual technique that assists students in organizing prior knowledge, key concepts, and main ideas; comparing and contrasting information; and understanding cause and effect (Friend & Bursuck, 2005; Vaughn & Edmonds, 2006). To use a graphic organizer, the teacher or students choose a topic. Then the class brainstorms key words or main ideas related to the topic and places them into the graphic organizer. (See Figure 8.7.)

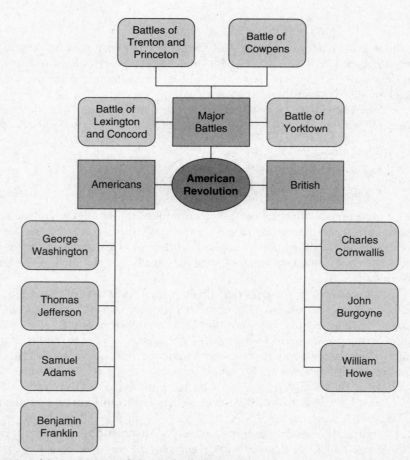

**FIGURE 8.7**    Graphic Organizer of the American Revolution.

Mnemonics is another type of delivery of instruction that is effective for students with emotional and behavior disorders (Cade & Gunter, 2002). Mnemonics is a technique that helps students remember information by using rhymes, songs, or visual images. They are ways to encode information so that it can easily be retrieved (Mastropieri & Scruggs, 1998). Common mnemonic devices include "Columbus sailed the ocean blue in fourteen hundred and ninety-two" to remember the year that Columbus reached America and "Every Good Boy Does Fine," using the first letter of each word to remember the notes on the lines of the treble clef musical staff. Mnemonics can also be used to remember the spelling of words. For example, "A Rat In Tom's House Might Eat Tom's Ice Cream" uses the first letter in each word to spell *arithmetic*.

Pegwords are a mnemonic strategy that can help students remember numbered information. Pegwords are rhyming words for numbers. These rhyming words are similar to the words in the nursery rhyme "This Old Man."

| | |
|---|---|
| One is bun, | six is sticks, |
| Two is shoe, | seven is heaven, |
| Three is tree, | eight is gate, |
| Four is door, | nine is vine, |
| Five is hive, | ten is hen. |

Pegwords are used instead of the number to be remembered and are associated with the other information. To remember that insects have six legs and spiders have eight legs, students create a mental image of an insect on sticks (six is sticks), and a spider on a gate (eight is gate) (Mastropieri & Scruggs, 1993).

Mnemonic devices can also be used to remember learning strategies. The RAP strategy can help students improve reading comprehension (Deschler, Ellis, & Lenz, 1996):

**R**ead a paragraph.

**A**sk yourself, "What is the main idea?"

**P**araphrase the content of the paragraph.

Mnemonic strategies are not comprehension strategies, but only memory strategies. They help students perform better on comprehension tests because the students remember more information that can be applied on the tests (Mastropieri & Scruggs, 1998). For many students (and adults), mnemonic strategies are fun, which makes them even more effective as memory aids.

*Manipulatives* are concrete objects such as beans, sticks, or marbles that teachers can use to teach mathematical concepts (Furner et al., 2005). Manipulatives can be used to teach addition, subtraction, multiplication, division, and fractions. The school may purchase commercial manipulative sets or teachers can create their own. Students comprehend abstract concepts more easily when they use manipulatives to solve mathematical problems (Freer Weiss, 2006), and they enjoy using them. Students who have emotional and behavior disorders, students who have other disabilities, and English language learners can all "benefit from instruction structured from concrete to abstract" (Furner et al., 2005, p. 17).

In addition to changing the delivery of instruction, teachers may wish to change the method by which students perform. Peer tutoring and cooperative learning activities are two alternative strategies for student performance. Allowing the student to tape-record the lesson or to record an oral recitation of a report instead of writing it are other accommodations that can be made in the general education classroom.

Finally, teachers can accommodate assessments of students' progress by providing more time for tests, reducing the number of questions on tests, or reading the test questions orally to students. These are simple accommodations that can easily be adapted to the general education setting.

**MODIFICATIONS**    Unlike accommodations, *modifications* are changes to the curriculum, instructional objectives, and methodology. They may be more difficult to implement in the general education setting than accommodations because of the time and effort they require. Three types of modifications are multilevel instruction, curriculum overlapping, and tiered assignments.

To implement multilevel instruction, the teacher engages all the students in the same curriculum, but assigns them different goals and provides material with different levels of difficulty. For example, Mrs. Smart is teaching her entire class a lesson on double-digit multiplication. After modeling the lesson, she writes a math problem on the board. She applies multilevel instruction by allowing the students who have difficulties with math to use manipulatives to solve the problem while the higher functioning math students solve the problem on paper.

To use curriculum overlapping, the teacher provides opportunities for students to pursue individually appropriate learning outcomes from different curricula within the same class. For example, while some students are completing their mathematics worksheet on double-digit multiplication, Mrs. Smart asks Timmy, a student with limited math skills and poor social skills, to pick up the manipulatives from other students while using the words "please" and "thank you." Curriculum overlapping could also involve a student beginning an assignment in one classroom and finishing it in another (Fisher & Frey, 2001). The method gives students with emotional and behavior disorders more time to complete the assignment. For instance, the social studies teacher could allow a student with a disability to type the answers to an essay question in computer class. The student would get credit for answering the essay question in social studies class and for writing a Word document in computer class.

With tiered assignments, the teacher models the lesson and then provides different assignments to the students depending on their individual ability levels. For example, students in a high school language arts class do a unit on *To Kill a Mockingbird*. The teacher assigns some students to write a summative report of the book, some students to write a play or create a storyboard of the book, and other students to make a video of the book.

Accommodations and modifications can easily be designed and implemented in the general education setting. Students with emotional and behavior disorders have a right to receive accommodations and modifications in the general education classroom through the IEP process, and these adaptations provide opportunities for these students to succeed academically.

## ACADEMIC INSTRUCTIONAL TIME

Students with emotional and behavior disorders often display inappropriate behaviors during "down time," or time when they are not engaged in instructional activities. It is important for the classroom teacher to consistently occupy students with instructional activities in order to prevent them from engaging in disruptive behavior. Instructional activities are not necessarily activities related to reading, writing, and arithmetic; they can also include social skills training, leisure activities, and reinforcement time. The instructional time should be meaningful and designed to meet the needs of the student (Keefe & Jenkins, 2005).

Instructional time has four levels: allocated time, actual academic instructional time, engaged time, and academic learning time (Kauchak & Eggen, 1993). *Allocated time* is the amount of time that the teacher has decided to spend on a lesson. This time is often determined by the amount of time in a class period. The teacher may have to spend some time taking attendance and listening to school announcements at the beginning of the period, and preparing for the transition to the next class at the end of the period. If the class period is 55 minutes long, the teacher may decide to devote 45 minutes to the lesson.

*Actual academic instructional time* is the amount of instructional time actually delivered to students. This is the time that the teacher spends actively teaching or presenting the lesson. Actual academic instructional time would encompass the first four steps of direct instruction (reviewing previous learning, stating the goals of the current lesson, modeling the lesson, and giving clear instructions). When students are engaged in peer tutoring, actual academic instructional time is the time that the teacher spends providing students with strategies to promote successful peer-tutoring activities.

*Engaged time* refers to the actual time that the students are engaged in instructional activities, or the time that they are on task. Students are engaged when they are actively paying attention to the teacher's presentation, responding appropriately to questions, and successfully completing instructional materials (Johns, Crowley, & Guetzole, 2002). Students should be actively engaged in learning during all aspects of teacher-mediated, peer-mediated, and child-mediated academic intervention. Peer tutoring has been very effective in increasing students' engaged time (Spencer et al., 2003).

*Academic learning time* is the amount of time that students are successful while they are engaged in learning. Academic learning time affects student self-esteem and the way that the student views learning. There is a positive relationship between academic learning time and academic achievement (Salend, 2000).

Teachers can enhance instructional learning time by allotting more time for the lesson, reducing interruptions, and planning smooth transitions between activities. Unfortunately, much instructional learning time is lost due to interruptions and activities beyond the teacher's control. Transitions from one class to another, fire drills, and pep rallies reduce instructional learning time. Teacher in-services during regular class days reduce instructional learning time because teachers who must attend the in-services generally leave busy work such as worksheets for substitute teachers. Many school districts are asking teachers to spend more class time preparing students to take state-mandated tests by giving them benchmark tests and practice tests and by teaching them test-taking strategies (Berliner & Biddle, 1995; Graves, 2002; Johnson & Johnson, 2002). The time that teachers spend preparing for these tests reduces the amount of instructional learning time they have left for lessons.

Actively engaging students with emotional and behavior disorders in instructional learning time has been shown to reduce inappropriate behavior and increase academic achievement in these students. It is important for teachers to allocate appropriate time and develop appropriate materials to promote learning in their classrooms for all students.

## ACADEMIC REINFORCEMENTS

The most difficult academic problem for teachers of students with emotional and behavior disorders is how to motivate them. Unfortunately, many of these students have experienced repeated academic failures and feel incapable of succeeding. Their low self-efficacy impedes their academic achievement and creates self-fulfilling prophecies of failure and learned helplessness (Margolis & McCabe, 2006). It is important for teachers to help students believe that they can achieve academically.

Certain methods of instruction, especially peer-tutoring or child-mediated interventions, can help students feel positive about academics. These interventions can increase a student's time on task, provide more opportunity for the student to practice and to receive feedback, and accommodate the different ability levels of students within the same classroom. Accommodations and modifications can also provide opportunities for these students to succeed academically. Another intervention that might improve students' academic performance is using academic reinforcements.

As discussed in Chapter 6, positive reinforcement can be used to increase the probability that a certain behavior will reoccur. *Academic reinforcements* can be anything that motivates a student to work harder on class assignments. There are many kinds of academic reinforcements. Some students are motivated by additional time on the computer. Others would rather spend a quiet lunch with the teacher. The reinforcements reward students for making appropriate efforts, being persistent, and correctly using strategies (Margolis & McCabe, 2006). As with accommodations, academic reinforcements can be simple to implement. It is amazing what many children at the elementary level will do for stickers or "stars," and these rewards are very powerful reinforcements. Verbal praise is also an effective reinforcement that can increase a student's feeling of self-efficacy. Teachers who provide students with high rates of praise have increased numbers of students responding during academic lessons (Sutherland et al., 2002).

A token economy that reinforces academics can be tailor-made for the classroom. For example, in Mrs. Swift's special education classroom, students receive $100 in monopoly money every time they receive 100% on an assignment. These assignments can be from the general education classroom as well as the special education classroom. Students show Mrs. Swift assignments on which they have earned 100%. She marks them so that students cannot present them again and gives them the monopoly money. During math class, the students deposit their money into a simulated checking account set up by the teacher. When the students have enough money saved up, they can purchase various items from the classroom store at the end of the day. Items in the store were chosen from a list compiled by the students, and range from candy bars to CDs. To purchase an item, the students write a check for the item and deduct it from their balance. The students are responsible for keeping their accounts updated and balanced.

Critics who argue that reinforcements are nothing but bribes need to remember that individuals are usually bribed to do something unethical or illegal. They argue that bribery takes away students' desire to do well on their own account and replaces it with the desire for extrinsic rewards. According to behaviorists, however, all behavior is reinforced by consequences. Motivating a student to do better in school is not unethical or illegal, and it may help the student feel better about himself or herself. Most of us do things for self-gratification. For example, a college student studies hard to get good grades so she can graduate and get a good job, which will allow her to purchase items (television, an automobile, a home, etc.).

Many teachers receive reinforcement and gratification from helping students. All behaviors are reinforced in some manner, and providing reinforcements to students to improve their academic performance is simply good teaching.

## Summary

Strategies for teaching academic content to students with emotional and behavior disorders are based on the assumptions that they want to be successful and that they can learn from a more intensive version of the same curriculum that is taught to other students. Providing effective interventions is one way to improve the problem of academic underachievement. The three types of academic interventions include teacher-mediated academic interventions, peer-mediated academic interventions, and child-mediated academic interventions.

Teachers are responsible for implementing interventions by managing antecedents and/or consequences with teacher-mediated academic interventions. The most common strategy is direct instruction, a sequential method of instruction that is designed primarily to teach an entire class the same lesson simultaneously.

In peer-mediated academic interventions, students implement teacher-selected instruction for their peers. Peer-mediated intervention strategies include peer tutoring, class-wide peer tutoring, peer-assisted learning strategies, and cooperative learning. Peer-Assisted Learning Strategies are a class-wide peer tutoring program that supplements reading and math instructions in the classroom.

Students have the responsibility for implementing and managing their own academic interventions in child-mediated interventions. The Personalized System of Instruction is a child-mediated academic intervention that places the responsibility of the student's education on the student.

Students with emotional and behavior disorders often have deficits in reading, writing, and mathematics. They need these basic skills in order to learn other skills and other content areas. A number of strategies are available to help students improve their basic academic skills, including Collaborative Strategic Reading, dialogue journals, manipulatives, peer tutoring strategies, and organizational strategies.

Two approaches for adapting instruction and the curriculum to meet the needs of students with emotional and behavior disorders are the Universal Design of Learning and traditional accommodations and modifications. A teacher using the Universal Design of Learning system would consider the needs of all children within the classroom before developing the curriculum. Accommodations and modifications are adaptations that are made for students with emotional and behavior disorders in the general education classroom. Accommodations are changes to the delivery of instruction, method of student performance, or method of assessment. Accommodations do not significantly change the content or the difficulty level of the curriculum. Modifications are changes to the curriculum, instructional objectives, and methodology. The implementation of modifications generally takes more time and effort on the part of the teacher.

It is important for teachers to consistently engage students in meaningful instructional time in order to prevent these students from displaying disruptive behaviors. Instructional time has four levels: allocated time, actual academic instructional time, engaged time, and academic learning time. Allocated time is the amount of time that the teacher has decided to spend on a lesson. Actual academic instructional time is the amount of instructional time actually delivered to students. Engaged time refers to the actual time that the students are engaged in instructional activities. Academic learning time is the amount of time students are successful while engaged in learning.

The most difficult academic problem for teachers of students with emotional and behavior disorders is how to motivate them. Academic reinforcements can motivate students to work harder on class assignments.

A number of interventions and strategies are available for teachers to improve the academic performance of students with emotional and behavior disorders. Many of these interventions and strategies are effective not only for students with emotional and behavior disorders, but also for students who do not have disabilities. Effective interventions and strategies can reduce inappropriate behaviors, increase academic achievement, and motivate students to achieve goals and improve their self-efficacy.

## Review Questions

1. What are the goals of academic instruction for students with emotional and behavior disorders?
2. Compare and contrast the three types of academic interventions and give examples of each.
3. Why is it important for students with emotional and behavior disorders to be proficient in the academic content areas?
4. What is the Universal Design for Learning, and how is it different from traditional accommodations and modifications in the general education classrooms?
5. What are the four levels of instructional time?
6. Describe several strategies for reinforcing academic performance.

# CHAPTER 9

# Meeting the Emotional Needs of Students With Emotional and Behavior Disorders

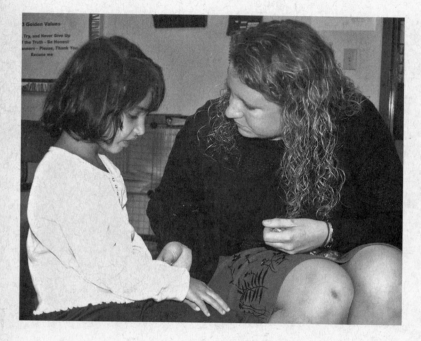

**After reading this chapter, you should be able to**

- Identify different counseling strategies teachers could use to address the emotional needs of students with emotional and behavior disorders, and describe differences and similarities between the strategies.

- Explain how reality therapy can help students meet their four basic human needs.

- List and describe the six therapeutic steps of the life space crisis intervention.

- Describe the similarities and differences between the various school-based mental health programs.

- Identify the four goals of a system-of-care program, and explain how these goals can help guide the development of a program in the public schools.

- Describe the five types of restrictive and intensive settings for students with emotional and behavior disorders.

---

Mr. Parelius, the U.S. History teacher at Franklin Pierce Middle School, was monitoring his students as they completed a worksheet on the events leading to World War I.

Several times he stopped at a student's desk and provided feedback.

After helping a student with a question, he noticed that Timothy was at his desk crying.

Unlike academic and behavioral concerns, the emotional and mental health needs of students with emotional and behavior disorders are seldom addressed in the public schools. Many administrators, general education teachers, and special education teachers feel that they are inadequately prepared to deal with the broad range of physical health, mental health, social, and psychological difficulties that students with emotional and behavior disorders may present (Anderson, Wright, Smith, & Kooreman, 2007; Epstein & Walker, 2002; Robertson, Anderson, & Meyer, 2004). The curricula of many teacher preparation programs do not address child or adolescent mental health beyond the Psychology 101 class (Daly et al., 2006). Unfortunately, many students with diagnosable disorders do not receive any counseling or mental health care.

Timothy was a student with emotional and behavior disorders who had been included in the U.S. History class but who had never given Mr. Parelius any problems.

Mr. Parelius walked over to Timothy and asked if he was all right. Timothy began crying harder and laid his head on his desk. Mr. Parelius was baffled. He had not noticed any antecedents that could have triggered Timothy's behavior, nor had he noticed any unusual behaviors from Timothy in the past.

Mr. Parelius gently asked Timothy if he would like to go into the hallway and talk about what was troubling him, but Timothy did not respond. His sobbing was gaining the attention of other students in the classroom, but Mr. Parelius did not know what else to do. He was completely unprepared for Timothy's behavior.

Because a large number of children with mental illnesses and emotional disorders attend public schools, it is logical for schools to become an important location for delivering mental health services to students. Interventions available to help meet the emotional needs of students with emotional and behavior disorders, include therapeutic timeouts, reality therapy, and life space crisis intervention. School-based health centers, system-of-care, and wraparound services are examples of the growing interdisciplinary efforts to provide mental health care for students with emotional and behavior disorders in public schools (Brown, 2006; Kutash & Duchnowski, 2004; Paternite, 2005). These interventions and services are crucial to meeting the emotional needs of students with emotional and behavior disorders.

## CLASSROOM COUNSELING TECHNIQUES

The role of counselor and advisor has always been a familiar one to teachers. Teachers are usually the first to respond to a student's inappropriate behavior and the first to respond to the student's psychological and emotional turmoil in school (Pirtle & Perez, 2003).

Teachers are not trained to be counselors. Many teacher preparation programs do not offer courses in counseling, but teachers can be trained to use "basic" counseling strategies that are relevant to the classroom. These strategies can be employed in the general education setting, but are more applicable in the special education classroom, especially for students with emotional and behavior disorders. Not surprisingly, many of the components of the strategies overlap, making it simple for teachers to use multi-intervention strategies when counseling students.

### Therapeutic Removal

Sometimes, the best action for the teacher to take when a student with emotional and behavior disorders is beginning to have behavioral difficulties is to remove the student from the classroom environment. This action is not an exclusionary time-out or a disciplinary removal, but simply an opportunity for the student to regain composure. Therapeutic removal may be the only intervention the student needs in order to refocus on the academic task. Sometimes the teacher may have to engage in basic counseling techniques as well as removing the student from the situation.

Before the teacher can "counsel" students, he or she must have an authentic and positive relationship with the students. The teacher needs to display unconditional positive regard, congruence, and empathy toward students in order to develop and maintain relationships with them (Gatongi, 2007; Pirtle & Perez, 2003; Rogers, 1980). Teachers who display these attitudes are in a position to create positive changes in their students' lives through the use of basic counseling techniques.

*Unconditional positive regard* means that the teacher accepts the student no matter what that student says or does. It is sometimes a challenge for teachers to maintain this attitude, especially when they are working with students with emotional and behavior disorders. It is difficult for a teacher to accept a student who is disrupting the class and behaving inappropriately, but unconditional positive regard is a prerequisite for establishing and maintaining a positive relationship with students. The teacher needs to accept the student regardless of the behavior he exhibits or despite what other teachers may have said about the student. For example, when the IEP Team decided to place Johnny in Mr. Poteet's classroom, Mrs. Smart, his math teacher, told Mr. Poteet that Johnny would be one of the worst students he had ever had. Had Mr. Poteet taken Mrs. Smart's words to heart, he would not have developed a positive relationship with Johnny.

If the teacher has genuine intentions to help a student or sees teaching as a noble and important profession, then he or she displays *congruence*. The student–teacher relationship in these cases will be based on trust, honesty, warmth, and dignity (Cornelius-White, 2007). The students need to feel that their teacher is *real*—that she genuinely cares for her students. Students can often tell the difference between a teacher who sees teaching as just an 8:00-to-3:00 job and a teacher who is passionate about her profession.

Finally, the teacher needs to be empathic toward the student's world and to appreciate the factors that may have significant impacts on the student's behavior in school. Students with emotional and behavior disorders may come from abusive homes, from single-parent homes where the parent works nights, or from homes where they do not have enough food to eat. Having empathy may help teachers understand their students' behaviors. Empathy does not mean that teachers must excuse inappropriate behaviors. Society expects individuals to behave in an acceptable manner, and part of a student's education is learning to behave appropriately and follow school rules.

**WALK AND TALK INTERVENTION**    Therapeutic removal integrates counseling with removing the student from the classroom setting before the student's inappropriate behavior can escalate. One such strategy for meeting the emotional needs of students with emotional and behavior disorders is the *walk and talk intervention*.

Using this intervention, the special education teacher identifies a student who appears to be having emotional difficulties and whose behavior may be on the verge of escalating. The teacher asks the student to go for a walk (preferably outside), and "talks" with him about what is triggering the behavior.

The walk and talk intervention has its foundation in Bronfenbrenner's (1979) ecological theory of behavior, which emphasizes the mutual dependence between the behavior of the child and the environment in which the behavior occurs. (See Chapter 3.) The student

Removing the student from the classroom environment is helpful in preventing an escalation of the inappropriate behavior.

experiences emotional or behavioral problems when there is a conflict between the student and the components of the student's ecological system. Through therapeutic removal, the teacher is attempting to return the balance to the student's interactions with his or her environment.

The walk and talk intervention uses three components to engage students: the counseling component, the ecopsychology component, and the physiological component (Doucette, 2004).

In the course of counseling the student, the teacher needs to maintain a positive regard for the student. The teacher should be nonjudgmental about the student and the behavior while helping the student find a more appropriate solution to the event that triggered the behavior. For example, Michael made a derogatory remark about Johnny's mother, and Johnny responded by shoving Michael. The teacher took Johnny for a walk and had him explore other ways to respond to Michael's remark (such as ignoring the remark or telling Michael that the remark was not appreciated).

The ecopsychology component of the intervention is associated with the psychological bonding that individuals have to the natural world (Doucette, 2004). The disconnection from nature that characterizes most people's lives and the fast pace of everyday life contribute to stress, anxiety, and depression (Abrams, Theberge, & Karan, 2005). There is something relaxing and nurturing about walking outside, away from the confines of the classroom. Removing the student from the environment in which the antecedent event occurred also helps to prevent an escalation of the inappropriate behavior.

The physiological component is the final component of the walk and talk intervention. It is based on the premise that exercise reduces stress and provides a sense of well-being (Nagel & Brown, 2003). The student experiences multiple benefits from physical activity.

The walk and talk intervention could also be incorporated into other counseling techniques. Two psychodynamic counseling strategies that could easily encompass it are reality therapy and life space crisis interventions.

## Reality Therapy

The premise of reality therapy is that all of us choose to behave in certain ways in order to satisfy basic human needs. For example, some individuals interact with a number of people in social situations to fulfill the basic need of belonging, whereas others choose to develop intimate relationships with a few people to meet the same need. The four basic needs include love and belonging, power, pleasure, and freedom (Fuller, 2007; Glasser, 2001). Of course, the most basic need of all is *survival*, which includes the necessary anatomical functions for life. These functions include respiration, digestion, and reproduction and are often beyond the purview of teachers providing basic counseling for students with emotional and behavior disorders. Thus, survival is not included in this text as one of the basic needs that reality therapy can address.

*Love and belonging* is probably the most important need (Glasser, 1998, 2001). All of us to some degree have a need for family and friends, for acceptance by others, and for feeling that we are loved. A student with emotional and behavior disorders who does not feel that he is cared for by others may have difficulties interacting with peers and adults.

*Power* is the need to feel important and recognized and to feel a sense of accomplishment. Overachievers may have a strong desire to accomplish goals in their lives, especially to gain recognition from a distant parent. Students who do not feel important may have low self-worth. They may feel that no matter how hard they try, they will not receive the recognition they need, so they may give up.

*Pleasure* is having fun, and although fun should be separate from work, learning can and should be fun. In 1969, Glasser criticized schools for taking the fun out of learning by emphasizing tests, lectures, and grades, but that trend has only intensified today with No Child Left Behind's emphasis on accountability and testing. Ask any student today if he or she thinks that school is fun, and the likely answer will be "no."

*Freedom* is the ability to make decisions that affect one's life. When students are given the opportunity to make decisions about their education, they often are more likely to pursue their educational goals. However, if students do not feel they have any choices, they may not take responsibility for their behaviors and may blame others (Fuller, 2007; Peterson, 2000).

Reality therapy follows the philosophy that students choose to behave a certain way in order to satisfy the basic human needs. When these needs are not met, students may develop emotional and behavioral difficulties.

To use reality therapy with students with emotional and behavior disorders, the teacher should have an established rapport with the student that is based on an authentic and positive relationship. The teacher's role is to help the student examine his or her behavior, take responsibility for the behavior, and choose a more responsible alternative behavior in the future (Passaro, Moon, Wiest, & Wong, 2004; Peterson, 2000). The teacher can accomplish this by asking the student four simple questions:

1. What do you want?
2. What are you doing?
3. Is what you are doing getting you what you want?
4. What is a better way for you to get what you want?

For example Ana took Michelle's pencil from the top of her desk. Michelle went over to Ana and started screaming at her. Then she snatched her pencil from Ana's hand and broke it into pieces. The teacher takes Michelle for a walk and initiates reality therapy. After establishing a rapport, the teacher asks Michelle what she wanted from Ana. Michelle replies that she wanted her pencil. This clarifies Michelle's goal in the situation. The teacher asks what Michelle did in the classroom to get her pencil back. Michelle acknowledges that she screamed at Ana and broke the pencil. Eliciting this statement encourages the student to recognize her present behavior. The teacher continues by asking Michelle if she got what she wanted. When Michelle responds that she did not get her pencil back, she recognizes that her behavior did not help her achieve her goal. The teacher then asks Michelle to suggest a better way to get her pencil back. Some appropriate solutions could be to ask Ana for the pencil back, tell the teacher that Ana took her pencil, or just ask the teacher for another pencil. Once a plan has been made to handle future incidents of this type, Michelle must agree to follow it.

Michelle's behavior was an attempt to meet the basic need of power. When Ana took the pencil, she was negating Michelle's sense of self-worth. Because Ana took the pencil, Michelle felt that she did not deserve the pencil. When Michelle finally did retrieve the pencil, she broke it because she still felt that she did not deserve the pencil. Another interpretation of the incident involved Michelle's need to be recognized as the owner of the pencil. She broke the pencil to show Ana that even if she took things from Michelle, she would not get to use them.

Reality therapy is designed to help students identify and evaluate their behavior and to make appropriate choices that meet their basic needs. Reality therapy can be an effective counseling technique that meets the emotional needs of students with emotional and behavior disorders.

## Life Space Crisis Intervention

Students with emotional and behavior disorders often overreact to stressful situations and display a pattern of self-defeating behaviors. Life space crisis intervention (LSCI) is a competency-based, psychodynamic counseling strategy designed to solve the social and emotional conflicts of students (Dawson, 2003; Forthun, McCombie, & Freado, 2006; Grskovic & Goetze, 2005). LSCI uses a crisis as an opportunity for change and helps students develop positive adaptive strategies to deal with stress, take responsibility, build emotional insight, and stop repetitive inappropriate behavior (Duggan & Dawson, 2004; Marston, 2001).

There are six therapeutic steps in the LSCI process (Amendola & Oliver, 2003; Cullinan, 2007; D'Oosterlinck, Goethals, Boekaert, Schuyten, & De Maeyer, 2008; Duggan & Dawson, 2004; Forthun et al., 2006). The first three steps provide students with "emotional first aid" by helping them to calm down and quickly return to the classroom. The last three steps provide students with skills that they can employ to change a pattern of self-defeating behaviors. The six steps of LSCI include (1) de-escalation, (2) timeline, (3) central issue, (4) insight, (5) new skills, and (6) transfer of training.

*De-escalation:* The teacher acknowledges the student's emotional distress and attempts to reduce or de-escalate the student's intense emotional state of mind without being judgmental. A good way to do this is to remove the student from the setting of the crisis event by taking him or her for a walk. The teacher can also make some nonjudgmental statements aimed at reducing the student's emotional state. For example, the teacher might say "Johnny, I know you are upset, and I want you to tell me what happened. You need to calm down so we can talk about it." These statements acknowledge the student's feelings but also let the student know that he needs to regain emotional control.

*Timeline:* The teacher asks the student to explain what happened, including what preceded the crisis event (antecedent) and what resulted from the crisis event (consequences). Information from this step can be incorporated into an FBA. (See Chapter 6.) This step also validates the student's perception of the event.

*Central Issue:* The teacher determines whether the crisis event was a separate incident that was unrelated to the student's typical pattern of behavior or whether it was a repetitive behavioral theme related to his emotional and behavior disorder. If the crisis event was a separate incident, the teacher should return the student to the classroom once the student has regained emotional control. If the crisis event was related to the student's emotional and behavior disorder or has occurred repeatedly, then the teacher needs to provide further therapeutic interventions.

*Insight:* If the crisis event has been determined to be related to the student's emotional and behavior disorder, then the teacher needs to determine whether the event represents one of six patterns of self-defeating behavior. Helping the student recognize that an event was part of a pattern enhances his or her personal insight and accountability. (See Table 9.1.) This step can be useful in determining the type of intervention that

**TABLE 9.1   Six Types of LSCI Interventions**

| Self-Defeating Pattern | Common Issues Addressed | Teacher-Mediated Intervention |
|---|---|---|
| **Red Flag:** Student brings problem to school and displays anger, defiance, and outbursts. | Personal issues. Family issues. Peer relationships. Inappropriate classroom behavior. | Help student recognize displacement of anger. Teach student to ask for help during a crisis event. |
| **Reality Rub:** Student has misperception of crisis event. | Incomplete assignments Peer relationships. Problems with school staff. Personal issues. | Use timeline to explain what happened. Identify cause and effect. Help student see a different perception. |
| **New Tools:** Student has good Intentions, but does not have appropriate social skills | Inappropriate behavior toward peers. Follow-up on previous LSCI. | Teach social skills. Acknowledge student's good intentions. |
| **Symptom Estrangement:** Student justifies inappropriate social behavior. | Does not follow directions. Unexcused absences: skipping classes, tardies. | Reference school rules. Confront behavior and rationalization. |
| **Massaging Numb Values:** Student acts impulsively, violates personal values, then feels worthless. | Personal issues. | Help student recognize own strengths. Promote development of self-control. Stop self-depreciation and self-abuse. |
| **Manipulation of Body Boundaries:** Manipulation by other students. | Aggressive/manipulative behavior by peers. Peer relationships. | Use timeline to explain how peers manipulated students. |

*Source:* Center for Effective Collaboration and Practice, 2000; Duggan & Dawson, 2004; Forthun, McCombie, & Freado, 2006

will be most valuable and the replacement behavior that can be used as the behavioral goal of the student's BIP. (See Chapter 6.)

*New Skills:* The teacher instructs the student in alternative ways of managing crisis events. Interventions for overcoming self-defeating behaviors could include social skills programs and problem-solving skills. (See Chapter 7.)

*Transfer of Training:* The teacher helps the student generalize the new skills to a variety of situations. The student practices the skills in different settings, usually in the special education or general education classroom. Generalization involves collaboration with other teachers, who need to know that the student will be attempting to practice the new skills in their classrooms and should encourage the student.

## Case Study 9.1

### Johnny

Johnny walked into his special education classroom and immediately went to the desk where Jimmy was sitting.

"Get out of my seat," Johnny demanded.

Jimmy looked up at Johnny in disgust. "I'm sitting here."

Johnny shoved the desk, nearly knocking Jimmy from his seat. "I said get out of my seat!" he yelled.

"Make me!" fumed Jimmy, and Johnny started to shove the desk again when Mr. Poteet called him.

"Johnny," said Mr. Poteet calmly, "let's go for a walk." Mr. Poteet turned to the paraprofessional and said, "Mrs. Amazi, Johnny and I are going for a walk. Please keep an eye on the class." Mrs. Amazi nodded as Mr. Poteet walked outside the classroom and paused, waiting for Johnny to follow him. After a moment's hesitation, Johnny left the classroom.

Johnny and Mr. Poteet walked silently through the hallways and out the front door of the school.

"Johnny, you were really upset," acknowledged Mr. Poteet. Johnny grunted.

"What was going on?"

"Jimmy was in my seat," complained Johnny.

"So why did you want that seat?"

Johnny explained. "It's closer to the door. I feel more comfortable sitting closer to the door."

"Well, what were you doing to get the seat?" asked Mr. Poteet.

"I was yelling at Jimmy," admitted Johnny, "and threatening him."

"Was that getting what you wanted?"

"No, but Jimmy just made me really mad," replied Johnny. "I wanted that seat."

Mr. Poteet continued. "Was there a better way you could have handled it, Johnny?"

Johnny thought for a moment. "I guess I could've asked Jimmy to move...."

"And if that didn't work?" prompted Mr. Poteet.

"I guess I could've talked to you about it."

"That's a much better way you could have handled the situation," agreed Mr. Poteet.

They walked for a few more minutes outside the school. Mr. Poteet decided that Johnny's incident was not related to his pattern of behavior, and decided that Johnny could return to the classroom.

As they walked into the school, Mr. Poteet asked, "What are you going to do next time?"

Johnny smiled slightly, and said, "Ask Jimmy to move, or come talk to you."

Students with emotional and behavior disorders need multiple LSCIs in order to accomplish long-term and generalized change (Marston, 2001). Opponents of LSCI feel that the program may actually serve to reinforce the unacceptable behavior (Gardner, 1990), but LSCI has been shown to be effective in school settings that include the expectations, routines, and consistent implementation found in school-wide PBS systems (Marston, 2001). Research has shown that schools using LSCI have a significant reduction in the number of student crises, an increase in student attendance, and an increase in the number of students partially included in general education (Dawson, 2003; Forthun et al., 2006). LSCI can be a useful intervention for helping teachers to determine and understand the causes of crisis events and for helping students learn insight, responsibility, and alternative behaviors to stressful events. (See Case Study 9.1.)

## SCHOOL-BASED MENTAL HEALTH CARE

An increasing number of students have mental health problems, but many of them do not receive adequate mental health services. Some of the barriers preventing these students from receiving services include the cost of services, the difficulty in obtaining referrals and finding providers (Mark & Buck, 2006), the need to arrange transportation to service sites, long waiting lists for appointments, and the stigma of seeking mental health care. Because children and young adolescents are required to attend school, it is logical for the education system to serve as a primary mental health provider for students with emotional and behavior disorders. School-based system-of-care, wraparound programs, and school-based therapists are several options available for serving the mental health needs of students with emotional and behavior disorders.

### School-Based System-of-Care

One strategy for meeting the mental health needs of students with emotional and behavior disorders is the school-based system-of-care. School-based system-of-care programs remove barriers to accessing mental health services and may promote increased communication and collaboration among school districts, families, and community services to help meet the needs of children with emotional and behavior disorders (Anderson et al., 2007; Zanglis, Furlong, & Casas, 2000).

A *system-of-care program* provides a comprehensive range of mental health and other necessary services in a concerted effort to meet the multiple and changing needs of students with emotional and behavior disorders (Stroul & Friedman, 1986). School personnel work closely with community service agencies and families to bring the services needed by students to the school. System-of-care programs are family-driven, community-based, and culturally competent (Anderson et al., 2007). The goals of a system-of-care program are (1) to meet the emotional and mental health needs of students with emotional and behavior disorders and their families, (2) to involve mental health agencies in a multidisciplinary team, (3) to promote parental participation in the development of the program, and (4) to recognize how cultural differences affect the development of the program (Bullock & Gable, 2006).

Before they can develop a school-based system-of-care program, school personnel have to recognize the need for such a program. Many school personnel do not believe that schools are responsible for providing mental health and other social services to students and are reluctant to create system-of-care programs due to budget restraints, legal concerns, and other priorities such as increasing test scores. Yet mental health centers in school settings greatly increase access to treatment for students with emotional and behavior disorders and clearly are serving a need (Costello-Wells, McFarland, Reed, & Walton, 2003). School-based system-of-care programs remove many of the barriers to providing mental health and community services to students and families. These programs have helped students with emotional and behavior disorders improve in functioning at home and school, improve in behavior, and continue attending their neighborhood schools and community-based settings (Costello-Wells et al., 2003; Wright, Russell, Anderson, Kooreman, & Wright, 2006).

The first step in developing a school-based system-of-care program is to create a multidisciplinary team that includes the student and his or her parents, school personnel, local mental health agencies, child welfare professionals, and community members. The school administrator, director of special education, or special education teacher should take the lead in contacting key personnel for the multidisciplinary team and arranging times for meetings. Because this team is responsible for collaboratively developing interventions and sharing information relating to the student, care and time should be taken to develop good team relationships (Costello-Wells et al., 2003). The multidisciplinary team needs to work together efficiently and effectively. Each member should rely on the others' expertise as they together develop an appropriate plan for the student.

Just as IDEA requires parents to participate in the development of IEPs and ITPs, the system-of-care program requires the active involvement of the student's family in developing a program for the child. A system-of-care program is more likely to be effective in meeting the needs of the student if the parents play an integral role in developing goals and strategies (Walker & Schutte, 2004). Conversely, if they are not involved in the program, parents may be wary of the school's involvement in their child's mental health (Samuels, 2007).

Cultural competence is another aspect of the system-of-care program. Ethnically and culturally diverse students are more likely to be identified as having emotional and behavior disorders but less likely to receive mental health services. Families are often unaware that services are available and feel that they will receive unequal or compromised treatment because of their cultural background (Ho, Yeh, McCabe, & Hough, 2007). The multidisciplinary team needs to recognize that families from different cultures will view mental health services differently. African Americans are less likely than European Americans to use mental health services because they have had past experiences with discrimination, Hispanic Americans are unlikely to use mental health services because of language and cultural barriers, and Asian Americans are unlikely to use mental health services because they have associations of shame surrounding mental illness. Cultural competence requires the team members to understand and accept cultural differences through training and in-services, self-assess their own cultural beliefs and attitudes, and adapt services to meet the needs of ethnically and culturally diverse students (Ho et al., 2007; Pumariega, Rogers, & Rothe, 2005).

## Wraparound Programs

The wraparound concept emerged from the system-of-care process and provides the necessary planning to improve services for students with emotional and behavior disorders and families. It matches the individualized needs of students to effective services and supports (Bruns, Walrath, & Sheehan, 2007). In essence, services are "wrapped" around students and their families (Stambaugh et al., 2007). A case manager or other designated individual works with the family to arrange the mental health and other services they need. These services could include respite care, parent partners, child-care, individual and group therapy, assistance in transportation, and programming and compliance issues in the school (Eber, Sugai, Smith, & Scott, 2002). The 10 basic elements of the wraparound approach are as follows: (1) Services and supports must be community-based; (2) services and supports must be individualized and tailored to the student's strengths; (3) the process must be culturally competent; (4) the process involves the family as active participants at every level; (5) the process must be team based; (6) the agencies involved must have access to flexible funding; (7) the plan of care must include a balance of formal and informal community and family resources; (8) services must be provided on an unconditional commitment; (9) treatment plans should be developed and implemented based on a community, interagency, collaborative process; and (10) outcomes must be determined and measured at every level of service (Burns & Goldman, 1999).

There are several advantages to using schools as the entry point for the wraparound approach. First, children and adolescents spend a significant part of their day in school. Second, schools can provide well-trained staff, access to supportive services, and the use of mandated service delivery mechanisms (Epstein et al., 2005). For students with emotional and behavior disorders, wraparound services could be arranged through special education procedures (such as IEP team meetings, transition planning, etc.). Finally, the wraparound approach could be incorporated into a school-wide PBS program. In a PBS program, tertiary, or comprehensive, intervention provides extensive, individualized supports (Walker et al., 2005). The wraparound approach could be one type of tertiary intervention for students with emotional and behavior disorder (Eber et al., 2002; Epstein et al., 2005; Scott & Eber, 2003).

Consistent with the ecological system surrounding students (Bronfenbrenner, 1979; Walker & Schutte, 2004), wraparound planning has been successful in improving the social, behavioral, and academic functioning of students with emotional and behavior disorders, and it is an effective preventive intervention for students who are at risk for developing emotional difficulties (Scott & Eber, 2003). Wraparound planning has also decreased the number of restrictive and alternative placements for students (Eber et al., 2002). However, the wraparound approach has been hindered when teams could not agree about guidelines for effective implementation of services. Schools, families, and wraparound providers need to avoid excessive conflict arising from different perspectives and work together to provide effective wraparound services that meet the needs of the student. The team needs to identify and summarize all the needs of the student and his or her family, prioritize these needs, and develop a plan similar to the IEP that includes the names of individuals who will be responsible for implementation and evaluation of the plan.

## School-Based Therapist

Another approach to meeting the emotional needs of students with emotional and behavior disorders is assigning the student to a full-time, school-based therapist. The goal of the therapeutic program is to meet students' needs in a public school setting by providing intensive support.

School-based therapist programs have the following objectives:

1. To provide intensive coordinated and comprehensive services within the school setting.
2. To increase the student's ability to internalize methods of coping with problems and solving problems related to his or her personal and social life.

**3.** To give students the skills to return to the general education setting.
**4.** To increase parents' and family members' abilities to cope with the child's emotional and behavior disorder and to provide needed support for the child at home.
**5.** To give students the opportunities to succeed academically.

One aspect of the therapeutic component of the program is individual therapy. The student meets with the therapist at various times throughout the day to discuss issues ranging from family and peer relationships to developing self-esteem. The program uses several therapeutic methods, including play therapy, reality therapy, LSCI, goal setting, and stress management.

Group therapy is another important aspect of the therapeutic interventions that is critical to the success of the program. Either the program staff or the students should decide the topic of discussion, which may range from conflict resolution to how to deal with an absent father. The therapist helps the students develop problem-solving skills to deal with peer conflict and disruptive behavior. The students contribute suggestions to the group discussion. The most obvious advantage of group therapy is that it encourages cooperation between peers.

Recreation and leisure therapy encourages students to manage personal behavior and growth by developing skills and interests in a variety of areas. It is important for students with emotional disabilities to learn to use their leisure time appropriately. During recreation and leisure therapy, students can build model cars, play card games, draw pictures, and read books. The staff designs these activities to help students deal with stress, frustration, and anxieties.

Many students with mental health needs do not have access to services outside of school. School-based systems of care, wraparound programs, and school-based therapist programs could meet many of the mental health needs of students, improve these students' academic performance and behavior, and reduce the number of children and adolescents who are placed in alternative educational settings. Despite these benefits, mental health services for students with emotional and behavior disorders have not been included in school reform efforts (Vanderbleek, 2004), and schools tend to marginalize efforts to address mental health concerns (Adelman & Taylor, 1998, 2000). In fact, many schools that have initiated educational reforms to meet the mandates of No Child Left Behind have remained "dysfunctional" in providing the mental health needs of all children (Dwyer, 2002). Until these comprehensive services are available, the outcomes for many students with emotional and behavior disorders will likely remain poor.

## RESTRICTIVE AND INTENSIVE SETTINGS

Because mental health services are not always available through the public schools, many students with emotional and behavior disorders end up in the child protection or juvenile justice systems. These students are often removed from their homes and placed in out-of-home settings. Students with emotional and behavior disorders are more likely to be placed in restrictive settings than youth with any other disability classification (U.S. Department of Education, 2002), and students exhibiting clinically significant behavior problems are more than four times as likely to enter intensive and restrictive settings (James et al., 2006).

There are five types of restrictive and intensive settings, serving as a continuum of services for students with emotional and behavior disorders. (See Figure 9.1.) These settings

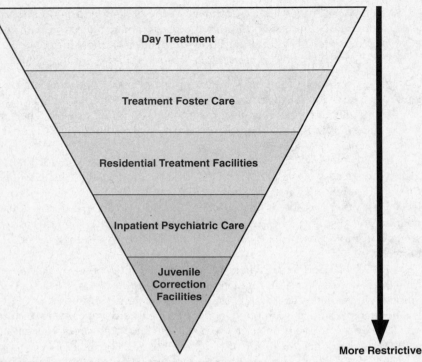

**FIGURE 9.1**  Five Types of Restrictive and Intensive Settings

are structurally different and provide different services. The five settings are day treatment, treatment foster care, residential treatment facilities, inpatient psychiatric care, and juvenile correctional facilities.

## Day Treatment

Day treatment programs provide educational and mental health services in a separate setting from the public school. Students attend day treatment programs in lieu of attending public school and return home each night.

Day treatment programs use a multimodal approach to address students' academic, behavioral, and emotional needs. They provide students with greater behavioral and therapeutic support than do public schools by maintaining a balance between education and therapeutic issues (Gagnon & McLaughlin, 2004). Day treatment teachers provide academic support, and counselors provide individual and group interventions. However, the allotment of some time to therapeutic issues takes away time from academic issues in day treatment programs, making it difficult for the programs to comply with the increasingly rigorous academic requirements mandated by No Child Left Behind. The day treatment curriculum may be unrelated to the general education curriculum (Gagnon & McLaughlin, 2004). As a result, when students spend a period of time in a day treatment program and then return to a public school, they may have difficulties achieving success in the general education classroom.

There is also little follow-up between day treatment programs and public schools once the students have exited the day treatment program and returned to their home school. If day treatment programs do not help students to develop follow-up activities that build on and extend their experiences in day treatment, students are unlikely to be successful reintegrating into their home schools and communities (Gagnon & Leon, 2005).

## Treatment Foster Care

Treatment foster care is an intensive round-the-clock treatment program for students with emotional and behavior disorders that includes opportunities for development and growth within a family and community setting (Farmer, Wagner, Burns, & Richards, 2003). Treatment foster care programs are the least restrictive residential option. Students are removed from their home environments and placed with a different family. The student also generally receives special education services that are provided by the public school in the school setting or in a homebound program.

Treatment foster care programs include an intense therapeutic component that can include behavior management training, counseling, and individual, family, and group interventions. The treatment foster parents often implement many of these interventions. The foster parents are trained to provide specialized care, and they receive additional support from mental health care and social service professionals (Dore & Mullin, 2006).

Many children placed in treatment foster care have experienced multiple residential placements, and treatment foster care is sometimes used as an intermediate step between residential treatment placements (see discussion that follows) and reintegration into the home environment (Farmer, et al., 2003). Because it has a family-based milieu, treatment foster care may be more effective than other residential placements in teaching children community values that they can apply after they return to their homes (Burns, Hoagwood, & Mrazek, 1999; Chamberlain & Moore, 1998), and it may be the preferred treatment residential option for students with emotional and behavior disorders (Farmer, Dorsey, & Mustillo, 2004).

## Residential Treatment Facilities

When community-based mental health interventions are ineffective or when the behavior of a student with emotional and behavior disorders is extremely severe, the student may be placed in residential treatment facilities. Children placed in these facilities usually have prior involvement in the juvenile justice system, the mental health system, or the child welfare system (Dale, Baker, Anastasio, & Purcell, 2007).

Students live at residential treatment facilities 24 hours a day for periods ranging from several weeks to several years. Residential treatment facilities often provide on-grounds schools, sessions that teach daily living skills, and individual and group therapy implemented by multidisciplinary teams (Burns et al., 1999; Hair, 2005). The goals of residential treatment centers are to provide a consistent, nurturing environment with predictable, consistent expectations (Rosen, 1998). Students attend the on-grounds school and/or counseling sessions during the day and are expected to complete chores and learn daily living skills during the evenings and weekends.

It is critical for residential treatment facilities, like other out-of-home placements, to offer aftercare service. Students with emotional and behavior disorders are more likely to be successful once they have been discharged from these facilities if they receive ongoing support (Hair, 2005). Without aftercare support, they are likely to have problems in the public school and home settings.

## Inpatient Psychiatric Care

Inpatient psychiatric hospitalization is the most restrictive type of residential care in the continuum of restrictive and intensive settings for students with emotional and behavior disorders. Psychiatric disorders are the leading reason for hospitalization among 5- to 19-year-olds, and they represent approximately 10% of the total mental health inpatient population (Geller & Biebel, 2006; Pottick, McAlpine, & Andelman, 2000).

In many states, the length of time that individuals stay in inpatient psychiatric care facilities has been reduced. Policymakers incorrectly assumed that services once provided by inpatient psychiatric care would be replaced by community-based services. Instead, the shorter stays and lack of community-based mental health aftercare have been associated with higher recidivism rates in psychiatric hospitalization (Geller & Biebel, 2006; James et al., 2006).

## Juvenile Correction Facilities

More than 134,000 youths are incarcerated in public and private juvenile correctional facilities in the United States (Sickmund, 2002). Many of these youths have committed criminal offenses and are receiving special education services.

Youths incarcerated in juvenile correction facilities are disproportionately male, poor, African American, Native American, or Hispanic. These youths often have learning disabilities or emotional and behavior disorders (Quinn et al., 2005; Sickmund, 2005; Zabel & Nigro, 2007).

Responses by the justice system to juvenile delinquency are usually reactive, or tailored to the particular criminal incident committed by the youth. One response is diversion. Diversion allows first-time offenders charged with minor crimes to be diverted away from the juvenile court systems and referred for services. Another response is the compensation of the victim. Youths convicted of juvenile delinquency often spend some time in juvenile correction centers. Yet little research has been done to determine the appropriate ways to prevent youth with disabilities from becoming incarcerated or how to provide them with the aftercare services they need when they are released. Only a few of these youths return to high school and obtain high school diplomas or GEDs. The remainder do not have the opportunity to learn academic, social, and life skills. Without appropriate transitions and aftercare, these youths have a high rate of unemployment and recidivism and experience multiple arrests (Bullis, Yovanoff, Mueller, & Havel, 2002; Zabel & Nigro, 2007).

## Implications of Restrictive and Intensive Settings

The role of the general and special education teachers in the education of students with emotional and behavior disorders in restrictive and intensive settings varies. In many cases, the public school is still responsible for developing and implementing the student's IEP and providing special education services. The home school district might not be responsible for implementing the IEP if the out-of-school placement is associated with a different public school district. However, if placement in a public or private residential program is necessary to provide special education and related service to a child with a disability, the program must be free for the parents of the child (IDEA, 2004; § 300.104).

Factors associated with the placement of youth in restrictive and intensive settings include male gender, older age, presence of clinical behavior problems, and multiple placements prior to entry into an out-of-school/out-of-home placement (James et al., 2006). The disproportionate placement of linguistically and culturally diverse youths in these settings is of concern. African American youths were more likely than European Americans to be placed in juvenile correctional facilities and treatment foster care. European American youths were more likely than African Americans to be hospitalized (Sheppard & Benjamin-Coleman, 2001).

The numbers of students with mental health issues and emotional and behavior disorders are increasing. If teachers and public schools can effectively meet the emotional and mental health needs of students through basic counseling techniques or through school-based mental health programs, then they can avoid some unnecessary placements of students in restrictive and intensive settings.

## Summary

The emotional and mental health needs of students are seldom addressed in public schools. School personnel feel that they are not adequately prepared to handle the physical health, mental health, social, and psychological needs of students with emotional and behavior disorders. However, as the numbers of these students attending public schools increase, it is logical for schools to become a focal point of mental health services.

Teachers are usually the first to respond to a student's inappropriate behavior or emotional distress. There are several basic counseling techniques they can use to de-escalate the student's feelings of turmoil. One simple strategy for assisting a student in crisis is to remove him or her from the classroom environment. When this is not effective, the teacher may need to counsel the student. Effective counseling depends on the warmth of the relationship the teacher has with the student. The teacher needs to display unconditional positive regard, congruence, and empathy toward the student.

The teacher can take the student for a walk and talk with him about his behavior. The walk and talk intervention uses the counseling component, the ecopsychology component, and the physiological component to engage the student. It can also be used in conjunction with reality therapy and life space crisis intervention (LSCI).

Reality therapy is founded on the choices individuals make to meet certain basic human needs. The teacher's role is to ask the student simple questions that will help the student to examine his behavior, assume responsibility for the behavior, and choose a more responsible behavior in the future.

LSCI uses a crisis as an opportunity for change. The steps of LSCI help the student calm down and develop skills to change a pattern of self-defeating behaviors. LSCI can help teachers determine the causes of crisis events and help students gain the insight to find alternative behaviors to stressful events.

Many students with emotional and behavior disorders who need more intensive interventions do not receive the mental health services they need. School-based mental health programs remove barriers to services by providing coordinated services at school. A system-of-care program provides a comprehensive range of mental health and other services by maintaining communication among schools, families, community mental health services, and social services. System-of-care programs are designed to meet the mental health needs of students with emotional and behavior disorders and their families.

Wraparound services provide the necessary planning process to improve mental health and other services for students with emotional and behavior disorders and their families. The effective services and supports are essentially "wrapped" around the student and his or her family. Wraparound services can also be incorporated in a school-wide PBS program at the tertiary level.

A school-based therapist can provide comprehensive services in the school setting. The school-based therapist provides individual and group therapy to students and their families and can manage crisis events.

Students with emotional and behavior disorders are more likely to be placed in intensive and restrictive settings than other students with disabilities. These settings include day treatment, treatment foster care, residential treatment facilities, inpatient psychiatric care, and juvenile correctional facilities. Day treatment programs provide educational and mental health services in a separate school-like setting. Treatment foster care is a round-the-clock treatment program that includes an intense therapeutic component in a family setting. Residential treatment facilities provide on-grounds schools, sessions that teach daily living skills, and individual and group therapy to residents 24 hours a day. Inpatient psychiatric care in hospitals is the most restrictive type of residential care. Finally, students who are convicted of criminal offenses are placed in juvenile correction facilities. The response of the judicial system to juvenile delinquency is often reactive and involves diversion or compensation for the victim.

It is crucial that students receive transition and aftercare when they are reintegrated from any restrictive and intensive setting. If they do not receive appropriate aftercare, students are likely to be returned to residential settings or incarcerated in juvenile detention facilities.

The public school is responsible for special education services for students in restrictive and intensive settings, and these placements must be at no cost to the parents if they are necessary. However, if the public school can meet the emotional and mental health needs of students with emotional and behavior disorders, restrictive and intensive settings may not be needed.

## Review Questions

1. What are the similarities and differences between the Walk and Talk Intervention, Reality Therapy, and LSCI? How can these counseling strategies be used in conjunction with each other?
2. What are the four basic human needs? Why is the basic human need for survival not included in reality therapy?
3. What are the differences between the first three therapeutic steps of LSCI and the last three steps? How are these steps significant for the special education teacher?
4. Should schools provide school-based mental health programs? Why or why not? Should these programs be developed for all students or just students with emotional and behavior disorders?
5. Is it or is it not fair to say that schools have marginalized efforts to address the mental health needs of students in the public school?
6. Of the five restrictive and intensive settings, which seems the most effective in meeting the emotional and mental health needs of students with emotional and behavior disorders, and why?

# CHAPTER 10

# Collaboration

**After reading this chapter, you should be able to**

- Identify a number of strategies for developing a positive parent–teacher relationship.
- Explain Patterson's Family Types and the interventions that could be prescribed to each type of family.
- Describe six different methods of demonstrating appreciation and respect toward paraprofessionals.

- Describe the differences between the four styles of co-teaching.
- Describe how to develop a positive working relationship with administrators.

## WORKING WITH PARENTS

IDEA 2004 requires that all parents of children with disabilities have the opportunity to participate in the development and implementation of their child's education. Parental consent is required before a multifaceted, comprehensive evaluation of the child can be conducted and before the child can receive special education services. IDEA recognizes that parents are the experts about their child. Unfortunately, teachers and administrators have more difficulty developing partnerships with parents of students with emotional and behavior disorders than they do with parents of other students.

Typically, schools have tended to blame, marginalize, and ignore parents of students with emotional and behavior disorders (Koroloff, Friesen, Reilly, & Rinkin, 1996). Some school personnel feel that the parents of these students are part of the problem and not part of the solution. Schools have had difficulties reaching out to these parents and encouraging them to participate. Making this connection is even more problematic with culturally and linguistically diverse parents (Osher, Quinn, & Hanley, 2002). Many parents of culturally and linguistically diverse students have a tradition of deference to authority (Harry, 2008). These parents often leave the decisions about their child's education to teachers and administrators, and they seldom participate in team meetings. It is vital that schools overcome such barriers and cultivate parental participation in their children's educational development.

## Parent–Teacher Relationships

It is the nature of the profession that teachers will need to interact with parents, and it is often the responsibility of teachers to develop a viable parent–teacher relationship. Teachers of students with emotional and behavior disorders often have a more arduous time cultivating that relationship due to a variety of factors. There are several strategies teachers can employ to foster good parent–teacher relationships.

First, teachers need to recognize that parents are the experts about their own child. Parents can provide valuable information on the child's sociodevelopmental history, their family's relationships, and any atypical environmental influences that may have affected the child. Second, teachers need to refrain from assigning blame for the child's emotional and behavioral problems to the parents. It is easy to assign blame to parents for students' behavioral problems, especially students with emotional and behavior disorders. Whereas some theorists state that children's behavior is learned or that disturbance is due to an imbalance between the child and his or her environment, it is not productive to assign blame. The focus needs to be on developing an educational program that will be beneficial for the student.

Parents' attitudes and perceptions can also be barriers to developing good parent–school relationships. Some parents—especially those who had some difficulties when they were students—do not have positive childhood memories of school. For them, school might not have been a welcoming place, and meeting the principal could bring back some uncomfortable memories. This innate and often illogical fear of the principal is not unusual. Even teachers may feel a twinge of dread when they are called to the principal's office.

Parents of students with emotional and behavior disorders often feel that no one is there to support them and that they are being judged by school personnel (Ditrano & Silverstein, 2006). Teachers and administrators need to remember that if a student is having academic and behavioral difficulties in school, then those same challenging behaviors are most likely present at home. Many times parents do not know how to deal with the behavior, do not understand the problems of their child, and do not know to whom to turn for assistance. Parents may feel isolated and misunderstood.

The age of the student also affects the level of parental involvement. Parents tend to be more involved in their child's education when the child is younger. As the child gets older, parental involvement tends to decrease, possibly because adolescents are actively striving to be more independent. As a result, teachers at the secondary level see parents less often and frequently do not work to encourage parental involvement.

Yet it is crucial that teachers promote parental involvement of students with emotional and behavior disorders. They should take a proactive approach that may be implemented in any of several ways.

About 2 weeks before the beginning of the academic year, the teacher can take his or her student list and send postcards to the parents of the students. This postcard can include a positive welcome that also conveys a willingness to include the parents in their child's educational process. (See Figure 10.1.)

Teachers can also make weekly *positive* contacts with parents throughout the year. This task can be accomplished by making phone calls or sending notes home. These notes can be simple and time efficient—for example, "Johnny did well on his math test today" or "Johnny had a good day today." Usually, the first time parents hear from teachers or administrators is when their child is having difficulties in school. Parents who have caller ID on their phones can easily ignore telephone calls from the school, especially if the only calls they receive from the school are negative. Hearing only bad news discourages parental involvement. By sending home positive messages on a regular basis, teachers can develop a professional, interactive relationship with parents. Once this positive parent–teacher relationship has been established, if the teacher does have to contact the parent about their child's inappropriate behavior, the parent is more likely to work with the teacher to improve the child's behavior.

Parents should have access to teachers' school e-mail addresses. Having this information allows parents to contact teachers at their convenience if they have any concerns about

Dear Parent(s),

My name is David Poteet, and your child, John, will be in my high school class this year. I am looking forward to getting to know your child and hope that this will be an exceptional school year. I have a number of exciting activities planned and will share those with you as the year progresses. If you ever have any concerns about your child's progress, please do not hesitate to contact me at 956-789-9653 or dpoteet@bfp.k12.tx.us.

*David Poteet*

Benjamin Franklin Pierce High School
1701 Enterprise Lane
Laredo TX  78049

*Home of the Javalinas*

**Kathleen Martin
9843 Jacinto Road
Laredo, TX  78049**

**FIGURE 10.1**  Postcard to Parents.

their child's academic progress or behavior in school. Teachers need to respond to parents' e-mail in a timely fashion. Quick, helpful responses give parents the sense that teachers value their involvement and care about their child.

IEP Team meetings can be extremely intimidating to parents. Parents see themselves on one side of the table facing a number of educated professionals. During IEP Team meetings, teachers should do everything they can to help parents understand the process. School personnel should avoid using special education acronyms. Never assume that a parent knows the meanings of IEP, ITP, LD, MR, EBD, or other terms with which most educators are familiar. The administrator or facilitator of the meeting could encourage parental participation by regularly asking parents if they have any questions or if they understood what was discussed. If parents disagree with an approach recommended by other members of the team, the team, in a professional and positive manner, should present the approach as best practice or as the approach most likely to have positive results for their child's academic and functional performance. If parents still disagree, the team could implement the plan anyway, without the parent's support, because decisions are made by the consensus of the team.

Presenting information in a positive manner is another strategy for increasing parent involvement at IEP Team meetings. For example, the teacher could start the discussion by talking about the student's strengths instead of starting with the student's weaknesses or deficits. Parents want to hear positive things about their child, and they may be more receptive to a discussion of the student's shortcomings after having had a discussion of his or her intrinsic worth.

The parent–teacher conference is another practical approach for encouraging parental involvement in their child's education, but teachers commonly report that the only parents they see at parent–teacher conferences are those parents whose children are doing well in school. Teachers of students with emotional and behavior disorders sometimes do not see any parents at parent–teacher conferences. Again, the key to parental involvement is to develop a positive parent–school relationship prior to conferences. Teachers could conduct parent conferences in neutral and nonthreatening settings such as conference rooms in public libraries or in community centers. Teachers could also meet at the parents' homes instead of at the school, but only if teachers feel comfortable doing so and only if someone goes with them. When schools are tracking parent–teacher conferences, they should include informal meetings with parents at grocery stores or other public places as bona fide parent–teacher conferences.

## Patterson's Family Types

Most parents are cooperative and responsive to schools and their children's academic needs, but some parents of children with emotional and behavior disorders tend to be resistant to interventions outside the school walls. It is important for special education teachers, general education teachers, and administrators to have some understanding of the principles of family dynamics and know how to provide appropriate interventions that will benefit the parents and the child. Patterson (1982) has identified seven family typologies involving interactions between the parents and the child. Patterson's family types include (1) the friend, (2) the unattached parent, (3) the special child, (4) the overwhelmed parent, (5) the sadomasochistic arabesque family, (6) the perfect parents, and (7) the misattribution parents.

**THE FRIEND**  The parent in this family type usually behaves like a friend of the child instead of like a responsible parent. The parent seldom has any outside interactions with other adults. By trying to be "buddies" with her child, the parent does not provide guidance or parameters for the child's behavior. The parent does not establish or enforce rules and discipline. School-sponsored interventions for this parent could include behavioral management skills, social skills, and opportunities to interact with other adults.

**THE UNATTACHED PARENT**   The parent in this family type does not need nor want the child's affection or love. Such a parent does not want to be involved in the child's life. The parent does not establish rules for the child, nor does he or she provide any type of discipline for inappropriate behaviors. This parent rarely attends parent–teacher conferences, IEP Team meetings, or any other school-related activities. School personnel have difficulties getting this type of parent to participate in his or her child's educational program or attend parent trainings, even though the parent and child could benefit from such trainings. The unattached parent needs behavioral management skills and probably some type of counseling.

**THE SPECIAL CHILD**   The parent in this family type treats his or her child as special. Whereas other children in the family may be expected to follow rules and experience consequences for their behaviors, the special child has "diplomatic immunity." The special child does not have to abide by established rules and is not held accountable for his or her actions. The parent not only needs behavioral management skills, but needs encouragement to apply them to the child.

**THE OVERWHELMED PARENT**   These parents are often inundated by life's problems and responsibilities. They are generally struggling economically because of job situations, health issues, or family dynamics (single-parent, large family, etc.). Although these parents may understand behavioral management strategies, they do not use them effectively because they are often too tired or are absent. The parent is typically exhausted and often leaves the child unsupervised during the parent's physical and emotional absences. Parents in this category need respite care and assistance from social services. Schools can provide information about services to meet the needs of this family type.

**THE SADOMASOCHISTIC ARABESQUE FAMILY**   The sadomasochistic arabesque family is a particular challenge for school-based interventions. In this family, one parent is harsh and punitive (often abusive), and the other parent is permissive and inconsistent. The permissive parent undermines the punitive parent, usually in an attempt to make it up to the child for the abuse he has endured from the punitive parent. Marital problems are frequently associated with this family type. Teaching the parents behavioral management skills is not effective because the parents cannot agree on rules and discipline—and even if they did agree, the good parent–bad parent dyad would continue; the permissive parent would enforce rules and consequences inconsistently, and the punitive parent would apply them harshly and excessively. This type of family may need professional counseling before the school can provide any parent training intervention. Child abuse can be associated with this family type and needs to be reported if suspected. (See Chapter 11.)

**THE PERFECT PARENTS**   These parents see themselves as experts at raising children. They use reason and logic to manage the child's behavior without setting limits. For example, if the child steals something from a store, the parents sit down with the child and calmly explain why his or her actions were inappropriate and harmful. When the child feigns remorse for misbehaving, the parents believe that the child has changed. The teacher of such a child will not receive any parental support if the child displays behavioral difficulties in class. The child will portray the teacher as iniquitous, and the parents will regularly side with their child. Convincing these parents to attend parent training on behavioral management will be difficult because they believe that they are experts. If school personnel do get these parents to attend an in-service, they should attempt to explain to them the importance of consistently providing reinforcements and consequences for their child's behavior.

**THE MISATTRIBUTION PARENTS**    In this type of family, the parents' expectations of the child are too high. The parents mistakenly attribute abilities to their child with respect to achieving certain goals when the child actually is incapable of accomplishing those goals. They expect the child to be an honor student, captain of the basketball team, or star of the school play, but no matter what the child does, he cannot please them. When the child does not meet the parents' expectations, they view him or her as a failure. Behavior management strategies that emphasize positive reinforcements and age-appropriate behaviors should be emphasized. Child abuse can sometimes be associated with this family type and must be reported if suspected (Morgan & Jenson, 1988; Patterson, 1982).

Administrators, general education teachers, and teachers of students with emotional and behavior disorders need to understand how the aversive interactions between a parent and a child can affect the behaviors of the child in the school setting. Many of the child's behaviors are maintained by familial negative reinforcement (Kaufmann, 2005), which increases the frequency or strength of a behavior through avoidance of the stimulus. (See Chapter 6.) When school personnel understand the parent–child interactions that affect students with emotional and behavior disorders, they may be better equipped to provide appropriate interventions for both the parents and the child.

## Parent Training

Schools should also offer in-service training for parents of children with emotional and behavior disorders. These parent-training sessions could help parents understand their rights under IDEA.

Family-centered interventions may be crucial in improving outcomes for students with emotional and behavior disorders. These students often need interventions that go beyond the classroom, and it is advantageous to have parents continue academic and behavioral interventions at home. Parent-training interventions have been effective in treating behavioral problems at home (McCart, Priester, Davies, & Azen, 2006) and in improving parent–child interactions. Two types of parent training interventions are behavioral parent training and cognitive–behavioral therapy.

*Behavioral parent training* (BPT) provides parents with the behavioral strategies to reinforce appropriate behavior and decrease inappropriate behavior. BPT encourages parents to increase their child's appropriate behavior by giving the child positive reinforcements (praise and rewards) and setting effective and reasonable limits (setting a firm bedtime, requiring the child to finish homework before watching television, etc.). Parents also learn to use natural consequences for inappropriate behaviors ("you don't get dessert unless you eat your vegetables") (Cartwright-Hatton, McNally, White, & Verduyn, 2005; McCart et al., 2006).

| TABLE 10.1 | Cognitive Behavior Theory Treatment Strategies | |
|---|---|---|
| **Domains** | **Treatment** | **Activities** |
| Cognitive | Cognitive Restructuring Technique | Teach Individuals to reduce negative thoughts and increase positive healthy thoughts. |
| Behavioral | Exposure | Use systematic exposure, in-vivo exposure. |
| | Response Prevention | Discontinue escape response to tears and anxieties. |
| | Activity Scheduling | Provide positive social interactions, activities that make individuals feel useful, and intrinsically pleasant activities. |
| | Skills Training | Identify skills deficit, learn the new skill, shape and generalize the new skill. |
| | Interpersonal Skills | Provide assertiveness training, social skills training. |
| | Contingency Procedures | Give reinforcements. |
| | Problem Solving | Define problem, generate solutions, choose a solution, implement a solution. |
| Physiological | Imagery | Imagine a pleasant person, place, thing or event. |
| | Meditation | Provide quiet time, focusing on a single thought. |
| | Relaxation Procedures | Use progressive muscle relaxation, diaphragmatic breathing. |

*Source:* McGinn & Sanderson, 2001

*Cognitive–behavioral therapy* (CBT) interventions teach strategies for building skills and focus on the remediation and amelioration of symptoms or problems. Strategies for reducing symptoms such as depression could include cognitive restructuring of depressive cognitions (reducing negative talk and increasing healthy self-talk). Strategies for problems such as social disconnection and relationship stress could include relaxation training and problem-solving skills. (See Table 10.1.) CBT addresses three domains that are common to emotional and behavior disorders: cognition, behavior, and physiology (McCart et al., 2006; McGinn & Sanderson, 2001).

Family-centered intervention programs such as BPT and CBT have been effective in helping parents improve their interactions with children with emotional and behavior disorders (Cartwright-Hatton et al., 2005; McCart et al., 2006). Unfortunately, it may be difficult to maintain parents' engagement in these interventions. Some problems include low parental attendance rates, attrition (high rates of premature family dropout), lack of parent participation throughout the intervention process, and failure of the parents and child to maintain the positive changes achieved during the intervention (Assemany & McIntosh, 2002; Lim, Stormshak, & Dishion, 2005).

As with school-based mental health programs, schools are the logical setting for parent training because parents have an inherent connection to their child and the school. Parent training provided through the schools may help remove the barriers of low parental involvement and maintain parents' engagement longer than training provided through other venues.

# WORKING WITH PARAPROFESSIONALS

Paraprofessionals are noncertified staff members who assist the teacher in carrying out the educational instruction of students. They play an integral role in providing special education services to students with emotional and behavior disorders. Their participation is important in general education classrooms where paraprofessionals provide assistance to students with disabilities. Their roles are even more crucial when they provide assistance to *all* students in inclusionary classrooms.

Yet despite the importance of their positions, paraprofessionals tend to be overworked, underpaid, and underappreciated. The shortage of paraprofessionals and the high attrition rate can be attributed to low wages, limited opportunities for advancement, lack of administrative support, and lack of respect (Ghere & York-Barr, 2007; Giangreco, Edelman, & Broer, 2001). Paraprofessional attrition can affect programs, staff, and students.

Expressing appreciation and respect for paraprofessionals can encourage them to remain involved in the classroom. Some ways of doing this are (1) making gestures of appreciation, (2) increasing their compensation, (3) entrusting them with high-level responsibilities, (4) making sure that they do not have exclusively nonacademic responsibilities, (5) asking for their input and making sure that they are working well with teachers, and (6) providing them with orientation and support (Giangreco et al., 2001).

Making gestures of appreciation is probably the easiest method of showing respect to paraprofessionals. Special education teachers and general education teachers can show their appreciation by thanking paraprofessionals for the job they do in the classroom or by letting paraprofessionals know how much teachers depend on their services. Taking the paraprofessional out to lunch or dinner is another way of showing appreciation and respect. Introducing paraprofessionals to parents whenever possible helps them to feel that they are important to the program. This appreciation means more coming from people with whom the paraprofessionals work the most and who are aware of their work, such as special education teachers.

School districts are sometimes limited in how much they can compensate paraprofessionals. Providing fringe benefits, such as health insurance, is a step in the right direction, but many schools pay paraprofessionals only slightly more than minimum wages. This is especially incongruous considering that No Child Left Behind requires many paraprofessionals to be "highly qualified." Highly qualified paraprofessionals must have completed two years of study at an institution of higher education, must have obtained an associate's degree or higher, or must meet rigorous standards of quality and demonstrate the ability to assist teachers in instructing reading, writing, and mathematics (U.S. Department of Education, 2004). The compensation for their work should reflect the paraprofessionals' highly qualified status.

Highly qualified paraprofessionals should also be entrusted with higher levels of responsibilities. Their responsibilities could include teaching at a high level in the special education and general education classrooms. Their roles are especially pertinent in inclusionary classrooms where paraprofessionals provide instruction to all students, or in special education classrooms where they use tiered assignments. Paraprofessionals are also invaluable to special education teachers who use basic counseling techniques that require removing the student from the classroom. The paraprofessionals could take over instructional activities while the teacher provides tertiary interventions for individual students.

It may be part of their job description to perform nonacademic tasks such as making copies, putting up bulletin boards, and supervising recess, but paraprofessionals should not be assigned exclusively to these tasks, or they may feel devalued.

Paraprofessionals should also have input into the educational programs of the students they service. They often work with the students as much as general and special education teachers do, and they may have insights that bear consideration. Giving paraprofessionals a voice in the development and implementation of special education programs helps them to feel like part of a team.

Teamwork is essential between the paraprofessional and the special education teacher. Conflicts between the paraprofessional and the teacher make the demanding nature of special education worse by creating a hostile work environment and are a factor in attrition for paraprofessionals (Ghere & York-Barr, 2007).

Providing paraprofessionals with orientation and ongoing support also makes them feel that they are an important component of the special education program. District-wide orientation provides paraprofessionals with information on school policies and procedures, whereas school-wide orientation provides a tour of the school, introduces paraprofessionals to school personnel, and familiarizes them with building procedures (Carroll, 2001). General and special education teachers generally have 2 to 4 days of in-services prior to the beginning of the academic year, and 2 to 4 days of in-services throughout the academic year. Paraprofessionals either do not attend any in-services or are randomly sent to in-services that are not designed specifically to meet their needs. In-services and orientations should be deliberately calculated to provide paraprofessionals with the training and skills they need to effectively provide services for students with emotional and behavior disorders.

Administrators, general education teachers, and especially special education teachers should not underestimate the importance of paraprofessionals. Highly qualified paraprofessionals are an important component of special education programs, and they play increasingly prominent roles in providing effective special education and related services.

## WORKING WITH GENERAL EDUCATION TEACHERS

Many general education teachers are reluctant to have students with emotional and behavior disorders in their classrooms. They perceive these students as having behavioral difficulties and do not want them to disrupt their classrooms. They may also feel that they are not adequately trained to teach students with emotional and behavior disorders (Wagner et al., 2006).

Although the majority of these students receive services in more restrictive settings, the number of students with emotional and behavior disorders in the general education classroom is increasing. As a result, paraprofessionals and special education teachers who teach students with emotional and behavior disorders are working more and more with general education teachers.

### Collaboration and Consultation

Special education teachers who teach students with emotional and behavior disorders often collaborate with, and provide consultation to, general education teachers. Special education teachers provide support, assist in problem-solving, provide information, and prescribe strategies to help general education teachers meet the needs of students with disabilities in the general education setting. The special education teacher usually meets with the classroom teachers to keep track of student progress and to provide assistance with modifications (Thousand, Villa, & Nevin, 2006).

## Case Study 10.1

### Johnny

At the last IEP/ITP Meeting, Johnny expressed an interest in pursuing a career in auto mechanics. As a result, the team developed an ITP to meet Johnny's vocational goals. These goals included *knowing safety principles and practices, knowing the proper care and use of tools,* and *developing skills to maintain, service, and repair different types of transportation vehicles.* As part of Johnny's ITP, he would take the Industrial Technology (IT) class at Franklin Pierce High School, but when Mr. Poteet discussed the issue with Mr. Johnson, the IT teacher, he adamantly opposed Johnny's inclusion in the class.

Mr. Johnson insisted that anyone taking his class had to do what was required of other students and that he was not going to be responsible for injuries occurring due to Johnny's behavior. Mr. Poteet assured Mr. Johnson that with minor modifications to class assignments and structure, Johnny would not pose any problems for the class, but Mr. Johnson was not convinced.

Nonetheless, Mr. Johnson allowed Johnny into this class. To allay Mr. Johnson's fears, Mr. Poteet accompanied Johnny to class. He sat inconspicuously at the back of the class and kept an eye on Johnny. After Johnny had displayed appropriate behavior for several weeks, Mr. Poteet began leaving the IT class after 20 minutes and returning 5 minutes before class was over. After 4 weeks, he began leaving after class had started and returning prior to the end of class. After 6 weeks, Mr. Poteet met with Mr. Johnson after class and discussed Johnson progress.

While Johnny did have a few minor incidents of inappropriate behavior that Mr. Poteet addressed immediately, Mr. Johnson had accepted Johnny as a member of his class by the end of the semester. Due to Mr. Poteet's support and assurances, Mr. Johnson gladly accepted Johnny into his class for the second semester. In addition, Mr. Johnson was also willing to accept other students from Mr. Poteet's class.

### Co-teaching

One way to demonstrate compliance with the federal requirement in No Child Left Behind that teachers demonstrate competency in all subject areas they teach is by forging collaborative partnerships between general and special education teachers. Each type of teacher has a different kind of expertise in learning strategies, pedagogy, and content skills. Each professional brings his or her own strengths to the classroom and has much to contribute to reciprocal teaming and co-teaching partnerships.

Co-teaching occurs when general and special education teachers share responsibility for delivering substantial instruction to all the students in a classroom (Cook & Friend, 1998; Thousand et al., 2006; Vaughn, Bos, and Schumm, 2007). When it is implemented correctly, co-teaching can increase the positive outcomes for all students in the general education classroom and increase student performance on high-stakes assessments. Co-teaching is a practical way to meet the needs of students with disabilities, including students with emotional and behavior disorders, in inclusionary settings (Dieker, 1998; Friend, 2007; Murawski & Dieker, 2004; Thousand et al., 2006).

**CO-TEACHING STYLES**    There are four different co-teaching styles: (1) supportive teaching, (2) parallel teaching, (3) station teaching, and (4) interactive team teaching.

In *supportive teaching*, one teacher, usually the general education teacher, takes the lead and instructs the students in the course content while the other teacher, usually the special education teacher, monitors student progress and provides feedback. This co-teaching style may be effective in an inclusionary classroom. However, it puts the special education teacher in an awkward position by making him or her more like a glorified teacher assistant than a teacher (Walsh & Jones, 2004).

In *parallel teaching*, students within the classroom are divided into two smaller groups. The teachers plan the lesson collaboratively; then each teacher takes a group and presents the same material. Sometimes one teacher provides the lesson at a more advanced level. However, for the students to achieve optimal learning, the two groups should be divided into mixed ability groups. Dividing them into students with disabilities and students without disabilities creates a segregated classroom. The main advantage of parallel teaching is that it reduces the student–teacher ratio.

In *station teaching*, students rotate among different learning centers, where they work independently or with assistance from teachers stationed at the centers. At each station, students learn a different aspect of the lesson. At independent stations, students are active learners in their education, whereas at teacher-run stations, teachers work with students in small groups.

*Interactive team teaching* is a truly shared form of co-teaching. The general education teacher and the special education teacher plan the lessons collaboratively. The teachers take turns presenting the lesson, monitoring student progress, providing feedback, and providing guided practice, dividing the content material on the basis of their own strengths and weaknesses. The general education teacher might provide a lesson on multiplication one week while the special education teacher provides support to all students, and the next week, the special education teacher might provide a lesson on division while the general education teacher provides support. This form of co-teaching presents both individuals as full teachers to the students in the classroom (Dettmer, Thurston, & Sellberg, 2005; Thousand et al., 2006; Walther-Thomas, Korinek, McLaughlin, & Williams, 2000).

Despite the benefits that co-teaching programs can bring, developing these programs in schools has been problematic. Co-teaching is often implemented to solve the problem of needing to place students with disabilities in the general education setting, and not because it is a method of providing effective instructional delivery (Weiss, 2004). Instruction is an afterthought. This attitude is due to the comparatively small amount of time that teachers spend planning and developing co-teaching programs, and the difficulties that arise in planning a shared curriculum when the general education and special education teacher seldom share the same planning periods. Teachers' unwillingness to share their classrooms with other teachers is another problem of co-teaching. Due to century-old traditions, the culture, and the nature of education, teachers are often territorial and used to teaching in isolation.

When teachers are beginning a co-teaching program, they need to get to know each other and respect each other's abilities. Administrative support is crucial in promoting co-teaching programs and making sure that teachers share the same period for planning. Without support from the school administration, special education teachers end up as classroom assistants, which is an abhorrent waste of talent and resources.

## WORKING WITH ADMINISTRATORS

Administrators, especially the school principal, probably influence the school environment more than any other factor. The relationships between administrators and teachers affect the relationships among teachers, students, and parents (Barth, 2006). Teachers who perceive their administrators to be supportive and encouraging are less likely to leave the field (Billingsley, 2004). The literature contains abundant examples of what principals can do to improve the work environment of teachers, reduce attrition among special education teachers, and provide support to teachers.

But what can special education teachers do to foster a positive working relationship with administrators? Sometimes it is difficult for them. Special education teachers sometimes seem like the stepchildren of education. They are left out of the loop, not included in school activities, and treated differently from their general education counterparts. Special education teachers often do not receive the recognition they deserve for their work from principals and other teachers (Wasburn-Moses, 2005). This failure generally stems from the misconception that special education is a separate educational program, instead of a supplemental program. Teachers who teach students with emotional and behavior disorders are further isolated because they teach the students nobody else wants to teach. What can a teacher of students with emotional and behavior disorders do when the principal states that he does not believe in offering special education services to these children?

Teachers of students with emotional and behavior disorders need to be passionate about their profession and believe in the teaching program they follow. They need to believe that their students can achieve academically and improve socially, emotionally, and behaviorally. If a teacher does not believe in his or her program, neither will the school principal. The special education teacher also needs to be forthright and honest with the principal. It is not an admission of incompetence for the special education teacher to admit to not knowing how to solve a student's behavioral difficulties or to refuse to be personally responsible for a student's inappropriate behavior.

The special education teacher can also be a team player. He or she can volunteer to help with extracurricular activities or serve on school teams, taking care, of course, not to become overextended. This participation will go a long way to change the perception that special education is a separate educational program.

## Summary

Parents are the experts about their own children and so can be valuable members of the team that addresses their children's behavior, but school personnel sometimes have difficulties developing partnerships with parents of children with emotional and behavior disorders. It often falls to the special education teacher to cultivate a positive parent–teacher relationship and to overcome any negative attitudes and perceptions of the parents toward the school that are barriers to developing that relationship. There are several proactive strategies that teachers can use to foster that relationship. The main one is for teachers to make positive contacts with parents throughout the year using postcards, notes, and phone calls. By sending home positive messages on a regular basis, teachers can develop a professional, interactive relationship with parents.

Schools need to provide interventions to help parents of children with emotional and behavior disorders, but some parents are resistant to any outside interference. Patterson (1982) has described seven types of families that make it difficult for schools to provide interventions. School personnel need to have some understanding of these family types in order to provide appropriate interventions that will benefit the parents and the child. Family-centered interventions may be crucial in improving outcomes for students with emotional and behavior disorders.

There are two types of parent training interventions. Behavioral parent training provides parents with the behavioral strategies to reinforce appropriate behavior and decrease inappropriate behavior. Cognitive–behavioral therapy teaches parents strategies for building skills and focuses on the remediation and amelioration of symptoms or problems. Although both training interventions have been effective in helping parents improve their interactions with children who have emotional and behavior disorders, it is difficult to retain parents' engagement in the program, and without parental implementation, the child often fails to generalize skills.

The role of paraprofessionals in the special education classroom and inclusionary classrooms is crucial. Yet despite their importance, paraprofessionals tend to be overworked, underpaid, and underappreciated, and the shortage of paraprofessionals is alarming. The shortage of paraprofessionals and their high attrition rate can be attributed to low wages, limited opportunities for advancement, lack of administrative support, and lack of respect. When teachers and administrators show appreciation and respect to paraprofessionals, it can decrease paraprofessional attrition rates.

As growing emphasis is placed on including students with emotional and behavior disorders in the general education setting, special education teachers are working more and more with general education teachers. Special education teachers can provide consultation or teach in the classroom with the general education teacher.

Co-teaching allows general education teachers and special education teachers to share the responsibility for delivering instruction to all the students in a classroom. A number of different styles of co-teaching programs have been implemented in general education classrooms. Unfortunately, co-teaching is often focused more on coping with the inclusion of students with disabilities in the general education setting than on instruction itself. It is crucial for teachers to plan, cooperate, and receive administrative support as they develop and implement co-teaching programs.

Administrators greatly influence the school environment and the relationships among teachers, parents, and students. Administrators who are supportive and encouraging create a positive work environment. Special education teachers who are dedicated, forthright, and involved can foster a positive relationship with school administrators.

## Review Questions

1. What are some strategies that a teacher of students with emotional and behavior disorders can use to foster a positive relationship with parents?
2. In the last couple of months, you have called Johnny's mother several times and complained about his inappropriate behavior in your class. The mother has been polite, but you get the feeling that she really is not concerned about your problems with Johnny. What has contributed to this poor relationship between you and Johnny's mother? What can you do to improve it?
3. Kathleen Martin, Johnny's mother, works three menial jobs in order to make ends meet and is seldom home until late evening. After school, Johnny roams the streets and gets into minor trouble.

When this occurs, Kathleen tells him that he is confined to the house, but she rarely enforces this punishment. Describe Kathleen's and Johnny's family type. What interventions could the school provide that would benefit Kathleen?
4. What is a unique way a teacher can show respect and appreciation for a paraprofessional who works with students with emotional and behavior disorders?
5. You are a teacher of students with emotional and behavior disorders. During your first meeting with your new principal, Mr. Rosenberg, he tells you that he does not believe in special education. What can you do to foster a positive teacher–administrator relationship?

# CHAPTER 11

# Legal and Ethical Issues Associated with Teaching Students Who Have Emotional and Behavior Disorders

### After reading this chapter, you should be able to

- Discuss the significant changes that distinguish the different versions of IDEA.

- Describe the three important components of inclusion and explain how they align with IDEA.

- Describe the legal requirements of maintaining student records under IDEA and FERPA.

- Explain the legal and ethical considerations of the behavioral management strategies that teachers implement with students who have emotional and behavior disorders.

- Discuss the differences between short-term and long-term disciplinary removals, the same-treatment rule, change of placement, and manifestation determination.

- Explain the importance of knowing and adhering to a professional code of ethics and upholding ethical principles.

- Identify the four classifications of mal-treatment and child abuse, and list their symptoms.

- Identify the four major types of medications that students with emotional and behavior disorders may use, the effects these medications may have on students, and the teacher's role regarding medication.

## BRIEF OVERVIEW OF IDEA 2004

IDEA 2004 is the latest reauthorization of a series of special education legislation that began in 1975 with the Education for All Handicapped Children Act (EAHCA, PL 94-142). This far-reaching legislation provided public education for all children with disabilities. EAHCA also established the six principals of special education legislation: zero reject, nondiscriminatory evaluation, appropriate education, least restrictive environment, procedural due process, and parent participation.

When Congress reauthorized EAHCA in 1990, it dispensed with the "handicapped" term and used the politically correct practice of people-first language (for example, *students with disabilities* instead of *disabled students*). Retitled the Individuals with Disabilities Education Act (IDEA), the law included traumatic brain injury and autism as new disability categories. The addition of autism was a significant change because, up to that point, students with autism often received services under the category of emotional disturbance and were placed in classrooms along with students who had emotional and behavior disorders.

IDEA was reauthorized in 1997 with several major new provisions that directly affected students with emotional and behavior disorders. Those provisions included positive behavior support plans, functional behavior assessments, behavioral intervention plans (see Chapter 6), and a requirement for the IEP team to conduct a manifestation determination if a school suspends or expels a child with a disability for more than 10 days. (See Chapter 1 and also discussion later in this chapter.)

When Congress reauthorized IDEA in 2004, the law was retitled the Individuals with Disabilities Education Improvement Act (IDEIA); however, most teachers, administrators, and professionals still refer to the law as IDEA or IDEA 2004. The reauthorization aligns IDEA 2004 with the No Child Left Behind Act (NCLB 2001) and includes changes that affect the services provided for students with emotional and behavior disorders. Some of these changes are briefly discussed in the following sections.

### Highly Qualified Teachers

IDEA 2004 defines highly qualified special education teachers the same way that No Child Left Behind defines highly qualified teachers. *Highly qualified* means that a special education teacher holds a bachelor's degree, meets the certification or licensing requirements of the individual state in which he or she is teaching, and demonstrates mastery of academic content and skills to serve students with disabilities (IDEA, 2004; Jameson & Huefner, 2006). Unfortunately, a number of students with emotional and behavior disorders are placed in self-contained classrooms with special education teachers who teach multiple academic subjects (Bradley et al., 2004). It may not be reasonable to expect them to demonstrate competency in several academic subjects in order to achieve highly qualified status. Thus, the requirements of No Child Left Behind and IDEA 2004 may make it difficult to fill positions with qualified teachers. These laws may actually exacerbate the shortage of teachers (Hyatt, 2007).

IDEA also requires that states take "measurable steps to recruit, hire, train, and retain highly qualified personnel" to meet the needs of students with disabilities (20 U.S.C. § 300.155[d]). This is a formidable task, considering that recruiting and retaining teachers of students with emotional and behavior disorders is already problematic. The greatest shortage of special education teachers is in the field of emotional and behavior disorders, and the demand for these teachers is much greater than the supply (Henderson et al., 2005; Katsiyannis, Zhang, & Conroy, 2003).

## Nondiscriminatory Evaluations

The purpose of nondiscriminatory evaluations is to determine whether a student has a disability and whether the student needs special education services. IDEA requires schools to conduct a multifaceted, comprehensive evaluation of every child who is referred for special education services. This evaluation includes diagnostic assessments, social and development histories, observations, and emotional and behavioral assessments. The process is codified to avoid referring students who do not need special education services, yet ethnically and linguistically diverse students are still overrepresented in special education. Compared with European American or Hispanic American males, African American males are 2 to 5 times as likely to be identified as having emotional and behavior disorders (Coutinho et al., 2002). Many teachers, administrators, and professionals are not familiar with the social and behavioral characteristics of different ethnic groups in the United States and perceive behavior influenced by the microculture to be inappropriate on the basis of the societal norms of the macroculture. As a result, a disproportionate number of ethnically and linguistically diverse students are referred and subsequently classified for special education services (Wilder et al., 2007).

Placement of a student in special education was once based on the IEP/Case Conference Team's decision, and if a parent disagreed with special education placement, the school could request a due process hearing. IDEA 2004 now specifically states, "if the parent refuses to consent for special education and related services," the school "is not required to convene an IEP Team meeting or develop an IEP, nor will the school be held accountable for providing special education and related services" (20 U.S.C. § 300.300 [b][1–4]). IDEA 2004 now gives parents the right to refuse special education services for their child, and schools are no longer held accountable for not providing those services. If a student has a disability and needs special education services, the parent has the right to refuse those services. It is conceivable that the parent of a child who has been identified as having emotional and behavior disorders could refuse special education services. In such an event, the school would not be held accountable for providing services, but the decision would probably be harmful to the student, who needs academic, behavioral, and social skills; to the teachers, who will have to manage and teach the student in the general education classrooms; and to the student's peers, whose learning may be hindered by the student's inappropriate behaviors.

Although schools are no longer held accountable, the best practice for schools when a parent refuses special education and related services is still to request a due process hearing. Not only does a request for a due process hearing provide important documentation of the extraordinary efforts made by the school district to address the emotional and behavior needs of the student, but it could also provide information to community agencies that are charged with protecting children. In addition, school districts possess a moral and ethical responsibility to advocate on behalf of their students' educational interests.

## Developing IEPs

The key to ensuring that students with emotional and behavior disorders receive an appropriate education is a well-developed IEP. IDEA 2004 made some changes in the content of the IEP. The IEP must now include a statement of the student's present levels of academic achievement and *functional performance* (20 U.S.C. § 300.320 [a][1]). IDEA 2004 does not define "functional performance," nor does it explain how this performance relates to the student's unique needs or affects the student's education. On the basis of the summary comments in IDEA 2004, educators may assume that functional performance is similar to *functional academics*, in which students are taught skills for daily independent living. For students with emotional and behavior disorders, this statement of functional performance would encompass the behaviors they exhibit in the general and special education classrooms and the interpersonal relations they display with peers and adults. These functional skills could be evaluated through an FBA.

IEPs have been revised to eliminate short-term objectives, unless the student is scheduled to take an alternative assessment that is aligned to alternative achievement standards. If a student is scheduled to take such an assessment, the IEP should include a description of benchmarks or short-term objectives (20 U.S.C. § 300.320 [a][2] [ii]). The change in short-term objectives is not universally accepted, and the law does not specify whether short-term objectives should be developed for behavioral or social skills (Hyatt, 2007).

## LEAST RESTRICTIVE ENVIRONMENT AND INCLUSION

Placing students with emotional and behavior disorders in the general education classrooms has always been controversial. Teachers and administrators are often reluctant to include these students in general education classrooms because the students may engage in inappropriate and disruptive behaviors. Although IDEA does not specifically mention inclusion or mainstreaming, it does state that to the maximum extent appropriate, children with disabilities should be educated with children who do not have disabilities (20 U.S.C. § 300.114[a][2]). This least restrictive environment (LRE) presumes that the first placement consideration for students with disabilities is the general education classroom.

### Determining LRE

The IEP Team decides where a student with emotional and behavior disorders receives special educational services. The team includes the parents, a general education teacher, a special education teacher, a representative of the school (usually a principal or assistant principal), someone who can interpret evaluation results, and when appropriate, the student. (See Chapter 5.)

Placement decisions are intended to meet the needs of the student and are made only after the IEP has been developed. IDEA specifically states that the student's placement should be determined at least annually, should be made on the basis of the child's IEP, and, unless otherwise noted in the IEP, should occur in the student's home school (20 U.S.C. § 300.116[b-c]). The IEP Team should not base its placement decisions on the category of disability, severity of disability, availability of educational or related services, availability of space, or administrative convenience (Yell & Katsiyannis, 2004). Yet students with emotional and behavior disorders are often placed in programs on the basis of their disabilities or placed in self-contained classrooms or alternative educational settings. These placement determinations are not made on the basis of the students' individual needs and are usually decided prior to the development of their IEPs. The first placement consideration for a student with emotional and behavior disorders should not be the special education classroom but the setting that is most appropriate for addressing their learning needs. Determining placement on the basis of disability or availability of services and space is illegal and unethical. The IEP Team's placement decision will significantly and irrevocably affect the student for the rest of his life. It is extremely important for the IEP Team to first develop an IEP that meets the student's needs, and then determine educational placement setting on the basis of those needs.

## Implementing LRE

IDEA specifically states that, to the maximum extent appropriate, students who have disabilities should be educated with students who do not have disabilities; however, IDEA does not mandate that all students with disabilities be placed in the general education classroom. A more restrictive or specialized setting is sometimes appropriate for students with disabilities. For example, inclusionary classrooms that do not provide intensive remediation in social skills training or self-control training fail to meet the needs of students with emotional and behavior disorders, as opposed to self-contained classrooms that do provide these needed services.

It is also illegal for a school to include all students with disabilities in general education classrooms if the setting is not appropriate for a student's individual needs (Yell & Katsiyannis, 2004). Such a placement would set the student up to fail. In fact, IDEA requires school districts to have a continuum, or range, of alternative placements available to meet the needs of students with disabilities. These placements can range from less restrictive placements to intensive and specialized facilities. (See Figure 11.1.)

Schools also must reconsider a student's placement in the general education setting if the student's behavior is so disruptive that it impairs the education of other students (*Clyde K. and Sheila K. v. Puyallup School District*, 1994). In this case, the student's educational placement is no longer appropriate and is not meeting his or her needs.

No Child Left Behind also may have a detrimental effect on inclusion and LRE. Many schools have had to limit classroom-specific reforms such as inclusion in order to focus on

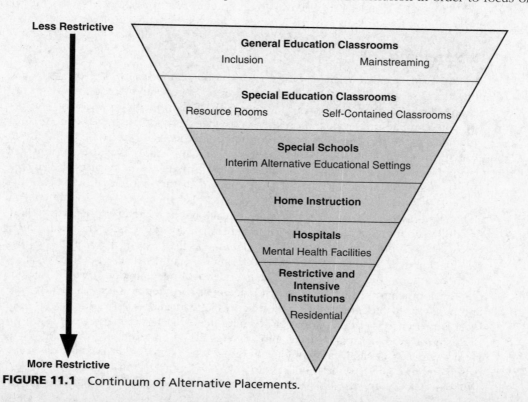

**FIGURE 11.1** Continuum of Alternative Placements.

high-stakes assessment (Sindelar, Shearer, Yendol-Hoppey, & Liebert, 2006). Because administrators and teachers are under extreme pressure to increase test scores, they have less time and resources to devote to activities that facilitate inclusion, such as instruction in functional life skills, self-control skills, and social skills, all of which should be integral components of inclusionary programs.

## Defining Inclusion

Inclusion is often resisted by teachers and not supported by school administrators because its parameters are not fully understood (Sindelar et al., 2006). Because it is not mentioned in IDEA, it does not have a standard operational definition, but inclusion is more than just including students with disabilities in the general education classroom. Inclusion requires schools to provide the necessary support to promote the learning of every student in the general education classroom within the neighborhood school. This definition of inclusion has three important components that are aligned with providing the least restrictive environment for students who have disabilities. These components are (1) providing the necessary support, (2) promoting the learning of every student, and (3) educating students in the neighborhood school.

**THE NECESSARY SUPPORT**    Necessary support for students with emotional and behavior disorders includes supplementary aids and services and administrative support.

IDEA requires the school to provide supplementary aids and services to students with disabilities who are being educated in the general education classroom. Supplementary aids and services can include consultation with special education teachers, the development of BIPs, assistance from paraprofessionals or itinerant special education teachers, assistive technology, teacher in-services, and any other support for the student and general education teacher (Yell & Katsiyannis, 2004). BIPs, social skills training, peer tutoring, and wraparound services are pertinent supplementary aids and services for students with emotional and behavior disorders.

There are two supplementary aids and services for students with emotional and behavior disorders that naturally blend into the archetype of the general education setting. The first is to add resources to the general education classroom by including the special education teacher as a coteacher, assigning a paraprofessional to the classroom, or reducing the class size. The second is to adapt how lessons are taught in the general education classroom by using academic interventions, accommodations, and modifications (McLeskey & Waldron, 2007). (See Chapter 8.)

Administrative support is also crucial to implementing inclusion in public schools. School administrators must provide teacher in-services on inclusion prior to and throughout the academic year. These in-services should define inclusion and explain expectations and classroom interventions related to it. The principal's affinity for, and commitment to, inclusion may affect whether it is successful and sustained (Sindelar et al., 2006). For example, if a paraprofessional has been assigned to assist a teacher in the general education classroom, the principal cannot repeatedly remove the paraprofessional from the inclusionary classroom and use her as a substitute teacher in another classroom.

**PROMOTING THE LEARNING OF EVERY STUDENT**    The implementation of inclusion is often incorrect. In many inclusionary classrooms, students with disabilities sit at the back of the room with a paraprofessional or special education teacher where they are taught lessons separately from the rest of the class. This approach is not inclusion; it is segregation and a violation of the LRE requirement of IDEA. Such an approach or perspective can prevent students with disabilities from being accepted among their peers. Inclusion should actually promote the learning of every student. While the general education teacher presents the lesson to the entire class, the paraprofessional should assist all students, including slower learners, students who are gifted and talented, and students who simply are struggling to understand the concepts being taught.

If an itinerant special education teacher is involved in the general education classroom, he or she should co-teach. The special education teacher should not be used as a glorified classroom assistant, as so often happens (Bouck, 2007). This is a waste of a highly trained and educated professional and can suggest to students without disabilities that special education teachers are not *real* teachers, but classroom aides.

Accepting a co-teacher in a classroom is difficult for some teachers. For nearly two centuries, teachers' classrooms were viewed as their inalienable domains. Teachers are responsible and held accountable for managing their classroom, planning the lessons, and educating the students placed under their care. Unfortunately, this view makes it difficult for teachers to abdicate their responsibilities and allow someone else to take the reins of their classroom.

In an inclusionary classroom, students with and without disabilities receive the same education, and every student is provided with assistance.

**THE NEIGHBORHOOD SCHOOL**    IDEA requires that a child with disabilities be placed in the closest possible setting to the child's home (20 U.S.C. § 300.116[b]). This requirement means that students with emotional and behavior disorders should remain in the public schools they have been attending, unless services cannot be provided to meet their needs. Unfortunately, students with emotional and behavior disorders are four times as likely as the average student with disabilities to receive an education in a separate public facility or in a separate private facility (Bradley et al., 2004). Students with emotional and behavior disorders are often automatically placed in programs according to their disability category. In other words, even though the first placement consideration should be the general education classroom, instead it is often a self-contained classroom set aside for students with emotional and behavior disorders. Many times, these self-contained classrooms are located in schools other than the student's home school. As a result, students with emotional and behavior disorders are further segregated from their peers and the division of their educational services in this manner is frequently detrimental to their academic and social development.

**INCLUDING STUDENTS WITH EMOTIONAL AND BEHAVIOR DISORDERS**    Students with emotional and behavior disorders are often excluded from the general classroom because of their inappropriate behaviors. But when they are excluded, these students lose opportunities to interact with their peers. According to Bandura (1986), most human behavior is learned from watching others. Students with emotional and behavior disorders are more likely to learn appropriate and acceptable social behavior from students who do not have disabilities than they are from other students with emotional and behavior disorders in self-contained classrooms.

IDEA 2004 extends the definition of the LRE to include extracurricular and other nonacademic activities (20 U.S.C. § 300.320[a][5]). These activities can include school sports, involvement in clubs and student activities, field trips, lunch periods, and recess periods. The inclusion of extracurricular and nonacademic activities is an important consideration for students with emotional and behavior disorders. At many schools, these students have recess at different times from their peers or they have lunch in the school cafeteria before or after the regular lunch period. They also may go on separate field trips (or no trips at all), and they seldom participate in sports. If students with emotional and behavior disorders are not involved in extracurricular or nonacademic activities, their IEPs must explain why they will not participate in these activities. Appropriate supplementary aids and services determined by the student's IEP Team must be provided for the student to participate in extracurricular and nonacademic activities as well as in academics (20 U.S.C. § 300.117).

Teachers and administrators have ethical, moral, and legal obligations to meet the needs of students with emotional and behavior disorders and to teach them in the least restrictive environment. Students with disabilities should have opportunities to participate as much as possible in general education classrooms, extracurricular activities, and nonacademic settings.

## STUDENT RECORDS

Schools maintain records that can include student grades, attendance, disciplinary records, and results of standardized tests and state-mandated examinations. The records of students with emotional and behavior disorders may contain sensitive information such as psychological tests and reports or teacher reports regarding child abuse (filed anonymously to protect the teacher's privacy). These records are generally confidential and released only to those individuals who have a legitimate need to see the information. The confidentiality of student records means that teachers, administrators, and counselors who interact in an educational capacity with the student, as well as parents, have a right to examine the student's records. The Family Education Rights and Privacy Act (FERPA) and IDEA define and set policies regarding student records. FERPA protects the privacy of student records in all educational institutions that receive federal funding. This protection covers public schools and state colleges and universities. Much of the discussion relating to student records in FERPA is reflected in IDEA.

Under FERPA (20 U.S.C. § 1232g; 34 CFR Part 99) and IDEA (§ 300.610-627), parents or eligible students (age 18 or over) have the right to inspect and review any of the student's records that are collected, maintained, or used by the school. Personal records, such as a daily log or journal maintained by teachers or counselors, are not part of the school's records, and parents do not have the right to view them. However, if these notes are shared with other school personnel—for example, at an IEP Team meeting—then the parents' request to see those personal records must be honored.

Parents have the right to request the school to correct their student's records if they believe the records are inaccurate, misleading, or in violation of the privacy or other rights of the child. School officials must either amend the information within a reasonable time or inform parents of their refusal to amend the information. If the school decides not to amend the record, the parents have the right to initiate a formal hearing. If the school still decides not to amend the record, the parents have the right to file a letter of disagreement with the student's records explaining why they disagree with information in those records.

Generally, schools must obtain a parent's written permission in order to release any information from a student's education record. However, schools can disclose education records without parental consent to teachers and other professionals with legitimate educational interests, to public schools to which a student is transferring (a release is required for private schools), to individuals who are involved in providing financial aid to a student, to officials who request the records in the case of a judicial order or lawfully issued subpoena, or to state and local authorities within a juvenile justice system. Under IDEA (§ 300.622[b]), parental consent is not required to release education records to a hearing officer because a hearing officer is considered a school official.

Schools can transmit disciplinary information about students with disabilities only if that information is also included in and transmitted with the records of students who do not have disabilities. Disciplinary information may include a description of the student's inappropriate behavior that required discipline, a description of the discipline that was applied, and any other information that is relevant to the safety of the student and others involved with the student (IDEA, § 300.229). This disciplinary record is especially pertinent to students with emotional and behavior disorders because they often display inappropriate behaviors.

If a student is transferring to another school, IDEA requires the new school to take reasonable steps to promptly obtain the student's records: the student's IEP, supporting documents, and any records involving the provisions of special education and related services. In addition, the student's original school must take reasonable steps to promptly respond to the request from the new school (§ 300.323[g]).

Schools are required to keep a record of all the individuals who obtain access to students' education records. These records include the name of the individual, the date that access was given, and the reason the individual accessed the records. The school does not always require teachers and parents to sign a record log when they access a student's record, but it is best practice and a good policy to require them to do so in case legal questions arise regarding student records.

Because students with disabilities are guaranteed a free and appropriate public education between the ages of 3 and 21 years, students with disabilities are sometimes still receiving services after they turn 18 years old. According to FERPA and IDEA, the rights of parents regarding student records are transferred to the student at age 18 (FERPA, § 99.5[a]; IDEA, § 300.625). Students may then inspect their own records, and the records cannot be released without their consent, except to teachers and other professionals with legitimate interests in the student's education.

## BEHAVIOR MANAGEMENT ISSUES

Behavior management of students is a growing concern for all teachers, especially for teachers of students with emotional and behavior disorders. The difficulties they face are directly and indirectly related to the behavior of their students.

Behavior management strategies for students with emotional and behavior disorders often go beyond the traditional behavior management methods of the general education classroom and into the area of individualized treatment. As a result, teachers need to understand the legal implications of informed consent, BIPs, time-outs, punishment, restraints, suspension and expulsion, and manifestation determinations.

### Informed Consent

Informed consent is the requirement that a parent be fully informed of all information that applies to the activity for which the parent's consent is sought. "Fully informed" means that the parent receives an explanation of the special education and related services that his or her child needs, in the parent's native language or other mode of communication, such as sign language. The parents also must agree in writing to any activity for which informed consent is sought (20 U.S.C. § 300.9).

Activities requiring informed consent include the initial evaluation to determine whether a child qualifies as having a disability, any reevaluation of a child with a disability, any excusal of a member of the IEP Team from an IEP Team meeting, any release of personally identifying information to parties other than school officials, and the provision of special education and related services to the child (20 U.S.C. § 300.300[b]). Specifically, parents must give their consent to behavior management techniques before they are initiated. The parents must be informed of any risks and benefits involved in the behavior management technique that is being proposed and must be told why alternative interventions are not appropriate. By obtaining informed consent, teachers and educational professionals satisfy the legal requirements of consulting with parents prior to implementing any traditional behavior management activities or other activities that go beyond traditional interventions. The requirement that the school obtain informed consent also involves parents more actively in their child's education.

## Restraint

As more students with emotional and behavior disorders move from alternative educational settings to the general and special education classroom, teachers in these classrooms are more likely to encounter situations in which they must restrain students to protect themselves and others from injury. Physical restraint can be physically and emotionally trying for both the teacher and the student. To minimize any potential for harm and any potential legal ramifications of using restraint procedures, a teacher needs to receive adequate training, supervision, and support.

*Restraint* is defined as any physical method of restricting an individual's freedom of movement by reducing the person's ability to move his or her arms, legs, or head; reducing his or her physical activity; or restricting the person's normal access to his or her body (International Society of Psychiatric and Mental Health Nurses, 1999; Van Haren & Fiedler, 2004).

There are three different types of restraint procedures: mechanical, ambulatory, and chemical. *Mechanical restraint* is defined as the restriction of an individual's body movement by mechanical means such as straps, a papoose board, or calming blanket wraps. Limited forms of mechanical restraint, including safety straps for children with physical disabilities and blanket wraps to calm a child with autism, are permitted in the public schools.

*Ambulatory restraint* involves one or more individuals using their bodies to restrict another person's body movement. Only trained personnel should perform ambulatory restraint. School districts should provide the training that teachers and staff need to perform ambulatory restraint.

*Chemical restraint* uses medication to restrict an individual's movement. This type of restraint is typically used only in institutional settings and is not used in the public schools (Ryan & Peterson, 2004).

In the case of a student whose previous or present behavior might lead to a situation where a restraint is necessary, the IEP Team should give serious consideration to including restraint procedures in the student's comprehensive BIP. The school's Human Subjects

Review Board or a team of professionals (including the Director of Special Education) should be involved in the decision to use restraint. Teachers need to understand the importance of gaining prior approval and receiving administrative and parent support before they implement a controversial management technique such as restraint. A teacher should not use restraint unless the principal or other administrators are aware that a restraint procedure might be used in the school and support the potential use of this procedure.

The proposed restraint procedure should be fully explained to the parent and included in the student's IEP and BIP. School districts should keep written procedures for the use of restraint. Only teachers and educational professionals trained in restraint procedures are authorized to use restraint, and if possible, the teacher should receive help restraining a student.

Restraint is used primarily as a protective procedure to prevent self-injury or injury to others. When using restraint, teachers and educational professionals "must use the safest method available, using the minimal amount of force necessary," and the restraint should be "discontinued as soon as possible" (Ryan & Peterson, 2004, p. 164). Any restraint that is excessive or prolonged is likely to be found illegal by the courts (Van Haren & Fiedler, 2004). Once the student has calmed down, the teacher should explain the reason for the restraint to the student and give the student an opportunity to explain his or her behavior.

Restraint should be used only in extreme circumstances, because it carries a heightened potential for harm. Teachers need to be aware that restraining a student could lead to *physical harm or even death*. (See Case Study 11.1.) FBAs, BIPs, and positive behavior support should be used to reduce behavior that may lead to restraint.

## Case Study 11.1

### Roxanna (1972–1989)

Roxanna and another resident at a residential treatment facility for troubled teenagers were missing from their rooms on a Friday night. Both teenagers were found hiding in the recreation room. Roxanna refused to return to her room and became combative. Two staff workers restrained her, using a procedure in which one person holds the legs and the other person holds the arms. After serving 90 minutes in an isolation room, Roxanna was escorted to her bedroom by the staff workers, where she once again became combative.

The two women repeated the restraint procedure. Struggling, they fell on the bed.

Roxanna wound up face down on her pillow. Unable to turn her head because of the restraint, she could not breathe. After several minutes, she stopped struggling, and the two staff workers left the room. Ten minutes later, they returned to check on Roxanna, only to discover that she had not moved and had no pulse. The two women called emergency medical services and administered CPR while they waited for the ambulance. At the hospital, Roxanna was placed on life support. Nearly a week later, life support was discontinued by court order. Twenty minutes later, Roxanna died.

## DISCIPLINE

Contrary to what many administrators and teachers think, students with disabilities, including those with emotional and behavior disorders, can be disciplined, suspended, and expelled. Receiving special education services does not make students with disabilities immune from suspension or expulsion (Cambron-McCabe, McCarthy, & Thomas, 2003). However, removing a student with a disability from the school must be done in accordance with a complex set of regulations.

Under IDEA 2004, students with disabilities are guaranteed a free and appropriate public education, but long-term suspension or expulsion may threaten that right. So IDEA provides for alternative disciplinary approaches for students with disabilities, such as positive behavior support and BIPs. These alternative disciplinary approaches are designed to promote positive behavior and social skills and to keep students with emotional and behavior disorders in school (Skiba, 2002). If such approaches are unsuccessful, administrators and teachers may consider suspension and expulsion, but they must understand the provisions for short-term disciplinary removal, long-term disciplinary removal, and manifestation determination of students with disabilities.

## Short-Term Disciplinary Removal

The Supreme Court ruling in *Honig v. Doe* (1988) and administrative rulings by the Office for Civil Rights (1988) and the Office of Special Education Programs (1995) set 10 school days as the maximum number for which students with disabilities can be suspended without the school considering a change of placement. During the suspension, school districts can discipline students with emotional and behavior disorders in the same manner as students without disabilities, which may or may not include the continuation of educational services while the student is suspended. The continuation of educational services at this point is dependent on the policy of the school district (Ryan, Katsiyannis, Peterson, & Chmelar, 2007). However, if the student is suspended for more than 10 school days and the behavior is a manifestation of or related to the student's disability, then school districts must initiate the procedures related to a change of placement and the school must continue to provide educational services (IDEA, § 300.530[d][3]).

For example, LeVar, a student with emotional and behavior disorders, was caught stealing magazines from the school library. School personnel reviewed LeVar's past and current school records, disciplinary referrals, and IEP, which showed that he had no history of stealing. On the basis of that information and direct observations from his teachers, the school determined that LeVar's behavior was not a manifestation of his disability. The school administrator had the right to suspend him for 3 days, the same period of time that would be applied to a student without disabilities, and the school was required to provide educational services during the suspension only if its policy was to provide services to a suspended student without disabilities. It is important to remember that schools may invoke the "same treatment" rule for students with disabilities only if their removals are 10 school days or fewer. If a student with a disability is removed for more than 10 consecutive school days, or if the removals add up to more than 10 school days in an academic year, then the removals amount to a change of placement.

**CHANGE OF PLACEMENT**   Removing a student with a disability for more than 10 school days is considered a "change of placement." School districts are required to convene a manifestation determination review within 10 days of any decision to change the placement of a student with a disability because the student violated a code of student conduct. The Review Team includes school administrators, counselors, the student's parents, and relevant members of the student's IEP Team. Under IDEA 2004, the Review Team no longer needs to consider whether the IEP or the original placement of the student was appropriate, but they must decide whether the student's behavior was related to his disability or whether the behavior was a direct result of the school's failure to implement the IEP (Arnberger & Shoop, 2006).

It is often difficult to determine whether inappropriate behaviors are related to emotional and behavior disorders. The Review Team needs to consider all relevant information in order to make this decision. Relevant information may include the following:

1. Evaluations and diagnostic results
2. Pertinent information provided by the parent
3. Observations of the student
4. The student's IEP and placement
5. Any previous record of the inappropriate behavior (Arnberger & Shoop, 2006, p. 18)

The Review Team needs to determine whether the student's disability impaired his or her ability to understand the impact and consequences of the behavior in question or whether it impaired his or her ability to control the behavior. If the student's disability affected his or her understanding of, or the ability to control, the behavior, then the behavior is a manifestation of the student's disability (Skiba, 2002). If there is no indication that a prior behavioral concern exists about the type of behavior that prompted the suspension, it is likely that the behavior is not related to the student's disability. In short, the disciplinary procedures for a student with disabilities are the same as for students without disabilities, except that the school *must continue to provide educational services* if the student is suspended for more than 10 days or expelled. The services must be provided in an alternative setting, or a teacher must provide the services in the student's home.

The Review Team also needs to review the student's IEP. If the student is consistently receiving the educational and related services that are outlined in the IEP, then it is unlikely that the student's inappropriate behavior is due to the school's failure to implement the IEP. If the school has not been consistent in implementing the IEP or has neglected to provide all the required services, then the student's behavior may be due to the school's failure to implement the IEP.

Once the Review Team has determined that the student's behavior was a manifestation of his or her disability, an FBA must be conducted and a BIP must be developed and implemented. If the student already has a BIP, the plan needs to be reviewed and modified where necessary to address the student's behavior. Unless the parent and the school agree to a change in placement as part of the behavioral intervention plan, the student should return to the placement from which he or she was removed.

## Long-Term Disciplinary Removal

The school can unilaterally remove a student with a disability to an interim alternative educational setting for a maximum of 45 schools days for possession of a weapon, possession of illegal drugs, or infliction of serious bodily injury on another person at school, on school premises, or at a school function. This alternative interim placement means that a temporary educational setting may need to be established for a student with a disability who exhibits

## Case Study 11.2

### Johnny

Johnny was in his high school art class working on a clay project when Michael walked by and purposely bumped Johnny's table. This caused Johnny to mess up his project. "Hey," he complained as he tried to fix his project.

Knowing that Johnny was from the special education classroom, Michael responded, "Retard."

Johnny ignored the comment and focused on his artwork.

Fifteen minutes later, Michael walked by and looked at the clay cup that was forming under Johnny's hands.

"That looks like your mama's face," he laughed.

Enraged, Johnny told Michael to shut up.

"Oooo," chortled Michael. "Your mom must have had sex with a dog to give birth to someone like you."

Johnny jumped up, knocking over his chair, and shoved Michael hard. Caught off guard, Michael fell to the floor, spraining his wrist. Johnny reached over and grabbed Michael by his shirt collar. He was raising his fist when Mrs. Blanco, the art teacher, intervened. Without asking Johnny what had happened, she told him that she did not tolerate violence in her classroom and sent him to the principal's office.

After Johnny had arrived in the office, Mr. Price, the principal, called Mr. Poteet to the office. Mr. Poteet was the special education teacher.

Mr. Price told Mr. Poteet that the school had a zero-tolerance policy about violence and that Johnny would be expelled and sent to an interim alternative education setting. Mr. Poteet informed the principal that this alternative setting would be considered a change in placement and that he would have to call a manifestation determination review. If Johnny's behavior was related to his disability, or if it was the direct result of the school's failure to implement Johnny's IEP, then the school would have to consider alternative disciplinary actions.

Two days later, a Review Team reconvened. Always a strong advocate for his students, Mr. Poteet had interviewed Johnny, Mrs. Blanco, and Michael, who had not received any disciplinary actions. Mrs. Blanco had not observed the two students' interactions prior to Johnny's assault on Michael, and Michael was reluctant to disclose his role in the incident. Fortunately, after talking to Mr. Poteet and Mr. Price, Michael confessed to having antagonized Johnny.

Johnny's emotional and behavior disorder was influenced by the death of his father in an automobile accident when Johnny was 5 years old. As a result of this death, Johnny was overprotective of his mother. Michael's comments regarding Johnny's mother had triggered the behavior. After reviewing the antecedents of Johnny's behavior, the Review Team concluded that Johnny's behavior was related to his disability. As a result, Johnny could not be disciplined in the same manner as a student without a disability. The team developed a new behavioral intervention plan and Johnny remained in his current placement.

prohibited behaviors at school dances, school-sponsored field trips, off-campus physical education classes, or any other academic, nonacademic, and extracurricular activities in and out of the school setting.

When a student with a disability brings a weapon or drugs to school or inflicts serious bodily injury on another person, the school does not need to determine whether the behavior is a manifestation of the student's disability. This type of dangerous action is aligned with the Gun-Free Schools Act (1994) and the zero-tolerance policies adopted by many school districts. Once the decision has been made to remove the student because he or she has violated a code of student conduct, the school must inform the parents and provide them with a copy of procedural safeguards. The student continues to participate in the general education curriculum and receives special education and related services in the interim alternative educational setting (Etscheidt, 2002).

A student who has not yet been determined to be eligible for special education and related services is protected by IDEA from disciplinary action if the school has knowledge of the child's disability. The school is deemed to have that knowledge if the student's parent has expressed concern in writing to school personnel, if the parent has requested an evaluation of the child, or if school personnel have expressed specific concerns about a child's behavior to administrators (IDEA, §300.534). If the school has knowledge that a student may have a disability, the student is entitled to receive the same protection as a student who has been identified as having a disability. This could include a manifestation determination and the 45-school-day interim alternative setting.

Proponents of the 45-school-day interim alternative education setting believe that these provisions create a balance between the LRE and the guarantee of safe schools. Opponents believe that the provisions are unfair because they reduce the number of days that students with disabilities can be suspended compared with the number of days that students without disabilities can be suspended (Skiba, 2002). Opponents also contend that it is not fair that a student without a disability who is expelled does not receive continued educational services, whereas a student with a disability who is expelled for the same offense does continue to receive educational services. At the high school level, this unequal disciplinary approach could mean the difference between graduating on time and waiting another semester. Yet in education, fairness is often about providing what a student needs to be successful in school, not about providing equal services for all students.

A number of professionals have also criticized the zero-tolerance policies of public schools. Zero-tolerance policies were intended to protect students from the threatening and potentially dangerous behavior of others in the school environment, but these policies have resulted in harsh punishments for innocent and minor infractions. For example, a middle school student was awarded a pocketknife during a weekend Boy Scout camping trip for earning the most merit badges. He inadvertently left the knife in his jacket, which he wore to school the following Monday. School officials discovered that he had the knife. The student was suspended from school and sent to an alternative education setting for the remainder of the semester. It was an innocent infraction of the zero-tolerance policy, and no student was in any danger, yet the inflexibility and rigidity of the policy required the student to be punished in a manner that was out of proportion to his action.

The zero-tolerance policies pose an even greater danger to students whose emotional and behavior disorders might predispose them to engage in impulsive behaviors that others sometimes interpret as threats (Kaplan & Cornell, 2005). Despite the protections they receive under IDEA, students with emotional and behavior disorders are suspended or expelled at double or even triple the rates for the entire school population, and they often receive harsher punishments (Achilles, McLaughlin, & Croninger, 2007; Kaplan & Cornell, 2005; Zhang, Katsiyannis, & Herbst, 2004).

Students with emotional and behavior disorders need continued academic, behavioral, social, and emotional interventions. When they are suspended or expelled, these strategies and interventions are interrupted, which reduces their effectiveness (Krezmien et al., 2006). Administrators, teachers, and other educational professionals need to consider the impact that disabilities have on the behavior of students with emotional and behavior disorders. By honestly implementing manifestation determinations and limiting the influence of zero-tolerance policies, schools can reduce the disproportionately high rates of suspension of students with disabilities and provide opportunities for these students to be successful in school.

## LEGAL AND ETHICAL CONSIDERATIONS

Because they deal almost exclusively with children, teachers are expected to conduct themselves in an ethical, moral, and professional manner at all times—even when they are outside the classroom. Parents and community leaders gauge the actions of teachers at grocery stores, malls, movie theaters, and other community settings. For better or worse, teachers are teachers 24 hours a day, 7 days a week. They hold a special place in society, and they are expected to comply with certain societal expectations.

### Professional Code of Ethics

Within the classroom, special education teachers are ethically bound to provide educational opportunities for all children, to respect individual differences, and to advocate for the rights and needs of all students (Crockett, 2002). The Council for Exceptional Children (CEC) has developed a Code of Ethics for special education professionals that includes the following principles:

1. Help students with disabilities meet their full academic potential and improve the quality of their lives.
2. Maintain a high level of professional competence and integrity.
3. Engage in professional activities.
4. Demonstrate unbiased ethical and professional judgment.
5. Commit to lifelong learning in the field of special education.
6. Operate within state and national standards.
7. Be actively involved in the implementation and improvement of special education laws, regulations, and policies.
8. Never engage in unethical or illegal acts or violate the CEC professional standards (CEC, 2003).

### Ethical Considerations

There are several issues worth noting that may affect the ethical principles held by teachers of students with emotional and behavior disorders. These teachers conceivably see more aggression, violence, abuse, or even death than other public school teachers. First and foremost, in order to interact with their students in an ethical manner, teachers of students with emotional and behavior disorders cannot take their students' behaviors personally. Perceiving the students' actions as a personal assault will affect how the teachers interact with them.

Second, teachers and educational professionals need to make sure that their own biases and societal expectations do not influence how they determine disability eligibility and placement in special education or how they discipline students from different cultures and socioeconomic levels.

The overrepresentation of ethnically and linguistically diverse students is a growing concern. African Americans are the most overrepresented group in special education and are 1.92 times more likely than European Americans to be identified as having emotional and behavior disorders (Skiba et al., 2006). General education teachers, special education teachers, and school administrators are ethically and legally bound to identify and provide special education services on the basis of students' disabilities and needs, not on the basis of teachers' own cultural and societal biases. When they are determining identification eligibility and placement of students with disabilities, teachers should keep several things in mind:

1. Race and culture matter in the placement of students.
2. Placement decisions should be made on the basis of students' needs and not on their racial, cultural, or socioeconomic identities.
3. A language difference should never be perceived as a lack of intelligence.
4. Providing the least restrictive environment is always the appropriate placement and reduces the exclusion of students from classroom and extracurricular activities.
5. Racial, cultural, and socioeconomic differences are not deficits and should be valued in a pluralistic, diverse society (Obiakor, 2007).

Teachers frequently believe that ethnically and linguistically diverse students display the highest potential for behavior problems. As a result, students from different cultures and socioeconomic levels are disciplined more often than are middle-class, European American students (Walker-Dalhouse, 2005).

To make classroom management practices more culturally responsive, teachers from both the majority and minority cultures must recognize their own ethnocentrism and cultural biases. Teachers can begin this recognition of personal biases by analyzing and understanding their own culture, which many individuals, especially European Americans, take for granted. Next, teachers need to understand the cultural background of their students by exploring the cultural community and asking questions of colleagues who are part of the community. By understanding the culture and the community, teachers can respond appropriately to the behaviors of their students and develop culturally appropriate classroom strategies to help students take responsibility for their behaviors (Weinstein, Tomlinson-Clarke, & Curran, 2004).

## Reporting Child Abuse

Schools report more cases of child abuse and neglect than any other institutions (Dombrowski & Gischlar, 2006), and teachers of students with emotional and behavior disorders encounter more incidents of mental, physical, and sexual child abuse than other teachers (Malmgren & Meisel, 2004). Teachers have a moral, ethical, and legal obligation to report suspected child abuse and neglect to child protection services. All 50 states have policies mandating that school personnel report cases of suspected abuse; a teacher who fails to report abuse could be subject to criminal prosecution or other sanctions (Haeseler, 2006; Lowenthal, 2001).

Unfortunately, the law is vague about what constitutes "suspected" abuse. To complicate matters, many school districts do not have policies regarding child abuse, and others that do have established policies do not communicate them well to school personnel and the community (Dombrowski & Gischlar, 2006). This lack of internal policies or adequate communication makes it difficult for teachers who are reluctant to report suspected abuse because they know they might be mistaken, are concerned about possible retribution, or are ignorant regarding procedures.

All school personnel, including teachers of students with emotional and behavior disorders, need to be able to identify the signs of abuse, know how to report abuse, and use effective teaching strategies with students who have been reported as maltreated.

There are four categories of maltreatment and abuse: neglect, emotional abuse, physical abuse, and sexual abuse. The basic needs of a child who is *neglected* (such as food, clothing, and care) are not satisfied, either because the parents consciously withhold this care or because they are inattentive. In cases of *emotional abuse*, a parent inflicts psychological damage through threats and verbal harassment designed to destroy the child's self-esteem. *Physical abuse* involves hitting, kicking, shaking, or burning the child, and *sexual abuse* occurs when an adult uses the child for his or her own sexual gratification. These forms of maltreatment and abuse have different symptomatology (see Table 11.1), but they generally occur in some combination.

When the teacher suspects that a student is neglected or abused, the teacher must file a report with child protection services. A report is simply a request for an investigation of an

**TABLE 11.1   Four Categories and Signs of Abuse**

| Neglect | | Emotional Abuse | |
|---|---|---|---|
| Child: | Has frequent absences. Begs or steals food or money. Does not receive medical, dental and vision care. Is dirty and has severe body odor. Lacks sufficient clothing. Abuses alcohol or other drugs. States that there is no one at home to provide care. | Child: | Displays extreme behaviors. Acts inappropriately like an adult or like a much younger child. Shows delay in physical or emotional development. Has suicide ideation. |
| Parent: | Does not seem to care for the child. Seems apathetic or depressed. Behaves strangely. Abuses alcohol or other drugs. | Parent: | Constantly blames, belittles, or berates child. Does not seem to care for the child or want help for the child's problems. Seems to reject child. |

| Physical Abuse | | Sexual Abuse | |
|---|---|---|---|
| Child: | Has unexplained burns, bites, bruises, broken bones, or black eyes. Has fading bruises or other marks after an absence. Is afraid of parents and adults. Does not want to go home. Reports injury by a parent or another adult. | Child: | Has difficulty walking or sitting. Refuses to dress and participate in gym or other physical activities. Shows change in appetite. Has a variety of sexual knowledge. Becomes pregnant or contracts a sexually transmitted disease. Runs away. Reports sexual abuse by a parent or another adult. |
| Parent: | Cannot explain the child's injury. Describes the child as a "bad" child. Uses harsh physical discipline with the child. Has a history of abuse as a child. | Parent: | Is overly protective of child or severely limits child's interactions with others. Seems secretive and isolated. Acts jealous or controls family members. |

*Source:* Child Welfare Information Gateway, 2006.

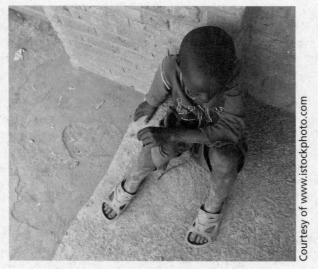

Teachers have a moral, ethical, and legal obligation to report suspected child abuse and neglect.

allegation of suspected neglect or abuse. The teacher is not required to prove that the neglect or abuse is taking place, only to report it (Lowenthal, 2001). In some states, the teacher may need to call a hotline network to report the abuse. Other states have online systems for reporting abuse. The report generally needs to include the name and address of the child, the dates and description of the injuries, the identities of the possible perpetrators and their relationship to the child, any statements made by the child, and how the teacher became aware of the suspected abuse. The reports are confidential, and teachers are protected from personal liability if their reports are made in good faith.

It is often a good idea for a teacher to inform the school principal that the teacher is filing a report; the teacher should not rely on the principal to file the report. It is the responsibility of the individual who suspects the abuse to file it.

Teachers of neglected or abused children can use a number of strategies and interventions to help them. Social skills training and positive behavior supports are appropriate socioemotional interventions (see Chapter 7), and peer tutoring and cooperative learning are effective teaching strategies (see Chapter 8). Most importantly, the teacher should create a safe and secure classroom environment for the student. Teachers of students with emotional and behavior disorders need to carefully reflect and plan how they discipline their students. Discipline should not be punitive or involve any physical or emotional discomfort. The discipline should address the problem and appear straightforward and reasonable. It should be delivered in a way that respects the individual student and his or her unique learning needs.

The teacher also needs to be careful about providing reinforcements for appropriate behavior. A pat on the back to praise a child for completing an assignment may evoke uncomfortable feelings in a child who has been abused. For this reason, it is extremely important for teachers to know their students.

Because they have daily contact with students, teachers are in the best position to identify and report abuse. Yet nearly 84% of all suspected abuse cases in schools are never reported, despite the fact that schools report more maltreatment and abuse than any other

| TABLE 11.2 Reporting Child Maltreatment and Abuse |
| --- |
| If you do suspect a child is being neglected or abused, contact your local child protective services agency or police department. For more information about where and how to file a report, call the Childhelp USA® National Child Abuse Hotline (1.800.4.A.CHILD) |

*Source:* Child Welfare Information Gateway, p. 2, 2006.

institution (Kesner & Robinson, 2002). Because of the devastating effects that maltreatment and abuse have on children, school districts need to develop policies that encourage teachers and other school personnel to report suspected abuse. (See Table 11.2.) Without some type of intervention, abused and neglected children are in danger of developing academic, behavioral, and social difficulties that will affect them for the rest of their lives.

## MEDICATION

An estimated 50% of students with emotional and behavior disorders have been prescribed at least one medication within a 3-year period (Mattison, 1999), and that number is increasing. Medication can improve a student's behavior, academic and cognitive functions, and positive social interactions among peers (Phelps, Brown, & Power, 2002).

Although teachers cannot prescribe medication, they can provide information to parents and their physicians about the effect medication is having on the behavioral, emotional, and academic performance of the student. It is important that teachers of students with emotional and behavior disorders have some understanding of the type and effect of medications that are used with these students. Their observations can aid in adjusting the dosage and type of medication to give the students the optimal benefits of psychopharmacological interventions.

### Types of Medications

Four major categories of medication are prescribed to students with emotional and behavior disorders: psychostimulants, antidepressants, neuroleptics, and mood-stabilizing agents (Sweeney, Forness, Kavale, & Levitt, 1997).

ADHD is the most commonly diagnosed psychiatric disorders among school-age children (National Institute of Mental Health, 2006). Among the many different medications used for ADHD, psychostimulants are probably the most common (Ryan, Reid, Epstein, Ellis, & Evans, 2005). Psychostimulants help students focus on tasks and, as a result, may reduce hyperactivity because students are no longer easily distracted. The psychostimulant Ritalin not only reduces the symptoms of ADHD, but also has been shown to improve academic, social, and behavior functioning (Connor, 2005). Other common psychostimulants include Adderall, Dexedrine, and Cylert; however, Cylert may seriously affect the liver and is not recommended as a first choice of treatment for ADHD (NIMH, 2006). Common side effects of psychostimulants include decreased appetite, stomachache, headache, and insomnia.

Another medication that was recently approved by the U.S. Food and Drug Administration (FDA) is Strattera, which is not a psychostimulant but a selective norepinephrine reuptake inhibitor. Atomoxetines like Strattera were shown to ameliorate the symptoms of ADHD and improve the quality of life for students (Wehmeier et al., 2008). However, the FDA has directed the manufacturer of Strattera to revise the labeling for this product to include a warning that Strattera increases the risk of suicidal thinking in children and adolescents with ADHD (FDA, 2005).

Antidepressants are prescribed to treat severe depression. Antidepressants are grouped into different types on the basis of the chemicals in the brain that they affect. The different groups include selective serotonin reuptake inhibitors (SSRIs), tricylics, serotonin and norepinephrine reuptake inhibitors (SNRIs), and norepinephrine and dopamine reuptake inhibitors (NDRIs). Celexa, Prozac, Tofranil, Effexor, and Wellbutrin are common antidepressants prescribed for children and adolescents for depression. Many of these medications are also used to treat obsessive–compulsive disorder, anxiety, and social phobia (Ginsburg & Grover, 2005). Common side effects of antidepressants include dry mouth, nausea, and headache.

Neuroleptic or antipsychotic medications are generally used to treat schizophrenia, mania, and delusional disorder and are sometimes used to treat bipolar disorder. Haldol, Risperdal, Zyprexa, and Seroquel are common neuroleptics prescribed for children. Many neuroleptics, like risperidone, improve behavioral and social symptoms in students with disruptive behavior disorders (Reyes, Buitelaar, Toren, Augustyns, & Eerdekens, 2006). Haldol is often used to control tics and the unintended utterances that are characteristics of Tourette's syndrome. Some common side effects of neuroleptics include agitation, anxiety, headaches, tremors, and drowsiness.

Mood stabilizers are commonly used to treat manic episodes and bipolar disorder. Lithium, Tegretol, Depakote, Topamax, and Neurontin are mood stabilizers that are used to decrease manic episodes and extreme anger. With the exception of lithium, mood stabilizers are also used as anticonvulsants. Some common side effects of mood stabilizers include nausea, stomachache, drowsiness, fatigue, and impairment of motor coordination. (See Table 11.3.)

## Role of the Teacher

Considering that about half of students with emotional and behavior disorders are on medication, teachers need to be knowledgeable about psychopharmacologic treatment and understand their role as collaborators with parents and physicians (Forness, Freeman, & Paparella, 2006; Forness, Walker, & Kavale, 2003-2004; Konopasek & Forness, 2004). Teachers should provide feedback on the effect or the absence of an effect that medication has on academic, behavioral, and social functioning during the course of the treatment (DuPaul & Carlson, 2005; Forness et al., 2006; Nardi & Barrett, 2005). For example, if a student starts taking lithium for bipolar disorder, the teacher needs to monitor whether the student's manic and depressive behaviors are reduced, remain at the same level, or increase in frequency or magnitude. The teacher also needs to report to the parents whether the student seems fatigued or sleepy after starting medication treatment. By monitoring and reporting the effects of medication on the student, teachers can help ensure that the student receives the appropriate dosage. If the medication does not appear to be effective, the teacher can suggest that it be replaced with a possibly more effective one.

It is critical for teachers to have a professional understanding of the adverse side effects of specific psychopharmacologic treatments. It is important for them to monitor the student for self-injurious behavior, suicidal ideation, or agitation (Nardi & Barrett, 2005). For example, nearly all antidepressants have package labels warning of a potential increase in suicidal thinking in children and adolescents.

**TABLE 11.3  Types of Medication and Possible Side Effects**

| Class of Drug | Brand and Generic Names | Possible Side Effects |
|---|---|---|
| **Psychostimulants** | Adderall (amphetamine)<br>Dexedrine (dextroamphetamine)<br>Cylert (pemoline)<br>Ritalin (methylphenidate) | Reduced appetite, stomachache, headache, and insomnia. |
| **Antidepressants** | | |
| *Selective Serotonin Reuptake Inhibitors (SSRIs)* | Celexa (citalopram)<br>Lexapro (escitalopram)<br>Prozac (fluoxetine)<br>Paxil, Pexeva (paroxetine)<br>Zoloft (sertraline) | Dry mouth, nausea, nervousness, insomnia, sexual problems, headache, and potential increase in suicidal thinking. |
| *Tricyclics* | Elavil (amitriptyline)<br>Norpramin (desipramine)<br>Tofranil (imipramine)<br>Aventyl, Pamelor (nortriptyline) | Dry mouth, blurred vision, constipation, difficulty urinating, worsening of glaucoma, impaired thinking and tiredness. |
| *Serotonin and Norepinephrine Reuptake Inhibitors (SNRIs)* | Effexor (venlafaxine)<br>Cymbalta (duloxetine) | Nausea and loss of appetite, anxiety and nervousness, headache, insomnia and tiredness. |
| *Norepinephrine and Dopamine Reuptake Inhibitors (NDRIs)* | Wellbutrin (bupropion) | Agitation, nausea, headache, loss of appetite, insomnia, and potential increase in suicidal thinking. |
| **Neuroleptics** | Haldol (haloperidol)<br>Risperdal (risperidone)<br>Zyprexa (olanzapine)<br>Seroquel (quetiapine) | Agitation, anxiety, constipation, drowsiness, dizziness, stomachache, headache, indigestion, insomnia, rapid or irregular heartbeat, restlessness, runny nose, sleepiness, nausea, and weight change. |
| **Mood Stabilizers** | Eskalith, Lithnate (lithium carbonate)<br>Biston, Tegretol (carbamazepine)<br>Depakote (valproate semisodium)<br>Topamax (topirimate)<br>Neurontin (gabapentin) | Nausea, stomachache, drowsiness, fatigue, motor coordination impairment, tremor, vision impairment, agitation, and anxiety. |

*Source:* Healthsquare, 2004–2007

Psychopharmacologic treatment along with behavioral or cognitive behavioral interventions produce normalized responses in a large number of students with emotional and behavior disorders. Teachers have an ethical and professional responsibility to monitor and provide feedback to parents and physicians regarding the effectiveness of the medication and need to take a proactive approach to collaborating with parents and physicians. Teachers also need to remember that they cannot talk to physicians about a student without parental permission.

## Summary

The Individuals with Disabilities Education Improvement Act (IDEA, IDEA 2004) was reauthorized in 2004 and has been aligned with the No Child Left Behind Act (NCLB; 2001). IDEA includes changes that affect the academic and related services provided for students with emotional and behavior disorders.

IDEA 2004 defines a highly qualified special education teacher as a special education teacher who holds a bachelor's degree, meets certification or licensing requirements, and demonstrates content knowledge and skills to serve students with disabilities. Unfortunately, teachers of students with emotional and behavior disorders may be required to demonstrate competencies in several academic subjects in order to be considered highly qualified, which makes it difficult to fill positions that already experience severe shortages of qualified teachers.

IDEA requires that schools conduct a multifaceted, comprehensive evaluation for every child referred for special education services. Yet despite this safeguard, ethnically and linguistically diverse students are still overidentified with emotional and behavior disorders. Students were once placed in special education on the basis of the decision of the IEP/Case Conference Team, which could overrule the parents' preferences, but IDEA 2004 now specifically states that if the parent refuses to consent to special education and related services, the school cannot provide special education services for the child.

IDEA 2004 has made some changes in the content of IEPs. IEPs now must include a statement of the student's functional performance and need not include short-term objectives.

*Inclusion* refers to providing the necessary support to promote the learning of every student in the general education classroom within the neighborhood school. Necessary support includes both the use of supplementary aids and services and administrative support. Appropriate supplementary aids and services for students with emotional and behavior disorders could include BIPs, social skills training, peer tutoring, and wraparound services. Inclusion should promote the learning of all students, including students with disabilities, slower learners, students who are gifted and talented, and students who simply are struggling with the concepts taught within the classrooms. Students with emotional and behavior disorders need an appropriate education in the general education classrooms within their home schools as much as possible.

Schools maintain records on every one of their students. The Family Education Rights and Privacy Act (FERPA) and IDEA define and set policies regarding student records to protect the privacy of students. Generally, only individuals who have a legitimate educational interest in the information can access student records.

Teachers need to understand the legal implications of the behavior management strategies they use for students with emotional and behavioral disorders. Parents should receive information that will give them a thorough understanding of all special education and related services that might be needed for their child.

As the numbers of students with emotional and behavior disorders in general and special education classrooms increase, the incidence of restraints in the schools has also increased. Restraint procedures, including mechanical, ambulatory, and chemical, should be used only when other methods of behavior management have been exhausted.

IDEA provides for alternative disciplinary approaches for students with disabilities. Schools are allowed to suspend students with emotional and behavior disorders in the same manner as students without disabilities if their removals are 10 school days or fewer. Removing a student with a disability for more than 10 school days is considered a change of placement, and in such cases school districts are required to reconvene a manifestation determination review to determine whether the student's behavior was related to his or her disability or whether the behavior was a direct result of the school's failure to implement the IEP.

Teachers are expected to conduct themselves in an ethical, moral, and professional manner at all times. Special education teachers should follow the professional code of ethics established by the Council of Exceptional Children. Teachers need to make sure that their own biases and societal expectations do not influence how they regard their students.

Teachers also have a moral, ethical, and legal obligation to report suspected child abuse and neglect to child protection services. Unfortunately, many school districts do not have policies regarding child abuse or do not communicate their policies clearly to school personnel and the community (Dombrowski & Gischlar, 2006). These failures make it difficult for teachers who may be reluctant to report suspected abuse because they know their suspicions might be mistaken, they fear possible retribution, or they are ignorant regarding procedures.

About half of students with emotional and behavior disorders are on medication, and teachers need to understand the benefits, risks, and possible side effects of common medications. Teachers should provide feedback to parents and physicians (with the parents' permission) on the effect of medication on the academic, behavioral, and social functioning of students.

By understanding the legal and ethical requirements of educating students with disabilities, teachers can provide the special education and related services needed to improve the academic, behavioral, and social skills of students with emotional and behavior disorders. IDEA and other federal and state laws guarantee students with disabilities the opportunity to receive an education in the least restrictive environment. This education will increase the success of students with disabilities in and out of the classroom.

## Review Questions

1. What happens if a parent refuses to give consent for special education and related services? What are the consequences for the parent? The student? The school?
2. Imagine that you are a special education teacher for students with emotional and behavior disorders and you are assigned to an inclusion program in the language arts classroom. The general education teacher seats the students with emotional and behavior disorders in a corner of the classroom and asks you to teach them separately from the rest of the class. Is this inclusion? How would you explain inclusion to the language arts teacher?
3. Which individuals are allowed to view students' records and why?
4. Read the story about Roxanna on p. 224. What went wrong? Do you think that the two staff workers should go to jail? Why or why not?

5. What are the two decisive factors that determine whether a student's inappropriate behavior is a manifestation of his or her disability?
6. Why is it important for special education teachers to abide by a Professional Code of Ethics?
7. Mary, an eighth grader, has recently started to act childish and has even started bringing a doll to class. Mary's mother constantly blames Mary for the problems the family is experiencing at home. As Mary's teacher, what do you think has triggered her behavior, and what should you do about it?
8. What are the advantages and disadvantages of the different types of medication prescribed to students with emotional and behavior disorders?

# CHAPTER 12

# Epilogue: Lessons Learned

**After reading this chapter, you should be able to**

- Discuss the factors that might lead to teacher burnout, stress, and attrition.
- Describe the three domains of teacher burnout.

- Describe some of the social, mental, and physical strategies that teachers can use to reduce their stress levels and prevent burnout.

---

Sandra Jones sat on the edge of her bed staring into space. The 6:30 A.M. alarm had gone off 15 minutes ago, but Sandra had not yet made any effort to get ready for work. Sandra was a certified elementary school teacher but she was currently teaching a self-contained unit for students with emotional and behavior disorders at the high school because she had taken some additional courses in special education. Her classroom seemed to be more of a dumping ground for juvenile delinquents than for children with disabilities. They were disrespectful and displayed an inordinate amount of inappropriate behaviors. Her principal had chided her several times for her lack of classroom management skills and had threatened to "write her up" if she didn't "get on the ball." Because she had

## THE LIFE OF A TEACHER

Yet, Mr. Poteet, who has been teaching students like Johnny for 8 years, does not have such vexations about teaching. Mr. Poteet takes pride in knowing that he does a job few other people could do. He appreciates the tiny incremental gains his students make in both academics and behavior. Mr. Poteet enjoys guiding his students over the course of their high school lives, while general education teachers have each student only for a year. What does David Poteet do differently from Sandra Jones to handle the stresses of teaching?

Teaching has often been considered one of the most stressful professions. Nearly 40% of teachers quit within the first 5 years (Carpenter, 2007), and in states like Texas, 50% of all beginning teachers leave the field within 5 years (Texas State

excessive paperwork to do and seldom received a preparation period, Sandra rarely had a chance to talk to the other teachers, and they ignored her when she walked into the teachers' lounge, as if she was not one of them. She had seven case conferences scheduled in the next 2 weeks, and she was tutoring most of her students after school in preparation for the state-mandated examinations required by No Child Left Behind. When she did finally get home, Sandra brought with her a pile of papers to grade. Her husband complained that they never had any time together anymore, and they argued more often these days. Each evening, after Sandra had finally graded her mountain of papers, she would watch a half hour of television and then go to bed, only to wake in the morning to start it all over again. But this morning, Sandra realized that she couldn't do it any more. She burst into tears. She wanted to teach children at the elementary school level, not high school delinquents. She couldn't do it any more. She just couldn't do it anymore.

Board for Educator Certification, 1998). Along with math and science, special education has the highest turnover of teachers (Billingsley, 2004), and special education teachers are more likely to leave teaching than any other teacher group (McLeskey, Tyler, & Saunders Flippin, 2004; Nichols & Sosnowsky, 2002). Nationally, 98% of school districts have reported a shortage of certified special education teachers and nearly 48,000 special education positions have been filled by teachers who are not fully certified (U.S. Department of Education, 2003). The greatest shortage of teachers is in the field of emotional and behavior disorders (American Association for Employment in Education, 2000, 2004; Katsiyannis et al., 2003). These teachers face immense instructional and management challenges, and the demand for teachers of students with emotional and behavior disorders greatly outweighs the supply (Henderson et al., 2005). Many factors have contributed to the serious shortage of these teachers, including high teacher attrition, a lack of new teachers entering the field, stress, and burnout (Billingsley et al., 2006; Henderson et al., 2005).

Teacher attrition, or the leaving of the teaching field by teachers, is one of the major reasons for the shortage of teachers who teach students with emotional and behavior disorders. Lack of appropriate qualifications, challenging work environment factors, and affective reactions to work are factors that influence attrition (Billingsley, 2004).

No Child Left Behind (2001) and IDEA (2004) mandate that all special education teachers be "highly qualified." Yet many individuals teaching students with emotional and behavior disorders are not fully certified and in fact are the least qualified of special education teachers. Nearly 27% of teachers of students with emotional and behavior disorders enter the field through alternative certification programs. More than half of the beginning teachers are not fully certified, 11% are certified in another field, and 39% hold an emergency certificate (Katsiyannis et al., 2003; SPeNSE, 2002a). Teachers who are not certified have a higher level of attrition than teachers who are well prepared in both content and pedagogy, and certified teachers are more likely to both enter and stay in teaching (Darling-Hammond, 2001).

The requirements of No Child Left Behind and IDEA 2004 may also exacerbate the shortage of special education teachers of students with emotional and behavior disorders. A teacher in a self-contained classroom who is required to meet the "highly qualified criteria" for every one of his or her students—in other words to demonstrate competency in multiple academic subjects—may feel overwhelmed by the expectation and may be inclined to leave the field (Thornton, Peltier, & Medina, 2007). Thus, No Child Left Behind and IDEA 2004 made it even more difficult to fill positions that already had severe shortages (Hyatt, 2007).

Working conditions also play a role in the attrition of teachers of students with emotional and behavior disorders. Many teachers leave the profession because they fail to receive administrative support, do not get respect or acceptance from the general education teachers, and are burdened by excessive paperwork (Billingsley, 2004; Billingsley, Carlson, & Klein, 2004; Council for Exception Children, 2001; Fore, Martin, & Bender, 2002).

Administrative support is an important aspect of the work environment that directly affects school climate and school culture (Thornton et al., 2007). When administrators have poor relationships with teachers, it creates a school environment that invites teacher burnout (Schlichte, Yssel, & Merbler, 2005). However, when principals provide strong administrative and emotional support by showing appreciation, taking an interest in teachers' work, and maintaining open lines of communication, general and special education teachers are more likely to remain in the classroom (Billingsley & Cross, 1992; Wasburn-Moses, 2005).

Special education teachers who do not receive respect and acceptance from colleagues often feel like stepchildren in the school setting and are inadvertently excluded from the school community. Teachers of students with emotional and behavior disorders are particularly ostracized, partly due to their association with students who have "behavioral problems" and partly because other teachers lack an understanding of emotional and behavior disorders. This state of affairs is unfortunate because teachers of students with emotional and behavior disorders are more likely to need the support of their colleagues due to the type of students they teach, and they are more likely to remain in the field when they have higher levels of support from colleagues (Billingsley, 2004).

Among the administrative duties and paperwork that special education teachers are required to carry out (more than general education teachers) are completing IEPs, student evaluations, and transition plans, and setting up and coordinating case conference meetings with all committee members. Teachers of students with emotional and behavior disorders may have the added duties of completing FBAs and BIPs and attending case conference meetings to determine manifestation and decide alternative placements. In one survey, 88% of special education teachers indicated that their administrative duties and paperwork interfered with their teaching duties (SPeNSE, 2003) and that these duties affected their desire to leave the profession (SPeNSE, 2002b).

The affective responses to a negative work environment are increased stress, lower job satisfaction, and reduced commitment to the profession (Billingsley, 2004). Unfortunately, general and special education teachers often cannot do much to change their work environments, but they can change their personal environments to prevent burnout.

## LEARNING TO STAY BALANCED

Special education teachers who felt that they were under a great deal of stress on a daily and weekly basis were more likely to leave the classroom, and those who taught students with emotional and behavior disorders reported higher levels of stress than other special education teachers (Billingsley, 2004; Cross & Billingsley, 1994; Center & Stevenson, 2001). Stress in teachers can cause anxiety and frustration, affect teaching performance, and damage interpersonal relationships at work and home (Kyriacou, 2001). Teachers who are under stress for a long time may experience burnout.

### Burnout

*Burnout* is a work-related syndrome that often affects human-service professionals such as social workers and nurses, but it affects teachers far more often (Farber, 2000; Friedman, 2000). Burnout has three domains: emotional exhaustion, depersonalization, and lack of accomplishment (Friedman, 2000; Wood & McCarthy, 2002). When teachers are emotionally exhausted, they feel that they do not have anything left to give. Teachers who feel depersonalized decrease their involvement at work and distance themselves from colleagues. They often verbally agree with the ideas and decisions of others, even though, at heart, they disagree, and they seldom express their own ideas or opinions. They sometimes exhibit depersonalization by having a poor attitude towards students and the work environment (Wood & McCarthy, 2002). Teachers who suffer from burnout feel incapable of accomplishing anything and feel that others do not value anything they do. They feel that they can no longer make a difference. This lack of self-worth is reinforced among teachers of students with emotional and behavior disorders. Unlike general education teachers who often see their efforts bear fruit in the academic and social progress of their students, teachers of students with emotional and behavior disorders may not see their successes until years later.

Burnout is a serious problem among general education teachers, special education teachers, and especially teachers of students with emotional and behavior disorders. Besides leaving the field, there is little teachers can do to change their work environment, but there are strategies they can implement to help themselves remain balanced.

First, teachers must recognize the symptoms of burnout so that they can take action to address the condition. Teachers experiencing burnout may have the following symptoms:

1. Dreading going to work and having an increased rate of absenteeism.
2. Finding it difficult to concentrate and complete work-related tasks.
3. Feeling devalued and worthless.
4. Avoiding interaction with peers and colleagues, or having a sense of being perpetually in conflict with them.
5. Sneaking out side doors or at carefully arranged times to avoid contact with colleagues.
6. Feeling that no one cares about them or feeling that they are under attack.
7. Disliking the school in which they work and always making negative comments about the school in general.
8. Experiencing headaches, insomnia, digestive disorders, depression, and anxiety.
9. Having difficulties behaving professionally in stressful situations.
10. Feeling exhausted all the time (Kyriacou, 2001; Troman & Woods, 2001).

When teachers experience burnout, they begin detaching themselves from their jobs. They become cynical and critical. Instead of doing their very best, teachers experiencing burnout try to get by with the bare minimum of effort (Leiter & Maslach, 2005).

Research has focused on the role of administrators, and particularly principals, in preventing teacher stress and burnout, but little work has been done on the role teachers could play in preventing burnout. These teacher strategies need to address the trinity of the human psyche: spirit, mind, and body.

## A TEACHER'S WELL-BEING

There are a number of things that principals can do to help prevent burnout and attrition, such as implementing mentor programs and providing administrative and emotional supports, but these interventions are often not in place. It falls to the individual teacher to develop strategies to prevent and address burnout. These strategies are designed to address the social, mental, and physical development of teachers, especially teachers of students with emotional and behavior disorders.

### Social Development

Teachers spend most of their time interacting with students, so they seldom have the opportunity to interact with their fellow teachers. Special education teachers are seldom involved in grade-level meetings or departmental planning meetings. As a result, they may not have the time to socialize with colleagues, the people in their lives who are most likely to understand the demands placed on them. This lack of socialization with colleagues puts teachers at greater risk for burnout (Wood & McCarthy, 2002).

Collegiality, or the sense of belonging and being part of a team, is an important variable in teaching, and collegial isolation is associated with burnout (Schlichte et al., 2005). Just as many general education teachers and administrators do not fully understand the nature of special education, they sometimes do not understand all the demands affecting special education teachers and have difficulties relating to special education teachers. Special education teachers have fewer opportunities for collegiality than general education teachers ("CEC Launches," 1998).

**BUILDING A SUPPORT GROUP**   In order to combat this isolation, special education teachers need to make a conscious effort to

Mr. Poteet, a teacher of students with emotional and behavior disorders, arrives at Franklin Pierce High School at 7:30 A.M. He quickly goes to the teacher's lounge and checks his mail, says a brief "hello" to anyone in the lounge, and then goes to his classroom to prepare for the day. At 7:50 A.M., he stands outside his classroom, monitors the students in the hallway, and greets students as they enter his classroom.

From 8:00 A.M. to 11:30 A.M., Mr. Poteet generally works in his classroom, teaching students and managing behavior. From 11:30 A.M. to noon, he eats lunch. Sometimes he eats in the teachers' lounge with other teachers, and sometimes he spends his lunchtime dealing with the behavioral difficulties of one of his students, but most times he eats alone in his classroom. The teachers' lounge is not a place of refuge for him. The other teachers often complain about the behavior of students, usually his students, and sometimes he feels that they don't accept him as a "real" teacher.

From noon to 2:15 P.M., Mr. Poteet once again teaches in his classroom. Occasionally, the routine is disrupted by a case conference. When it is not interrupted by extraneous events, his planning period begins at 2:15 P.M. During this time, Mr. Poteet grades papers, prepares for the following day's lessons, or prepares the paperwork for case conferences. His planning period and the school day end at 3:00 P.M. Mr. Poteet often stays after school to help tutor students who are having difficulties.

integrate themselves into school culture. Schools tend to be the social hub of many communities. Sports events, theatrical productions, and band and choir recitals are part of school life. Special education teachers need to attend these activities so that others will see them as being involved in the school and so that they will have opportunities to socialize with other active members of the school community. Attending these events also gives the teacher the opportunity to see students, especially students with disabilities, in a setting outside the classroom. It personalizes the school community and helps prevent depersonalization, which leads to burnout.

It is also important for teachers of students with emotional and behavior disorders to find someone at school to whom he or she may go to seek emotional support or vent frustrations. It is not common for schools to have more than one teacher of students with emotional and behavior disorders, but seeking another special education teacher for support may be helpful. Although no one except another teacher of children with emotional and behavior disorders can fully understand the demands of the profession, other special education teachers often feel similar stressors such as excessive paperwork, lack of administrative support, and indifference from other colleagues.

Teachers of students with emotional and behavior disorders often work closely with school counselors and may find that these individuals provide valuable and needed emotional support for the teacher. School counselors are not teachers, nor do they fit into the realm of administrators, so they may feel the same sense of isolation as special education teachers and may also be prone to emotional exhaustion and depersonalization leading to burnout (Wilkerson & Bellini, 2006). By including school counselors in their circle of support, special education teachers may be able to provide the same needed interventions for the counselors to prevent *them* from experiencing burnout.

It is important for teachers of students with emotional and behavior disorders to take the time and effort to develop a circle of support. Having support will help reduce stress, prevent burnout, and keep special education teachers in the field longer (Billingsley, 2004). It is also beneficial to the mental and emotional well-being of teachers who have students with emotional and behavior disorders.

**LIFE OUTSIDE THE CLASSROOM**   It is equally important for teachers to have a life outside the school community. This can be difficult for special education teachers because they need to be in better communication with the parents of their students than do other types of teachers. It is not uncommon for a special education teacher to run into a parent while shopping at the local grocery store and hold an impromptu parent conference. Such meetings are a wonderful way for special education teachers to build parental support, but they do not constitute having a life outside the classroom. Teachers of students with emotional and behavior disorders need to be involved in community activities. These could include church activities, bowling leagues, concerts, or any other activity that is not directly related to teaching or education. For example, a special education teacher should not volunteer or be asked to teach a children's Sunday school class, and if he or she does, it should be on a rotating basis. Otherwise, this becomes a sixth day of teaching, and a special education teacher may benefit more from engaging in other activities and socializing with other adults.

Having a life outside of school also means leaving work, and its associated problems, at school. Too often, general education teachers and special education teachers take their work home. Teachers need to go home empty handed, rather than taking papers to grade, lessons to prepare, or case conference forms to fill out. Of course, there will be times when taking home paperwork is necessary, but it should be the exception, not the rule. In nearly all studies regarding teacher attrition and burnout, teachers almost always list excessive paperwork as a factor. Not taking work home is a simple strategy, but it is one that many general education teachers and special education teachers have difficulty implementing.

Besides leaving the paperwork at school, teachers also need to leave many of their job-related problems there. It is beneficial for teachers to occasionally vent their frustrations about students, administrators, and school with a spouse or friends, but when it becomes a daily occurrence, it can have detrimental effects on the teacher's personal relationships. No one wants to be around someone who complains constantly.

Before leaving school, teachers should write down a list of the day's stressors and throw it in the trash as they go out the door. Or they might try tapping the mailbox as they get home and mentally leaving the stressors in the mailbox. The time teachers have outside the classroom is *their* time.

Teachers also need to learn to say "no" to requests that come from outside the immediate classroom when they are too overwhelmed to handle any more requests. Teachers are often asked to sponsor clubs or activities, coach sports, and attend school-related events. Being involved in some of these activities enhances the experience of teaching, but when a teacher is already involved in a number of activities or when the activity is not interesting to the teacher, agreeing to take it on does not benefit the teacher, the students, or the school. Unfortunately, teachers have a difficult time saying "no" because they feel obligated to agree, and they end up having trouble balancing work and home life. One way to avoid any potential guilt associated with the decision is to use assertive communication with "I" statements to say "no" (Nagel & Brown, 2003). For example, if the principal asks the special education teacher to sponsor the Drama Club, the teacher may respond by saying, "I really appreciate the opportunity, but I am already involved in a number of other activities. Maybe I will have more time next year." Using the "I" statement and justifying the reasons for not accepting the request will diminish the stress of saying "no."

Vacations are for rejuvenation, a time to relax and recover energy. We all have a biological need to occasionally disengage from the daily demands of life, but many teachers ignore this preventive measure. As a result of foregoing vacations, teachers may feel high levels of stress. Stress is now considered the fastest growing disability in the United States (Gorman, 2007). Teachers need to take summers off. Unfortunately, due to financial or professional considerations, many teachers spend the summer teaching summer school, taking college courses to maintain their licenses, or seeking a degree leading to a position outside the classroom.

Taking courses to maintain certification or, even better, taking a class for personal enjoyment is an excellent way to develop a support network with others in the teaching field. Unfortunately, teachers tend to overload on courses. They take more than two classes per semester during the academic year, while they are teaching, and up to four or more courses in the summer when they should be recharging. This overload of courses tends to negate the positive effect of continuous education and increase the probability of burnout.

Teachers receive a certain number of sick days per year that accumulate during the life of a teaching career. Occasionally, teachers may take a "mental health" day, a sick day they use when they feel stressed or frustrated and need a break from the classroom. Some principals actually encourage teachers to take mental health days because they know that it is beneficial for the teachers and the students.

Teaching is a job, not a life. It is a means to make a wonderful difference in the students that come into the classrooms, and it is a noble way to make a living, but it should not consume a person's life. As difficult as it may be for a teacher to separate teaching from his or her personal life, it is critical to do so, or the consequences will damage the teacher's emotional well-being. By not taking time out for themselves, teachers run the risk of burnout. Burnout will affect relationships with others, the energy teachers have to devote to teaching, and, ultimately, the quality of education they provide to students.

## Mental Development

Mental exercise is just as important as social interactions and physical exercise. It can relieve stress and provide a sense of individual satisfaction. A number of simple strategies are available for exercising the mind.

Crossword puzzles, logic problems, and sudoku puzzles are good mental exercises. These activities are a break from routine, mundane tasks. They require the use of logic, common sense, and concentration, which challenge the mind. However, they should be used in conjunction with other activities, such as playing music, taking dancing lessons, and physical exercise.

Music also has the ability to promote relaxation and reduce stress. In order to receive the full effect, the listener needs to sit down, preferably with eyes closed, and listen. When music is used as background noise or white noise, its therapeutic effect is diminished. Self-efficacy, self-esteem, and relaxation, which are countermeasures to stress, depersonalization, and lack of accomplishment, are some of the benefits of learning to play a musical instrument (Jutras, 2006). Music therapy has been shown to help teachers develop strategies for coping with stress by giving them opportunities for expression and helping them establish interpersonal relationships with colleagues (Cheek, Bradley, Parr, & Lan, 2003).

Meditation and diaphragmatic breathing (deep breathing) have been demonstrated to reduce stress, increase positive states of mind, and decrease negative emotions. Teachers who meditate for 20 minutes a day outside the classroom in quiet reflection may be able to reduce their stress levels (Chang et al., 2004; Lane, Seskevich, & Pieper, 2007; Nagel & Brown, 2003). Ideally, a teacher should meditate in the morning. In addition, taking short, quiet breaks of a minute or two throughout the day will help reenergize the teacher. One teacher who taught students with emotional and behavior disorders meditated in the time-out room for 15 minutes before school to prepare himself for the day and for 15 minutes after school to rejuvenate himself for the rest of the day.

Reading a book is another form of mental exercise. The teacher should choose a book that is not a textbook or anything related to education. Novels, science fiction, and mysteries are good choices for taking the teacher's mind off the classroom.

Other useful diversions include fine-motor activities such as building plastic models, crocheting, painting, and putting together jigsaw puzzles. These activities can provide mental exercise, give the teacher a sense of satisfaction, and reduce stress levels. The teacher needs to make a conscious effort to pursue and maintain such activities. The long-term benefits include reduced stress, prevention of burnout, and improved efficiency in the classroom.

## Physical Development

Much has been written about the long-term benefits of exercising, eating well, and getting enough sleep. These activities reduce stress and make the teacher feel better. Some school

| **TABLE 12.1    Steps to Developing a Wellness Program in School** |
|---|

1. Obtain Administrative Support: Provide administrators with benefits and a  list of activities of a Wellness Program.
2. Identify a School District Coordinator: This individual will be responsible for the implementation of the Wellness Program.
3. Organize a Team: Members of this team will plan, revise, and review the activities of the Wellness Program.
4. Gather and Analyze Data: Identify current health activities, concerns and interests of faculty and staff, health problems, and health costs.
5. Develop a Plan: A school wellness plan could include a mission statement, goals, activities, timelines, resource needs, budget, and an evaluation plan.
6. Promote Awareness: Develop activities that promote awareness of the Wellness Program.
7. Implement the Plan: Plan for and celebrate small, early successes.
8. Offer Incentives: Incentives can motivate teams and individuals.
9. Identify District Resources: A Wellness Program will require time, space, and equipment.
10. Evaluate and Adapt the Program: Evaluate aspects of the program that are successful, and improve the program as it develops.

*Source:* Kolbe et al., 2005.

districts have actually developed wellness programs for their faculty, staff, and administrators within the school setting. (See Table 12.1.) These programs are educational sessions addressing exercise concerns, providing nutritional guidelines, and promoting exercise. Program activities include weekly weigh-ins, blood pressure monitoring, body fat and weight-loss analyses, and physiological evaluations. The results of school-based wellness programs include reduced absenteeism, stress, and illnesses; increased productivity; improved staff retention; improved health and reduced health insurance costs; and the setting of a good example for students (Kolbe et al., 2005; Sell & Rees, 2005).

Besides helping a person feel better, physical exercise burns stress hormones and increases resiliency to stress (Nagel & Brown, 2003). That does not mean that teachers need to run out and join a fitness club; just walking daily can provide them with the benefits of exercise. Teachers can walk around the school building during their lunch breaks. A teacher of students with emotional and behavior disorders can take a student for a walk when the student is feeling frustrated, thus reaping the benefits of walking for him- or herself as well. Teachers can also use gym time as a reinforcer for their students. When the teacher takes his or her students to the gym, the teacher should participate in basketball, racquetball, or any other activities. This activity not only will help improve the wellness of the teacher, but it will improve the teacher's relationships with the students as well.

There are a number of other ways teachers can keep physically fit. They can join an adult sports league, such as a baseball, volleyball, golfing, or bowling league.

Eating a healthy diet is also important. Many teachers are aware of the components of a healthy diet: lots of fruits and vegetables; few fats, sweets, and red meats; and moderate serving sizes. Yet, like many Americans, teachers often do not follow good dietary rules. Teachers tend to eat too many foods and beverages that contain high fat and high sugar contents and consume too much caffeine. Even though most teachers oppose the availability of

Physical activity will not only help improve the wellness of the teacher but improve relationships with the students.

soft drink and snack vending machines for students, over 60% of teachers purchase soft drinks for themselves, over 30% purchase high-sugar or high-fat snacks from vending machines, and over 30% purchase these items from the à la carte line at lunch (Kubik, Lytle, Hannan, Story, & Perry, 2002). Foods such as soft drinks, doughnuts, and candies are often used as comfort foods that individuals consume when they are feeling sad or depressed. Unfortunately, most comfort foods have little or no nutritional values. Comfort foods become counterproductive in the fight against stress and burnout because they do not benefit the teacher's well-being and because a teacher who partakes of comfort food is less likely to employ the interventions and strategies that will reduce stress and burnout.

## The Final Say

The attrition rate for general education teachers, special education teachers, and especially teachers of students with emotional and behavior disorders is high. Many teachers leave the field due to the daily stress that leads to burnout. Much has been written regarding the principal's role in reducing burnout, but the personal role of the teacher in preventing stress and burnout has not been explored. Unfortunately, many teachers, like most Americans, do all the wrong things to combat stress. They frequently deal with chronic stress by watching television, not exercising, and eating foods that are high in fat and sugar. These coping mechanisms actively prevent teachers from using the strategies that do help reduce stress, such as socializing, exercising, and eating healthy foods (Gorman, 2007). As a result, many teachers who are currently in the field will not be teaching 5 years from now, and positions for special education teachers of students with emotional and behavior disorders will not be filled by qualified personnel.

There are many strategies teachers can use to reduce stress and prevent burnout, but they have to decide to implement and maintain these strategies. Individuals who do so will be happier and healthier teachers. Healthy, optimistic teachers are critical to effecting student well-being and academic achievement (Centers for Disease Control and Prevention, 2003; Kolbe et al., 2005). (See Table 12.2.)

| **TABLE 12.2**    **Tips for Reducing Stress and Preventing Burnout** |
| --- |
| • Develop a support group at school. |
| • Get involved in community activities that are not related to school. |
| • Leave work and school problems at school. |
| • Just say "no" to additional responsibilities. |
| • Take vacation time. |
| • Take a couple of classes. |
| • Take time each day for relaxation (hobbies, music, paint, etc.). |
| • Meditate, take a yoga class, or do deep breathing. |
| • Read a good book. |
| • Go walking. |
| • Go to bed earlier. |
| • Cut back on sodas and foods that are high in sugar and fat. |
| • Turn off your cell phone. |

## Summary

Teaching has often been considered one of the most stressful professions, and many teachers leave the field within the first 5 years. Special education teachers are more likely to leave teaching than any other teacher group, and the greatest shortage of special education teachers is of teachers of students with emotional and behavior disorders. Demanding teacher qualifications, a difficult work environment, and affective reactions to work are factors that influence the attrition of teachers who teach students with emotional and behavior disorders. Many special education teachers leave the profession because they do not receive administrative support, are not respected or accepted by the general education teachers, and are burdened by excessive paperwork.

Teachers of students with emotional and behavior disorders experience high levels of stress and may be at risk for burnout. Burnout has three domains: emotional exhaustion, depersonalization, and lack of accomplishment. Research shows that administrators can play a role in preventing teacher stress and burnout, but there has been little focus on the role of teachers. Strategies designed to address the social, mental, and physical needs of teachers may help reduce stress and prevent burnout. Unfortunately, many teachers do all the wrong things to reduce stress. Teachers need to make a conscious effort to implement strategies that will make them happier and healthier in their jobs.

## Case Study 12.1

### Johnny's Graduation

Mr. Poteet and Mrs. Martin sat together in the auditorium for the Franklin Pierce High School Commencement Ceremony. For Mrs. Martin, the road to this destination had been long and difficult. While Johnny still displayed bouts of anger and aggression, his behavior and academic performance had improved significantly thanks to people like

Mr. Poteet and other teachers, administrators, and professionals who had guided Johnny to this point in his life.

For special education teachers like Mr. Poteet, who seldom see the immediate fruit of their labor, watching Johnny cross the stage to receive his diploma gave Mr. Poteet a sense of satisfaction and accomplishment. He had worked with Johnny for the past 4 years, trying to meet his behavioral, social, academic, and emotional needs. That journey was now nearing the end.

Finally, Johnny's name was called. Dressed in his cap and gown, he walked across the stage to retrieve his diploma from Mr. Price, the principal. It was a milestone few people had thought Johnny would accomplish. Next week, he would start a job with an auto repair shop.

**Three Years Later**

Johnny was still working at the auto repair shop and had received a promotion. He was taking a few courses at a local technical school that had helped him with the promotion. Compared with other students who have emotional and behavior disorders, Johnny had beaten the odds. Three years after graduation, he was employed and had not had any involvement with the law.

**Four Years Later**

Mr. Poteet received an invitation to Johnny's marriage to a girl he had been dating for 2 years. In a personal, handwritten note included in the invitation, Johnny wrote that he hoped that Mr. Poteet could make it to the wedding.

Mr. Poteet would not have missed Johnny's wedding for anything.

## Review Questions

1. What are the factors that can lead to stress, burnout, and attrition for general education teachers, special education teachers, and teachers of students with emotional and behavior disorders?
2. How can teacher certification affect the attrition rate of teachers who teach students with emotional and behavior disorders?
3. How does No Child Left Behind exacerbate the shortage of teachers who teach students with emotional and behavior disorders?
4. What is burnout and what are its three domains?
5. What are some of the strategies used to maintain the social, mental, and physical health of teachers so that they can reduce stress and prevent burnout?

# REFERENCES

Aaroe, L., & Nelson, J. R. (2000). A comparative analysis of teachers', Caucasian parents', and Hispanic parents' views of problematic school survival behavior. *Education and Treatment of Children, 23*(3), 314–324.

Abrams, K., Theberge, S. K., & Karan, O. C. (2005). Children and adolescents who are depressed: An ecological approach. *Professional School Counseling, 8*(3), 284–292.

Achenbach, T. M., & Edelbrock, C. S. (1981). Behavioral problems and competencies reported by parents of normal and disturbed children aged 4 through 16. *Monographs of the Society for Research in Child Development, 46* (Serial No. 188).

Achenbach, T. M., & Edelbrock, C. S. (1983). *Manual for the child behavior checklist*. Burlington, VT: University of Vermont Department of Psychiatry.

Achenback, T. M., & Rescorla, L. A. (2000). *Manual for the ASEBA Preschool Forms and Profiles*. Burlington, VT: University of Vermont, Department of Psychiatry.

Achilles, G. M., McLaughlin, M. J., & Croninger, R. G. (2007). Sociocultural correlates of disciplinary exclusion among students with emotional, behavioral, and learning disabilities in the SEELS national dataset. *Journal of Emotional and Behavioral Disorders, 15*(1), 33–45.

Adelman, H. S., & Taylor, L. (1998). Mental health in schools: Moving forward. *School Psychology Review, 27*(2), 175–190.

Adelman, H. S., & Taylor, L. (2000). Promoting mental health in schools in the midst of school reform. *The Journal of School Health, 70*(5), 171–178.

Alber-Morgan, S. R., Ramp, E. M., Anderson, L. L., & Martin, C. M. (2007). Effects of repeated readings, error correction, and performance feedback on the fluency and comprehension of middle school students with behavior problems. *The Journal of Special Education, 41*(1), 17–30.

Alberto, P. A., & Troutman, A. C. (2006). *Applied behavior analysis for teachers*. Upper Saddle River, NJ: Merrill-Prentice Hall.

Al Otaiba, S., & Rivera, M. O. (2006). Individualizing guided oral reading fluency instruction for students with emotional and behavioral disorders. *Intervention in School and Clinic, 41*(3), 144–149.

Amendola, A. M., & Oliver, R. W. (2003). LSCI and aggression replacement training: A multi-modal approach. *Reclaiming Children and Youth, 12*(3), 181–185.

American Academy of Child and Adolescent Psychiatry Official Action. (2001). Practice parameter for the treatment of children and adolescents with schizophrenia. *Journal of the American Academy of Child and Adolescent Psychiatry, 40*, 4s–23s.

American Association for Employment in Education (AAEE). (2000). *Educator supply and demand*. Columbus, OH: AAEE.

American Association for Employment in Education (AAEE). (2004). *Educator supply and demand in the United States (executive summary)*. Columbus, OH: AAEE.

American Psychiatric Association. (2000). *Diagnostic and statistical manual of mental disorders* (4th ed., text rev.). Washington, DC: Author.

American Psychiatric Association Work Group on Eating Disorders. (2000). Practice guideline for the treatment of patients with eating disorders (revision). *American Journal of Psychiatry, 157* (1 Suppl): 1–39.

American Psychological Association. (1989). Council policy manual: XXVIII. Special education. Washington, DC: Author.

Anderson, J. A., Wright, E. R., Smith, J. S., & Kooreman, H. E. (2007). Educational profiles of students at enrollment in a system of care. *Remedial and Special Education, 28*(1), 9–20.

Anderson, R. N. (2002). Deaths: Leading causes for 2000. *National Vital Statistics Report, 50*(16), 1–86.

Anderson, R. N., & Smith, B. L. (2003). Deaths: Leading causes for 2001. *National Vital Statistics Report, 52*(9), 1–86.

The Annie E. Casey Foundation. (2003). Kids Count data book indicator: State profiles of poverty. Retrieved November 26, 2005, from http://www.aecf.org/kidscount/sld/compare_resul ts.jsp?i=240

Apter, S. J. (1977). Applications of ecological theory: Toward a community special education model for troubled children. *Exceptional Children, 43*, 366–373.

Apter, S. J., & Conoley, J. C. (1984). *Childhood behavior disorders and emotional disturbances.* Englewood Cliffs, NJ: Prentice-Hall.

Arnberger, K., & Shoop, R. (2006). A principal's guide to manifestation determination. *Principal Leadership, 6*(9), 16–21.

Arndt, S. A., Konrad, M., & Test, D. W. (2006). Effects of the self-directed IEP on student participation in planning meetings. *Remedial and Special Education, 27*(4), 194–101.

Ash, P. (2008). Suicidal behavior in children and adolescents. *Journal of Psychosocial Nursing & Mental Health Services, 46*(1), 26–31.

Assemany, A. E., & McIntosh, D. E. (2002). Negative treatment outcomes of behavioral parent training programs. *Psychology in the Schools, 39*(2), 209–219.

Bailey, M. K., Zauszniewski, J. A., Heinzer, M. M., & Hemstrom-Krainess, M. (2007). Patterns of depressive symptoms in children. *Journal of Child and Adolescent Psychiatric Nursing, 20*(2), 86–95.

Baker, S., Gersten, R., Dimino, J. A., & Griffiths, R. (2004). The sustained use of research-based instructional practice: A case study of Peer-Assisted Learning Strategies in mathematics. *Remedial and Special Education, 25*(1), 5–24.

Bandura, A. (1977). *Social Learning Theory.* Englewood Cliffs, NJ: Prentice-Hall.

Bandura, A. (1986). *Social foundations of thought and action: A social cognitive theory.* Englewood Cliffs, NJ: Prentice-Hall.

Bandura, A. (1997). *Self-efficacy: The exercise of control.* New York: Freeman.

Bandura, A., Ross, D. M., & Ross, S. A. (1963). Imitation of film-mediated aggressive models. *Journal of Abnormal and Social Psychology, 66*, 3–11.

Barkley, R. (2005). *Attention-deficit hyperactivity disorder: A handbook for diagnosis and treatment* (3rd ed.). New York: The Guilford Press.

Barkley, R. A., Fischer, M., Smallish, L., & Fletcher, K. (2004). Young adult follow-up of hyperactive children: Antisocial activities and drug use. *Journal of Child Psychology and Psychiatry, 45*(2), 195–211.

Barnard, L., Young, A. H., Pearson, A. D. J. Geddes, J., & O'Brien, G. (2002). A systematic review of the use of atypical antipsychotics in autism. *Journal of Psychopharmacology, 16*(1), 93–101.

Barth, R. S. (2006). Improving relationships within the schoolhouse. *Educational Leadership, 63*(6), 8–13.

Bartlett, C. W., Goedken, R., Vieland, V. J. (2005). Effects of updating linkage evidence across subsets of data: Reanalysis of the autism genetic resource exchange data set. *American Journal of Human Genetics, 76*(4), 688–695.

Barton-Arwood, S. M., Wehby, J. H., & Falk, K. B. (2005). Reading instruction for elementary-age students with emotional and behavioral disorders: Academic and behavioral outcomes. *Exceptional Children, 72*(1), 7–27.

Barton-Arwood, S. M., Wehby, J. H., Gunter, P. L., & Lane, K. L. (2003). Functional behavior assessment rating scales: Intrarater reliability with students with emotional or behavioral disorders. *Behavioral Disorders, 28*(4), 386–400.

Baumrind, D. (1994). The social context of child maltreatment. *Family Relations, 43*(4), 360–368.

Baumrind, D. (1995). *Child maltreatment and optimal caregiving in social contexts.* New York: Garland.

*Beattie v. Board of Education*, 169 Wis. 231, 172 N.W. 153 (1919).

Beatty, M. J., Heisel, A. D., Hall, A. E., Levine, T. R., & La France, B. H. (2002). What can we learn from the study of twins about genetic and environmental influences on interpersonal affiliation, aggressiveness, and social anxiety?: A meta-analytic study. *Communication Monographs, 69*(1), 1–18.

Becker, K. A. (2003). *Histories of the Stanford–Binet intelligence scales: Content and psychometrics.* (Stanford–Binet Intelligences Scales, Fifth Edition Service Bulletin No. 1). Itasca, IL: Riverside Publishing.

Beers, C. W. (1981). *A mind that found itself: An autobiography.* University of Pittsburgh Press.

Berliner, D. C., & Biddle. B. J. (1995). *The manufactured crisis: Myths, fraud, and the attack on America's public schools.* White Plains, NY: Longman.

Bergert, S., & Burnette, J. (2001). *Educating exceptional children: A statistical profile.* Arlington, VA: ERIC Clearinghouse on Disabilities and Gifted Education, EC 308407.

Bickhard, M. H. (1997). Piaget and active cognition. *Human Development, 40*(4), 238–244.

Billingsley, B. S. (2004). Special education teacher retention and attrition: A critical analysis of the research literature. *The Journal of Special Education, 38*(1), 39–55.

Billingsley, B. S., Carlson, E., & Klein, S. (2004). The working conditions and induction support of early career special educators. *Exceptional Children, 70*(3), 333–347.

Billingsley, B. S., Fall, A., & Williams, Jr., T. O. (2006). Who is teaching students with emotional and behavioral disorders?: A profile and comparison to other special educators. *Behavioral Disorders, 31*(3), 252–264.

Binet, A., & Simon, T. (1905). Méthodes nouvelles pour le diagnostic du niveau intellectuel des anormaux. *L'Année psychologique, 11*, 191–336.

Blake, C., Wang, W., Cartledge, G., & Gardner, R. (2000). Middle school students with serious emotional disturbances serve as social skills trainers and reinforcers for peers with SED. *Behavioral Disorders, 25*(4), 280–298.

Borgmeier, C., & Horner, R. H. (2006). An evaluation of the predictive validity of confidence ratings in identifying functional behavioral assessment hypothesis statements. *Journal of Positive Behavior Interventions, 8*(2), 100–105.

Bouck, E. C. (2007). Co-teaching … not just a textbook term: Implications for practice. *Preventing School Failure, 51*(2), 46–51.

Bower, E. M. (1960). *Early identification of emotionally handicapped children in school.* Springfield, IL: Thomas.

Bower, E. M. (1981). *Early identification of emotionally handicapped children in school* (3rd ed.). Springfield, IL: Thomas.

Bower, E. M. (1982). Defining emotional disturbance: Public policy and research. *Psychology in the School, 19*, 55–60.

Boyce, T. E., & Hineline, P. N. (2002). Interteaching: A strategy for enhancing the user-friendliness of behavioral arrangements in the college classroom. *The Behavior Analyst, 25*, 215–226.

Braaten, S. (2003). Remembering Arnold P. Goldstein. *Reclaiming Children and Youth, 12*(3), 130–131.

Bracken, B. A., & McCallum, R. S. (1998). *Universal Nonverbal Intelligence Test: Examiner's manual.* Itasca, IL: Riverside Publishing.

Bradley, R., Henderson, K., & Monroe, D. A. (2004). A national perspective on children with emotional disorders. *Behavioral Disorders, 29*(3), 211–223.

Bradley, R., Danielson, L., & Doolittle, J. (2005). Response to intervention. *Journal of Learning Disabilities, 38*(6), 485-486.

Brantlinger, E. (2001). Poverty, class, and disability: A historical, social, and political perspective. *Focus on Exceptional Children, 37*(7), 1–19.

Brendgen, M., Dionne, G., Girard, A., Boivin, M., Vitaro, F., & Pérusse, D. (2005). Examining genetic and environmental effects on social aggression: A study of 6-year-old twins. *Child Development, 76*(4), 930–946.

Brendtro, L. K. (2006). The vision of Urie Bronfenbrenner: Adults who are crazy about kids. *Reclaiming Children and Youth, 15*(3), 162–166.

Briones, E., Tabernero, C., & Arenas, A. (2007). Effects of disposition and self-regulation of self-defeating behavior. *The Journal of Social Psychology, 147*(6), 657–679.

Bronfenbrenner, U. (1979). *The ecology of human development: Experiments by nature and design.* Cambridge, MA: Harvard University Press.

Bronfenbrenner, U. (1995). The bioecological model from a life course perspective: Reflections of a participant observer. In P. Moen, G.H. Elder, Jr., & K. Luscher (Eds.), *Examining lives in context* (pp. 599–618). Washington, DC: American Psychological Association.

Bronfenbrenner, U. (2005a). Interacting systems of human development: Research paradigms: Present and future. In U. Bronfenbrenner (Ed.), *Making human beings human: Bioecological perspectives on human development* (pp. 67–93). Thousand Oaks, CA: Sage.

Bronfenbrenner, U. (2005b). Lewinian space and ecological substance. In U. Bronfenbrenner (Ed.), *Making human beings human: Bioecological perspectives on human development* (pp.41–49). Thousand Oaks, CA: Sage.

Browder, D. M., Wood, W. M., Test, D. W., Karvonen, M., & Algozzine, B. (2002). Reviewing resources on self-determination: A map for teachers. *Remedial and Special Education, 22*(4), 233–244.

*Brown v. the Board of Education,* 347 U.S. 483 (1954).

Brown, E. J. (2005). Psychosocial and psychiatric correlates and treatment of posttraumatic stress disorder in children and adolescents. *Psychiatric Annals, 35*(9), 758–765.

Brown, M. B. (2006). School-based health centers: Implications for counselors. *Journal of Counseling & Development, 84*, 187–192.

Brown, M. R. (2007). Educating all students: Creating culturally responsive teachers, classrooms, and schools. *Intervention in School and Clinic, 43*(1), 57–62.

Bruns, E. J., Walrath, C. M., & Sheehan, A. K. (2007). Who administers wraparound? An examination of the training, beliefs, and implementation supports for wraparound providers. *Journal of Emotional and Behavioral Disorders, 15*(3), 156–168.

Bullis, M., & Cheney, D. (1999). Vocational and transition interventions for adolescents and young adults with emotional or behavioral disorders. *Focus on Exceptional Children, 31*(7), 1–24.

Bullis, M., Yovanoff, P., Mueller, G., & Havel, E. (2002). Life on the "outs"—Examination of the facility-to-community transition of incarcerated youth. *Exceptional Children, 69*(1), 7–22.

Bullock, L. M., & Gable, R. A. (2006). Programs for children and adolescents with emotional and behavioral disorders in the United States: A historical overview, current perspectives, and future directions. *Preventing School Failure, 50*(2), 7–13.

Burns, B. J., & Goldman, S. W. (Eds.) (1999). *Promising practices in wraparound for children with serious emotional disturbance and the families. Systems of care: Promising practices in children's mental health* (1998 series, Vol. 4). Washington, DC: Center for Effective Collaboration and Practice, American Institute for Research.

Burns, B. J., Hoagwood, K., & Mrazek, P. J. (1999). Effective treatment for mental disorders in children and adolescents. *Clinical Child and Family Psychology Review, 2*(4), 199–254.

Buskist, W., Cush, D., & DeGrandpre, R. J. (1991). The life and times of PSI. *Journal of Behavioral Education, 1*, 215–234.

Cade, T., & Gunter, P. L. (2002). Teaching students with severe emotional or behavioral disorders to use a musical mnemonic technique to solve basic division calculations. *Behavioral Disorders, 27*(3), 208–214.

Calhoon, M. B. (2005). Effects of a peer-mediated phonological skill and reading comprehension program on reading skill acquisition for middle school students with reading disabilities. *Journal of Learning Disabilities, 38*(5), 424–433.

Calhoon, M. B., & Fuchs, L. S. (2003). The effects of peer-assisted learning strategies and curriculum-based measurement on the mathematics performance of secondary students with disabilities. *Remedial and Special Education, 24*(4), 235–245.

Callahan, C., & Smith, R. M. (1990). Keller's Personalized System of Instruction in a junior high gifted program. *Roeper Review, 13*, 39–44.

Cambron-McCabe, N. H., McCarthy, M. M., & Thomas, S. B. (2003). *Public school law: Teacher's and student's rights* (5th ed.). Boston: Allyn & Bacon.

Cameto, R. (2003). *Findings from the national longitudinal transition study-2* (NLTS2). Washington, D.C.: U.S. Department of Education, Office of Special Education Programs.

Canter, L., & Canter, M. (2001). *Assertive discipline: Positive management for today's classroom* (3rd ed.). Seal Beach, CA: Canter.

Carpenter, W. A. (2007). Top ten reasons to eliminate foundations courses from teacher education. *Educational Horizons, 85*(2), 83–91.

Carroll, D. (2001). Considering paraeducator training, roles, and responsibilities. *Teaching Exceptional Children, 34*(2), 60–64.

Carroll, J. B. (1993). *Human cognitive abilities: A survey of factor-analytic studies.* New York: Cambridge University Press.

Carter, E. W., & Lunsford, L. B. (2005). Meaningful work: Improving employment outcomes for transition-age youth with emotional and behavioral disorders. *Preventing School Failure, 49*(2), 63–69.

Cartledge, G., & Kourea, L. (2008). Culturally responsive classrooms for culturally diverse students with and at risk for disabilities. *Exceptional Children, 74*(3), 351–371.

Cartwright-Hatton, S., McNally, D., White, C., & Verduyn, C. (2005). Parenting skills training: An effective intervention for internalizing symptoms in younger children? *Journal of Child and Adolescent Psychiatric Nursing, 18*(2), 45–52.

Cawley, J., Parmar, R., Foley, T. E., Salmon, S., & Roy, S. (2001). Arithmetic performance of students: Implications for standards and programming. *Exceptional Children, 67*(3), 311–328.

Center, D. B., & Stevenson, C. (2001). The EBD teacher stressors questionnaire. *Education and Treatment of Children, 24,* 323–335.

Center for Effective Collaboration and Practice. (2000). The six life space crisis intervention strategies. Retrieved May 2, 2008, from http://cecp.air.org/interact/authoronline/april98/5.htm

Centers for Disease Control and Prevention. (2002). *National vital statistics.* Atlanta, GA: National Center for Injury Prevention and Control.

Centers for Disease Control and Prevention. (2003). *Stories from the field: Lessons learned about building coordinated school health programs.* Washington, DC: Department of Health and Human Services.

Chamberlain, P., & Moore, K. (1998). A clinical model for parenting juvenile offenders: A comparison of group care versus family care. *Clinical Child Psychology & Psychiatry, 2,* 375–386.

Chang, V. Y., Palesh, O., Caldwell, R., Glasgow, N., Abramson, M., Luskin, F., et al. (2004). The effects of a mindfulness-based stress reduction program on stress, mindfulness self-efficacy, and positive states of mind. *Stress and Health, 20,* 141–147.

Cheek, J. R., Bradley, L. J., Parr, G., & Lan, W. (2003). Using music therapy techniques to treat teacher burnout. *Journal of Mental Health Counseling, 25*(3), 204–217.

Chess, S., & Thomas, A. (1996). *Temperament: Theory and practice.* New York: Bruner-Mazel.

Child Welfare Information Gateway. (2006, April). *Recognizing child abuse and neglect: Signs and symptoms.* Retrieved April 26, 2007, from http://www.childwelfare.gov/pubs/factsheets/signs.cfm

Cho, S., Hudley, C., & Back, H. J. (2003). Cultural influences on ratings of self-perceived social, emotional, and academic adjustment for Korean American adolescents. *Assessment for Effective Intervention, 29*(1), 3–14.

Cillessen, A. H., & Bukowski, W. M. (2000). Conceptualizing and measuring peer acceptance and rejection. In A. H. Cillessen & W. M. Bukowski (Eds.), *Recent advances in the measurement of acceptance and rejection in the peer system* (pp. 3–10). San Francisco: Jossey-Bass.

*Clyde K. and Sheila K. v. Puyullup School District*, 35 F3d 1396 (9th Cir. 1994).

Cohen, M. K. (1994). Children on the boundary: The challenge posed by children with conduct disorders. Alexandria, VA: National Association of State Directors of Special Education.

Coie, J. D., Dodge, K. A., & Coppotelli, H. (1982). Dimensions and types of social status: A cross-age perspective. *Developmental Psychology, 18,* 557–570.

Coleman, M. C., & Vaughn, S. (2000). Reading interventions for students with emotional/behavioral disorders. *Behavioral Disorders, 25*(2), 93–104.

Coleman, M. C., & Webber, J. (2002). *Emotional and behavioral disorders: Theory and practice* (4th ed.). Boston: Allyn and Bacon.

The Conduct Problems Prevention Research Group. (2002). Evaluation of the first 3 years of the fast track prevention trial with children at high risk for adolescent conduct problems. *Journal of Abnormal Child Psychology, 30*(1), 19–35.

Connor, D. F. (2005). Stimulants. In R. A. Barkley (Ed.), *Attention-deficit hyperactivity disorder: A handbook for diagnosis and treatment* (3rd ed.). New York: Guilford.

Conners, C. K. (1985). *Conners' Parent Rating Scale.* North Tonawanda, NY: Multi-Health Systems, Inc.

Conners, C. K. (1985). *Conners' Teacher Rating Scale.* North Tonawanda, NY: Multi-Health Systems, Inc.

Conroy, M. A., & Brown, W. H. (2004). Early identification, prevention, and early intervention with young children at risk for emotional or behavioral disorders: Issues, trends, and a call for action. *Behavioral Disorders, 29*(3), 224–236.

Cook, L., & Friend, M. (1998). Co-teaching: Guidelines for creating effective practices. In E. L. Meyen, G. A. Vergason, & R. J. Whelan (Eds.), *Educating students with mild disabilities: Strategies and methods* (2nd ed., pp. 453–479). Denver: Love.

Coolican, J., Bryson, S. E., & Zwaigenbaum, L. (2008). Brief report: Data on the Stanford–Binet Intelligence Scale (5th ed.) in children with autism spectrum disorder. *Journal of Autism and Developmental Disorders, 38*(1), 190–197.

Cornelius-White, J. (2007). Learning-centered teacher–student relationships are effective: A meta-analysis. *Review of Educational Research, 77*(1), 113–143.

Costello-Wells, B., McFarland, L., Reed, J., & Walton, K. (2003). School-based mental health clinics. *Journal of Child and Adolescent Psychiatric Nursing, 16*(2), 60–70.

Costenbader, V., & Buntaine, R. (1999). Diagnostic discrimination between social maladjustment and emotional disturbance: An empirical study. *Journal of Emotional & Behavioral Disorders, 7*(1), 2–10.

Coster, W. J., & Haltiwanger, J. T. (2004). Social skills of elementary students with physical disabilities included in general education classrooms. *Remedial and Special Education, 25*(2), 95–103.

Council for Children with Behavior Disorders. (1989). Best assessment practices for students with behavioral disorders: Accommodation to cultural diversity and individual differences. *Behavioral Disorders, 14,* 263–278.

Council for Children with Behavioral Disorders. (1990). Position paper on provision of service to children with conduct disorders. *Behavioral Disorders, 15,* 180–189.

Council for Children with Behavioral Disorders. (2002). *School discipline policies for students with significantly disruptive behavior.* Reston, VA: Author.

Council for Children with Behavior Disorders. (2005). *About CCBD*. Retrieved November 19, 2005, from http://www.ccbd.net/content.cfm?categoryID=668B70E2-C09F-1D6F-F979C15CAF18E46F

Council for Exceptional Children. (1998). CEC launches initiative on special education teaching conditions. *CEC Today, 2*(7), 2.

Council for Exceptional Children. (2001). New study on special education working conditions. *CEC Today, 8*, 1–12.

Council for Exceptional Children. (2003). *What every special educator must know: Ethics, standards, and guidelines for special educators*. Arlington, VA: Author.

Coutinho, M. J., Oswald, D. P., Best, A. M., & Forness, S. R. (2002). Gender and sociodemographic factors and the disproportionate identification of culturally and linguistically diverse students with emotional disturbance. *Behavioral Disorders, 27*(2), 109–125.

Crockett, J. B. (2002). Special education's role in preparing responsive leaders for inclusive schools. *Remedial and Special Education, 23*(3), 157–168.

Cross, L. H., & Billingsley, B. S. (1994). Testing a model of special educators' intent to stay in teaching. *Exceptional Children, 60*(5), 411–421.

Cullinan, D. (2007). *Students with emotional and behavioral disorders: An introduction for teachers and other helping professionals* (2nd ed.). Upper Saddle River, NJ: Pearson.

Cullinan, D., & Sabornie, E. J. (2004). Characteristics of emotional disturbance in middle and high school students. *Journal of Emotional and Behavioral Disorders, 12*(3), 157–167.

Curtiss, V. S., Mathur, S. R., & Rutherford, Jr., R. B. (2002). Developing behavioral intervention plans: A step-by-step approach. *Beyond Behavior, 11*(2), 28–31.

Dadds, M. R., & Barrett, P. M. (2001). Practitioner review: Psychological management of anxiety disorders in childhood. *Journal of Child Psychology and Psychiatry and Allied Disciplines, 42*(8), 999–1011.

Dale, N., Baker, A. J. L., Anastasio, E., & Purcell, J. (2007). Characteristics of children in residential treatment in New York state. *Child Welfare, 86*(1), 5–27.

Daly, B. P., Burke, R., Hare, I., Mills, C., Owens, C., Moore, E., & Weist, M. D. (2006). Enhancing No Child Left Behind–school mental health connections. *The Journal of School Health, 76*(9), 446–451.

D'Amico, R., & Blackorby, J. (1992). Trends in employment among out-of-school youth with disabilities. In M. Wagner, R. D'Amico, C. Marder, L. Newman, & J. Blackorby (Eds.), *What happens next? Trends in postschool outcomes of youth with disabilities* (pp. 4.1–4.47). Menlo Park, CA: SRI International.

D'Amico, R., & Marder, C. (1991). *The early work experiences of youth with disabilities: Trends in employment rates and job characteristics. A report from the National Longitudinal Transition Study of Special Education Students*. Menlo Park, CA: SRI International.

Darling-Hammond, L. (2001). The challenge of staffing our schools. *Educational Leadership, 58*(8), 12–17.

Darling-Hammond, L. (2002). Research and rhetoric on teacher certification: A response to "teacher certification reconsidered." *Education Policy Analysis Archives, 8*. Retrieved September 6, 2002, from http://epaa.asu.edu/epaa/v10n36.html

Dawson, C. A. (2003). A study on the effectiveness of life space crisis intervention for students identified with emotional disturbances. *Reclaiming Children and Youth, 11*(4), 223–230.

Day-Vines, N. L. (2007). The escalating incidence of suicide among African-Americans: Implications for counselors. *Journal of Counseling & Development, 85*(3), 370–377.

*Department of Public Welfare v. Haas*, 154 N.E. 2nd 265 (Ill. 1958).

DeRosier, M. E., & Thomas, J. M. (2003). Strengthening sociometric prediction: Scientific advances in the assessment of children's peer relations. *Child Development, 74*(5), 1379–1392.

Deshler, D. D., Ellis, E. S., & Lenz, B. K. (1996). *Teaching adolescents with learning disabilities: Strategies and methods*. Denver, CO: Love Publishing.

Dettmer, P., Thurston, L. P., Sellberg, N. J. (2005). *Consultation, collaboration, and teamwork for students with special needs* (5th ed.). Boston: Allen & Bacon.

Dieker, L. (1998). Rationale for co-teaching. *Social Studies Review, 37*(2), 62–65.

DiStefano, C. A., & Kamphaus, R. W. (2007). Development and validation of a behavioral screener for preschool-age children. *Journal of Emotional and Behavioral Disorders, 15*(2), 93–102.

Ditrano, C. J., & Silverstein, L. B. (2006). Listening to parents' voices: Participatory action research in the schools. *Professional Psychology: Research and Practice, 37*(4), 359–366.

Dombrowski, S. C., & Gischlar, K. L. (2006). Supporting school professionals through the establishment of a school district policy on child maltreatment. *Education, 127*(2), 234–243.

D'Oosterlinck, F., Goethals, I., Boekaert, E., Schuyten, G., & De Maeyer, J. (2008). Implementation and effect of life space crisis intervention in special schools with residential treatment for students with emotional and behavioral disorders (EBD). *Psychiatric Quarterly, 79*(1), 65–79.

Dore, M. M., & Mullin, D. (2006). Treatment family foster care: Its history and current role in the foster care continuum. *Families in Society, 87*(4), 475–482.

Doucette, P. A. (2004). Walk and talk: An intervention for behaviorally challenged youth. *Adolescence, 39*(154), 373–388.

Downing, J. A. (2007). *Students with emotional and behavioral problems: Assessment, management, and intervention strategies.* Upper Saddle River, NJ: Pearson.

Driver, J. (2005). Consequentialism and feminist ethics. *Hypatia, 20*(4), 183–239.

Drotar, D. (2004). Detecting and managing developmental and behavioral problems in infants and young children: The potential role of the DSM-PC. *Infants and Young Children, 17*(2), 114–124.

Duggan, D., & Dawson, C. A. (2004). Positive behavior support infused by life space crisis intervention in New York City's special education district. *Reclaiming Children and Youth, 13*(1), 37–42.

Duke, N. K., & Pearson, P. D. (2002). Effective practices for developing reading comprehension. In A. Farstrup & S. Samuels (Eds.), *What research has to say about reading instruction* (pp. 205–242). Newark, DE: International Reading Association.

Duncan, G. J., & Brooks-Gunn, J. (1997). *Consequences of growing up poor.* New York: Sage.

DuPaul, G. J., & Carlson, J. S. (2005). Child psychopharmacology: How school psychologists can contribute to effective outcomes. *School Psychology Quarterly, 20*(2), 206–221.

Dwyer, K. P. (2002). Mental health in the schools. *Journal of Child and Family Studies, 11*(1), 101–111.

D'Zurilla, T. J., & Goldfried, M. R. (1971). Problem solving and behavior modification. *Journal of Abnormal Psychology, 78*(1), 107–126.

Eber, L., Sugai, G., Smith, C. R., & Scott, T. M. (2002). Wraparound and positive behavioral interventions and supports in the schools. *Journal of Emotional and Behavioral Disorders, 10*(3), 171–180.

Eddy, J. M., Reid, J., & Curry, V. (2002). The etiology of youth antisocial behavior, delinquency, and violence and a public health approach to prevention. In M. Shinn, H. Walker, & G. Stoner (Eds.), *Interventions for academic and behavior problems* (2nd ed., pp. 27–52). Bethesda, MD: National Association of School Psychologists.

Edscheidt, S. (2002). Discipline provisions of IDEA: Misguided policy or tacit reform initiatives? *Behavioral Disorders, 27*(4), 408–422.

Elksnin, L. K., & Elksnin, N. (1998a). Teaching social skills to students with learning and behavior problems. *Intervention in School and Clinic, 33*(3), 131–140.

Elksnin, L. K., & Elksnin, N. (2003). Fostering social–emotional learning in the classroom. *Education, 124*(1), 63–75.

Elksnin, N., & Elksnin, L. K. (1998b). *Teaching occupational social skills.* Austin, TX: Pro-Ed.

English, D. J., Graham, J. C., Litrownik, A. J., Everson, M., & Bangdiwala, S. I. (2005). Defining maltreatment chronicity: Are there differences in child outcomes? *Child Abuse & Neglect, 29*(5), 575–595.

Epstein, M. H., Nordness, P. D., Gallagher, K., Nelson, R., Lewis, L., & Schrepf, S. (2005). School as the entry point: Assessing adherence to the basic tenets of the wraparound approach. *Behavioral Disorders, 30*(2), 85–93.

Epstein, M. H., & Walker, H. H. (2002). Special education: Best practices and first steps to success. In B. Burns & K. Hoagwood (Eds.), *Community and treatment for youth: Evidence-based interventions for severe emotional and behavioral disorders* (pp. 179–197). New York: Oxford University Press.

Erath, S. A., Flanagan, K. S., & Bierman, K. L. (2007). Social anxiety and peer relations in early adolescence: Behavioral and cognitive factors. *Journal of Abnormal Child Psychology, 35*(3), 405–416.

Erickson, M. J., Stage, S. C., & Nelson, J. R. (2006). Naturalistic study of the behavior of students with EBD referred for functional behavioral assessment. *Journal of Emotional and Behavioral Disorders, 14*(1), 31–40.

Erikson, E. H. (1959). Identity and the life cycle. *Psychological Issues, 1,* 1–171.

Erikson, E. H., & Erikson, J. M. (1997). *The life cycle completed: Extended version with new chapters on the ninth stage of development.* New York: Norton & Company.

Etscheidt, S. (2006). Behavioral intervention plans: Pedagogical and legal analysis of issues. *Behavioral Disorders, 31*(2), 223–243.

Executive Committee of the Council for Children with Behavioral Disorders. (1989). White paper on best assessment practices for students with behavioral disorders: Accommodation to cultural diversity and individual differences. *Behavioral Disorders, 14,* 263–278.

Fairbanks, S., Sugai, G., Guardino, D., & Lathrop, M. (2007). Response to intervention: Examining classroom behavior support in second grade. *Exceptional Children, 73*(3), 288–310.

Falk, K. B., & Wehby, J. H. (2001). The effects of peer-assisted learning strategies on the beginning reading skills of young children with emotional or behavioral disorders. *Behavioral Disorders, 26*(4), 344–359.

*Family Educational Rights and Privacy Act* (FERPA) (20 U.S.C. § 1232g; 34 CFR Part 99).

Farber, B. A. (2000). Treatment strategies for different types of teacher burnout. *Journal of Clinical Psychology, 56*(5), 675–689.

Farmer, E. M. Z., Dorsey, S., & Mustillo, S. A. (2004). Intensive home and community interventions. *Child and Adolescent Psychiatric Clinics of North America, 13*(4), 857–884.

Farmer, E. M. Z., Wagner, H. R., Burns, B. J., & Richards, J. T. (2003). Treatment foster care in a system of care: Sequences and correlates of residential placements. *Journal of Child and Family Studies, 12*(1), 11–15.

Farmer, T. W. (2000). Misconceptions of peer rejection and problem behavior: Understanding aggression in students with mild disabilities. *Remedial and Special Education, 21*(4), 194–208.

Farmer-Dougan, V., Viechtbauer, W., & French, T. (1999). Peer-prompted social skills: The role of teacher consultation in student success. *Educational Psychology, 19*(2), 207–219.

Farrell, D. T., Smith, S. W., & Brownell, M. T. (1998). Teacher perceptions of level system effectiveness on the behavior of students with emotional or behavioral disorders. *The Journal of Special Education, 32*(2), 89–98.

Feingold, B. F. (1975). *Why your child is hyperactive.* New York: Random House.

Fisher, D., & Frey, N. (2001). Access to the core curriculum: Critical ingredients for student success. *Remedial and Special Education, 22*(3), 148–157.

FitzGerald, J. L., & Watkins, M. W. (2006). Parents' rights in special education: The readability of procedural safeguards. *Exceptional Children, 72*(4), 497–510.

Fives, C. J., & Flanagan, R. (2002). A review of the Universal Nonverbal Intelligence Test (UNIT): An advance for evaluating youngsters with diverse needs. *School Psychology International, 23*(4), 425–448.

Ford, D. Y., Grantham, T. C., & Whiting, G. W. (2008). Culturally and linguistically diverse students in gifted education: Recruitment and retention issues. *Exceptional Children, 74*(3), 289–306.

Fore III, C., Martin, C., & Bender, W. N. (2002). Teacher burnout in special education: The causes and the recommended solutions. *The High School Journal, 86*(1), 36–44.

Forness, S. R. (2003). Barriers to evidence-based treatment: Developmental psychopathology and the interdisciplinary disconnect in school mental health practice. *Journal of School Psychology, 41,* 61–67.

Forness, S. R., Freeman, S. F. N., & Paparella, T. (2006). Recent randomized clinical trials comparing behavioral interventions and psychopharmacologic treatment for students with EBD. *Behavioral Disorders, 31*(3), 284–296.

Forness, S. R., & Knitzer, J. (1992). A new proposed definition and terminology to replace "serious emotional disturbances" in Individuals with Disabilities Education Act. *School Psychology Review, 21,* 12–20.

Forness, S. R., Walker, H. M., & Kavale, K. A. (2003–2004). Psychiatric disorders and their treatment: A primer for school professionals. *Report on Emotional and Behavioral Disorders of Youth, 4,* 3–6, 20–23.

Forthun, L. F., McCombie, J. W., & Freado, M. (2006). A study of LSCI in a school setting. *Reclaiming Children and Youth, 15*(2), 95–102.

Freer Weiss, D. M. (2006). Keeping it real: The rationale for using manipulatives in the middle grades. *Mathematics Teaching in the Middle School, 11*(5), 238–242.

Fremont, W. P. (2003). School refusal in children and adolescents. *American Family Physician, 68*(8), 1555–1560.

Freud, S. (1962). *A general introduction to psychoanalysis* (J. Riviere, Trans.). New York: Washington Square Press. (Original work published 1923)

Freud, S. (1975). *The ego and the id* (J. Riviere, Trans.). New York: Vintage/Ebury. (Original work published 1923)

Freud, S. (1989). *An outline of psycho-analysis* (J. Strachey, Trans.). New York: W. W. Norton & Company. (Original work published 1938)

Frick, P. J. (2004). Serving youth who show severe aggressive and antisocial behavior. *Psychology in the Schools, 41*(8), 823–834.

Friedman, I. A. (2000). Burnout in teachers: Shattered dreams of impeccable professional performance. *Journal of Clinical Psychology, 56*(5), 595–606.

Friend, M. (2007). The coteaching partnership. *Educational Leadership, 64*(5), 48–52.

Friend, M., & Bursuck, W. D. (2005). *Including students with special needs: A practical guide for classroom teachers.* Boston: Allyn & Bacon.

Fuchs, D., & Fuchs, L. S. (2005). Peer-assisted learning strategies: Promoting word recognition, fluency, and reading comprehension in young children. *The Journal of Special Education, 39*(1), 34–44.

Fuchs, D., Fuchs, L. S., Mathes, P. G., & Simmons, D. C. (1997). Peer-Assisted Learning Strategies: Making the classrooms more responsive to diversity. *American Educational Research Journal, 34*, 174–206.

Fuchs, D., Fuchs, L. S., Reeder, P., Gilman, S., Fernstrom, P., Bahr, M., et al. (1989). *Mainstream assistance teams: A handbook on prereferral intervention.* Nashville, TN: Peabody College of Vanderbilt University.

Fuchs, D., Mathes, P. G., & Fuchs, E. S. (1997). Peer-Assisted Learning Strategies: Reading methods for grades 2–6. Available from Douglas Fuchs, Box 328 Peabody, Vanderbilt University, Nashville, TN 37203 (or http://kc.vanderbilt.edu/pals/library/08%20PALS%202-6.html).

Fuchs, L. S., Fuchs, D., Karns, K., & Phillips, N. (1994). Peer-mediated mathematics instruction: A manual. Available from Douglas Fuchs, Box 328 Peabody, Vanderbilt University, Nashville, TN 37203 (or http://kc.vanderbilt.edu/pals/teachmat/MathMaterials.html).

Fuchs, L. S., Fuchs, D., & Speece, D. L. (2002). Treatment validity as a unifying construct for identifying learning disabilities. *Learning Disability Quarterly, 25*, 33–45.

Fujiura, G. T., & Yamaki, K. (2000). Trends in demography of childhood poverty and disability. *Exceptional Children, 66*(2), 187–199.

Fuller, G. B. (2007). Reality therapy approaches. In H. T. Prout & D. T. Brown (Eds.), *Counseling and psychotherapy with children and adolescents: Theory and practice for school and clinical settings* (4th ed., pp. 332–382). Hoboken, NJ: John Wiley & Sons, Inc.

Furner, J. M., Yahya, N., & Duffy, M. L. (2005). Teach mathematics: Strategies to reach all students. *Intervention in School and Clinic, 41*(1), 16–23.

Gagnon, J. C., & Leon, P. E. (2005). Elementary day and residential schools for children with emotional and behavioral disorders. *Remedial and Special Education, 26*(3), 141–150.

Gagnon, J. C., & McLaughlin, M. J. (2004). Curriculum, assessment, and accountability in day treatment and residential schools. *Exceptional Children, 70*(3), 263–283.

Gallagher, P. (1997). Promoting dignity: Taking the destructive D's out of behavior disorders. *Focus on Exceptional Children, 29*(9), 1–19.

Gacono, C. B., & Hughes, T. L. (2004). Differentiating emotional disturbance from social maladjustment: Assessing psychopathy in aggressive youth. *Psychology in the Schools, 41*(8), 849–860.

Gardner, R., III. (1990). Life space interviewing: It can be effective, but don't … *Behavioral Disorders, 15*(2), 110–126.

Gardner, R., Cartledge, G., Seidl, B., Woolsey, M. L., Schley, G. S., & Utley, C. A. (2001). Mt. Olivet after-school program: Peer-mediated interventions for at-risk students. *Remedial and Special Education, 22*(1), 22–33.

Garmon, M. A. (1998). Using dialogue journals to promote student learning in a multicultural–teacher education course. *Remedial and Special Education, 19*(1), 32–45.

Garrick Duhaney, L. M. (2003). A practical approach to managing the behaviors of students with ADD. *Intervention in School and Clinic, 38*(5), 267–279.

Gartin, B. C., & Murdick, N. L. (2005). IDEA 2004: The IEP. *Remedial and Special Education, 26*(6), 327–31.

Gatongi, F. (2007). Person-centred approach in schools: Is it the answer to disruptive behaviour in our classrooms? *Counselling Psychology Quarterly, 20*(2), 205–211.

Gaughan, E. (1995). Family assessment in psychoeducational evaluations: Case studies with the Family Adaptability and Cohesion Scales. *Journal of School Psychology, 33*, 7–28.

Gay, G. (2002). Preparing for culturally responsive teaching. *Journal of Teacher Education, 53*(2), 106–116.

Gaylord, N. K., Kitzmann, K. M., & Lockwood, R. L. (2003). Child characteristics as moderators of the association between family stress and children's internalizing, externalizing, and peer rejection. *Journal of Child and Family Studies, 12*(2), 201–213.

Geller, J. L., & Biebel, K. (2006). The premature demise of public child and adolescent inpatient psychiatric beds. Part I: Overview and current conditions. *Psychiatric Quarterly, 77*(3), 251–271.

Ghere, G., & York-Barr, J. (2007). Paraprofessional turnover and retention in inclusive programs: Hidden costs and promising practices. *Remedial and Special Education, 28*(1), 21–32.

Giangreco, M. F., Edelman, S. W., & Broer, S. M. (2001). Respect, appreciation, and acknowledgement of paraprofessionals who support students with disabilities. *Exceptional Children, 67*(4), 485–498.

Gibb, G. S., & Dyches, T. T. (2007). *Guide to writing quality individualized education programs: What's best for students with disabilities?* (2nd Ed.). Boston: Allyn & Bacon.

Gibbs, J. C., Basinger, K. S., Grime, R. L., & Snarey, J. R. (2007). Moral judgment development across cultures: Revisiting Kohlberg's universality claims. *Developmental Review, 27*(4), 443–500.

Gilligan, C. (1982). *In a different voice: Psychological theory and women's development.* Cambridge, MA: Harvard University Press.

Gingerich, K. J., Turnock, P., Liftin, J. K., & Rosen, L. A. (1998). Diversity and attention deficit hyperactivity disorder. *Journal of Clinical Psychology, 54*(4), 415–426.

Ginsburg, G. S., & Grover R. L. (2005). Assessing and treating social phobia in children and adolescents. *Pediatric Annals, 34*(2), 119–27.

Girls and Boys Town. (n.d.). *The girls and boys town education model.* Retrieved March 1, 2006, from http://www.boystown.org/pros/training/education/ed_model_obj.asp

Glasser, W. (1969). *Schools without failure.* New York: Harper & Row.

Glasser, W. (1998). *Choice theory: A new psychology of personal freedom.* New York: Harper Collins.

Glasser, W. (2001). *Choice theory in the classroom* (Rev. ed.). New York: Harper Collins.

Goldman, L. S., Genel, M., Bezman, R. J., & Slanetz, P. J. (1998). Diagnosis and treatment of attention-deficit/hyperactivity disorder in children and adolescents. *Journal of the American Medical Association, 279*(14), 1100–1107.

Goldstein, A. P. (1999). *The Prepare Curriculum: Teaching prosocial competencies.* Champaign, IL: Research Press.

Goldstein, A. P., & McGinnis, E. (1997). Skillstreaming the adolescent: New strategies and perspectives for teaching prosocial skills. Champaign, IL: Research Press.

Gollnick, D. M., & Chinn, P. C. (2005). *Multicultural education in a pluralistic society* (7th ed.). Upper Saddle, NJ: Prentice Hall.

Gorman, C. (2007, January 29). 6 lessons for handling stress. *Time, 169*(5), 80.

Gould, M. S., Greenberg, T., Velting, D. M., & Shaffer, D. (2003). Youth suicide risk and preventive interventions: A review of the past 10 years. *Journal of the American Academy of Child and Adolescent Psychiatry, 42*(4), 386–405.

Graden, J. L., Casey, A., & Bronstrom, O. (1985). Implementing a prereferral intervention system: Part I. The model. *Exceptional Children, 51*, 377–387.

Grant, C., & Sleeter, C. (2006). *Turning on learning: Five approaches for multicultural teaching plans for race, class, gender and disability* (4th ed.). Hoboken, NJ: Wiley Jossey-Bass.

Graves, D. H. (2002). *Testing is not teaching: What should count in education.* Portsmouth, NH: Heinemann.

Greenberg, M. T., Kam, C., Henirichs, B., & Conduct Problems Prevention Research. Group. (2003, June). *The cumulative effects of the PATHS curriculum: Outcomes at Grade 3.* Paper presented at annual meeting of the Society for Prevention Research, Washington, DC.

Greenman, J. (2005). Missing the mark: A response to Grineski's 'Misidentified problems and mistaken solutions.' *The Teacher Educator, 41,* 126–139.

Greenwood, C. R., & Delquadri, J. (1995). Classwide peer tutoring and the prevention of school failure. *Preventing School Failure, 39*(4), 21–25.

Gresham, F., M., Elliot, S. N., & Evans-Fernandez, S. E. (1992). *Student Self-Concept Scale*. Circle Pines, MN: American Guidance Service.

Gresham, F. M. (2002). Social skills assessment and instruction for students with emotional and behavioral disorders. In K. L. Lane, F. M. Gresham, & T. E. O'Shaughnessy (Eds.), *Interventions for children with or at risk for emotional and behavioral disorders* (pp. 242–258). Boston: Allyn & Bacon.

Gresham, F. M. (2005). Response to intervention: An alternative means of identifying students as emotionally disturbed. *Education and Treatment of Children, 28*(4), 328–345.

Gresham, F. M., Cook, C. R., Crews, S. D., & Kern, L. (2004). Social skills training for children and youth with emotional and behavioral disorders: Validity considerations and future directions. *Behavioral Disorders, 30*(1), 32–46.

Gresham, F. M., & Elliot, S. N. (1990). *The social skills rating system (SSRS)*. Circle Pines. MN: American Guidance Service.

Gresham, F. M., Lane, K. L., & Beebe-Frankenberger, M. (2005). Predictors of hyperactive-impulsive-inattention and conduct problems: A comparative follow-back investigation. *Psychology in the Schools, 42*(7), 721–736.

Grskovic, J. A., & Goetze, H. (2005). An evaluation of the effects of life space crisis intervention on the challenging behavior of individual students. *Reclaiming Children and Youth, 13*(4), 231–235.

Guetzloe, E., & Rockwell, S. (1998). Fight, flight, or better choices: Teaching nonviolent responses to young children. *Preventing School Failure, 42*(4), 154–159.

Gulley, T. J., Burke, R. V., & Hensley, M. M. (2003, April). *Collaborative efforts to improve students' social behavior: A four-step process for helping staff work together*. A paper presented at the National Association of Elementary School Principals Conference, Anaheim, CA.

*Gun-Free School Act of 1994*, Public Law 103-382, 108 Statute 3907, Title 14.

Habel, J. C., & Bernard, J. A. (1999). School and educational psychologists: Creating new service models. *Intervention in School and Clinic, 34*(3), 156–162.

Haeseler, L. A. (2006). Children of abuse and school discourse: Implications for teachers and administration. *Education, 126*(3), 534–540.

Hagie, M. U., Gallipo, P. L., & Svien, L. (2003). Traditional cultural versus traditional assessment for American Indian Students: An investigation of potential test item bias. *Assessment for Effective Intervention, 29*(1), 15–25.

Hanson, E. M. (1996). *Educational administration and organizational behavior* (4th ed.). Boston, MA: Allyn & Bacon.

Hair, H. J. (2005). Outcome for children and adolescents after residential treatment: A review of research from 1993 to 2003. *Journal of Child and Family Studies, 14*(4), 551–575.

Hallahan, D. P., & Kaufmann, J. M. (2003). *Exceptional learners: Introduction to special education* (9th ed.). Boston: Allyn & Bacon.

Hammill, D. D., Pearson, N. A., & Wiederholt, J. L. (1997). *Examiner's manual: Comprehensive Test of Nonverbal Intelligence*. Austin, TX: Pro-Ed.

Hansen, S. D., & Lignugaris/Kraft, B. (2005). Effects of a dependent group contingency on the verbal interactions of middle school students with emotional disturbance. *Behavioral Disorders, 30*(2), 170–184.

Hardin, B. J., Roach-Scott, M., & Peisner-Feinberg, E. S. (2007). Special education referral, evaluation, and placement practices for preschool English language learners. *Journal of Childhood Education, 22*(1), 39–54.

Haring, N. G., & Phillips, E. L. (1962). *Educating emotionally disturbed children*. New York: McGraw-Hill.

Harry, B. (2008). Collaboration with culturally and linguistically diverse families: Ideal versus reality. *Exceptional Children, 74*(3), 372–388.

Hazel, J. S., Schumaker, J. B., Sherman, J. A., & Sheldon-Wildgen, J. (1982). *Asset: A social skills program for adolescents*. Champaign, IL: Research Press.

Healthsquare. (2004–2007). *Drugs and medicine*. Retrieved May 28, 2007, from http://www.healthsquare.com/drugmain.htm

Henderson, K., Klein, S., Gonzalez, P., & Bradley, R. (2005). Teachers of children with emotional disturbance: A national look at preparation, teaching conditions, and practices. *Behavioral Disorders, 31*(1), 6–17.

Henry, G. T., Gordon, C. S., Mashburn, A., & Ponder, B. D. (2001). *Pre-K longitudinal study: Finding from the 1999–2000 school year.* Atlanta: Georgia State University, Applied Research Center of the Andrew Young School of Policy Studies.

Heron, M. (2007). Deaths: Leading causes for 2004. *National Vital Statistics Reports, 56*(5), 1–96.

Hester, P. P., Baltodano, H. M., Hendrickson, J. M., Tonelson, S. W., Conroy, M. A., & Gable, R. A. (2004). Lessons learned from research on early intervention: What teachers can do to prevent children's behavior problems. *Preventing School Failure, 49*(1), 5–10.

Heward, W. L. (2006). *Exceptional children: An introduction to special education* (8th ed.). New Jersey: Prentice Hall.

Hinshaw, S. P. (1992). Externalizing behavior problems and academic underachievement in childhood and adolescence: Causal relationships and underlying mechanisms. *Psychological Bulletin,* 111, 127–155.

Hintze, J. M., Volpe, R. J., & Shapiro, E. S. (2002). Best practices in the systematic direct observation of student behavior. In A. Thomas & J. Grimes (Eds.), *Best practices in school psychology IV* (pp. 993–1006). Bethesda, MD: National Association of School Psychologists.

Hitchcock, C., Meyer, A., Rose, D., & Jackson, R. (2002). Providing new access to the general curriculum. *Teaching Exceptional Children, 35*(2), 8–17.

Ho, J., Yeh, M., McCabe, K., & Hough, R. L. (2007). Parental cultural affiliation and youth mental health services use. *Journal of Youth and Adolescence, 36*(4), 529–542.

Hoff, K. E., DuPaul, G. J., & Handwerk, M. L. (2003). Rejected youth in residential treatment: Social affiliation and peer group configuration. *Journal of Emotional and Behavioral Disorders, 11*(2), 112–121.

*Honig v. Doe.* 484 U.S. 305 (1988).

Hooper, S. R., Roberts, J. E., Zeisel, S. A., & Poe, M. (2003). Core language predictors of behavioral functioning in early elementary school children: Concurrent and longitudinal findings. *Behavioral Disorders, 29*(1), 10–24.

Hooper, V. S., & Bell, S. M. (2006). Concurrent validity of the Universal Nonverbal Intelligence Test and the Leiter International Performance Scale-Revised. *Psychology in the Schools, 43*(2), 143–148.

Hops, H., Guild, J. J., Fleischman, D. H., Paine, S. C., Street, A., Walker, H. M., & Greenwood, C. R. (1978). *PEERS (Procedures for Establishing Relationships Skills).* Eugene, OR: CORBEH.

Horner, R. H., & Sugai, G. (2002). *School-wide positive behavior support: Implementers' blueprint and self-assessment.* Eugene, OR: OSEP Center on Positive Behavior Support.

Horner, R. H., Sugai, G., Todd, A. W., & Lewis, T. (in press). School-wide positive behavior support: An alternative approach to discipline in schools. In L. Bambara & L. Kern (Eds.), *Positive Behavior Support.* New York: Guilford.

Horner, R. H., Sugai, G., Todd, A. W., & Lewis, T. (2005). School-wide positive behavior support. In L. M. Bambara & L. Kern (Eds.), *Individualized supports for students with problem behaviors: Designing positive behavior plans.* New York: Guilford Press.

Hosp, J. L., Howell, K. W., & Hosp, M. K. (2003). Characteristics of behavior rating scales: Implications for practice in assessment and behavioral support. *Journal of Positive Behavior Interventions, 5*(4), 201–208.

Houck, G. M., & Spegman, A. M. (1999). The development of self: Theoretical understandings and conceptual underpinnings. *Infants and Young Children, 12*(1), 1–16.

Hyatt, K. J. (2007). The new IDEA: Changes, concerns, and questions. *Intervention in School and Clinic, 42*(3), 131–136.

Indiana University, Evansville. (2003). Human Intelligence: Jean-Marc Gaspard Itard. Retrieved October 12, 2005, from http://www.indiana.edu/~intell/itard.shtml

Individuals with Disabilities Education Improvement Act of 2004, P.L. 108-446, 20 U.S.C. § 300 *et seq.*

Inhelder, B., & Piaget, J. (1958). *The growth of logical thinking from childhood to adolescence: An essay on the construction of formal operational structures.* New York: Basic Books. (Original work published 1955)

International Society of Psychiatric and Mental Health Nurses. (1999). ISPN position statement on the use of restraint and seclusion. *Journal of Child and Adolescent Psychiatric Nursing, 14*(3), 100–102.

Irvine, J. J. (1990). *Black students and school failure: Policies, practices, and prescriptions.* New York: Greenwood.

Ishii-Jordon, S. R. (2000). Behavioral interventions used with diverse students. *Behavioral Disorders, 25*(4), 299–309.

Itard, J. M. G. (1962). *The wild boy of Aveyron.* (G. Humphrey & M. Humphrey, Trans.). New York: Appleton-Century-Crofts. (Original works published 1801 and 1806)

Jackson, N. F., Jackson, D. A., & Monroe, C. (1983). *Getting along with others: Teaching social effectiveness to children.* Champaign, IL: Research Press.

James, S., Leslie, L. K., Hurlburt, M. S., Slymen, D. J., Landsverk, J., Davis, I., et al. (2006). Children in out-of-home care: Entry into intensive or restrictive mental health and residential care placements. *Journal of Emotional and Behavioral Disorders, 14*(4), 196–208.

Jameson, J. M., & Huefner, D. S. (2006). "Highly qualified" special educators and the provision of a free appropriate public education to students with disabilities. *Journal of Law and Education, 35*(1), 29–50.

Jenkins, J. R., Antil, L. R., Wayne, S. K., & Vadasy, P. F. (2003). How cooperative learning works for special education and remedial students. *Exceptional Children, 69*(3), 279–292.

Jensen, P. S. (2000). Pediatric psychopharmacology in the United States: Issues and challenges in the diagnosis and treatment of attention-deficit/hyperactivity disorder. In L. L. Greenhill & B. B. Osman (Eds.), *Ritalin: Theory and practice* (2nd ed.). Larchmont, NY: Mary Ann Liebert, Inc.

Jim Thorpe Area School District, 28 IDELR 320 (SEA PA 1998).

Johns, B. H., Crowley, E. P., & Guetzloe, E. (2002). *Emotional and behavior disorders.* Denver, CO: Love Publishing.

Johnson, D. W., & Johnson, R. (1986). Mainstreaming and cooperative learning strategies. *Exceptional Children, 52*, 553–561.

Johnson, G. M. (1994). An ecological framework for conceptualizing educational risk. *Urban Education, 29*, 34–49.

Jolivette, K., Wehby, J. H., & Hirsch, L. (1999). Academic strategy identification for students exhibiting inappropriate classroom behaviors. *Behavioral Disorders, 24*(3), 210–221.

Jones, C., Caravaca, L., Cizek, S., Horner, R. H., & Vincent, C. G. (2006). Culturally responsive schoolwide positive behavior support: A case study in one school with a high proportion of Native American students. *Multiple Voices, 9*(1), 108–119.

Joseph, J. (2000). Not in their genes: A critical view of the genetics of attention-deficit hyperactivity disorder. *Developmental Review, 20*, 539–567.

Jurbergs, N., & Ledley, D. R. (2005). Separation anxiety disorder. *Psychiatric Annals, 35*(9), 728–735.

Jutras, P. J. (2006). The benefits of adult piano study as self-reported by selected adult piano students. *Journal of Research in Music Education, 54*(2), 97–110.

Kaiser, A. P., Cai, X., Hancock, T. B., & Foster, E. M. (2002). Teacher-reported behavior problems and language delays in boys and girls enrolled in Head Start. *Behavioral Disorders, 28*, 23–29.

Kam, C., Greenberg, M. T., & Kusche, C. A. (2004). Sustained effects of the PATHS curriculum on the social and psychological adjustment of children in special education. *Journal of Emotional and Behavioral Disorders, 12*(2), 66–78.

Kamps, D. M., Ellis, C., Mancina, C., & Greene, L. (1995). Peer-inclusive social skills groups for young children with behavioral risks. *Preventing School Failure, 39*(4), 10–15.

Kanner, L. (1962). Emotionally disturbed children: A historical review. *Child Development, 33*, 97–102.

Kanner, L. (1973). Historical perspective on developmental deviations. *Journal of Autism and Childhood Schizophrenia, 3*, 187–98.

Kaplan, S. G., & Cornell, D. G. (2005). Threats of violence by students in special education. *Behavioral Disorders, 31*(1), 107–119.

Kaplow, J. B., Dodge, K. A., Amaya-Jackson, L., & Saxe, G. N. (2005). Pathways to PTSD, Part II: Sexually abused children. *The American Journal of Psychiatry, 162*(7), 1305–1310.

Kaslow, N., Morris, M., & Rehm, L. (1997). Childhood depression in the practice of child therapy (3rd ed., pp. 48–90). Boston: Allyn & Bacon.

Katsiyannis, A., Zhang, D., & Conroy, M. (2003). Availability of special education teachers: Trends and issues. *Remedial and Special Education, 24*(4), 246–253.

Kauchak, D., & Eggen, P. (1993). *Learning and teaching.* Boston: Allyn and Bacon.

Kauffman, J. M. (2004). The President's Commission and the devaluation of special education. *Education & Treatment of Children, 27*(4), 307–324.

Kauffman, J. M. (2005). *Characteristics of emotional and behavioral disorders of children and youth* (8th ed.). Upper Saddle River, NJ: Merrill/Prentice Hall.

Kawakami, A. J., & Dudoit, W. (2000). Ua ao Hawai'i/Hawai'i is enlightened: Ownership in a Hawaiian language immersion classroom. *Language Arts, 77*(5), 384–390.

Kea, C. D., Campbell-Whatley, G. D., & Bratton, K. (2003). Culturally responsive assessment for African American students with learning and behavioral challenges. *Assessment for Effective Intervention, 29*(1), 27–38.

Kearney, C. A., Bates, M. (2005). Addressing school refusal behavior: Suggestions for frontline professionals. *Children & Schools, 27*(4), 207–216.

Keefe, J. W., & Jenkins, J. M. (2005). Personalized instruction. *Phi Delta Kappa Fastbacks, 532,* 1–49.

Kehle, T. J., Bray, M. A., Theodore, L. A., Zhou, Z., & McCoach, D. B. (2004). Emotional disturbance/social maladjustment: Why is the incidence increasing? *Psychology in the Schools, 41*(8), 861–865.

Keith, C. (1991). Psychodynamic theory and practice. In J. L. Paul & B. C. Epanchin (Eds.), *Educating emotionally disturbed children and youth: Theories and practices for teachers* (2nd ed., pp. 116–147). New York: Merrill.

Keller, F. S. (1968). Good-bye teacher … *Journal of Applied Behavior Analysis, 1,* 79–89.

Keller, F. S. (1981). PSI and educational reform. *Journal of College Science Teaching, 11,* 37–38.

Keller, G. (1921). *Der grune Heinrtch: Vol. I.* Munich: Deutsch-Meister-Verlag.

Keltner, N. L., Hogan, B., & Guy, D. M. (2001). Dopaminergic and serotonergic receptor function in the CNS. *Perspectives in Psychiatric Care, 37*(2), 65–73.

Keogh, B. K. (2000). Risk, families, and schools. *Focus on Exceptional Children, 33*(4), 1–10.

Keogh, B. K. (2003). *Temperament in the classroom: Understanding individual differences.* Baltimore: Brookes.

Kerbeshian, J., & Burd, L. (2005). Moving target: The developing social brain and psychopathology. *Psychiatric Annals, 35*(10), 839–852.

Kerr, M. M., & Nelson, C. M. (2006). *Strategies for addressing behavior problems in the classroom* (5th ed.). Upper Saddle River, NJ: Pearson.

Kesner, J. E., & Robinson, M. (2002). Teachers as mandated reporters of child maltreatment: Comparison with legal, medical, and social services reporters. *Children & Schools, 24*(4), 222–231.

Kidd, P. M. (2003). An approach to the nutritional management of autism. *Alternative Therapies in Health and Medicine, 9*(5), 22–32.

Kidder-Ashley, P., Deni, J. R., Azar, K. R., & Anderson, J. B. (2000). Comparison of 40 states' procedures for identifying students with serious educational problems. *Education, 120*(3), 588–569.

Killu, K., Weber, K. P., Derby, K. M., & Barretto, A. (2006). Behavior intervention planning and implementation of positive behavioral support plans: An examination of states' adherence to standards for practice. *Journal of Positive Behavior Interventions, 8*(4), 195–199.

Klingner, J. K., & Edwards, P. A. (2006). Cultural considerations with response to intervention models. *Reading Research Quarterly, 41*(1), 108–117.

Klingner, J. K., Vaughn, S., Arguelles, M. E., Hughes, M. T., & Leftwich, S. A. (2004). Collaborative Strategic Reading: "Real-world" lessons from classroom teachers. *Remedial and Special Education, 25*(5), 291–302.

Kohlberg, L. (1969). Stage and sequence: The cognitive–developmental approach to socialization. In D. A. Goslin, (Ed.), *Handbook of socialization theory and research* (pp. 347–480). Chicago: Rand McNally.

Kolbe, L. J., Tirozzi, G. N., Marx, E., Bobbitt-Cooke, M., Riedel, S., Jones, J., & Schmoyer, M. (2005). Health programmes for school employees: Improving quality of life, health and productivity. *Promotion & Education, 12*(3/4), 157–197.

Konold, T. R., Hamre, B. K., & Pianta, R. C. (2003). Measuring problem behaviors in young children. *Behavioral Disorders, 28*(2), 111–123.

Konold, T. R., Walthall, J. C., & Pianta, R. C. (2004). The behavior of child behavior ratings: Measurement structure of the Child Behavior Checklist across time, informants, and child gender. *Behavioral Disorders, 29*(4), 372–383.

Konopasek, D. E., & Forness, S. (2004). Psychopharmacology in the treatment of emotional and behavioral disorders. In R. B. Rutherford, M. M. Quinn, & S. R. Mathur (Eds.), *Handbook of research in emotional and behavioral disorders* (pp. 352–368). New York: Guilford.

Koroloff, N. M., Friesen, G. J., Reilly, L., & Rinkin, J. (1996). The role of family members in systems of care. In B. A. Stroul (Ed.), *Children's mental health: Creating systems of care in a changing society* (pp. 409–426). Baltimore: Brookes.

Koyanagi, C., & Gaines, S. (1993). *All systems failure: An examination of the results of neglecting the needs of children with serious emotional disturbance*. Alexandria, VA: National Mental Health Association.

Krezmien, M. P., Leone, P. E., & Achilles, G. M. (2006). Suspension, race, and disability: Analysis of statewide practices and reporting. *Journal of Emotional and Behavioral Disorders, 14*(4), 217–226.

Kube, D. A., Petersen, M. C., & Palmer, F. B. (2002). Attention deficit hyperactivity disorder: Comorbidity and medication use. *Clinical Pediatrics, 41*(7), 461–469.

Kubik, M. Y., Lytle, L. A., Hannan, P. J., Story, M., & Perry, C. L. (2002). Food-related beliefs, eating behavior, and classroom food practices of middle school teachers. *The Journal of School Health, 72*(8), 339–345.

Kusche, C. A., & Greenberg, M. T. (1994). *The PATHS curriculum*. Seattle: Developmental Research and Programs.

Kutash, K., & Duchnowski, A. J. (2004). The mental health needs of youth with emotional and behavioral disabilities placed in special education programs in urban schools. *Journal of Child and Family Studies, 13*(2), 235–248.

Kyriacou, C. (2001). Teacher stress: directions for future research. *Educational Review, 53*(1), 28–35.

Lambros, K. M., Ward, S. L., Bocian, K. M., MacMillan, D. L., & Gresham, F. M. (1998). Behavioral profiles of children at-risk for emotional and behavioral disorders: Implications for assessment and classification. *Focus on Exceptional Children, 30*(5), 1–16.

Lane, J. D., Seskevich, J. E., & Pieper, C. F. (2007). Brief meditation training can improve perceived stress and negative mood. *Alternative Therapies in Health and Medicine, 13*(1), 38–44.

Lane, K. L., Gresham, F. M., & O'Shaughnessy, T. E. (2002). *Interventions for children with or at risk for emotional and behavioral disorders*. Boston: Allyn and Bacon.

Lane, K. L. (2004). Academic instruction and tutoring interventions for students with emotional/behavioral disorders: 1990 to present. In R. B. Rutherford, M. M. Quinn, & S. R. Mathurs (Eds.), *Handbook of research in emotional and behavioral disorders* (pp. 462–486). New York: Guilford Press.

Lane, K. L., Menzies, H. M., Barton-Arwood, S. M., Doukas, G. L., & Munton, S. M. (2005). Designing, implementing, and evaluating social skills interventions for elementary students: Step-by-step procedures based on actual school-based investigations. *Preventing School Failure, 49*(2), 18–26.

Lane, K. L., Wehby, J. H., & Cooley, C. (2006). Teacher expectations of students' classroom behavior across the grade span: Which social skills are necessary for success? *Exceptional Children, 72*(2), 153–167.

Larsson, J., Larsson, H., & Lichtenstein, P. (2004). Genetic and environmental contributions to stability and change of ADHD symptoms between 8 and 13 years of age: A longitudinal twin study. *Journal of the American Academy of Child and Adolescent Psychiatry, 43*(10), 1267–1275.

Lassiter, K. S., Matthews, T. D., & Feeback, G. (2007). An examination of the CTONI utilizing CC-GF theory: A comparison on the CTONI and WJ-III. *Psychology in the School, 44*(6), 567–577.

Laursen, E. K. (2003). Principle-centered discipline. *Reclaiming Children and Youth, 12*(2), 78–82.

Lee, J. W., & Cartledge, G. (1996). Native Americans. In G. Cartledge & J. F. Milbrun, *Cultural diversity and social skills instruction* (pp. 205–243). Champaign, IL: Research Press.

Leiter, M. P., & Maslach, C. (2005). *Banishing burnout: Six strategies for improving your relationship with work*. New York: Jossey-Bass.

Leiter, V., & Krauss, M. W. (2004). Claims, barriers, and satisfaction: Parents' requests for additional special education services. *Journal of Disability Policy Studies, 15*(3), 135–146.

Levy, S., Coleman, M., & Alsman, B. (2002). Reading instruction for elementary students with emotional/behavioral disorders: What's a teacher to do? *Beyond Behavior, 11*(3), 3–10.

Lewis, T. J., & Sugai, G. (1999). Effective behavior support: A systems approach to proactive schoolwide management. *Focus on Exceptional Children, 31*(6), 24–47.

Li, H., & Prevatt, F. (2007). Fears and related anxieties across three age groups of Mexican American and white children with disabilities. *The Journal of Genetic Psychology, 168*(4), 381–396.

Lian, M. J. (1996). Teaching Asian American children. In E. Duran (Ed.), *Teaching students with moderate/severe disabilities, including autism: Strategies for second-language learners in inclusive settings* (pp. 239–253). Springfield, IL: Charles C. Thomas.

Lieberman, L. J., Lytle, R. K., Clarcq, J. A. (2008). Getting it right from the start: Employing the Universal Design for Learning approach to your curriculum. *Journal of Physical Education, Recreation & Dance, 79*(2), 32–39.

Lilienfeld, S. O. (2005). Scientifically unsupported and supported interventions for childhood psychopathology: A summary. *Pediatrics, 115*(3), 761–764.

Lim, M., Stormshak, E. A., & Dishion, T. J. (2005). A one-session intervention for parents of young adolescents: Videotape modeling and motivational group discussion. *Journal of Emotional and Behavioral Disorders, 13*(4), 194–199.

Linan-Thompson, S., Vaughn, S., Prater, K., & Cirino, P. T. (2006). The response to intervention of English language learners at risk for reading problems. *Journal of Learning Disabilities, 39*(5), 390–398.

Liljequist, L., & Renk, K. (2007). The relationships among teachers' perceptions of student behaviour, teachers' characteristics, and ratings of students' emotional and behavioural problems. *Educational Psychology, 27*(4), 557–571.

Liu, C. H., & Matthews, R. (2005). Vygotsky's philosophy: Constructivism and its criticisms examined. *International Education Journal, 6*(3), 386–399.

Lloyd, J. W., Kauffman, J. M., Landrum, T. J., & Roe, D. L. (1991). Why do teachers refer pupils for special education? An analysis of referral records. *Exceptionality, 2*, 115–126.

Lo, Y., Loe, S. A., & Cartledge, G. (2002). The effects of social skills instruction on the social behaviors of students at risk for emotional or behavioral disorders. *Behavioral Disorders, 27*(4), 371–385.

Lohman, D. F. (2003). *The Woodcock–Johnson III and the Cognitive Abilities Test (Form 6): A concurrent validity study.* Retrieved March 21, 2008, from http://faculty.education.uiowa.edu/dlohman/pdf/CogAT_WJIII_final_2col%202r.pdf

Long, N. J., Morse, W. C., & Hewman, R. G. (1965). *Conflict in the classroom: The education of emotionally disturbed children.* Belmont, CA: Wadsworth.

Lopez, M. L., Tarullo, L. B., Forness, S. R., & Boyce, C. (2000). Early identification and intervention: Head Start's response to mental health challenges. *Journal of Early Childhood Education and Development, 11*, 265–282.

Lorimer, P. A., Simpson, R. L., Myles, B. S., & Ganz, J. B. (2002). The use of social stories as a preventative behavioral intervention in a home setting with a child with autism. *Journal of Positive Behavioral Intervention, 4*(1), 53–60.

Lowenthal, B. (2001). *Abuse and neglect: The educator's guide to the identification and prevention of child maltreatment.* Baltimore: Brookes.

Luckasson, R., & Reeve, A. (2001). Naming, defining, and classifying in mental retardation. *Mental Retardation, 39*(1), 47–52.

Maag, J. W. (2004). *Behavior management: From theoretical implications to practical applications* (2nd ed.). Belmont, CA: Wadsworth/Thomson Learning.

Maag, J. W. (2005). Social skills training for youth with emotional and behavioral disorders and learning disabilities: Problems, conclusions, and suggestions. *Exceptionality, 13*, 155–172.

Maag, J. W., & Katsiyannis, A. (2006). Behavioral intervention plans: Legal and practical considerations for students with emotional and behavioral disorders. *Behavioral Disorders, 31*(4), 348–362.

Maag, J. W., & Kemp, S. E. (2003). Behavioral intent of power and affiliation. Implications for functional analysis. *Remedial and Special Education, 24*(1), 57–64.

Maccini, P., & Calvin Gagnon, J. C. (2006). Mathematics instructional practices and assessment accommodations by secondary special and general educators. *Exceptional Children, 72*(2), 217–234.

Malmgren, K. W., Meisel, S. M. (2004). Examining the link between child maltreatment and delinquency for youth with emotional and behavioral disorders. *Child Welfare, 83*(2), 175–188.

Malmgren, K. W., Trezek, B. J., & Paul, P. V. (2005). Models of classroom management as applied to the secondary classroom. *The Clearing House, 79*(1), 36–39.

Mancini, C., Van Ameringen, M., Bennett, M., Patterson, B., & Watson, C. (2005). Emerging treatments for child and adolescent social phobia: A review. *Journal of Child and Adolescent Psychopharmacology, 15*(4), 589–607.

Margolis, H., & McCabe, P. P. (2006). Improving self-efficacy and motivation: What to do, what to say. *Intervention in School and Clinic, 41*(4), 218–227.

Marin, G., & Marin, B. (1991). *Research with Hispanic populations.* Newbury Park, CA: Sage Publications.

Mark, T. L., & Buck, J. A. (2006). Characteristics of U.S. youths with serious emotional disturbance: Data from the National Health Interview Survey. *Psychiatric Services, 57*(11), 1573–1578.

Markwardt, F. (1998). *Peabody Individual Achievement Test-Revised-Normative update.* Circle Pines, MN: American Guidance Service.

Marston, J. R. (2001). LSCI in functional behavior assessment and positive behavioral intervention. *Reclaiming Children and Youth, 10*(1), 57–60.

Martin, J. (2002). Transition: The foundation of secondary educational programs. *Beyond Behavior, 12*(1), 27–28.

Martin, J. E., Marshall, L. H., Maxson, L., & Jerman, P. (1997). *Self-directed IEP.* Longmont, CO: Sopris West.

Martin, J. E., Marshall, L. H., & Sale, P. (2004). A 3-year study of middle, junior high, and high school IEP meetings. *Exceptional Children, 70*(3), 285–297.

Martin, J. E., Van Dycke, J. L., Christensen, W. R., Greene, B. A., Gardner, J. E., & Lovett, D. L. (2006). Increasing student participation in IEP meetings: Establishing the self-directed IEP as an evidence-based practice. *Exceptional Children, 72*(3), 299–316.

Martin, T. L., Pear, J. J., & Martin, G. L. (2002). Analysis of proctor marking accuracy in a computer-aided personalized system of instruction course. *Journal of Applied Behavior Analysis, 35*(3), 309–312.

Mastropieri, M. A., & Scruggs, T. E. (1993). *A practical guide for teaching science to students with special needs in inclusive settings.* Austin, TX: PRO-ED.

Mastropieri, M. A., & Scruggs, T. E. (1998). Enhancing school success with mnemonic strategies. *Intervention in School and Clinic, 33*(4), 201–208.

Mattison, R. (1999). Use of psychotropic medications in special education students with serious emotional disturbance. *Journal of Child and Adolescent Psychopharmacology, 9*, 143–155.

Maudsley, H. (1880). *The pathology of the mind.* D. Appleton & Co.

Max, J. E., Schachar, R. J., Levin, H. S., Ewing-Cobbs, L., Chapman, S. B., Dennis, M., Saunders, A., & Landis, J. (2005). Predictors of secondary attention-deficit/hyperactivity disorder in children and adolescents 6 to 24 months after traumatic brain injury. *Journal of the American Academy of Child and Adolescent Psychiatry, 44*(10), 1041–1049.

Mayes, S. D., & Calhoun, S. L. (2008). WISC-IV and WIAT-II profiles in children with high-functioning autism. *Journal of Autism and Developmental Disorders, 38*(3), 428–439.

McCarney, S. B., & Leigh, J. E. (1990). *Behavior Evaluation Scale-2.* Columbia, MO: Hawthorne Educational Services.

McCart, M. R., Priester, P. E., Davies, W. H., & Azen, R. (2006). Differential effectiveness of behavioral parent-training and cognitive–behavioral therapy for antisocial youth: A meta-analysis. *Journal of Abnormal Psychology, 34*(4), 527–543.

McCarthy, J., Downes, E. J., & Sherman, C. A. (2008). Looking back at adolescent depression: A qualitative study. *Journal of Mental Health Counseling, 30*(1), 49–68.

McConaughy, S., & Ritter, D. (2002). Best practices in multidimensional assessment of emotional or behavioral disorders. In A. Thomas & J. Grimes (Eds.), *Best practices in school psychology IV* (pp. 1303–1336). Bethesda, MD: National Association of School Psychologists.

McDermott, R. P., & Varenne, H. (1996). Culture, development, disability. In R. Jessor, A. Colby & R. A. Shweder (Eds.) *Ethnography and human development* (pp. 101–126). Chicago: The University of Chicago Press.

McGinn, L. K., & Sanderson, W. C. (2001). What allows cognitive behavioral therapy to be brief: Overview, efficacy, and crucial factors facilitating brief treatment. *Clinical Psychology: Science and Practice, 8*(1), 23–37.

McLaughlin, K. A., Hilt, L. M., & Nolen-Hoeksema, S. (2007). Racial/ethnic differences in internalizing and externalizing symptoms in adolescents. *Journal of Abnormal Psychology, 35*(5), 801–816.

McLeskey, J., Tyler, N. C., Saunders Flippin, S. (2004). The supply of and demand for special education teachers: A review of research regarding the chronic shortage of special education teachers. *The Journal of Special Education, 38*(1), 5–21.

McLeskey, J., & Waldron, N. L. (2007). Making differences ordinary in inclusive classrooms. *Intervention in School and Clinic, 42*(3), 162–168.

McMaster, K. L., Kung, S., Han, I., & Cao, M. (2008). Peer-assisted learning strategies: A "tier 1" approach to promoting English learners' response to intervention. *Exceptional Children, 74*(2), 194–214.

McSwain, A. (2002). The effects of multicultural and bilingual training on preserve students' self-reported level of competency. *Multiple Voices for Ethnically Diverse Exceptional Learners, 5*(1), 54–65.

Meadows, N., Neel, R. S., Parker, G., & Timo, K. (1991). A validation of social skills for students with behavioral disorders. *Behavioral Disorders, 16,* 200–210.

Mendez, L. M. R., & Knoff, H. M. (2003). Who gets suspended from school and why: A demographic analysis of schools and disciplinary infractions in a large school district. *Education and Treatment of Children, 26*(1), 30–51.

Mental Health America. (2006). History of the organization and the movement. Retrieved December 10, 2005, from http://www. mentalhealthamerica.net/index.cfm?objectId=DA2 F000D-1372-4D20-C8882D19A97973AA

Meo, G. (2008). Curriculum planning for all learners: Applying universal design for learning (UDL) to a high school reading comprehension program. *Preventing School Failure, 52*(2), 21–30.

Merrell, K. W., & Walker, H. M. (2004). Deconstructing a definition: Social maladjustment versus emotional disturbance and moving the EBD forward. *Psychology in the Schools, 41*(8), 899–910.

Miller, J. D., Lynam, D., & Leukefeld, C. (2003). Examining antisocial behavior through the lens of the five factor model of personality. *Aggressive Behavior, 29,* 497–514.

Miller, M. D., Brownell, M., & Smith, S. W. (1999). Factors that predict teachers staying in, leaving, or transferring from the special education classroom. *Exceptional Children, 65*(2), 201–218.

Miller, M. J., Lane, K. L., & Wehby, J. (2005). Social skills instruction for students with high-incidence disabilities: A school-based intervention to address acquisition deficits. *Preventing School Failure, 49*(20), 27–39.

Miller, T. R., & Taylor, D. M. (2005). Adolescent suicidality: Who will ideate, who will act? *Suicide & Life-Threatening Behavior, 35*(4), 425–435.

Miller-Johnson, S., Coie, J. D., Maumary-Gremaud, A., & Bierman, K. (2002). Peer rejection and aggression and early starter models of conduct disorder. *Journal of Abnormal Child Psychology, 30*(3), 217–230.

*Mills v. Washington, DC, Board of Education.* 348 F. Supp 866 (D.DC 1972); contempt proceedings, EHLR 551:643 (D.DC 1980).

Minnameier, G. (2001). The new "Stairway to Moral Heaven"? A systematic reconstruction of stages of moral thinking based on a Piagetian "logic" of cognitive development. *Journal of Moral Education, 30*(4), 317–337.

Mojica, A., O'Neill Fichtner, L., Johnson, S., Gemma, G., Lindley, M., & Burke, R. (2005, February). *A collaborative project to improve student behavior and academic performance.* Paper presented at the National Association of Secondary School Principals Convention, San Francisco, CA.

Mooney, P., Denny, R. K., & Gunter, P. L. (2004). The impact of NCLB and the reauthorization of IDEA on academic instruction of students with emotional or behavioral disorders. *Behavioral Disorders, 29*(3), 237–246.

Mooney, P., Epstein, M. H., Reid, R., & Nelson, J. R. (2003). Status and trends of academic intervention research for students with emotional disturbance. *Remedial and Special Education, 24*(5), 273–287.

Morgan, D. P., & Jenson, W. R. (1988). *Teaching behaviorally disordered students: Preferred practices.* New York: Merrill Publishers.

Morrier, M. J., Irving, M. A., Dandy, E., Dmitriyev, G., & Ukeje, I. C. (2007). Teaching and learning within and across cultures: Educator requirements across the United States. *Multicultural Education, 14*(3), 32–40.

Mueller, F., Jenson, W. R., Reavis, K., & Andrews, D. (2002). Functional assessment of behavior can be as easy as A-B-C. *Beyond Behavior, 11*(3), 23–27.

Murawski, M. W., & Dieker, L. A. (2004). Tips and strategies for co-teaching at the secondary level. *Teaching Exceptional Children, 36*(5), 52–58.

Murray, C., & Greenbert, M. T. (2006). Examining the importance of social relationships and social contexts in the lives of children with high-incidence disabilities. *The Journal of Special Education, 39*(4), 220–233.

Myles, B. S., Moran, M. R., Ormsbee, C. K., & Downing, J. A. (1992). Guidelines for establishing and maintaining token economies. *Intervention in School and Clinic, 27*(3), 164–169.

Nagel, L., & Brown, S. (2003). The ABCs of managing teacher stress. *The Clearing House, 76*(5), 255–258.

Nardi, D. A., & Barrett, S. (2005). Potential effects of antidepressant agents on the growth & development of children & adolescents. *Journal of Psychosocial Nursing & Mental Health Services, 43*(1), 22–35.

National Center for Children Exposed to Violence. (2003). Retrieved November 26, 2005, from http://www.nccev.org/resources/statistics.html#domestic

National Council of Teachers of Mathematics. (2000). *Principle and standards for school mathematics.* Reston, VA: Author.

National Institute of Mental Health. (2001). *Blueprint for change: Research on child and adolescent mental health.* Washington, D.C.: Author.

National Institute of Mental Health. (2002). *Depression.* Washington, D.C.: Author.

National Institute of Mental Health. (2005). *Schizophrenia.* Washington, D.C.: Author.

National Institute of Mental Health. (2006). *Attention deficit hyperactivity disorder* (NIH Publication Number: NIH 3572). Retrieved May 27, 2007, from http://www.nimh.nih.gov/publicat/adhd.cfm

National Institute of Mental Health. (2006). *Childhood-onset schizophrenia: An update from the National Institute of Mental Health.* Washington, D.C.: Author.

National Institute of Mental Health. (2007). *Depression.* Washington, D.C.: Author.

Negrao II, C., Bonanno, G. A., Noll, J. G., Putnam, F. W., & Trickett, P. K. (2005). Shame, humiliation, and childhood sexual abuse: Distinct contributions and emotional coherence. *Child Maltreatment, 10*(4), 350–363.

Nelson, J. R., Benner, G. J., Cheney, D. (2005). An investigation of the language skills of students with emotional disturbance served in public school settings. *The Journal of Special Education, 39*(2), 97–105.

Nelson, J. R., Benner, G. J., Lane, K., & Smith, B. W. (2004). Academic achievement of K–12 students with emotional and behavioral disorders. *Exceptional Children, 71*(1), 59–73.

Nelson, J. R., Martella, R. M., & Marchand-Martella, N. (2002). Maximizing student learning: The effects of a comprehensive school-based program for preventing problem behaviors. *Journal of Emotional and Behavioral Disorders, 10*(3), 136–148.

Nettles, S. M., Caughy, M. O., O'Campo, P. J. (2008). School adjustment in the early grades: Toward an integrated model of neighborhood, parental, and child processes. *Review of Educational Research, 78*(1), 3–32.

Nichols, A. S., & Sosnowsky, F. L. (2002). Burnout among special education teachers in self-contained cross-categorical classrooms. *Teacher Education and Special Education, 25*(1), 71–86.

Nickerson, A. B., & Brosof, A. M. (2003). Identifying skills and behaviors for successful inclusion of students with emotional or behavioral disorders. *Behavioral Disorders, 28*(4), 401–409.

Nicolson, R., & Rapoport, J. L. (1996). Childhood onset schizophrenia: Rare but worth studying. *Biological Psychiatry, 46,* 1418–1428.

Nieto, S. (2002). *Language, culture, and teaching: Critical perspectives for a new century.* Nahwah, NJ: Lawrence Erlbaum Associates.

No Child Left Behind, 20 U.S.C. §16301 *et seq.*

Obenchain, K. M., & Taylor, S. S. (2005). Behavior management: Making it work in middle and secondary schools. *The Clearing House, 79*(1), 7–11.

Obiakor, F. E. (2003). *The eight-step approach to multicultural learning and teaching* (2nd ed.). Dubuque, IA: Kendall/Hunt.

Obiakor, F. E. (2007). Multicultural special education: Effective intervention for today's schools. *Intervention in School and Clinic, 42*(3), 148–155.

Obiakor, F. E., & Utley, C. A. (2004). Educating culturally diverse learners with exceptionalities: A critical analysis of the Brown Case. *Peabody Journal of Education, 79*(2), 141–156.

Ochoa, S. H., Robles-Pina, R., Garcia, S. B., & Breunig, N. (1999). School psychologists' perspectives on referrals of language minority students. *Multiple Voices for Ethnically Diverse Exceptional Learners, 3*(1), 1–13.

Odom, S. L., & Strain, P. S. (1984). Peer-mediated approaches to promoting children's social interaction: A review. *American Journal of Orthopsychiatry, 54,* 544–557.

Oetting, J. B., Cleveland, L. H., & Cope, R. F., III. (2008). Empirically derived combinations of tools and clinical cutoffs: An illustrative case with a sample of culturally/linguistically diverse children. *Language, Speech, and Hearing Services in School, 39*(1), 44–53.

Office of Civil Rights (OCR) Letter of Finding. EHLR 307.06 (Office for Civil Rights, 1988).

Office of Special Education Programs. (1995). [OSEP Memorandum 95–16, 22 IDELR 531]. Washington, DC: Author.

Olympia, D., Farley, M., Christiansen, E., Pettersson, H., Jenson, W., & Clark, E. (2004). Social maladjustment and students with behavioral and emotional disorders: Revisiting basic assumptions and assessment issues. *Psychology in the Schools, 41*(8), 835–847.

Ortiz, A. A., Wilkinson, C. Y., Robertson-Courtney, P., & Kushner, M. I. (2006). Considerations in implementing intervention assistance teams to support English language learners. *Remedial and Special Education, 27*(1), 53–63.

Osher, D. M., Quinn, M. M., & Hanley, T. V. (2002). Children and youth with serious emotional disturbance: A national agenda for success. *Journal of Child and Family Studies, 11*(1), 1–11.

Paige, L. Z. (2007). Obsessive–compulsive disorder. *Principal Leadership, 8*(1), 12–15.

Paolucci, E. O., Genuis, M. L., & Violato, C. (2001). A meta-analysis of the published research on the effects of child sexual abuse. *The Journal of Psychology, 135*(1), 17–36.

Passaro, P. D., Moon, M., Wiest, D. J., & Wong, E. H. (2004). A model for school psychology practice: Addressing the needs of students with emotional and behavioral challenges through the use of an in-school support room and reality therapy. *Adolescence, 39*(155), 503–517.

Paternite, C. E. (2005). School-based mental health programs and services: Overview and introduction to the special issue. *Journal of Abnormal Child Psychology, 33*(6), 657–663.

Patterson, G. R. (1982). *Coercive family process.* Eugene, OR: Castalia.

Pear, J. J., & Crone-Todd, D. E. (1999). Personalized system of instruction in cyberspace. *Journal of Applied Behavior Analysis, 32*(2), 205–209.

Peel, J., & McCary, C. E., III. (1997). Visioning the "Little Red Schoolhouse" for the 21st century. *Phi Delta Kappan*, 698–705.

Penno, D. A., Frank, A. R., & Wacker, D. P. (2000). Instructional accommodations for adolescent students with severe emotional or behavioral disorders. *Behavioral Disorders, 25*(4), 325–343.

*Pennsylvania Association for Retarded Citizens (PARC) v. Pennsylvania.* 334 F. Supp. 1257, 343 F. Supp. 279 (1971, 1972).

Perry, D. F. (2007). A missed opportunity: Categorical programs fail to meet the needs of young children and their caregivers. *Journal of Early Intervention, 29*(2), 107–110.

Peterson, A. V. (2000). Choice theory and reality therapy. *TCA Journal, 28*(1), 41–49.

Peyton, J., & Staton, J. (1993). *Dialogue journals in the multilingual classroom: Building language fluency and writing skills through written interaction.* Norwood, NJ: Ablex.

Peyton, J. K. (1997). Dialogue journals: Interactive writing to develop language and literacy. *Emergency Librarian, 24*(5), 46–48.

Phelps, L., Brown, R. T., & Power, T. (2002). *Pediatric psychopharmacology: Combining medical and psychological interventions.* Washington, DC: American Psychological Association.

Piacentini, J., & Roblek, T. (2002). Recognizing and treating childhood anxiety disorders. *Western Journal of Medicine, 176*(3), 149–151.

Piaget, J. (1997). *The moral judgment of the child* (M. Gabain, Trans.). New York: The Free Press. (Original work published 1932)

Piaget, J. (2001). *The psychology of intelligence* (2nd Ed.) (M. Piercy and D. E. Berlyne, Trans.). New York: Routledge. (Original work published 1950)

Piaget, J. (2008). Intellectual evolution from adolescence to adulthood. *Human Development, 51*(1), 40–47.

Pierce, C. D., Reid, R., & Epstein, M. H. (2004). Teacher-mediated interventions for children with EBD and their academic outcomes. *Remedial and Special Education, 25*(3), 175–188.

Pirtle, T. N., & Perez, P. (2003). *Survival counseling skills for new teachers.* (ERIC Document Reproduction Service No. ED479644)

Pisha, B., & Coyne, P. (2001). Smart from the start: The promise of universal design for learning. *Remedial and Special Education, 22*(4), 197–203.

Pisha, B., & Stahl, S. (2005). The promise of new learning environments for students with disabilities. *Intervention in School and Clinic, 41*(2), 67–75.

*Plessy v. Ferguson,* 163 U.S. 537, 16 S. Ct. 1138 (1986).

Polya, G. (2004). *How to solve it: A new aspect of mathematical methods.* New Jersey: Princeton University Press.

Pottick, K. J., McAlpine, D. D., & Andelman, R. B. (2000). Changing patterns of psychiatric inpatient care for children and adolescents in general hospitals, 1988–1995. *American Journal of Psychiatry, 157*(8), 1267–1273.

Prater, M. A., Serna, L., & Nakamura, K. K. (1999). Impact of peer teaching on the acquisition of social skills by adolescents with learning disabilities. *Education and Treatment of Children, 22*(1), 19–35.

Pumariega, A. J., Rogers, K., & Rothe, E. (2005). Culturally competent systems of care for children's mental health: Advances and challenges. *Community Mental Health Journal, 41*(5), 539–555.

Putnam, J., Markovchick, K., Johnson, D. W., & Johnson, R. T. (1996). Cooperative learning and peer acceptance of students with learning disabilities. *The Journal of Social Psychology, 136*(6), 741–752.

Qi, C. H., & Kaiser, A. P. (2003). Behavior problems of preschool children from low-income families: Review of the literature. *Topics in Early Childhood Special Education, 23,* 188–216.

Quay, H. C., & Peterson, D. R. (1987). *Manual for the Behavior Problem Checklist.* Miami, FL: Authors.

Quinn, M. M., Osher, D., Warger, C., Hanley, T., Bader, B. D., Tate, R., et al. (2000). *Educational strategies for children with emotional and behavioral problems.* Washington, DC: American Institutes for Research, Center for Effective Collaboration and Practice.

Quinn, M. M., Rutherford, R. B., Leone, P. E., Osher, D. M., & Poirier, J. M. (2005). Youth with disabilities in juvenile corrections: A national survey. *Exceptional Children, 71*(3), 339–345.

Rapport, M. D., Scanlan, S. W., & Denny, D. B. (1999). Attention-deficit/hyperactivity disorders and scholastic achievement: A model of dual developmental pathways. *Journal of Child Psychology Psychiatry, 40,* 1169–1183.

Rasmussen, E. R., Neuman, R. J., Heath, A. C., Levy, F., Hay, D. A., & Todd, R. (2004). Familial clustering of latent class and DSM-IV defined attention-deficit/hyperactivity disorder (ADHD) subtypes. *Journal of Child Psychology and Psychiatry, 45*(3), 589–598.

Redl, F., & Wineman, D. (1951). *Children who hate.* New York: The Free Press.

Redl, F., & Wineman, D. (1957). *The aggressive child.* New York: The Free Press.

Regan, K. S., Mastropieri, M. A., & Scruggs, T. E. (2005). Promoting expressive writing among students with emotional and behavioral disturbance via dialogue journals. *Behavioral Disorders, 31*(1), 33–50.

Reisner, A. D. (2005). The common factors, empirically validated treatments, and recovery models of therapeutic change. *The Psychological Record, 55*(3), 377–399.

Reyes, M., Buitelaar, J., Toren, P., Augustyns, I., & Eerdekens, M. (2006). A randomized, double-blind, placebo-controlled study of risperidone maintenance treatment in children and adolescents with disruptive behavior disorders. *The American Journal of Psychiatry, 163*(3), 402–410.

Reynolds, C. R., & Kamphaus, R. W. (1992). *Behavior Assessment System for Children manual.* Circle Pines, MN: American Guidance Services.

Rhee, S., & Waldman, I. D. (2002). Genetic and environmental influences on antisocial behavior: A meta-analysis of twin and adoption studies. *Psychological Bulletin, 29,* 490–529.

Rieck, W. A., & Wadsworth, D. E. D. (2005). Assessment accommodations: Helping students with exceptional learning needs. *Intervention in School and Clinic, 41*(2), 105–109.

Rivera, L. M., Chen, E. C., Flores, L. Y., Blumberg, F., & Ponterotto, J. G. (2007). The effects of perceived barriers, role models, and acculturation on the career self-efficacy and career consideration of Hispanic women. *The Career Development Quarterly, 56*(1), 47–61.

Robertson, D. C., Anderson, J. A., & Meyer, R. (2004). Individual focus, systemic collaboration: The current and potential role of schools in the integrated delivery of mental health services. In K. Robinson (Ed.), *School-based mental health: Best practices and program models* (pp. 5.1–5.13). Kingston, NJ: Civic Research Institute.

Robin, A., Schneider, M., & Dolnick, M. (1976). The turtle technique: An extended case study of self-control in the classroom. *Psychology in the Schools, 13,* 449–453.

Robison, L. M., Skaer, T. L., Sclar, D. A., & Galin, R. S. (2002). Is attention deficit hyperactivity disorder increasing among girls in the U.S.? Trends in diagnosis and the prescribing of stimulants. *CNS Drugs, 16*(2), 129–137.

Rogers, C. (1980). *A way of being.* Boston: Houghton Mifflin.

Roid, G. H. (2003). *Stanford Binet Intelligence Scales* (5th ed.). Itasca, IL: Riverside Publishing.

Rose, D. H., & Meyer, A. (2002). *Teaching every student in the digital age: Universal Design for Learning.* Alexandria, VA: ASCD.

Rosen, M. (1998). *Treating children in out-of-home placements.* New York: The Haworth Press.

Rosenberg, M. S., Wilson, R., Maheady, L., & Sindelar, P. T. (2004). *Educating students with behavior disorders* (3rd ed.). Boston: Pearson.

Rosenfeld, A. (2005). The benefits of board games. *Scholastic Parent & Child, 12*(4), 52–55.

Rosenshine, B. (1976). Classroom instruction. In N. Gage (Ed.), *The psychology of teaching methods: Seventy-fifth yearbook of the National Society for the Study of Education.* Chicago: University of Chicago Press.

Rosenshine, B., & Stevens, R. (1986). Teaching functions. In M. C. Writrock (Ed.), *Handbook of Research on Teaching* (3rd ed.). New York: Macmillan.

Rothstein, L. F. (2000). *Special education law* (3rd ed.). New York: Longman.

Rotter, K. M. (2004). Simple techniques to improve teacher-made instructional materials for use by pupils with disabilities. *Preventing School Failure, 48*(2), 38–43.

Russell, J. (1999). Counseling and the social construction of self. *British Journal of Guidance and Counseling, 27*(3), 339–352.

Rutter, M. (1996). Maternal deprivation. In M. H. Bornstein (Ed.), *Handbook of parenting: Vol. 4. Applied and practical parenting* (pp. 3–31). Mahwah, NJ: Erbaum.

Ryan, J. B., Katsiyannis, A., Peterson, R. L., & Chmelar, R. (2007). IDEA 2004 and disciplining students with disabilities. *National Association of Secondary School Principals. NASSP Bulletin, 91*(2), 130–140.

Ryan, J. B., & Peterson, R. L. (2004). Physical restraint in school. *Behavioral Disorders, 29*(2), 154–168.

Ryan, J. B., Reid, R., & Epstein, M. H. (2004). Peer-mediated intervention studies on academic achievement for students with EBD. *Remedial and Special Education, 25*(6), 330–335.

Ryan, J. B., Reid, R., Epstein, M. H., Ellis, C., & Evans, J. H. (2005). Pharmacological intervention research for academic outcomes for students with ADHD. *Behavioral Disorders, 30*(2), 135–154.

Ryan, J. B., Sanders, S., Katsiyannis, A., & Yell, M. L. (2007). Using time-out effectively in the classroom. *Teaching Exceptional Children, 39*(4), 60–67.

Sachs, J. S. (2004). The truth about sugar. *Parenting, 18*(5), 140–144.

Safran, S. P. (2006). Using the effective behavior supports survey to guide development of schoolwide positive behavior support. *Journal of Positive Behavior Interventions, 8*(1), 3–9.

Safran, S. P., & Oswald, K. (2003). Positive behavior supports: Can schools reshape disciplinary practices? *Exceptional Children, 69*(3), 361–373.

Saifer, S., & Barton, R. (2007). Promoting culturally responsive standards-based teaching. *Principal Leadership, 8*(1), 24–28.

Saklofske, D. H., Prifitera, A., Weiss, L. G., Rolfhus, E., & Zhu, J. (2005). Clinical interpretation of the WISC-IV FSIQ and GAI. In A. Prifitera, D. H. Saklofske, & L. G. Weiss (Eds.), *WISC-IV clinical use and interpretation* (pp. 33–65). New York: Elsevier.

Salend, S. J. (2000). Strategies and resources to evaluate the impact of inclusion programs on students. *Intervention in School and Clinic, 35*(5), 264–271.

Salend, S. J. (2001). *Creating inclusive classrooms: Effective and reflective practices* (4th ed.). Upper Saddle River, NJ: Prentice Hall.

Salvia, J., & Ysseldyke, J. E. (2001). *Assessment in special and remedial education* (8th ed.). Boston: Houghton Mifflin.

Salvia, J., & Ysseldyke, J. E. (2004). *Assessment in special and inclusive education* (9th ed.). Boston: Houghton Mifflin.

Samuels, C. A. (2007). Schools' role in mental-health care uneven, experts say. *Education Week, 26*(35), 14.

Sansosti, F. J., & Powell-Smith, K. A. (2006). Using social stories to improve the social behavior of children with Asperger syndrome. *Journal of Positive Behavior Interventions, 8*(1), 43–57.

Savage, R. C. (2005). The great leap forward: Transitioning into the adult world. *Preventing School Failure, 49*(4), 43–52.

Saville, B. K., Zinn, T. E., & Elliott, M. P. (2005). Interteaching versus traditional methods of instruction: A preliminary analysis. *Teaching of Psychology, 32*(3), 161–163.

Schlichte, J., Yssel, N., & Merbler, J. (2005). Pathways to burnout: Case studies in teacher isolation and alienation. *Preventing School Failure, 50*(1), 35–40.

Schroeder, C. S., & Riddle, D. B. (1991). Psychodynamic theory and practice. In J. L. Paul & B. C. Epanchin (Eds.), *Educating emotionally disturbed children and youth:* theories and practices for teachers (2nd ed., pp. 148–179). New York: Merrill.

Scott, T. M. (2003). Making behavior intervention planning decisions in a schoolwide system of positive behavior support. *Focus on Exceptional Children, 36*(1), 1–18.

Scott, T. M., & Barrett, S. B. (2004). Using staff and student time engaged in disciplinary procedures to evaluate the impact of school-wide PBS. *Journal of Positive Behavior Interventions, 6*(1), 21–27.

Scott, T. M., & Eber, L. (2003). Functional assessment and wraparound as systemic school processes: Primary, secondary, and tertiary systems examples. *Journal of Positive Behavior Interventions, 5*(3), 131–143.

Section 504 of the Rehabilitation Act of 1973, 29 U.S.C. §794 *et seq.*

Segurado, R., Conroy, J., Meally, E., Fitzgerald, M., Gill, M., & Gallagher, L. (2005). Confirmation of association between autism and the Mitochondrial Aspartate/Glutamate Carrier SLC25A12 Gene on Chromosome 2q31. *The American Journal of Psychiatry, 162*(11), 2182–2184.

Seidman, L. J., Pantelis, C., Keshavan, M. S., Faraone, S. V., Goldstein, J. M., Horton, N. J., Makris, N., & Falkai, P. (2003). A review and a new report of medial temporal lobe dysfunction as a vulnerability indicator for schizophrenia: A MRI morphometric family study of the parahippocampal gyrus. *Schizophrenia Bulletin, 29,* 803–808.

Sell, K. M., & Rees, K. (2005). Wellness programming: A pilot study of a rural public school and university partnership. *Research Quarterly for Exercise and Sport, 76*(1), A45–A46.

Sergiyenko, Y. (2005). A revolution in cognitive developmental psychology. *Social Sciences, 36*(2), 91–102.

Serna, L. A., Lamros, K., Nielsen, E., & Forness, S. R. (2002). Brief Head Start children at risk for emotional or behavioral disorders: Behavior profiles and clinical implications of a primary prevention program. *Behavioral Disorders, 27*(2), 137–141.

Serna, L. A., & Lau-Smith, J. A. (1995). Learning with a purpose: Self-determination skills for students who are at risk for school and community failure. *Intervention in School and Clinic, 30,* 142–146.

Serna, L. A., Nielsen, E., Lambros, K., & Forness, S. (2000). Primary prevention with children at risk for emotional or behavioral disorders: Data on a universal intervention for Head Start classrooms. *Behavioral Disorders, 26*(1), 70–84.

Serna, L. A., Nielsen, E., Mattern, N., & Forness, S. (2003). Primary prevention in mental health for head start classrooms: Partial replication with teachers as intervenors. *Behavioral Disorders, 28*(2), 124–129.

Shepherd, T. L., & Brown, R. D. (2003). Analyzing certification options for special education teachers. *Teaching Exceptional Children, 35*(6), 26–30.

Shepherd, T. L., Linn, D., & Brown, R. D. (2005). The disproportionate representation of English language learners for special education services along the border. *Journal of Social and Ecological Boundaries, 1*(1), 101–112.

Sheppard, V. B., & Benjamin-Coleman, R. (2001). Determinants of service placements for youth with serious emotional and behavioral disturbances. *Community Mental Health Journal, 37*(1), 53–65.

Sickmund, M. (2002). *Juvenile offenders in residential placement: 1997–1999.* Washington, DC: U. S. Department of Justice, Office of Juvenile Justice and Delinquency Prevention.

Sickmund, M. (2005). New survey provides a glimpse of the youth reentry population. *Corrections Today, 67*(2), 30–32.

Sindelar, P. T., Shearer, D. K., Yendol-Hoppey, D., & Liebert, T. W. (2006). The sustainability of inclusive school reform. *Exceptional Children, 72*(3), 317–331.

Skiba, R. J. (2002). Special education and school discipline: A precarious balance. *Behavioral Disorders, 27*(2), 8–97.

Skiba, R. J., & Grizzle, K. (1991). The social maladjustment exclusion: Issues of definition and assessment. *School Psychology Review, 20*(4), 580–598.

Skiba, R. J., Poloni-Staudinger, L., Gallini, S., Simmons, A. B., & Feggins-Azziz, R. (2006). Disparate access: The disproportionality of African American students with disabilities across educational environments. *Exceptional Children, 72*(4), 411–424.

Skinner, B. F. (1953). *Science and human behavior.* New York: The Free Press.

Skinner, B. F. (1994). Selection by consequences. In A. C. Catania & S. Harnad (Eds.), *The selection of behavior: The operant behaviorism of B. F. Skinner: Comments and consequences* (pp. 11–76). Cambridge, MA: Cambridge University Press.

Smith, S. W., & Coutinho, M. J. (1997). Achieving the goals of the National Agenda: Progress and prospects. *Journal of Emotional and Behavioral Disorders, 5,* 2–5.

Smokowski, P. R. (2003). From mad to worse: Anger management for Grades 3–4. *Journal of Technology in Human Services, 21*(3), 69–72.

Spencer, V. G. (2006). Peer tutoring and students with emotional or behavioral disorders: A review of literature. *Behavioral Disorders, 31*(2), 204–222.

Spencer, V. G., Scruggs, T. E., & Mastropieri, M. A. (2003). Content area learning in middle school social studies classrooms and students with emotional or behavioral disorders: A comparison of strategies. *Behavioral Disorders, 28*(2), 77–93.

SPeNSE. (2002a). *Recruiting and retaining high-quality teachers: Study of personnel needs in special education summary sheet.* Retrieved February 4, 2007, from http://ferdig.coe.ufl.edu/spense/Results.html

SPeNSE. (2002b). *Paperwork in special education.* Retrieved February 5, 2007, from http://ferdig.coe.ufl.edu/spense/Results.html

SPeNSE. (2003). *Study of personnel needs in special education: Final report of the paperwork substudy.* Retrieved February 5, 2007, from http://ferdig.coe.ufl.edu/spense/Results.html

Spiker, D. (1999). The role of genetics in autism. *Infants and Young Children, 12*(2), 55–63.

Spirito, A. & Overholser, J. C. (2003). *Evaluating and treating adolescent suicide attempters: From research to practice.* New York: Academic Press.

Spivack, G., Spotts, J., & Haimes, P. E. (1967). *Devereux Adolescent Behavior (DAB) Rating Scale.* Devon, PA: The Devereux Foundation.

Spivack G., & Spotts, J. (1966). *The Devereux Child Behavior (DCB) Rating scale.* Devon, PA: The Foundation.

Sprague, J., & Walker, H. (2000). Early identification and intervention for youth with antisocial and violent behavior. *Exceptional Children, 66,* 367–379.

Stambaugh, L. F., Mustillo, S. A., Burns, B. J., Stephens, R. L., Baxter, B., Edwards, D., & DeKraai, M. (2007). Outcomes from wraparound and multisystemic therapy in a center for mental health services system-of-care demonstration site. *Journal of Emotional and Behavioral Disorders, 15*(3), 143–155.

Stein, M. B., & Stein, D. J. (2008). Social anxiety disorder. *The Lancet, 371*(9618), 1115–1125.

Stein, S., and Merrell, K. W. (1992). Differential perceptions of multidisciplinary team members: Seriously emotionally disturbed vs. socially maladjusted. *Psychology in the Schools, 29,* 320–331.

Steuer, F. B. (1994). *The psychological development of children.* Pacific Grove, CA: Brooks/Cole Publishing Company.

Stone, W. S., Faraone, S. V., Seidman, L. J., Olson, E. A., & Tsuang, M. T. (2005). Searching for the liability to schizophrenia: Concepts and methods underlying genetic high-risk studies of adolescents. *Journal of Child and Adolescent Psychopharmacology, 15*(3), 403–417.

Storch, E. A., Brassard, M. R., & Masia-Warner, C. L. (2003). The relationship of peer victimization to social anxiety and loneliness in adolescence. *Child Study Journal, 33*(1), 1–18.

Stroul, B., & Friedman, R. (1986). *A system of care for severely emotionally disturbed children and youth.* Washington, DC: Georgetown University Child Development Center, CASSP Technical Assistance Center.

Sugai, G., & Horner, R. H. (2003). Introduction to the special series on Positive Behavior Support in Schools. *Journal of Emotional and Behavioral Disorders, 10*(3), 130–135.

Sugai, G., Horner, R. H., & Sprague, J. R. (1999). Functional-assessment-based behavior support planning: Research to practice to research. *Behavioral Disorders, 24*(3), 253–257.

Sugai, G., Lewis-Palmer, T., & Hagan, S. (1998). Using functional assessments to develop behavior support plans. *Preventing School Failure, 43*(1), 6–13.

Sugai, G., Horner, R. H., Dunlap, G., Hieneman, M., Lewis, T. J., Nelson, C. M., et al. (2000). Applying positive behavior support and functional behavioral assessment in schools. *Journal of Positive Behavior Interventions. 2*(3), 131–143.

Sullivan, P. F. (1995). Mortality in anorexia nervosa. *American Journal of Psychiatry, 152*(7), 1073–1074.

Sutherland, K. S., Copeland, S., & Wehby, J. H. (2001). Catch them while you can: Monitoring and increasing the use of effective praise. *Beyond Behavior, 11*(1), 46–49.

Sutherland, K. S., & Snyder, A. (2007). Effects of reciprocal peer tutoring and self-graphing on reading fluency and classroom behavior of middle school students with emotional or behavioral disorders. *Journal of Emotional and Behavioral Disorders, 15*(2), 103–118.

Sutherland, K. S., Wehby, J. H., & Yoder, P. J. (2002). Examination of the relationship between teacher praise and opportunities for students with EBD to respond to academic requests. *Journal of Emotional and Behavioral Disorders, 10*(1), 5–13.

Sweeney, D. P., Forness, S. R., Kavale, K. A., & Levitt, J. G. (1997). An update on psychopharmacologic medication: What teachers, clinicians, and parents need to know. *Intervention in School and Clinic, 33*(1), 4–21, 25.

Swick, K. J., & Williams, R. D. (2006). An analysis of Bronfenbrenner's bio-ecological perspective for early childhood educators: Implications for working with families experiencing stress. *Early Childhood Education Journal, 33*(5), 371–378.

Talbott, E., & Lloyd, J. W. (1997). Raters' views of the problems and competence of adolescent girls. *Exceptionality, 7*(4), 229–243.

Talbott, E., & Thiede, K. (1999). Pathways to antisocial behavior among adolescent girls.

*Journal of Emotional and Behavioral Disorders, 7,* 31–39.

Taylor, R. L. (2003). *Assessment of exceptional students: Educational and psychological procedures* (6th ed.). Boston: Allyn and Bacon.

Texas State Board for Educator Certification. (1998). *Report of the panel on novice teacher induction support system.* Austin: SBEC.

Thelen, E. (2005). Dynamic systems theory and the complexity of change. *Psychoanalytic Dialogues, 15*(2), 255–283.

Thelen, E., & Smith, L. B. (1994). *A dynamic systems approach to the development of cognition and action.* Cambridge, MA: MIT Press.

Thornton, B., Peltier, G., & Medina, R. (2007). Reducing the special education teacher shortage. *The Clearing House, 80*(5), 233–238.

Thousand, J. S., Villa, R. A., & Nevin, A. I. (2006). The many faces of collaborative planning and teaching. *Theory Into Practice, 45*(3), 239–248.

Tissington, L. D., & Grow, A. (2007). Alternative certified teachers and children at risk. *Preventing School Failure, 51*(2), 23–27.

Toffalo, D. A. D., & Pedersen, J. A. (2005). The effect of a psychiatric diagnosis on school psychologists' special education eligibility decisions regarding emotional disturbance. *Journal of Emotional and Behavioral Disorders, 13*(1), 53–60.

Townsend, B. (2000). Disproportionate discipline of African American children and youth: Culturally-responsive strategies for reducing school suspensions and expulsions. *Exceptional Children, 66,* 381–391.

Trent, S. C., & Artiles, A. J. (2007). Today's multicultural, bilingual, and diverse schools. In R. Turnbull, A. Turnbull, M. Shank, & S. J. Smith (Eds.), *Exceptional lives: Special education in today's schools* (5th ed., pp. 56–79). Upper Saddle River, NJ: Pearson.

Trent, S. C., Kea, C. D., & Oh, K. (2008). Preparing preservice educators for cultural diversity: How far have we come? *Exceptional Children, 74*(3), 328–350.

Troman, G., & Woods, P. (2001). *Primary teachers' stress.* New York: Routledge/Falmer.

Trout, A. L., Nordness, P. D., Pierce, C. D., & Epstein, M. H. (2003). Research on the academic status of children with emotional and behavioral disorders: A review of the literature from 1961 to 2000. *Journal of Emotional and Behavioral Disorders, 11*(4), 198–210.

Tucker, B. F., Singleton, A. H., & Weaver, T. L. (2002). *Teaching mathematics to all children: Designing and adapting instruction to meet the needs of diverse learners.* Upper Saddle River, NJ: Prentice Hall.

Tulviste, T., & Koor, M. (2005). "Hands off the car, it's mine!" and "The teacher will be angry if we don't play nicely": Gender-related preferences in the use of moral rules and social conventions in preschoolers' dyadic play. *Sex Roles, 53*(1/2), 57–66.

Turnbull, A. P., Edmonson, H., Griggs, P., Wickham, D., Sailor, W., Freeman, R., et al. (2002). A blueprint for schoolwide positive behavior support. *Exceptional Children, 68*(3), 377–402.

Turnbull, A. P., & Turnbull, H. R. (1996). Self-determination within a culturally responsive family systems perspective: Balancing the family mobile. In L. E. Powers, G. H. S. Singer, & J. Sowers (Eds.), *On the road to autonomy: Promoting self-competence for children and youth with disabilities* (pp. 195–220). Baltimore: Brookes.

U.S. Department of Education, Code of Federal Regulations, 34 CFR 300.

U.S. Department of Education. (1999). Assistance to states for the education of children with disabilities and the early intervention program for infants and toddlers with disabilities. Final regulations. *Federal Register, 64*(48), CFR Parts 300 and 303.

U.S. Department of Education. (2002). *Twenty-fourth annual report to Congress on the implementation of the Individuals with Disabilities Education Act.* Washington, DC: Author.

U.S. Department of Education. (2003). *Individuals with Disabilities Education Act (IDEA) data.* Available at www.ideadata.org/index.html

U.S. Department of Education. (2004). *Title 1 paraprofessionals: Non-regulatory guidance.* Washington DC: U.S. Government Printing Office.

U.S. Department of Education. (2006). Assistance to states for the education of children with disabilities and the early intervention program for infants and toddlers with disabilities. Final regulations. *Federal Register, 71*(156), CFR Parts 300 and 301.

U.S. Department of Education, National Center for Education Statistics. (2002). *The Condition of Education 2002, NCES 2002–025.* Washington, DC: U.S. Government Printing Office. Retrieved

June 9, 2004, from http://nces.ed.gov/pubsearch/pubsinfo.asp?pubid=2002025

U.S. Department of Health and Human Services, National Center on Child Abuse and Neglect. (2002). *Child maltreatment.* Washington, DC: U.S. Government Printing Office.

U.S. Department of Health and Human Services, Substance Abuse and Mental Health Services Administration. (n.d.). *PATHS-Promoting Alternative Thinking Strategies.* Washington, DC: U.S. Government Printing Office.

U.S. Food and Drug Administration. (2005). *Public health advisory: Suicidal thinking in children and adolescents being treated with Strattera (atomoxetine).* Retrieved May 18, 2007, from http://www.fda.gov/cder/drug/advisory/atomoxetine.htm

U.S. Public Health Service. (1999). *The Surgeon General's Call to Action to Prevent Suicide.* Washington, DC: Author.

U.S. Public Health Service. (2000). *Report of the Surgeon General's Conference on Children's Mental Health: A National Action Agenda.* Washington, DC: Author.

Vanderbleek, L. M. (2004). Engaging families in school-based mental health treatment. *Journal of Mental Health Counseling, 26*(3), 211–224.

VanDerHeyden, A. M., Witt, J. C., & Gilbertson, D. (2007). A multi-year evaluation of the effects of a response to intervention (RTI) model on identification of children for special education. *Journal of School Psychology, 45*(2), 225–256.

Van Garderen, D., & Whittaker, C. (2006). Planning differentiated, multicultural instruction for secondary inclusive classrooms teaching. *Exceptional Children, 38*(3), 12–20.

Van Haren, B. A., & Fiedler, C. (2004). Physical restraint and seclusion of students with disabilities. *Beyond Behavior, 13*(3), 17–19.

Varela, R. E., Weems, C. F., Berman, S. L., Hensley, L., & de Bernal, M. C. R. (2007). Internalizing symptoms in Latinos: The role of anxiety sensitivity. *Journal of Youth & Adolescence, 36*(4), 429–440.

Vaughn, S., Bos, C. S., & Schumm, J. S. (2007). *Teaching exceptional, diverse, and at risk students in the general education classroom* (4th ed.). Upper Saddle River, NJ: Merrill.

Vaughn, S., & Edmonds, M. (2006). Reading comprehension for older readers. *Intervention in Schools and Clinics, 41*(3), 131–137.

Vaughn, S., Klingner, J. K., & Bryant, D. P. (2001). Collaborative Strategic Reading as a means to enhance peer-mediated instruction for reading comprehension and content-area learning. *Remedial and Special Education, 22*(2), 66–74.

Vierhaus, M., & Lohaus, A. (2008). Children and parents as informants of emotional and behavioural problems predicting female and male adolescent risk behavior: A longitudinal cross-informant study. *Journal of Youth and Adolescence, 37*(2), 211–224.

Vikan, A., Camino, C., & Biaggio, A. (2005). Note on a cross-cultural test of Gilligan's ethic of care. *Journal of Moral Education, 34*(1), 107–111.

Viney, W., & Zorich, S. (1982). Contributions to the history of psychology XXIX: Dorothea Dix. *Psychological Reports, 50,* 211–218.

Vygotsky, L. S. (1978). *Mind in society: The development of higher psychological processes.* Cambridge, MA: Harvard University Press.

Wagner, M., Friend, M., Bursuck, W. D., Kutash, K., Duchnowski, A. J., Sumi, W. C., et al. (2006). Educating students with emotional disturbances: A national perspective on school programs and services. *Journal of Emotional and Behavioral Disorders, 14*(1), 12–30.

Wagner, M., Kutash, K., Duchnowski, A. J., Epstein, M. H., & Sumi, W. C. (2005). The children and youth we serve: A national picture of the characteristics of students with emotional disturbances receiving special education. *Journal of Emotional and Behavioral Disorders, 13*(2), 79–96.

Wagner, M., Newman, L., Cameto, R., Garza, N., & Levine, P. (2005). *After high school: A first look at the post school experiences of youth with disabilities. A report from the National Longitudinal Transition Study-2 (NLTS2).* Menlo Park, CA: SRI International.

Walker, B., Cheney, D., Stage, S., & Blurn, C. (2005). Schoolwide screening and positive behavior supports: Identifying and supporting students at risk for school failure. *Journal of Positive Behavior Interventions, 7*(4), 194–204.

Walker, H. M. (1983). *The Walker Behavior Identification Checklist* (2nd ed.). Los Angeles: Western Psychological Services.

Walker H. M., & McConnell, S. R. (1995). *Walker-McConnell Scale of Social Competence and School Adjustment.* Belmont, CA: Wadsworth Publishing.

Walker, H. M., McConnell, S. R., Holmes, D., Todis, B., Walker, J., & Golden, N. (1983). *ACCEPTS: A Children's Curriculum for Effective Peer and Teacher Skills.* Austin: Pro-Ed.

Walker, H. M., Ramsey, E., & Gresham, F. M. (2004). *Antisocial behavior in school: Strategies and best practices* (2nd ed.). Pacific Grove, CA: Brooks/Cole.

Walker, H. M., Severson, H. H., & Feil, E. G. (1995). *User manual. Early Screening Project: A proven child find process.* Longmont, CO: Sopris West.

Walker, H. M., & Severson, H. H. (1990). *Systematic screening for behavior disorders (SSBD).* Longmont, CO: Sopris West.

Walker, H. M., & Severson, H. H. (1994). Replication of the Systematic Screening for Behavior Disorders (SSBD) procedure for the identification of at-risk children. *Journal of Emotional & Behavioral Disorders, 2*(2), 66–77.

Walker, H. M., & Severson, H. H. (2002). Developmental prevention of at-risk outcomes for vulnerable antisocial children and youth. In K. L. Lane, F. M. Gresham, & T. E. O'Shaughnessy (Eds.), *Interventions for children with or at-risk for emotional and behavioral disorders* (pp. 175–194). Boston: Allyn & Bacon.

Walker, H. M., Severson, H. H., Stiller, B., Williams, G., Haring, N., Shinn, M., & Todis, B. (1988). Systematic screening of pupils in the elementary age range at risk for behavior disorders: Development and trial testing of a multiple gating model. *Remedial and Special Education, 9*(3), 8–14.

Walker-Dalhouse, D. (2005). Discipline: Responding to socioeconomic and racial differences. *Childhood Education, 82*(1), 24–30.

Walker, J. S., & Schutte, K. M. (2004). Practice and process in wraparound teamwork. *Journal of Emotional and Behavioral Disorders, 12*(3), 182–192.

Walsh, J. M., & Jones, B. (2004). New models of cooperative teaching. *Teaching Exceptional Children, 36*(5), 14–20.

Walther-Thomas, C., Korinek, L., McLaughlin, V. L., & Williams, B. T. (2000). *Collaboration for inclusive education: Developing successful programs.* Boston: Allyn & Bacon.

Wasburn-Moses, L. (2005). How to keep your special education teachers. *Principal Leadership, 5*(5), 35–38.

Waschbusch, D. A. (2002). A meta-analytic examination of comorbid hyperactive–impulsive–attention problems and conduct problems. *Psychological Bulletin, 128,* 118–150.

*Watson v. the City of Cambridge,* 157 Mass. 561, 32 N.E. 864 (1893).

Watson, J. B., & Raynor, R. (1920). Conditioned emotional reactions. *Journal of Experimental Psychology, 3,* 1–14.

Wechsler, D. (1974). *Manual for the Wechsler Intelligence Scale for Children-Revised.* Cleveland, OH: Psychological Corporation.

Wechsler, D. (2002). *Wechsler Individual Achievement Test* (2nd ed.). San Antonio, TX: Psychological Corporation.

Wechsler, D. (2003). *Wechsler Intelligence Scale for Children—4th Edition (WISC-IV).* San Antonio, TX: Psychological Corporation.

Wehby, J. H., Lane, K. L., & Falk, K. B. (2003). Academic instructions for students with emotional and behavioral disorders. *Journal of Emotional and Behavioral Disorders, 11*(4), 194–197.

Wehmeier, P. M., Dittmann, R. W., Schacht, A., Minarzyk, A., Lehmann, M., Sevecke, K, et al. (2008). Effectiveness of atomoxetine and quality of life in children with attention-deficit/hyperactivity disorder as perceived by patients, parents, and physicians in an open-label study. *Journal of Child and Adolescent Psychopharmacology, 17*(6), 813–829.

Wehmeyer, M. L., Agran, M., & Hughes, C. A. (1998). *Teaching self-determination to students with disabilities.* Baltimore: Brookes.

Wehmeyer, M. L., & Schwartz, M. (1997). Self-determination and positive adult outcomes: A follow-up study of youth with mental retardation or learning disabilities. *Exceptional Children, 63,* 245–255.

Weinstein, C. S., Tomlinson-Clarke, S., & Curran, M., (2003). Toward a conception of culturally responsive classroom management. *Journal of Teacher Education, 55*(1), 25–38.

Weiss, M. P. (2004). Co-teaching as science in the schoolhouse: More questions than answers. *Journal of Learning Disabilities, 37*(3), 218–223.

Witt, J. C., Elliott, S. N., Daly III, E. J., Gresham, F. M., & Kramer, J. J. (1998). *Assessment of at-risk and special needs children* (2nd ed.). Boston: McGraw Hill.

Wilder, L. K., Dyches, T. T., Obiakor, F. E., & Algozzine, B. (2004). Multicultural perspectives on teaching students with autism. *Focus on Autism and Other Developmental Disabilities, 19*(2), 105–113.

Wilder, L. K., Shepherd, T. L., Murry, F., Rogers, E., Heaton, E., & Sonntag, A. W. (2007). Teacher ratings of social skill competence across ethnic groups for students with mild disabilities: Implication for teacher education. *Curriculum and Teaching, 22*(1), 47–66.

Wilhoit, B. E., & McCallum, R. S. (2002). Profile analysis of the Universal Nonverbal Intelligence Test standardization sample. *School of Psychology Review, 31*(2), 263–281.

Wilkerson, K., & Bellini, J. (2006). Intrapersonal and organizational factors associated with burnout among school counselors. *Journal of Counseling and Development: JCD, 84*(4), 440–450.

Williams, G. J., & Reisberg, L. (2003). Successful inclusion: Teaching social skills through curriculum integration. *Intervention in School and Clinic, 38*(4), 205–210.

Wimmer, M. (2008). School refusal. *Principal Leadership, 8*(8), 10–14.

Winzer, M. A. (1993). *The history of special education: From isolation to integration.* Gallaudet University Press: Washington, DC.

Wood, F. H. (1999). CCBD: A record of accomplishment. *Behavioral Disorders, 24*(4), 273–283.

Wood, T., & McCarthy, C. (2002). *Understanding and preventing teacher burnout.* Washington, DC: ERIC Clearinghouse on Teaching and Teacher Education. (ERIC Document Reproduction Service No. ED477726)

Wood, W. M., Karvonen, M., Test, D., Browder, D., & Algozzine, B. (2004). Self-determination instruction in special education: Getting SD into the IEP. *Teaching Exceptional Children, 36*(3), 8–16.

Woodcock, R. W., McGrew, K. S., & Mather, N. (2001). *Woodcock–Johnson-III Test of Cognitive Abilities and Test of Achievement.* Itasca, IL: Riverside Publishing Company.

Woolley, M. E., & Curtis, H. W. (2007). Assessing depression in latency-age children: A guide for school social workers. *Children & Schools, 29*(4), 209–218.

Wright, E. R., Russell, L. A., Anderson, J. A., Kooreman, H. E., & Wright, D. E. (2006). Impact of team structure on achieving treatment goals in a system of care. *Journal of Emotional and Behavioral Disorders, 14*(4), 240–250.

Yeh, M., Forness, S. R., Ho, J., McCabe, K., & Hough, R. L. (2004). Parental etiological explanations and disproportionate racial/ethnic representation in special education services for youths with emotional disturbances. *Behavioral Disorders, 29*(4), 348–358.

Yell, M. L. (2006). *The law and special education* (2nd ed.). New Jersey: Upper Saddle River.

Yell, M. L., & Katsiyannis, A. (2004). Placing students with disabilities in inclusive settings: Legal guidelines and preferred practices. *Preventing School Failure, 49*(1), 28–35.

Yell, M. L., Rogers, D., & Lodge Rodgers, E. (1998). The legal history of special education: What a long, strange trip it's been! *Remedial & Special Education, 19*(4), 219–228.

Yonan, A. L., Alarcon, M., Cheng, R., Magnusson, P. K., Spence, S. J., Palmer, A. A., Grunn, A., Juo, S. H., Terwilliger, J. D., Liu, J., Cantor, R. M., Geschwind, D. H., & Gilliam, T. C. (2003). A genomewide screen of 345 families for autism-susceptibility loci. *The American Journal of Human Genetics, 73*, 886–897.

Zabel, R., & Nigro, F. (2007). Occupational interests and aptitudes of juvenile offenders: Influence of special education experience and gender. *Journal of Correctional Education, 58*(4), 337–355.

Zanglis, I., Furlong, M. J., & Casas, J. M. (2000). Case study of a community mental collaborative: Impact on identification of youths with emotional or behavioral disorders. *Behavioral Disorders, 25*(4), 359–371.

Zhang, D., Katsiyannis, A., & Herbst, M. (2004). Disciplinary exclusions in special education: A four-year analysis. *Behavioral Disorders, 29*(4), 337–347.

Zimbardo, P. G., & Gerrig, R. J. (2004). *Psychology and life* (17th ed.). Boston: Allyn & Bacon.

# Name Index

# Subject Index